THE TEXTURE OF BEING

STUDIES IN PHILOSOPHY
AND THE HISTORY OF PHILOSOPHY

General Editor: Jude P. Dougherty

Studies in Philosophy
and the History of Philosophy   Volume 46

The Texture of Being
Essays in First Philosophy

Kenneth L. Schmitz

Edited by Paul O'Herron

THE CATHOLIC UNIVERSITY OF AMERICA PRESS
Washington, D.C.

Copyright © 2007
The Catholic University of America Press
All rights reserved
Printed in the United States of America

The paper used in this publication meets the minimum requirements of the American National Standards for Information Science—Permanence of Paper for Printed Library Materials, ANSI Z39.48-1984.
∞

LIBRARY OF CONGRESS CATALOGING-IN-PUBLICATION DATA
Schmitz, Kenneth L.
The texture of being : essays in first philosophy/Kenneth L. Schmitz ; edited by Paul O'Herron.
     p. cm. — (Studies in philosophy and the history of philosophy ; v. 46)
Includes bibliographical references and index.
ISBN-13: 978-0-8132-1468-9 (cloth : alk. paper)
ISBN-13: 978-0-8132-2760-3 (pbk.)
     1. Metaphysics. 2. Philosophical theology. 3. Catholic Church—Doctrines. I. O'Herron, Paul. II. Title. III. Series.
B21.S78 vol. 46
[BT50]
100 s—dc22
[1
                                  2006004941

Contents

Preface	vii
Introduction by Paul O'Herron	ix

PART I. BEING

1. Metaphysics: Radical, Comprehensive, Determinate Discourse	3
2. Analysis by Principles and Analysis by Elements	21
3. From Anarchy to Principles: Deconstruction and the Resources of Christian Philosophy	37
4. Neither with nor without Foundations	54
5. Another Look at Objectivity	74
6. Enriching the Copula	88
7. Created Receptivity and the Philosophy of the Concrete	106
8. The Solidarity of Personalism and the Metaphysics of Existential Act	132

PART II. MAN

9. The Geography of the Human Person	149
10. Immateriality Past and Present	168
11. The First Principle of Personal Becoming	183
12. Purity of Soul and Immortality	200
13. Is Liberalism Good Enough?	221

PART III. GOD

14. Theological Clearances: Foreground to a
    Rational Recovery of God ... 245

15. God, Being, and Love: New Ontological
    Perspectives Coming from Philosophy ... 265

16. The Death of God and the Rebirth of Man ... 283

17. The Witness of Beauty: The Profile of God ... 300

Bibliography ... 317

Index of Names ... 325

Preface

The present volume has come about through many helpful persons: the editor, Paul O'Herron, and a trio of friends—Dave McGonagle, Director of the Catholic University of America Press; Jude Dougherty, Dean Emeritus of the School of Philosophy at the Catholic University of America; and Gladys Sweeney, Dean of the Institute for the Psychological Sciences. They were ably assisted in the preparation of the manuscript by the following students of the Institute: Rosella Allison, Leah Boelte, Jill Bohacik, Donna Darbellay, Bernadette Devine, Gaelyn Felix, Eric Gudan, Michael Horne, Irene Lagan, Peter Martin, Jesslyn McManus, Linda Montagna, Elena Sanches, Kelly Sheftall, Andrew Sodergren, and Genevieve Yep, who organized and directed their efforts. John Cicala, Ellen Coughlin, Jenna Garofalo, Heather Hill, Christine Leon, Peggy Murphy, and Keneisha Williams were a great help to the editor.

I am deeply indebted to all, as well as to the staff of the press, and to those unnamed teachers, friends, and colleagues who helped me along the path of many years towards a clearer understanding of the texture of being. The Philosopher spoke in truth when he observed that

Without friends no one would choose to live, though he had all other goods . . . for with friends men are more able to think and to act. (Ethics 1155ff.)

Introduction

Kenneth L. Schmitz has taken giant strides toward doing what Hegel said he wanted to do: to reconcile the "being of the ancients" with the "subjectivity of the moderns." In the first part of this introduction, I try to set up this issue.

Intellectual reconciliation itself is not his goal. It is rather "to make one single philosophical life." The seventeen articles gathered here make an arc from the firstness of being to the newness of being. In the second part of the introduction, I mark off how, on the warp of the old, Professor Schmitz shuttles the woof of the new to weave a rich tapestry for our own life and thought.

To account for a physical thing Aristotle elaborated four causes or "responsibles" *(aitia):* the matter (material cause), form (formal cause), agent (efficient cause), and end (final cause). He analyzed place, time, motion, genus, and species. He categorized types of human beings (virtuous, continent...) and types of regimes (monarchy, oligarchy...). He created a table of virtues (fortitude, magnificence...) and sketched the types of argumentation and figures of speech. He perfected a logic of classes and types.

Aristotle's thought is remarkably suited to physical things of determinate kinds. His thought is not limited to physical beings (it was he who taught us much about the blessings of friendship, the structure of drama, and the sublimity of contemplation) but remains anchored in them.

Descartes began with consciousness. Doubting mind cannot doubt its own doubting. With Hume, consciousness imploded into "separate impressions" or what Thomas Prufer called "uncollected timeless flashes illuminating nothing for nobody." Kant rebuilt the structure of consciousness, but with a price tag—we do know what is outside of us but what is known are the appearances of things.

For Kenneth Schmitz, Hegel is the prime contrast to Aristotle. A triple beat pulses though Hegel's work. A position is staked out and fortified (thesis). Then its weaknesses are probed, its opponents are brought out and strengthened (antithesis). But the two sides do not cancel nor do they make a peace treaty. Rather they are resolved or pushed up into a new understanding (synthesis). The German word *aufheben*, whose root meaning seems to be "to lift (hay) up on a wagon," covers all three aspects of the "dialectic."

Hegel showed how the insidious perfume of Enlightenment drifts across the classroom of simple faith. He demonstrated that Skepticism and Stoicism simply can't hold on as lifetime stances toward reality.

He told how consciousness becomes self-consciousness when one looks into the eyes of another who looks back. But for him, gazing on gazing is a troubled beginning as each seeks to dominate the other. And, in one of his most stunning passages (sometimes called the "Master-Slave" section), he showed how the winner by pushing too hard loses. Yes, the master dominates the slave, but he is also dependent on him. And as his dominance/dependence increases so does his helplessness. The slave is less helpless. He, at least, knows his work or controls part of nature.

For Hegel, dialectical vectors are but "moments" (motions and notions in or of the cosmic spirit that pours forth its own infinitude). But what is this "cosmic spirit"? Is it a sort of mega-being that you and I are inside of? It is not the Christian God. You don't pray to *Geist*. Absolute Spirit didn't create the world in play.

And there is little play or rest in Hegelian dialectic. Instead of give and take or friendly communication, dialectical moves involve pushing-off-of or falling-over-into. Differences imply an othering. Othering is opposition. Opposition is contradiction. The dialectic moves by tension and negation. In general, happiness must be constricted into loss-overcome or contradiction-reconciled. Joy is demoted into victory. Like a skylight in the *Phenomenology* is the praise of Antigone. The love between brother and sister is a rare exception to dialectical tension.

Let us contrast the "being of the ancients" and the "subjectivity of the moderns."

Hegel more or less speaks past causality. Forms and final causes are ignored. The dialectic doesn't help us count the planets or fill in the periodic table.

Aristotle sets out everything from place and time to virtue and vice. But there is little sense of the historical, of the times in which we were born, of the longings that go with a certain place or face, of crushed hope or ecstatic prayer.

Hegel is rich with the descriptions of the inner spirit of classical China or India. He lights up the shift from classicism to romanticism in art. Oswald Spengler's *Decline of the West* traces a series of world-historical epochs. In a parallel way, each epoch works from its own rich dream-like inwardness to its formalized outer achievement. Sense or nonsense, the very claim that there are inner workings in the life of a whole people, such as Magian Man or Faustian Man, is a kind of applied Hegelianism.

To reemphasize: the reconciliation issue is acute because both "sides" do have a lot to say yet the very styles of thought seem contradictory. How, for instance, can we juxtapose the aspiration to make one's mark, to shake the world, with the recipes for virtue in the *Nicomachean Ethics*?

Could these contrasting philosophical styles be bridged by what came in the middle-time, by medieval philosophy? Some accept one or more of the modern thinkers and set aside ancient and medieval philosophy as largely irrelevant to an expanding, evolutionary reality. Others hold that philosophy got derailed somewhere (either going into the Middle Ages or coming out of them). They reject as darkness what we've been taught to call "Enlightenment." Martin Heidegger's appropriation of earlier thought is complex. Thomas Prufer's Heidegger "has taught us that the otherness of hiddenness and truth to each other is not an otherness of loss or contradiction: they rest in each other; they are not violently wrested from each other."

Kenneth Schmitz says, "I do not think the history of philosophy is a pointless tale." One may borrow from another without accepting the other's overall system. Aquinas borrowed much from Aristotle. Yet a central Christian idea—that God loves us—is explicitly rejected by Aristotle (*Nicomachean Ethics* 1159a) and certainly St. Thomas would not agree with his mentor's view in the *Politics* at 1335b!

Schmitz starts at the start. Principles are first. Causes are the chief principles. It is obvious that we didn't make the world or construct our own language. Reflection on the obvious (philosophers' favorite sport) turns us to others, to the Source and to the gift of existence. From Aquinas, he learned that each non-self-subsisting entity receives its to-be *(esse)* along with its nature. The metaphysics of *esse* is combined with treasures found along the path of mind's history to display our three dimensions: the inward, the outward, and the upward. Philosophy begins in wonder.[1] Each creature wakes up and is stunned at the news of its own existence. It's the kind of news you never really get over.

Does it deepen our excitement at a painting to have it called baroque? Labels can cast more shadow than light. But for those who must: Kenneth Schmitz draws deeply on Aristotle, Aquinas, and Hegel. He has

---

1. See also Kenneth L. Schmitz, *The Recovery of Wonder: The New Freedom and the Asceticism of Power* (Montreal: McGill-Queen's University Press, 2005).

intellectual cousins in Maurice Blondel, Gabriel Marcel, and Karol Wojtyla as well as Etienne Gilson and Jacques Maritain.

The articles are arranged thematically. There is some overlap but such as tends to deepen the insights and thicken the texture of discourse.

Chapters 1 through 5 are preliminary. Chapter 3 acts like an interlude because its style of argumentation is by counterexample. These five sharpen the tools of thought and build up to the central metaphysics of Chapters 6 and 7. Chapter 8 acts as a bridge from being in general to personal being. Chapters 9 through 13 speak of human existence—its interiority, intimacy, and immateriality. Chapter 14 is a bridge to theology. Chapters 15 and 17 examine and elaborate Karol Wojtyla's engagement with phenomenology and traditional metaphysics. Chapter 16 is a sort of interlude countering death-of-God prophecies.

Please consider what follows as an invitation to Schmitz's thought, not a condensation of it.

For Aristotle, the science of being as being is first philosophy. But the history of philosophical discourse has led metaphysics to where it feels it must defend its own possibility. If this challenge is accepted, metaphysics is no longer first. Epistemology or something else is. In Chapter 1, Schmitz neatly flanks the issue by starting with firstness itself: principles (*principium, archē*). Principles are sources from which consequences follow in an order that depends upon the nature of the principle.

Modern natural science explains by quantitative elements. Millions of organic reactions are explained (and some even predicted) by the positioning of electrons or energy levels. Experiments measure the wavelength of red light. Such analyses tend to be reductionist because we think of elements as prior and thus more real. The unity of anything not an element is undermined. Fragmented and compartmentalized understandings are frustrating. But knowledge is for happiness. In Chapter 2 Schmitz shows us how we may hold on to the brilliance of modern science and retain all explanatory factors. There can be progression from affirmation through negation to the joy of beauty.

In Chapter 3, the author moves quickly to deconstruct deconstructionism. Some recent philosophers attack principles because, like princes, they dominate. To them principles hide being, clamp down on choice, and stamp out variety. To Reiner Schürmann's Heidegger technology is metaphysics' tightest grip and its last gasp. Schmitz offers counterexamples from Christian theology: Rather than flat unity the Trinity is inherently social. Rather than a bullying First Power, the creator gives life and in the Incarnation gives and shares His own life. Finally, rather than hiding being, the Christian God dwells with us and within us. "He pitched his tent among us" (Jn 1:14).

How shall we speak of entity? In Chapter 4, Schmitz develops the term "contextualized singular" to illuminate entity as both individual and yet open to and constituted by community.

Here he also advances a theory of the origin of theory in ancient Greece through a distancing between mind and thing and within the mind itself. Schmitz doesn't discuss the stage just before this but I think it may have been the development of the full alphabet. Semitic languages wrote only consonants. To say a word, the reader would have to know or guess its grammatical context. Borrowing from Semitic, Greek put vowels in place of consonants they did not pronounce: *'ayin* became *omicron* and *yodh* became *iota*. Looking for the first time at a writing, the Greek could say what he was seeing and then, in a distancing shift, begin to see what he was saying.

Reacting, perhaps, to reductionist tendencies in science, some thinkers want to reject objectivity altogether. In Chapter 5, the author counters that we need this "keystone of theoretical knowledge" because it discloses a transcognitional terminus and value within cognition itself. There is an imperative in us to gather, be critical of, build on, make one's own, rest in, and pass on truth. Although actual knowledge is limited by perspective, we complete our knowledge "in principle by comprehending its actual incompleteness."

Hegel complained that the "is" of "A is B" remained undeveloped in Kant. Since there are languages, e.g., Russian, which do not even use the copula, some assume the issue is purely verbal. But all human thinking involves affirming or denying, i.e., joining. Further, we all recognize the difference between speech that is about something and speech that blabbers on emptily.

Thought outstrips language, but language is an aid to thought not a trap for it. Starting with these observations, Schmitz in Chapter 6 develops with great keenness the senses of being, presence, and union involved in things, thoughts of things, and thought itself as a thing. Chapters 6 and 7 contain the core of his metaphysics. Any attempted summary would be a short circuit. Fortunately, the voltage of Professor Schmitz's thought pushes the reader through the "long circuit."

Some of the themes in Chapter 7 were articulated also in his book *The Gift: Creation*. In creation, the creature is given both existence *(esse)* and the capacity to receive existence (essence). The receptivity in a creature is like the receptivity of a host who welcomes a guest to his home. It is an active potency which implies interiority in each created being. A gift is incomplete unless accepted—but what is this first act of response?

In Chapters 7 and 8 Schmitz sees a sort of *conatus*, a self-affirmation in each being. Aquinas said the wish to be happy is voluntary but not a matter of free choice. The wish does come from us but we couldn't wish to be unhappy. Similarly for Schmitz, there is a freedom deeper than free choice. It lies in this self-affirmation. No caused being is a closed being. Interiority and relationship run through all being, not just persons.

For created spirit a secondary act of response is called for: seek the Giver, search for the true and the good of the community. He cites Gabriel Marcel: the fortunes of being depend in some significant way upon the use we make of our freedom.

As a comment on the unfolding of being, Schmitz says that as we can know things without changing them, so God can know/love things without mutating himself.

Chapters 9 and 13 contribute to political philosophy and to an emergent philosophy of normative psychology. Psychology is of perennial interest but its study has been irregular. Ethics and rational psychology are too external; novels or tracts on spirituality may get at the inner person but they are not philosophical; phenomenology speaks of the call, or guilt, or gossip, but in a free-floating way. Abnormal psychology is just that—abnormal. True, we have learned a lot by studying diseases and defects. But shall we learn to paint in oils by consulting only colorblind people?

In Chapter 9 Schmitz precisely distinguishes privacy, familiarity, and intimacy. Privacy and intimacy, as defined, are almost opposites. There is no privacy between humans and God. But among us, some privacy is needed to preserve the space for intimacy. Totalitarian regimes try to destroy even the will to both privacy and intimacy. Everyone in Moscow had to live in apartments so that under the glare of everyone else there could be no shared secrets.

However protecting the individual by privacy is too fragmented and lonely. The concept of person provides the basis for mutual association in society. It nourishes uniqueness via "distinctness with its variety and abundance."

A true understanding of the individual frees from hurtful isolation or mass madness. Collectivisms have killed hundreds of millions while millions have been aborted under the banner of individual privacy. Political wisdom, though more urgent than ever, is rationed: in almost every country either the government controls the media or the media controls the government.

In Chapter 13 classical liberalism is set aside. The individual is not an "atomic-subject" nor an "elector-self" who chooses how/when to relate to others. Schmitz speaks of the "constitutive individual" who receives his/her constitution from and through causes and relatedness to others. There is an ontological equality within that grounds the equality among individuals and between each person and the state. We should not flee the public sphere in confusion nor rush to trade freedom for empire.

Medieval thinkers contrasted the immaterial directly with the material. Material things undergo change and bear the imprint of what changes them, each immersed in its own space and time. "Immaterials," then, are characterized by self-display, immanence (dwelling-within), and transcendence of space and time.

There has been a "change of weather." Modern "subjectivity" is characterized by openness, intentionality, aspiration for comprehension, and limits of situation such as perspective or historical setting.

In Chapter 10 Schmitz sees affinities between these two camps and develops them. For example, the past *as past* is not in the tree or the canyon. Pastness is an immaterial "property" true of the thing but manifest only through association with the temporal cadence and spatial perspective of situated intelligence. Marcel claims that works of art *themselves* increase in being as looked upon through the ages and understood and enjoyed by appreciating minds.

Personal becoming is the coming-to-be of spirit in the flesh. In Chapter 11 Schmitz notes a shift in the sense of spirit. Spirit as *forma* (specifying principle) becomes spirit as *Geist* (dynamic inner expression of unity). Religious interiority looks to reach God through purgation, prayer, and charity. Modern subjectivity faces a field of objects that it cannot identify with except by techno-mastery. But both recognize a certain insufficiency in the world.

Another contrast: for modern physics the primary action is motion transferring matter or energy. Rest is stale, sterile, or at best recuperative. But Aristotle said our rest in the bliss of friendship or pure contemplation is the highest activity.

The key to spirit is communication without loss. When we teach something, we don't lose the knowledge that the other gains. Learning is a spiritual mutation or quasi-mutation. Indifference, apathy, evil deeds are real spiritual setbacks. The interaction of human cultures, mutual friendships, beautiful art, new persons—are real enhancements. Immateriality—it matters!

Chapter 12 is an exposition and expansion of Aquinas' argument that the intellectual operations of the soul are incorporeal. Intellect can have knowledge of all corporeal things—not that we know each material thing but that we know "what it is to be a material thing." Human intelligence in grasping meanings "transcends the particular conditions from which and within which it discerns them." The world may run out of vanilla but even vanished essences remain for thought. "Knowing is not an ordinary traffic between bodies."

In Chapter 14, Schmitz says discourse about God is unique. "We must not play at the fiction that we simply start thinking and accidentally stumble upon the argument that, step by step, proves the existence of such a God."

Thomas' arguments for the existence of God do not work rhetorically without a modern background (or foreground). Anselm, Eckhart, and Cusa help us set up the notion of what we are trying to prove. Nicholas of Cusa said: God is so transcendent that he is not even "other" from his creation, not that he is the same as us, but that he is so transcendent that he cannot be fitted into the category of same and other.

Schmitz deepens and tunes senses of nature, nearness, motion, etc. For example, he invites us to think beyond Newton's Third Law. The "reciprocity" of reception is itself nonreciprocal. "It is a free acknowledgment that adds nothing physical to the original communication." Armed with more "modern weapons" and with a full sense of causality, we are sent back to Aquinas' arguments.

Chapters 15 and 17 are an explication of and comment on Karol Wojtyla/John Paul II's *Fides et ratio* placed in the context of his earlier works and of the traditional relation between philosophy and theology. In searching for truth (Chapter 15), we glimpse a personal God who desires friendship with all who inquire. Though inquiry is a kind of struggle, insight comes as a gift.

John Paul II speaks of the newness of being. Phenomenology describes the horizon, the inside of human experience as such. Metaphysics situates beings within a community of beings. Each being has an active, interior, yet given principle—the to-be *(esse)*. Combining phenomenology with the metaphysics of *esse* allows us a more radical appreciation of the inside of being itself—the dearest freshness deep down things.

Kenneth Schmitz has some fun at the expense of certain coroners in Chapter 16. Thrice God was pronounced dead. The morticians expected a new Man to arise in his stead. Instead they had to prepare three more coffins. Diderot's superfluous God died and Metaphysical Man did too. The dangerous God was put away and Nietzsche interred Rational Man. Finally Comte pronounced the negligible God dead and in Robbe-Grillet's novel *Jealousy*, man simply isn't there.

Is there a way out of this spiral of deflation and fatigue? The author suggests we review and consolidate some real gains of the Enlightenment: a greatly increased knowledge of the workings of nature, including the size and age of the universe; the history of existence including the earth and the fragile environment; a sharpened sense of individuality; expansion of options such as going all around the world; an expansion of imagination in the novel, plastic arts, and music. If being has a history, these four hundred years are a part of it. We are to probe again the texture of being starting with the good because, as Plato pointed out, no one willingly accepts substitutes or a merely apparent good.

In Chapter 17, we hear Anselm: "Your face, O Lord! I long to see your Face; I was made to see your Face and I have not yet done that for which I was made." The call to vision is also John Paul II's call to courage, the Angel Gabriel's "fear not." But how to hear and see in the noise of a blighted landscape?

Nietzsche made war against the Good and the True. But he could not overcome Beauty—indeed he was overcome by it. "Where power becomes gracious [*gnädig*] and descends into the visible—such descent I call beauty" and "It is not in satiety that his desire shall grow silent and be submerged, but in beauty." Schmitz comments on Aquinas' three qualities of beauty: harmony, integrity, and radiance (so beloved by James Joyce's Stephen Daedalus).

But the Christian cannot simply idle in the idyll of the beautiful. Not yet. We must help redeem the ugly. We do not value ugliness. We try to replace and heal it.

In Buddhism, the saved one, the Bodhisattva, immediately gets back in the boat to bring the others over. So the Christian gazing on the stricken face of the Lord on the cross makes a transvaluation to see the Face of God in the unlovely faces of the poor, the ignorant, and the hurt.

Like philosophy itself, the arc of Kenneth Schmitz's thought rises in wonder and awe at existence and beauty. Like a rainbow after clouds, colorful mystery lifts us.

Paul O'Herron

PART I

BEING

Chapter 1

METAPHYSICS
Radical, Comprehensive, Determinate Discourse

Metaphysics is the most controversial and controverted of the philosophical disciplines. I want to argue, nevertheless, that if it did not already exist in some form, then it would be necessary to invent it. For the need to think fundamentally is not incidental to the inquiring energy of the human mind. That energy has taken form as myth, meditation, and reflection among a variety of peoples of diverse cultures. In our rather abstract and articulate culture, however, fundamental thinking has taken the rational, argumentative, and conceptual form of discourse.

Discourse. By "discourse" I mean a modification of language that makes its use more selective than it ordinarily is—more tightly organized, and more deliberate, disciplined, and reflective. Language serves a host of human interests, of course; it is often directed towards the expression of feelings or the implementation of actions. Discourse, as I understand the term,[1] is language pressed into the service of cognitive ends. It aims at making statements that are true assertions about things. For that reason, discourse strives to be methodical, and functions with a more or less explicit theory of what counts for truth, a more or less worked out theory of what counts as evidence, and a more or less developed set of canons for valid and acceptable argumentation.

Reprinted from the *Review of Metaphysics* 39 (June 1986): 675–94. Copyright © 1986 by the *Review of Metaphysics*

1. For a more extended development of the concept of discourse along these lines, see "The Philosophy of Religion and the Redefinition of Philosophy," *Man and World* 3 (1970): 54–82 (reprinted in *The Challenge of Religion*, ed. F. Ferré, J. Kockelmans, and J. E. Smith [New York: Seabury, 1982], 3–26); "Restitution of Meaning in Religious Speech," *International Journal for Philosophy of Religion* 5 (1974): 131–51; "Natural Imagery as a Discriminatory Element in Religious Language," in *Experience, Reason and God: Studies in Philosophy and the History of Philosophy*, vol. 8, ed. E. T. Long (Washington, D.C.: The Catholic University of America Press, 1980), 159–76.

The origins of discourse lie in the Greek cities of the seventh and eighth centuries before our present era.[2] The poetic and religious heritage of the Greeks gave expression to an apportioned order *(kosmos)*, presided over by the implacable and irrevocable decrees of Fate (*Moira*, cf. *moirao:* to apportion, *meros:* part). Against the backdrop of the *mythos* of ordered partitioning, *logos* took shape as rational discourse. In the process, a quite general alteration of attitude seems to have taken place. For the Greeks were now able to put themselves mentally at a distance from things within the world, and thereby to lay before their minds several spheres of inquiry: the substance of things (philosophy), the architectonic of numbers (mathematics), the course of human events (history), and even the functions of language itself (grammar). A sort of "objectification" took place, a new way of seeing things, to which they later gave the name *Theoria*. Moreover, with that distancing, a mode of thought and expression arose which was relatively (i.e., never completely) free of the imagery of poetry and myth: the process of "conceptualization." "Objectification" and "conceptualization" together formed the tissue of rational discourse.

By the sixth century, theoretical discourse seems to have taken the four primary forms just indicated: (i) *philosophy* (including what we might call science as well as metaphysics or ontology), (ii) *mathematics*, (iii) *history*, and (iv) *linguistics* (including grammar, rhetoric, and logic), perhaps even in that order. The last to emerge out of the general sense of discursive rationality seems to have been conceptual reflection upon language in terms of the objective functions of the parts of speech (grammar), along with logic and rhetoric, for we have little evidence of them earlier than the fifth century. History seems to have taken shape also in the early fifth century, when the actions of the Greeks were taken as objective events in the world and the story of their deeds was told in terms of their causes and reasons—reasons *(aitiai)* which included their measure as noble or base (cf. aetiology). Mathematics, on the other hand, may well have been twinned with philosophy in the sixth century. Building upon the complex and even sophisticated calculations of the Egyptians and Babylonians, the Greeks gave an account of the things that are in the form of relationships made intelligible in terms of numerical values. Philosophy, on the other hand, seems to have pressed on towards the radical and comprehensive unity of things in terms of

---

2. I have presented my understanding of the historical origins and early formation of discourse at greater length in "Gibt es für den Menschen Wichtigeres, als zu uberleben? Das Erbe Griechenlands: Rationalität," trans. H. Scheit, in *Das europäische Erbe und seine christliche Zukunft*, ed. N. Lobkowicz (Cologne: Hans Martin Schleyer-Stiftung/Pontificium Consilium pro Cultura, 1985), 99–104 (English, 348–56).

some real substance that pervaded the whole of reality, accessible to human inquiry and to rational expression. Rather soon, this became an account in terms of being and essence *(on ousia)*—not, however, without competitors.

Since that ancient time, the four accounts have played out their varying fortunes—rendered in terms of being (philosophy), number (mathematics), time (history), and verbal expression (grammar). Although each has retained its native character with remarkable consistency, still there have been dramatic developments in each of them throughout our own intellectual traditions. Notably, the theological appropriation of ontology in the doctrinal councils of the Christian church during the fourth and fifth centuries of our era, as well as in the High Middle Ages. And again, the explosion of the mathematical account in the physics of the sixteenth century, an impetus that has not yet run its course, and that has tended over the past few centuries to crowd out the other modes of discourse. More recently, the spread of the historical mode into the earth sciences of the late eighteenth century, as well as into the biological, social, and human sciences during the nineteenth century is still in full steam. Finally, one needs scarcely remark upon the unprecedented progress made during the past century in the reflective and discursive study of language and logic. Metaphysics, too, has had its ups; especially during the later Greek period from Plato on, and again during the High Middle Ages and in the seventeenth century. Today, however, with a small number of exceptions, it is somewhat quiescent, and in some circles of thought there continues to be much talk about the overcoming of metaphysics: through dialectics, positivism, hermeneutics, or some other strategy. We can expect, then, that if metaphysics has survived, it may stand in need of resuscitation and will not be unaffected by the stormy career through which it has recently passed. It is, then, within the general context and tradition of metaphysics as ontology that I dare to pursue this question.

There is an advantage to putting the question as baldly as the conference has framed it. For if it were phrased in terms of the "possibility" of metaphysics, as it so often is, it would be difficult to avoid giving the palm to possibility, arguing from possibility towards some actual version of metaphysics. The possibility of something has been decided in one of two ways in our traditions. One way is by an appeal to possibility itself; the other is by defining the possible in terms of what is actual. In the former, an appeal is usually made to non-contradiction and a set of criteria adopted a priori—whether rationalist after the manner of Descartes, or empiricist after the manner of Hume, or even positivist. At that point metaphysics as the study of the ultimately real must give way to a first philosophy that speaks for epistemology, axiology, or some other interest. On the other hand, one gets a rather different metaphysics at the end of a road that is determined on the basis of what is actual, for example, after the manner of Aristotle or Hegel in contrast to the Latin Avicenna or Leibniz. It may well be that the growing influence of the historical mode of explanation today helps to reassert the primacy of the actual, without determining the ontological significance of what is actual.

In view of the pre-eminent role of actuality which I have asserted in the foregoing, it seems appropriate to register a note about the manner in which a metaphysics of the actual is to be proposed these days. Given the history of the multitude of metaphysical systems that have already been put forward in the long history of Western philosophical thought—to say nothing of the religious philosophies of non-Western cultures—it is no longer appropriate simply to advance yet one more system. It is just the plethora of seemingly incompatible metaphysical systems that makes the adoption of criteria of possibility so plausible, as though to ask: Why not go behind metaphysics in order to settle the issue of its possibility first, and then go on to realize its particular form? But then, of course, there would be a "first" *prior* to what has been traditionally taken to be first philosophy: an unacceptable solution to anyone who is not prepared to abandon metaphysics' claim to firstness in the order of discursive knowledge.

It is a narrow, hard place. For if it is no longer appropriate simply to advance yet one more system of metaphysics, and if it is not appropriate to settle upon criteria prior to doing metaphysics, where can one turn? It is necessary here to become as fully self-conscious as possible about the very activity of "doing" metaphysics. On the side of our own subjectivity, we must be more tentative and more exploratory than has been the case in more robust centuries. Yet we cannot become so tentative that we give up the making of truth claims, nor the thrust of conceptual analysis and rational argument on their behalf. For rational argumentation and the making of truth claims are the *minima* that must survive if we are to have philosophical discourse at all. But the adjustment of metaphysical tone requires more than a change of style, since its root concern lies deeper than rhetoric. For, on the objective side, there is the fact of the plurality of metaphysical systems with which to contend. Moreover, the plurality of metaphysical systems seems to indicate a pluralism that is endemic to metaphysics itself. Now, pluralism is not simply plurality: it is the recognition (aided by the growing force of the historical mode of discourse) of the persistence of a plurality of metaphysical insights, a plurality that does not seem to be reducible in any ordinary way to a single, overarching metaphysical idea. If there is such a single idea or even several, it or they do not seem to provide a conceptual unity in any of the usual senses—as for example "energy" might be said to be what physics is concerned with. Nor does the plurality of insights seem to have been given adequate expression in any one of the many systems. The pluralism of metaphysics consists in the irreducible diversity of answers to the question: What does it mean to think metaphysically?

Perhaps this is what is meant by the grandeur and the misery of metaphysics. According to my own mind, its grandeur of conception is to think radically, comprehensively, and determinately about whatever is, reaching down to the roots and out to the edges of all that is. Its misery of condition arises, however, because metaphysics is not a divine activity, but a reflection carried out by the human mind, reaching out from the particular cave of each metaphysician, a cave which he or she can never quite leave without ceasing to be human. In becoming aware of the caves of others, the metaphysician must formulate an understanding of what is radical, comprehensive, and determinate in the face of the tension between the perspectivity of the actual human condition and the comprehensivity of metaphysical ambition, between the strictures of human knowing and the openness of metaphysical hope. In terms of the question before us: Are that ambition and that hope empty?

Foundations? The metaphor of foundations has had a long career in Western philosophy, especially in reflection upon and discussion about the order of the sciences and disciplines. Thus, for example, there are foundations of algebra, foundations of political theory, foundations of economic analysis, and so on. When an algebraist is discoursing upon the foundations of his science or a physicist upon his fundamental research, certain pervasive conceptions are continually in play. They have sometimes been called "primitive terms," though they might better be termed "primary concepts." Now, I do not mean that such concepts play a merely peripheral role as part of a non-quantitative, non-mathematical, and non-technical commentary to the business at hand; nor that they serve as a mere pedagogical device for those who otherwise might not be able to follow the argument insofar as it is couched in technical terms. Rather, these fundamental conceptions are in the very mix of thought; they underlie, penetrate, and make up part of the meaning even of the special, technical, mathematical, and quantitative terms. And they are also present in the "qualitative" discourse of history, sociology, psychology, theology, and the like. They are largely presupposed in discourse, being implicit and operative rather than thematic. Discourse can proceed without thematizing them; and indeed, it does so in the special inquiries. Nevertheless, because they are the primary conceptions without which discourse itself could not proceed, they need to be thematized, if discourse is to take possession of itself. Some of them are: unity and multiplicity, sameness and diversity, activity and passivity, ordination and subsumption, and the like. I do not here offer a list, for that is the very task of metaphysics itself in its role as first philosophy.

The issue can be brought to focus, then, with the question: Do the relative senses of the term *foundation*—i.e., relative to algebra, economics, and other special inquiries—themselves stand in need of a foundation in knowing? Of course, we might want to look more carefully at the distinction between relative or special forms of discourse and primary or general terms which allegedly underlie all discourse. But it does seem that the relative senses of the term "foundation" already embody a deeper sense that needs to be made explicit and given methodical, discursive, conceptual formulation. Failing this, we might well ask whether discourse can purchase for itself the unity, coherence, and adequacy that it demands of its more special forms. Now, methodical, discursive, conceptual knowing that attends to the foundation of foundations is just what has been meant by first philosophy.

The answer a philosopher gives to this question depends in large measure upon the status that he or she accords to such conceptions as one and many, same and different, presence and absence. He may take them to be obvious and in need of no further consideration, so that metaphysics will consist of stating the self-evident. Or again, he may consider them truly primitive, neither standing in need of nor able to receive further articulation. As an illustration in favor of the need for such discourse about primary conceptions, however, let me point out an issue that suggests that the concept of *unity* is less than obvious, and that it stands in need of methodical, reflective discourse. It is an issue that has dogged the history of Western thought for a very long time, and may be put as follows: Is the primary conception of unity in its pristine form equivalent to the utterly *simple?* This convergence of unity and simplicity was the direction along which the thought of the ancient atomists moved; it was also the direction of the medieval nominalists; and at least until recently it was the sought-after discovery of particle theory. On the other hand, it was not the direction pursued by such thinkers as Aristotle, for whom the primary sense of unity is compatible with complexity. Indeed, according to him, the primary ontological unit—this something of a certain sort *(tode ti)*—is inherently complex in its constitution. And for Thomas Aquinas, unity *(unum)* was defined as undivided—not indivisible—being *(ens indivisum),* said analogously of diverse beings. Nor was the identification of unity with simplicity the direction of Hegel's thought, for whom unity is also inherently complex. Nor is it the expectation of those physicists today who look beyond the mechanism inherent in classical quantum mechanics. The illustration suggests that there are primary concepts and that they do need discursive articulation. The problem remains, however, how they might best receive it, and whether that articulation can meet acceptable standards of methodical discourse.

For the most pressing problem today arises, it seems to me, out of the suspicion that the foundations of our discursive conceptual knowing are not susceptible, after all, to rigorous methodical articulation and adequate conceptual clarification. Can we suppose any longer that the foundations of meaning are cut from the same intelligible cloth as discourse itself? Is it possible to maintain that the depths of our understanding move in the same pure atmosphere as discourse? It seems, rather, that the foundations do *not* share the same intellectual character as the concepts that make up the fabric of discourse. For discourse, as I have characterized it, intends to bring everything it talks about to intellectual clarity as far as possible; it pledges itself to render everything intelligible in the form of concepts. It may well be that it is still haunted by the lost dream of a pure, ontological grammar. To this medieval dream there is sometimes added in modern times the goal of an absolutely presuppositionless starting point, as though intellectual sight could peer down through the clear waters of life to grasp the foundations of its own knowing with the same conceptual clarity and definition with which it grasps a well-defined concept or a carefully worked out and coherent theory. Instead, it has learned that the waters are muddy, and sometimes surprisingly lively, with strange eddies of feeling, strong currents of motivation, and partly hidden turbulence. For psychology talks of hidden impulses and drives, anthropology discloses the limitations of each of our inherited cultures, and sociology traces out general forces that move the individual along paths scarcely discernible to him. Moreover, there is the suspicion that concepts themselves cannot sustain their meaning without the umbilical cord of experience, imagination, and human freedom—experience (the great compacter) with its sedimentation, partly unconscious, partly forgotten; imagination (the great profiler) with its pre-rational selectivity and the creativity that breathes an air that never was; and freedom with its subjective interest. It is not surprising, then, that any concepts put forward as foundational become suspect, and that they are likely to be judged inadequate, partial, derivative, and even arbitrary expressions of whatever foundations there may be. Indeed, this Heraclitean river seems to exclude the very possibility of foundations at all, for the metaphor of foundations draws upon a more stable world than either Heraclitus' river or the tangle of contemporary discourse seems likely to support.

Nevertheless, the recognition of the opacity of the foundations of discourse, though perhaps more acute today, does not pose an entirely new problem. On the one hand, the apparent incommensurability of the intelligible and the sensible orders has been marked by philosophies ranging from Plato's theory of forms, through Kant's critical idealism according to which the primary concepts (pure categories) cannot arise out of the sensible manifold of experience as out of their source, to pure formalists for whom the ideas of mathematics and the laws of logic are not derivable from a psychological or physical basis. On the other hand, the relation between conceptual discourse and its experiential basis has been reflected upon since Aristotle insisted upon the sensory origin of intellectual knowledge, and since scholastics spoke of abstracting the intelligible species from the sensible phantasm. It has also been inquired into since empiricism insisted in its own way upon the sensory origin of ideas.

In coming to grips with the problem of the adequacy of discourse to reach and express its own foundations, I have found helpful the way in which Hegel distinguishes between two senses of the term "foundation." He distinguishes a *basis (Grundlage)* from a *ground (Grund)*. The former signifies a substrate *upon which* a structure can be erected—in this instance, a structure of knowledge. The basis, then, plays a role not unlike the material cause of which Aristotle spoke *(hypokeimenon)*, though in Hegel the basis has systemic rather than substantive or entitative functions. When the foundation is taken to be the *ground* of knowledge, however, we have a richer and more active category. For the ground, in the senses in which it is spoken of by Leibniz, Hegel, and even Heidegger, is a modern way of gathering together the presuppositions of intelligibility into a single legitimizing conception. In Leibniz, the ground is the sufficient reason for the way things are and the rational justification for the knowledge we have of them. He traced it back to the divine intelligence and the divine will, giving the conception a theological character. For Hegel, on the other hand, the ground is both origin and result. Moreover, if we were to give it another name, it would be that of *system*—the totality of being and thought grasped in the complex unity of its own process of self-determination. The ground, then, in Hegel has a *systemic* character, and it has this character in much of the subsequent talk about foundations, whether the talk stems from him or from Leibniz or from Kant. For, after all, even in Kant the ground in its broadest sense is the foundation of the architectonic system, the *conceptus cosmicus* which gathers into a rational unity the essential needs of human reason, and thereby constitutes the appropriate form of philosophy itself.

We can put the difference between these two meanings of the term "foundation" in another way. The *basis* plays out its role by providing evidence for the activity of inquiring—data upon which knowing can rest its claim by tracing its results back to what has been given to it. And so the basis plays a decisive role in philosophies that accept the given as a starting point *(datum)*. The weakness of this understanding of foundation, however, is that it does not account for the givenness of the very *datum* to which the account appeals for its justification. And so, the given remains inert (simply there) and outside of knowledge; that is, it remains unrelated (or only externally attached) to the process of knowing. Moreover, an account of knowing based upon the givenness of evidence tries to guarantee the objectivity of knowledge, but it does not account for other factors which also play a role in the whole knowledge claim—such factors as the context of the inquiry, its approach and method, the perspective and disposition of the inquirer, the inquirer's interest and purpose, and the dynamism of inquiry itself. For that reason, some have conceded that the given is not an adequate basis for interpreting events and records in the social and cultural spheres; since in them, human subjectivity has already entered into the very constitution of the evidence—be it a social custom, a psychological attitude, a literary text, or the like—so that the human subject is already involved and the evidence already more than what is naturally given. It has been suggested, however, that the conception of the given is more appropriate to the natural sciences at least, since in them the evidence is supposedly already well defined prior to any human intervention; but that condition seems to hold less and less as the inquiry in those disciplines becomes more sophisticated and more and more explicitly involves the condition of the observer. It seems to me, therefore, that the conception of foundation as basis *(Grundlage)* or as given *(datum)* may serve as a limit in a partial theoretical inquiry, or as a convenient stopping place suitable to the practical interests of technology, but that it cannot withstand the pressure of a thoroughgoing theoretical inquiry into the fundamental nature of knowing.

The *ground*, on the other hand, plays out its role by providing the implicit context as well as the content and aim of knowledge—i.e., the horizon and contours as well as the matter and objectives of inquiry. In Hegel's philosophy, of course, the ground in the broader sense is fully systemic and rests upon the initial suspension of the dualism between knowing and reality, a dualism that is inherent in the concept of *basis* and in philosophies of the *given*. Moreover, there is no doubt that Hegel substituted the conception of *self-giving* for that of givenness, and that for him the process of self-giving was the ground of a fully self-determining system. It will become clear in what follows that I do not rest my argument upon these systemic features of the Hegelian philosophy, and that I have appealed to the distinction between the concepts of *basis* and *ground* only in order to acknowledge what I take to be their rival claims upon the conception of *foundation.*

Principles. What I propose, however, is that the very conception of foundation needs to be questioned, because—however well it may serve other sciences—it carries with it unsuitable traits and presuppositions when it is asked to serve as the characterization of metaphysics. Instead, the metaphor I should like to bring into play is that of *firstness,* so that I might recover in a modified way a conception that challenges *both* senses of foundation. Furthermore, it seems to me that a philosophy in search of firstness will be neither empty nor foundational. Now, it may be that the metaphor of foundations is more ancient than that of firstness, for the former may have been present at least implicitly ever since the first philosopher proposed moisture as the pervasive substance. Moreover, I am not sure just when the metaphor of foundations assumed the controlling power over our understanding of first philosophy that it now seems to enjoy. But I do know that the metaphor received a decisive emphasis in the shift that occurred in the sixteenth century and that was subsequently carried out by the scientific search for simple elements. These elements came to be thought of as building blocks—for some they were material, for others they were ideas or impressions—whose discovery and linkage was thought to yield the knowledge of foundations and all that rested thereupon.

Let me propose, then, that metaphysics as first philosophy does not seek foundations at all, neither as bases nor as grounds, and that, instead, it seeks *firstness.* By "firstness" here I mean to revive the old Greek notion of principle *(archē).* I understand by a principle *(principium)* a firstness or primacy, from which consequences *(principiata)* follow as from a source, and follow according to a certain order which is in keeping with the character of the principle that establishes such an order. Now, this order may be either real or mental or both; that is, it may be an order of things or of knowledge or of both. Thus, for example, the American Constitution prescribes an order of political relationships; the eight-tone scale institutes an order of musical intervals and consequent harmonies; and more generally, a goal ordains the means, even though the latter may be manifold and not at all obvious. In each case, the principle sets limits and allows possibilities to come forward, a certain differentiation becomes available. If we consider only a single principle, we may speak of that differentiation as an order, recognizing that a diffusion of principles results in a complex order, and that ultimately the universe is the order of orders. I have selected the examples to make the point that principles can emerge as new sources of new orders, either natural or social or historical, either technical, artistic, religious, or scientific. There is no need to defend the eternity of species and the fixity of the world order to recover the central point about principles. They do not bar what we call "creativity," and are compatible with an "open" universe, as long as "open" does not mean "without any order at all." Now, this search may eventually turn us along a path towards a theological conception of metaphysics, but I should like to suspend that possible outcome in order to examine the initial steps along the path towards firstness, if only because the very word "theological" is encrusted with differing and even incompatible, and not seldom vehement, associations that are drawn from dispositions towards or against institutional religion.

A little more needs to be said about principles in the sense intended. An element is a constitutive part of a composite, and its contribution *qua* element is restricted to its inclusion in the resultant whole of which it is an elemental part. A principle, on the other hand, generates its appropriate order of consequences—whether in the thing or also in our knowledge of it, or in knowledge alone, depending upon the nature of the principle. For a principle is generative of consequences that follow from the kind of principle that it is, and not from whether its status is at one time mental, at another real. A web of different principles, then, results in a complex and unified order of orders.

Now, Aristotle distinguished principles from elements in his analysis of things, although an element *(stoicheion)* can and almost always does function as a principle as well. A brick presumably is chiefly a material part of a wall, and hence an element; but many elements contribute to the new properties of a resultant chemical compound (e.g., Na in NaCl, in which Na is both an elemental part of the resultant compound and a co-principle or source of the new properties that emerge with it). Moreover, Aristotle took some principles, such as matter and form, to be constitutive causes of physical things. Now, precisely *qua* principles, they are the source not merely of a part of the complex thing; rather, they play out their role with regard to the whole of the thing. Thus, for example, the physical thing is through and through material: matter is not simply a part or element contained somehow in the thing. Or again, the thing is through and through its kind or type: the form or essence is not a part of the thing, it is the whole of it. Composition in this sense, then, is not a binding together of parts (synthesis), but is rather the unification of different orders of consequences whose sources are really diverse principles. And so, among various principles, we call a principle "primary" if it is the source of a distinctive and fundamental order. A "primary principle," then, is the source of an original order of consequences that is not reducible without loss to some other order, as color is not reducible without loss to wavelengths, or knowledge without loss to brain waves.

Implicit in this conception of principle is that each is an original fullness, i.e., a fullness relative to the order which results from it. In reviving the conception of principle, then, I am conscious of appealing to a notion of plenitude. It is this inherent plenitude that distinguishes the conception of principle as source *(archē)* from the more modern concept of totality *(Totalitätsbegriff)*. For the latter is understood as a result already aimed for (e.g., Kant's a priori idea), or as a context within which something comes to be (e.g., Husserl's *Horizont* or Heidegger's *Welt* or language as implicit system). A principle, on the other hand, is an origin. Indeed, even if the totality is taken—not as a fact achieved, but as a goal *(telos)* to be achieved—then *qua* principle, it is taken in its character of firstness and not as a result. It is this insight that led the scholastics to pronounce the final cause the "first of all causes." And it is just this difference that must be recognized between the Aristotelian principle of originating actuality *(energeia and entelecheia)*, on the one hand, and the modern concept of resultant actuality (*Wirklichkeit*, the facts or states of affairs), on the other.

Radical. Instead of the knowledge of foundations, then, metaphysics as first philosophy can be represented as knowledge of a web of interlocking primary principles. Each principle is first and source in its own order and determinant of its own kind of consequences; and together with other principles it is determinant of a complex order of orders. Nothing prevents us from calling such a principled web "foundational," since the first (the principle) must be present if the second (the principiates) are to be there too. But metaphors are important, since they exert a pull upon discourse, and the term "foundation" tends to carry us off into a metaphor of stability and external relations (superstructure) whose explication in either of the two senses traced earlier (base and ground) has systemic implications from which a metaphysics of principles is free. As sources, the metaphor appropriate for principles is that of roots *(radices)*; and the thinking appropriate to first philosophy is *radical* thinking, inasmuch as the term does not indicate eccentricity of opinions nor extremism of action, but thought pressing on towards its own sources.

Comprehensive. Such a metaphysics of principles has also been understood to be *comprehensive* knowing. In the long tradition stemming from Aristotle it has been known as the science of being as being *(to on he on)*—most comprehensive, since all that comes before the mind either is or is related in some way to whatever is. Even negations and privations fulfill such a broad requirement. Nevertheless, the nature of this comprehensive universality is not unproblematical. *Comprehensive* universality is no ordinary universality—neither genus, nor species, nor class, nor generality. Speaking of such terms as *being* and *unity,* Aristotle declared them to be equivocal, i.e., analogous. Thus, for example, taken in the entirety of each usage, each referent of the term *being* is simply diverse, and the full meaning of each referent is similarly diverse. A dictionary illustration may suffice: When a certain structure on an airplane is called a "wing," and a certain organ of a bird is also called a "wing," both the referent and the meaning of each taken as a whole is intentionally different. But their simple otherness is not the only appropriate word, and within this radical diversity the mind grasps an affinity or resonance in the meanings of the word, even as the tongue pronounces it. We can, of course, abstract (i.e., mentally attend to) a single function which they share: "to sustain flight," or some such univocal meaning; but if, seeking to remain closer to the real, the mind attends to each whole respectively (i.e., to the organ, then to the metal structure) so as to also acknowledge their differences (i.e., organic and artifactual), then the mind must recognize the similarity between them without being able to disengage that similarity from its divers contexts: and this is to recognize their "diversity-commonality." There are many such analogous universals, but what is relevant here is that the very term *principle* itself possesses just this sort of analogous universality. So that first philosophy conceived as a metaphysics of principles includes the study of radical analogous universals.

In the High Middle Ages metaphysics as the study of ontological principles centered upon the transcendental concomitants of being as being. The noteworthy pervasive universals usually listed were: being itself *(ens),* thing *(res),* unity *(unum),* truth *(verum),* goodness *(bonum),* and sometimes beauty *(pulchrum).* They are universal in the sense that they can be said in some way of everything that is; and they are analogous because they are said diversely of each thing. For this is what is meant by utterly comprehensive universality: an unrestricted presence that is quite different from the limited universality of definite kinds, that is, of genera, species, or classes. Now, this sense of unrestricted universality arose in the context of thinking about first principles; for although this understanding of transcendentals is not explicit in Aristotle, nevertheless several discussions in his *Metaphysics* regarding being and unity are compatible with it and even seem to imply something like an understanding of radical universals as principles that lie beyond the formal restrictions of every genus and species. A distinction suggests itself between primary universals that are the principles of generic orders and the absolutely "first" and radical principles that are the concern of metaphysics. Thomas Aquinas brought together the comprehensive nature of first principles and the analogous character of the terms that express them, so that first principles were understood by him to be radical, analogous, and comprehensive. What is at stake in such a conception of metaphysics is whether such trans-generic conceptions can provide sufficient unity and reality for an inquiry that strives to give discursive expression to the totality of whatever is.

The general understanding of principle that served for about eighteen hundred years in Western thought was this: a principle is a beginning *qua* source *(principium)* upon which consequences *(principiata)* follow, and a first principle is a universal whose consequences are unrestricted to any generic or specific kind. For reasons too complex to enter into here, this understanding of principle was deliberately and resolutely rejected in the seventeenth century by leaders of thought, such as Bacon, Hobbes, Descartes, Spinoza, and others, often in terms of an attack upon the Aristotelian causes, but sometimes by the translation of the Aristotelian terms into quite different meanings and into a quite different mode of thought.[3] It must not be forgotten, moreover, that the abandonment of thinking in terms of such ontological principles was part of a program that sought out foundations, conceived as elements of thought and reality, in order to rebuild in thought a structure that was intended to mirror nature more faithfully and to contribute to the commodiousness of human life more effectively. What is relevant in this context, however, is not past history as such, but the manner in which thinking in the light of principles operates, since it is just the trans-generic universality of first principles that has traditionally sustained the metaphysical claim to comprehensivity. And the question arises: By what means can one both reach and articulate such primary principles?

Determinate. Principles, then, are what are first in a certain order; as primary they are first in some irreducible order; and as metaphysically first they are trans-generic and radical sources of the order of orders. All principles play out their roles in the makeup of what actually is, i.e., actuality *qua* result. Now, actuality as result, i.e., as fact or state of affairs or *Wirklichkeit*, arises out of the interplay of the principles (sources) of actuality. As one or another of the principles come forward—in reality, or in the inquiring mind, or in both—they establish an actual order (of reality and/or knowledge) which contains consequent possibilities within it: actual and possible *principiata* arise out of *principia*. Nevertheless, while the

---

3. For a more detailed account of the shift from principles to elements, see "Analysis by Principles and Analysis by Elements," in *Graceful Reason: Essays in Ancient and Mediaeval Philosophy Presented to Joseph Owens, CSSR*, ed. Lloyd Gerson (Toronto: Pontifical Institute of Mediaeval Studies, 1983), 315–30. See chapter 2 below.

principles are principles of actuality, we need to distinguish within the open multitude of principles, those that are "actuality-principles," i.e., principles that are themselves actual, and precisely the source of actuality; for not all principles are sources of what can be called the *actuality* of what is actual. Thus, the American Constitution does not *of itself* and without any other principles playing their roles bring about the realization of a political order in keeping with it. Political action on the part of citizens is required. By "actuality-principles," then, I mean the sources of power, latent within the achieved actuality. At an earlier time, they were called "active potencies" or "active powers," and from them as from a source the other principles come into play and discharge their appropriate role in the actual order. Now, these actuality-principles are possessed of a fullness that carries actuality to new careers, as long as other principles do not inhibit them. Thus, for example, as long as a culture has resources of power and possibilities within it, it can continue to develop, unless hindered by extraneous forces. It is often feared today that talk of order, principles, and causes will inhibit emerging novelty in the realms of nature, history, and society. On the contrary, such a view of fullness is compatible with a universe that is open to new developments—whether the new potency arises out of a given fund of actuality which is there from the beginning (an eternal world), or from the continuing influx of a creative principle, either cosmological (after the manner suggested by some recent cosmologists) or theological. Now, these "actuality-principles" grasped in their radical character are existing agents, full-bodied sources of actual determinations. They are contextualized individuals at play fashioning the order of orders. Metaphysics is the recognition in universal terms of the agency of contextualized individuals open to developments in nature, history, and society.

The meaning of "contextualized individuals" must be made clear, however. To do this, it is necessary to rid the conception of "individual" of any bias in favor of the "individualized individual." In his basically sound battle against certain disciples of Plato, Aristotle insisted that the primary ontological unit is an individual being of some kind *(tode ti)*. Now, this insistence has often been interpreted in such a way that it has led to underestimating the status of the non-individual factors (the *ti*) of the individual. According to Aristotle, metaphysical thought takes shape as a science of primary substance, and primary substance is understood to be an individual entity of some definite kind. Nevertheless, although this is true and important, it is not the last word to be said about the constitution of the real. What is more, we must think here beyond the standard theories of meaning with their division into particularity (whether instance, member, or case) and universality (whether of kind or class or generality). What needs to be resisted is the separation of the universal facet (the *ti*) from the individual (the *tode*), for such a separation turns the individual into an exclusively individuated reality, and suppresses the reality of the non-individual aspects (the *ti*) of the individual. Thus, a mistaken identification of the real with the individual tends to play down the reality of the non-individual factors. The latter include the context in which the individual is real, in which it acts and possesses existence—i.e., its kind, and in man's case, his community, culture, and society, and ultimately the world. Now, if metaphysics is the science of being as being, and if it is to be truly comprehensive, then its principles need to be understood in the context of the order of orders that follows from the principles together. Put in other words, Aristotle's *Metaphysics* has often been read as though the world is no more than the result of the collection of relations between individuals; and hence as derivative. Something similar occurs when a social contract thinker or an existentialist identifies community or society with the collection of interpersonal relations among its members.[4] But, if world or community were merely derivative from individuals, then the individual could be understood without the context within which alone it can act and without which it cannot even be.

It may well be that Aristotle left the context less than explicitly accounted for, and that he tended to resolve the cosmos back into the constituent principles of individuals as its causes. The schoolmen went a bit further, working with the latent Platonism in Aristotle and even with the explicit use of Platonisms of various provenance. I have already mentioned the transcendental concomitants of being, and it is to these that metaphysics needs to look, for they form the web within which the context of individuals—i.e., the world, the order of orders—is constituted, even as the individuals themselves are constituted of them. But even Thomas Aquinas, who developed Aristotle's metaphysical inquiries with profundity, fell back, not only upon the substantive language of properties, but also upon an incomplete characterization of the transcendentals. Holding on to the exclusive primacy of the individual, Thomas seems to have agreed that, when the subject matter of metaphysics (being as being) is considered in its integrity and referred to as being in common *(ens commune)*, it is a construct of the human mind alone *(ens rationis)*. But, on the other hand, it is also true that both Aristotle and Thomas acknowledged the presence of contextual factors, even if they did not usually bring them to full articulation. For, although it seems to me correct to insist upon the primacy of the individual, still that pri-

---

4. For further development of the concept of "contextualized individuals," see "Community: The Elusive Unity," *Review of Metaphysics* 37 (1983): 243–64.

macy needs to be understood in such a way that it does not prevent us from recognizing the non-individuality of the contextualized individual. We need to articulate further the inherent worldliness of the individual and the way in which the reality of the context enters into the very being of the individual. I would even go so far as to say that, properly understood, *ens commune* (the subject of metaphysics) is not merely *ens rationis;* it is *ens reale* (real being as the order of orders). For although the context is not real in the way that individuals are real (for example, the context *does* nothing, it is not an agent), neither is it simply a mental construct. In a word, the context is not an afterthought; it is concomitant and constitutive reality.

Even though Thomas' language often suppresses the reality of the context in favor of the primacy of the substance and its properties, still he does acknowledge that reality in another way. For he insists that metaphysics is not a science of concepts, but that it is instead, and uniquely, a science of judgment. Judgment, however, not only unites or separates concepts; in so doing, it refers the mind to the original context out of which the concepts have been formed. Judgment embraces context; judgment returns the mind to the world. Now, the reality of the context has been recognized in recent philosophy—whether it be as explanatory framework, or language as semiotic system, or horizon of experience, or the worldedness of being—though under the aegis of some version of the concept of totality (*Totalitätsbegriff, System, Horizont, Welt,* etc.).

In considering actuality as principle *(energeia, entelecheia)* and not simply as result (the facts, the actual state of affairs, *Wirklichkeit*), metaphysics locates the immediate source of that result, and also the future that is pregnant within it. It does not attempt to specify the particular characteristics of the various forces, for that requires specific modes of inquiry (the special sciences and disciplines); instead, it understands them simply as actuality-principles. What is more—and it is this that Thomas Aquinas has made explicit—the context into which the principles are to be resolved as into actuality is the context of being taken precisely as actuality *(esse),* i.e., as the order of principles that are themselves ordained to their functions within the context of actuality. Now, it is just this resolution of all principles into actuality that is to be understood through the existential force of the judgment.[5] For, within the parameters of discourse as I understand it, and within the contours of knowing, judgment cashes out into *is* and *is not.* By means of judgment, knowing is rendered determinate by this resolution into the context of actuality, so that judg-

---

5. For a more extensive consideration of the existential force of the judgment, see "Enriching the Copula," *Review of Metaphysics, A Commemorative Issue: Thomas Aquinas 1224–1274* 27 (1974): 492–512. See chapter 6 below.

ment is the device by which thought and discourse realize their determinacy. For it is here that the ultimate determination is reached, because the context of *is* and *is not* is the determinacy that outstrips formal conditions. As the trans-conceptual science of judgment, rooted in being as actuality, metaphysics is the consideration of trans-formal determinacy. Paradoxically, the study of what is most common issues into the recognition of what is most determinate. In metaphysics, the term "principle" refers analogously, not only to the contextual principles, but, above all, to the sources of actuality (the agents). In the metaphysics of judgment thought finds the medium through which it can break beyond itself, and thereby recognize and give expression to the root that lies beyond formal principles and structures, beyond systems and beyond foundations just because it is the source of the actuality of them, and of thought about them. With the recognition of the existential force of judgment, metaphysical discourse (as the effort to understand being as being through principles) becomes radical, comprehensive, and determinate. Radical, because it is the knowing of first principles as sources; comprehensive, because it is knowing by means of trans-generic universals; and determinate, because it is recognition of the primacy of a determinacy that is the trans-formal principle *(archē)* of actuality as result. Metaphysics is the invitation to thought, awakened by its most radical, comprehensive, and determinate inquiries, to trace its own source back to contextualized individuals and the web of principles that constitutes the order of orders.

Chapter 2

ANALYSIS BY PRINCIPLES AND ANALYSIS BY ELEMENTS

In the sixteenth and seventeenth centuries widespread distrust of analysis by *principles* contributed to the acceptance of analysis by *elements*. More precisely, the challenge to the validity and significance of analysis by *ontological*[1] principles resulted in the rise of analysis by *quantitative* elements. The latter was not unknown hitherto, of course, but under new conditions of thought and life it assumed new forms and unprecedented power, leading in modern physics to the search for basic particles and in chemistry to the search for simple elements. The pervasive collapse of ontological analysis took place largely outside of the universities and north of the Alps and Pyrenees.[2] What was distinctive about the change was that analysis by quantitative elements broke loose from the subordinate role it had played within an ontological context. Moreover, it came to be associated with a quite general redefinition of the interests

---

Reprinted from *Graceful Reason: Essays in Ancient and Mediaeval Philosophy Presented to Joseph Owens, CSSR*, ed. Lloyd P. Gerson. Papers in Mediaeval Studies 4 (Toronto: Pontifical Institute of Mediaeval Studies, 1983), 315–30. © Pontifical Institute of Mediaeval Studies, 1983.

1. In the discussion that followed upon my first professional paper ("Natural Wisdom in the Manuals," *Proceedings of the American Catholic Philosophical Association* 30 (1956): 160–81) I was asked by Fr. Owens (rhetorically, I suspect) whether the term "ontological" ought to be used nowadays by someone in the Aristotelian or Thomistic metaphysical tradition. I replied that it ought not to be used, and I think that my answer then was prudent, given the context in Catholic intellectual circles. The meaning associated with Leibniz and Wolff, viz., that ontology was the study of *ens possible*, was being communicated indirectly through some of the scholastic manuals then in wide use. Moreover, the Heideggerian stress on ecstatic possibility *(existentialia)* was beginning to command quite general attention in North America. Since then, however, the preferred term "metaphysical" has also fallen upon ambiguity in the uses to which positivists and some linguistic analysts have put it; so that it seems to me to be desirable to retrieve a neutral meaning of the term ontological, viz., "analysis in terms of being," and to develop the further and more determinate meaning in the exposition itself.

2. The quite different situation that prevailed in Italy has often been remarked upon: for there the universities played a more important part in the change of thought. In Spain, of course, the older ontological analysis remained somewhat more secure.

and limits of knowledge underway in European culture, and even came to be its definitive factor. This did not mean, however, that ontological analysis was entirely eliminated; nor could it be. Fragments survived for a while and the language persisted long after its previous meaning had departed. There was still *talk* about matter and form, of essence and existence, of cause and end, but the whole status of ontological analysis itself was displaced into a kind of intellectual limbo. The underpinnings of scientific discourse were taken to be either obviously given (and so not in need of further clarification), or posited hypothetically (in the service of analysis undertaken with laudable motives), or matters of deeply rooted human belief (and so both inevitable and ineradicable). In any event, it was widely accepted that conceptions which lay beyond the reach of quantitative analysis neither needed nor could admit of rational articulation: nor could they receive rational justification. A curtain of primitive positivism descended upon a region of intellectual life that had hitherto been appreciated as the domain of first philosophy and of philosophical wisdom.

This redirection of philosophical effort—indeed, its reversal—is patent in the writings of the most influential early modern philosophers whose thoughts set down the framework surrounding the intellectual labors of the scientists. At the beginning of the seventeenth century Francis Bacon expressed a quite general hope for "the new philosophy or active science":

I have made a beginning of the work—a beginning, as I hope, not unimportant:— the fortune of the human race will give the issue;—such an issue, it may be, as in the present condition of things and men's minds cannot easily be conceived or imagined. For the matter in hand is no mere felicity of speculation, but the real business and fortunes of the human race, and all power of operation.[3]

His sometimes express contempt for Plato and Aristotle, his excoriation of the schoolmen as spinners of insubstantial spider's webs, his depiction of the idols to which the human mind is prey, his appeal for light-bearing and fruit-bearing experiments, and his search for middle axioms, neither too general nor too particular—these forged a strategy for the invention of a new logic, a new mode of discourse which placed human felicity at the forefront and center of human inquiry, but understood it primarily as mastery over nature. Bacon's sometime secretary, Thomas Hobbes, wrote that the language of first philosophy was threadbare, and that

---

3. From the Preface to *The Great Instauration,* the argument to the sixth part (*The English Philosophers from Bacon to Mill,* ed. E. A. Burtt [New York: Modern Library, 1939], 22–23).

the first grounds of all science are not only not beautiful, but poor, arid and, in appearance, deformed.[4]

Nevertheless, he urged that philosophy pursue these grounds, isolating them as corporeal elements, which could serve in the orderly construction of a body of knowledge; that body of knowledge would then serve to determine men in the performance of actions and the production of goods "for the commodity of human life." Descartes made the same point with more subtlety and learning. In a well-known passage from a letter to Abbé Picot, he had written:

> Thus all philosophy is like a tree, of which metaphysics is the root, physics the trunk, and all the other sciences the branches that grow off this trunk, which reduce to three principal ones: namely, medicine, mechanics and morals. . . . But just as it is not from the roots or the trunks of trees that we gather the fruit, but only from the extremities of their branches, so the chief use of philosophy depends on those of its parts which we can learn only last of all.[5]

With many of his contemporaries he shared the opinion that Aristotle and his followers had invented dubious "potencies," "forms," and "final causes" that obscured the plain and evident starting points of knowledge, the "seeds," *"principia,"* or *"initia."*[6]

Now, it is in a writing of one of the leading spokesmen of the older ontological analysis that we read the following:

> All sciences and arts are directed in an orderly way toward one thing, that is, to the perfection of man, which is his happiness.[7]

So that what is at issue is not the desirability of human happiness, nor the need that knowledge contribute to that happiness. What is at issue is how man ought to inquire in order to acquire that knowledge which can contribute to his happiness. At the deepest level of inquiry, is the philosopher to draw the highest wisdom from consideration of the source upon which all good depends—as Plato sought participation in the archetypal Forms, as Aristotle sought contemplation in self-thinking

---

4. *De corpore* 1.1.1 and 6 (*Body, Man and Citizen,* trans. R. S. Peters [London: Collier-Macmillan, 1962], 24 and 27).

5. From the Preface to the French translation of the *Principles of Philosophy* (in the English translation by John Veitch; cited from *A Discourse on Method* . . . [London: Dent, 1946], 156–157, and slightly emended by N. Kemp Smith, *New Studies in the Philosophy of Descartes* [New York: Russell and Russell, 1953], 31).

6. From a letter to Father Dinet: *Oeuvres de Descartes,* ed. C. Adam and P. Tannery (Paris: Cerf, 1904), 7: 580; in English: *The Philosophical Works of Descartes,* ed. E. S. Haldane and G. R. T. Ross (Cambridge, 1911, reprint 1970), 2: 359.

7. *Proemium* to St. Thomas Aquinas' *Commentary on Aristotle's Metaphysics,* trans. V. J. Bourke in *The Pocket Aquinas* (New York: Washington Square, 1960), 145.

Thought, or as St. Thomas sought to prepare himself for union with *Ipsum Esse Subsistens?* Or, was he to proceed from isolated elements—the simple natures of Bacon, the corpuscles of Hobbes, the seeds or clear and distinct ideas of Descartes—to composite knowledge, methodical production, and commodious results? The disjunction seems forced: why not both? After all, the ancients sought results (in the arts) and not only principles; and the moderns sought basics (the elements) and not only results. But the disjunction is severe because the question is about fundamental inquiry; it is a question of emphasis and primacy. It asks: In which direction is thought to flow when it is engaged at its deepest level? Does thought seek out foundations only in order to leave them for something better, or does it seek them out in order to unite itself with that which is highest and best? At least until rather recently in our culture, there have been two prevalent modes of discourse about foundations: discourse in terms of ontological principles and discourse in terms of quantitative elements.[8] With their contending claims in mind, it is instructive to read and reflect upon an early work of St. Thomas[9] in which he takes stock of his Aristotelian heritage, not without enriching it with his own understandings.[10] The struggle in the sixteenth and seventeenth centuries between the two contending modes of discursive analysis stands between us and St. Thomas, so that every attempt to understand his meaning becomes an effort to recover the ontological mode of discourse, and offers an opportunity for further self-knowledge.

In *On the Principles of Nature* St. Thomas distinguishes the term "principle" from the term "element" by the intermediary term "cause":

Principle is as it were a more extensive term than cause, and cause more extensive than element.[11]

---

8. "... recently ... prevalent": a third mode of discourse, the historical, is as ancient as the other two, but it has come to prominence as a candidate for foundational thinking only in the past century or so.

9. *De principiis naturae*, ed. J. J. Pauson (Fribourg: Société Philosophique, 1950).

10. Pauson, ibid., 72, remarks: "In *De principiis,* influences of Avicenna, Averroes, Boethius, and the translations of Aristotle from the Arabic are visible, but the synthesis belongs strictly to St. Thomas. No general integration of the works of these authors could possibly bring about this end product, even though the phraseology of almost every part of it can be duplicated from their works." For a general consideration of the nature and sources of St. Thomas' own positions regarding the distinction of the sciences, the nature of actuality, and the role of sacred doctrine insofar as they add to or diverge from Aristotle, see Joseph Owens, "Aquinas as Aristotelian Commentator," in *St. Thomas Aquinas: 1274–1974 Commemorative Studies* (Toronto: Pontifical Institute of Mediaeval Studies, 1974), 1: 213–38.

11. Translation by V. J. Bourke in *The Pocket Aquinas,* 70. The Latin (ed. Pauson, 93) reads: "... principium aliquomodo est in plus quam causa, et causa in plus quam elementum."

This lapidary statement bears scrutiny, since it might be misunderstood and taken as saying no more than that "principle" is the genus of "cause" and "element," and that the latter two are to be included in "principle" as two species of a common genus, "cause" being a superior species, and "element" an inferior one. Or, because we tend today to restrict the term "cause" to productive force, we might mistake "principle" as the broad genus that includes "cause" as a species along with other constitutive factors, such as "end," "form," and "matter," taken as other species; and then take "matter" as a more inclusive species that contains "element" as a subordinate and less inclusive species. Much more is meant, however; or rather, what is meant is not a classification into genera and species at all. This is borne out by what follows. For St. Thomas immediately takes up the divers senses of the term "cause."[12] A little further on[13] he makes explicit the analogous character of being and its principles; and he concludes the brief work with an insistence upon the radical diversity among the various principles of natural being. Even the matter, form, and privation considered in one category differ irreducibly from the same principles considered in another category. We may well ask: Do the terms "matter," "form," and "privation" retain a unity that survives the radical diversity of the categories? We may put St. Thomas' reply in other words: each term expresses a similarity of role played out by one item in a category in respect to other items in that category. Thus, "privation" indicates a certain non-being in the category of quantity, and again in the category of quality; but what it is to lack quantity is irreducibly other than what it is to lack quality. In his own words translated:

> Yet, the matter of substance and of quantity, and similarly their form and privation, differ generically [*differunt genere*] but agree only by way of proportion [*convenient solum secundum proportionem*]—in the sense that just as the matter of substance is related to the substance according to the characteristic meaning of matter [*in ratione materiae*], so, too, is the matter of quantity related to quantity.[14]

The distinction between "principle," "cause," and "element," then, is not meant to set forth the decreasing extension of genera and species, but to exhibit the network of analogously related features of being. The tension is created by the univocal tendency of human speech and the analogous diversity inherent in real being.

---

12. Ibid., ed. Pauson, 93–94; trans. Bourke, 70–71.
13. Ibid., ed. Pauson, 102–4: ". . . diximus quod substantia et quantitas differunt genere, sed sunt idem secundum analogiam"; trans. Bourke, 75–76.
14. Ibid., ed. Pauson, 104; trans. Bourke, 77.

St. Thomas concedes that we may sometimes use the term "principle" interchangeably with that of "cause"; but he insists that there is an important distinction between causal and non-causal principles. We may call something a "principle" simply because it is first in its own order, whether any real consequences *(esse posterioris)* follow from it or not. For

everything from which [*a quo*] a change takes its start is called a principle.[15]

Whereas a cause, strictly speaking, is

that sort of first item from which [*de illo primo, ex quo*] the existence of the consequent [*esse posterioris*] follows.[16]

And again, a cause is

that from whose being another being follows [*id ex cuius esse sequitur aliud*].[17]

And so, we must distinguish what is a principle in the weak, non-causal sense from what is a principle in the strong, causal sense. Thus, in the analysis of a change, we must distinguish between what is at the beginning as starting point only and what is at the beginning as source. It follows, too, that we must distinguish between what is "consequent upon" something and what is "consequent from" something.[18] In the alteration of a surface from black to white, therefore, the old paint is found at the beginning of the change as a starting point but not as its source: and the fresh paint is consequent upon *(a quo)* the old, but not at all a consequent of *(ex quo)* the old paint. The fresh paint is, rather, along with the painter a cause of the change.[19]

We may, then, legitimately use the term "principle" to designate an item as first in any given order without expecting real consequences *(esse posterioris)* to follow from it. Nevertheless, there will be at least implicit reference to other items in the order, including subordinate principles.

15. Ibid., ed. Pauson, 91; trans. Bourke, 68.
16. Ibid.
17. Ibid., ed. Pauson, 91; trans. Bourke, 69.
18. Ibid., ed. Pauson, 91; trans. Bourke, 69–70.
19. Ibid., ed. Pauson, 91: "sed quando aliquid movetur de nigredine ad albedinem, dicitur quod nigredo est principium illius motus, et universaliter omne id a quo incipit esse motus dicitur principium, tamen nigredo non est id ex quo consequitur *esse* albedinis. . . . Et propter hoc, privatio ponitur inter principia et non inter causas, qui privatio est id a quo incipit generatio" (italics added). Earlier (ed. Pauson, 82–83), in setting forth the three principles of nature—matter, form, and privation—St. Thomas seems to speak of privation as a principle *ex quo*: "forma est id ad quod est generatio. alia duo [scil., materia et privatio] sunt ex parte eius ex quo est generatio." But here privation is assimilated to matter which is a cause, and since it coincides with it, it is the same in subject and differs from it only in its meaning and function: that is, it is the matter *qua* lack, rather than *qua* passive potency: "Unde materia et privatio sunt idem subjecto, sed differunt ratione." Trans. Bourke, 63.

An order is a unified totality, i.e., a plurality of items brought into unity in some fashion. That which is the ground of the unity is the primary principle of the order and endows it with its distinctive character. The other items are its principiates; we might even say, its "consequences," though not necessarily *real* consequences. That is, the relationship of principle and principiates need not consist in the communication and reception of real being: the black is a principle of the change but not its source. Today, we might be tempted to call the black—that is, the black as the not-white in the order of color—a necessary "condition" for the change. But to the extent that the term "condition" suggests "circumstance" it is too external to satisfy the requirements of ontological analysis. For privation is no mere circumstance, since it is "constitutive" of the very subject at the starting point of its change, in the way that lack of health "belongs to" and is "part of" the very being of the patient undergoing cure. Privation, then, is "constitutive" of the order of changing beings.

Nevertheless privation is not a *primary* principle. St. Thomas writes that it is not a principle *per se*, but only a principle *per accidens*,[20] and he distinguishes this principle in the weak sense from the four causes which are principles in the strong sense, i.e., causes *per se*. Elsewhere[21] he remarks that each of the categories includes its own version of the incomplete *(imperfectus)* and the complete *(perfectus)*. Radically taken, these are privation and possession *(habitus)*, and the two form the primary contrariety within each categorial order. Finally, they reduce to non-being and being respectively. Now the order within which privation plays out its role is that of alteration, and the principiates are the consequences that both follow upon and follow from the principles operative in that alteration. The privation is a subordinate principle because the alteration is directed towards the possession of the new form and the new being. No institution of real consequences arises from it, whereas they do from form and the other causes.

These causes cooperate to produce a complex result in and through the change. St. Thomas remarks that the same thing *(idem)* may have several causes. Moreover, the same thing may be the cause of contrary effects. Even more, what is a source in one order or along one line of causality may be a consequent in another:

idem sit causa et causatum respectu eiusdem, sed diversimode: one thing [may] be both cause and effect with regard to another item, but in a different fashion.[22]

---

20. Ibid., ed. Pauson, 90; trans. Bourke, 68; also ed. Pauson, 83–84; trans. Bourke, 65.
21. In his *Commentary on the Physics of Aristotle*. 3.1, par. 8. Cf. *De principiis naturae*, ed. Pauson, 95–96; trans. Bourke, 71.
22. Ibid., ed. Pauson, 93; trans. Bourke, 70.

Thus, in the line of agency, the activity of walking may be a source of health *(principium);* and health can be its consequence *(principiatum).*[23] But conversely, in the line of finality, that same walking, the very same activity at the same time, may be a consequence: for, inasmuch as health is that for the sake of which the walking is done, health will be in a different way the source or principle of the activity, and walking will be its derivative or principiate. In sum, health will be principle in an order other than that within which walking is principle. The four causes, then—agency, end, form, and matter—are each first in their own order, and each contributes in its distinctive way to the complex resultant being. It need only be added[24] that, overall, i.e., in the interplay among the orders, the end is rightfully called "the cause of causes," since for its sake alone does the causality of the other causes come into play. The *interplay of orders* is not a random affair, but rather gives expression to the inherent unity-in-diversity that characterizes the analogical order appropriate to being and its beings.

It is important, moreover, to recognize that the analogical character of being does not result from the gathering of its divers principles into itself. On the contrary, being is the principle of principles: and so, their analogical character expresses the original diversity that characterizes being itself. The diversity, then, is not merely *between* principles; nor even between the embodiments of each principle within the various categorial orders. The analogical diversity is rooted *within* each principle itself. A thoroughgoing ontological analysis of change will show that each principle discharges quite opposite functions. At the first level of such an analysis it may be said that matter is the principle of continuity (as substrate or subject) and that form is the principle of difference (as definitive of the kind or qualification). But when the analysis is carried deeper, the analogous diversity inherent within each principle discloses itself.[25] Thus, matter cannot be identified simply with the substrate as the principle of continuity: for it is also the potential source of diversity. The coming into being of a child as the term of a change is its coming to be diverse from and other than its parents. Now matter plays a role in that diversification, since it is the root capacity for just such diversification even while it also provides both the link with the parents in the process and a real basis for the continuing relation between parents and child. Matter is, then, principle of both continuity and discontinuity in the order

---

23. The terms are not in the *De principiis,* but they express the general concept of order.

24. Ibid., ed. Pauson. 93–94; trans. Bourke, 70–71.

25. This point has been made in regard to the subject of becoming and the act of becoming by one of the most profound metaphysicians of the Thomistic revival, Gerard Smith, in *The Philosophy of Being* (New York: Macmillan, 1961), 29–30.

of potency. Or again, the form of something specifies it and sets it off from others unlike it. Form is, then, a principle of difference or definition. But in defining the thing, form establishes an agreement of that thing with others of its kind. In the coming to be of something the form is communicated by the causes: *omne agens agit sibi simili*. Form is, then, at once a principle of likeness and unlikeness, of continuity and discontinuity, of identity and non-identity.

It is this coincidence of being and non-being in ontological principles which Hegel sought to incorporate from Aristotle, but which he dispersed into a dialectical movement of negative and positive moments.[26] There is no such fundamental dialectic in Aristotle or St. Thomas, but rather a sort of "simultaneity" according to which a principle is the determinant and source of quite divers consequences *in its own order*. So that matter is not to be identified simply with and exhausted in its contribution to continuity within change; nor is form to be identified without qualification with and exhausted in its contribution to the differentiation that comes about in and through the change. As principles, they are the source at once of identity and non-identity, each within its own order: matter within the order of passive potency, form within the order of formal actuality, and other basic principles within their own orders. It is this inherent diversity that shows that they are principles (i.e., original) and not merely components (i.e., elementary). It seems to me that this more deeply embedded diversity within each principle is the basis for the diversity St. Thomas points out in regard to the four causes.[27]

In his brief consideration of the term "element" in the *Principles*[28] St. Thomas takes the term to stand for those items that contribute to the composition of some real thing by entering into it and becoming part of its matter. These components belong, therefore, in an order of causality, and precisely that of material causality; and so, they may be called "material causes." He writes of them in the plural, showing that he had in mind what may be called "secondary matters," items that are qualitatively formed in some way, rather than the pure indeterminacy of primary

---

26. Indeed, the Hegelian *moments* are neither ontological principles in the sense developed here, nor are they quantitative elements. But the articulation of their difference would carry us too far from our present theme. Suffice it to note here that the Hegelian moments have the nominalist units of late medieval and early modern thought as their remote ancestors—units of analysis that paved the way for the quantitative elements of particle analysis. Hegel attempted to break down their independence by implicating the units in a self-determining process of mutual constitution, i.e., of co-constitution within the system. Whereas ontological principles are co-determinant within their source, and whereas elements come together to constitute results, dialectical moments constitute each other within the system.

27. *De principiis naturae*, ed. Pauson, 93–96; trans. Bourke, 70–72.

28. Ibid., ed. Pauson, 91–93; trans. Bourke, 69–70.

matter. But, although they are secondary matters, they are primary components. That is, first of all, in the order of material composition, the elements are *components* out of which some material composite comes to be formed *(ex quibus est compositio rei)*.[29] And secondly, they are *primary* components, and not those parts *(membra)* of a body which are themselves made up of qualitatively different components, as the hand is made of flesh and bones, and the flesh and bones of still other qualitatively distinct components. Since elements enter into the composite itself, they are intrinsic principles. They continue to reside *(remanere, in ea)* in the composite, unlike bread which passes away into blood. And finally, although an element may be divided into quantitative parts, it is indivisible into qualitatively different parts, i.e., into parts which differ in kind *(quae differunt secundum speciem)*. Along with his contemporaries, St. Thomas thought that such bodies as water and earth were quantitatively divisible (into drops and pieces) but qualitatively simple; and so he took them to be elements. Analysis by quantitative elements was to show him wrong as to the fact: water is divisible into qualitatively distinct components. But that same mode of analysis was to agree that elements in their simplest form were those particles that would not yield—or at least had not yet yielded—to further analysis.

According to St. Thomas, then, the term "element" designates those items which enter as qualitatively simple components into any primary process of material composition. The term "principle" designates any item which, being first in its order, has consequences (principiates), at least implicitly, though not necessarily real consequences *(esse posterioris)*. The thrust of ontological analysis, then, is carried forward by those principles which are causes, and analysis by element-principles remains subordinate to material causality and the other causes. It is quite other with analysis by quantitatively determined elements. For in this mode of analysis, they focus the primary thrust of the mind as it probes nature and challenges the apparent indivisibility of the most recently discovered particle.

Analysis by quantitatively determined elements has had astounding success from the sixteenth century on to our own day. Francis Bacon can be seen as an interim thinker, slighting the use of mathematics in determining the nature of elements, and searching for qualitative elements that had an ill-defined material basis. These elements *(minima)*[30] had in

---

29. Ibid., ed. Pauson, 91; trans. Bourke, 69.
30. *Novum Organum*, 2: vi (ed. T. Fowler, 2nd ed. [Oxford: Clarendon. 1889], 354; Burtt, *The English Philosophers,* 92). These "real particles" (2: viii: Burtt, 94; Fowler, 357) are not atoms since they do not exist in a void. Their relation to the "simple natures" (2: v: Burtt, 90; Fowler, 351), which might almost be thought of as formal elements, remains

his own thought almost broken away from the earlier ontological context. The nature of distinctness had already begun to harden as early as the late thirteenth century, in part perhaps through a tendency in Platonism to make formal difference primary. In William of Ockham a radical nominalism implied in principle the impossibility of the Aristotelian metaphysical analysis as it was developed by St. Thomas. For mandatory for such an analysis is the possibility of an analogical diversity among the ontological principles, and even within them (as was indicated above). That is to say, the character of unity must be such that it can tolerate a diversity whose principles exist together in a real composite, so that one can speak of a "real composition," of a complexity belonging to the thing and not merely constructed by the mind. Later it became usual for schoolmen to speak in terms of a "real distinction" among the principles that constitute a being. Although used occasionally earlier, this less suitable, negative locution may have become prominent as a concession to pressure exerted upon scientific and philosophical discourse by nominalism and by analysis into quantitative elements. In any event, the distinguishing mark of the older metaphysics stemming from Aristotle was that its ontological principles could be really distinct without being really separate, To paraphrase the poet: *There* is being, two in one, *there* is number slain; *there* is really only one, yet two remain. Such a diversity of ontological principles is a diversity *in* being: it is not simply a division made for the convenience of the inquiring human mind. And yet, it need not be a diversity *of* beings; that is, it need not be a physical separation into numerically distinct, really existent entities. In a word, the diversity is not a distinction *in mente*, but rather a distinction *in re*, an otherness prior to the intervention of the human mind.[31]

During the seventeenth and eighteenth centuries any distinction that was not a distinction of reason *(in mente)*—and thereby grounded in the formal structure of the human mind—was being forced to take shape as a separation. If it failed to do that—as the faculties or powers of the

---

unclarified. For all that, each time one rereads Bacon there arises an expectation that his own road of inquiry retains a latent power of physical analysis that has been prematurely thrust aside by quantitative analysis. Regarding mathematics, see *Novum Organum*, 1: xcvi (Burtt, 67; Fowler, 300).

31. St. Thomas discusses how causes can coincide or differ in number and in kind, both with respect to the process of generation and to the thing that results from the generation (*De principiis naturae*, ed. Pauson, 97–98): "... tres causae possunt incidere in unum, scilicet forma, finis et efficiens, ... finis incidit cum forma in idem numero, quia illud idem numero quod est forma generate, est finis generationis. Sed cum efficiente non incidit in idem numero, sed in idem specie.... Materia autem non coincidit cum aliis. quia materia ex eo quod est ens in potentia. habet rationem imperfecti; sed aliae causae, cum sint actu, habent rationem perfecti; perfectum autem et imperfectum non coincidunt in idem." (Cf. trans. Bourke, 72–73.)

soul, for example, had been held to be really distinct from it without being separate from it—then that distinction risked and eventually would receive the charge of being unimportant, irrelevant, and unfruitful for scientific and even for philosophical purposes. The best known kinds of separation among the philosophers are perhaps the Cartesian dualism of body and soul, the separation of theology from philosophy, and the precise lines that guarded the clarity of one idea from another; but also the self-isolation of each Humean impression. Nevertheless, the units of seventeenth-century mechanics and eighteenth-century chemistry were undoubtedly even more influential. Physical things were analyzed in order to isolate their component parts. The convergence of mathematical learning and physical analysis-by-separation-into-numerically-determined-material-components led to a general quantification of rational discourse, so that other modes of rational discourse which had earlier been considered to be scientific in the broad sense and philosophical tended to be dismissed from the field of serious inquiry. To use the older language, form and matter were fused by quantification to become the primary units of explanation in the light of which reality itself was to be understood. New meaning was undoubtedly gained, but the horizon of intelligibility was reduced, for better and for worse. A simplification of discourse was underway, and with it the redefinition of the possibilities of human understanding.

A keen observer might have expected the fate that awaited the web of causes and other principles associated with ontological analysis. As the mode of quantitative analysis took control of the scientific reason, formal causality *(forma)* tended to dissolve into relations in the real order and ideas in the rational order. With Hobbes, forms were reduced to shapes brought about by the geometrical distances between points. With Descartes, they were mathematical-like relationships between the clear and distinct products of analysis. With Leibniz, they were internal relations of exemplarity; and his attempt to re-employ the principle of *entelechy* in order to ground *phenomena bene fundata* in the monads served a continuum of incorporeal monads ranging from the unconscious and obscure to the self-conscious and clear, rather than the gradation of specifically different, real substances formed by Aristotle's principle. With Locke, the metaphysical status of real essences was precarious, to say the least.[32] What quite generally disappeared from the mainstream of scien-

---

32. In confirmation of the foregoing see: Hobbes, *De corpore,* 1.1.5 (Peters, *Body,* 26–27); Descartes, *Discourse,* part 2. rule 3 (Haldane and Ross, *Works,* 1: 92; Adam and Tannery, *Oeuvres,* 6:18–19); Leibniz, *Monadology,* no. 18 (*The Monadology and Other Philosophical Writings,* ed. R. Latta [Oxford, 1898, reprint 1948], 229 and n. 32; *Opera philosophica quae exstant Latina . . .* , ed. J. E. Erdmann [1840], augmented by R. Vollbrecht [Aalen. 1959], 2: 706b); Locke, *Essay Concerning Human Understanding* 3.9, no. 12 (ed. J. W. Yolton, 2nd ed. [London: Dent. 1964, reprint 1972], 2: 82).

tific and philosophical thought, in any event, was the pre-quantitative and pre-qualitative ontological character of form as substantial form. Form was no longer *natura:* "that by which a thing has existence," that which "makes something to be actually."[33] There are no such natures in the work of Galileo, Hobbes, Descartes, or Spinoza, nor in Locke, Hume, and Kant; nor would they be welcome. The terms "form" and "formal" come to stand in the new thought-world for patterns, structures, designs, and interrelationships, i.e., for something formed, a result; they cease to stand for a principle. More precisely, form was no longer taken as the first item in a certain order of being from which real consequences follow. In a word, form ceased to be a cause.

So, too, with the final cause or end *(finis)*. The struggle against final causes neither began with Galileo nor ended with Molière and Voltaire, not even with Darwin and Thomas Huxley. Nevertheless, in the seventeenth century it was reduced to a feature of human agency, i.e., to purpose, the self-conscious motive for certain kinds of action. It was declared inappropriate as a principle of reality overall. Here again, Francis Bacon's ambiguity is telling.[34] With few exceptions (and those vague) he tends to relegate finality to theology and the divine purpose, on the one hand, and to morality and human activity, on the other. Of course, Bacon was not a mechanist, but in the matter of final causes his influence joined with that of mechanism to drive final causality into its merely subjective anthropological corner or to let it out of the world through a theological chimney flue.

Nor did agency or efficient causality *(causa efficiens)* escape the reduc-

33. *De principiis naturae,* ed. Pauson, 80–81: "omne a quo aliquid habet esse. sive substantiale sive accidentale, potest dici forma; . . . Et quia forma facit esse in actu, ideo forma dicitur esse actus. Quod autem facit actu esse substantiale, dicitur forma substantialis." (Cf. trans. Bourke, 62.)

34. The whole aphorism (*Novum Organum,* 2: ii: Burtt, 88; Fowler, 345–46) is worth noting: "In what an ill condition human knowledge is at the present time, is apparent even from the commonly received maxims. It is a correct position that 'true knowledge is knowledge by causes.' And causes again are not improperly distributed into four kinds: the material, the formal, the efficient, and the final. But of these the final cause rather corrupts than advances the sciences, except such as have to do with human action. The discovery of the formal is despaired of. The efficient and the material (as they are investigated and received, that is, as remote causes, without reference to the latent process leading to the form) are but slight and superficial, and contribute little, if anything, to true and active science. Nor have I forgotten that in a former passage I noted and corrected as an error of the human mind the opinion that forms give existence. For though in nature nothing really exists beside individual bodies, performing pure individual acts according to a fixed law, yet in philosophy this very law, and the investigation, discovery, and explanation of it, is the foundation as well of knowledge as of operation. And it is this law, with its clauses, that I mean when I speak of *forms;* a name which I adopt because it has grown into use and become familiar." Cited from *The English Philosophers from Bacon to Mill,* ed. E. A. Burtt (New York: Modern Library, 1939), 88–89. The last sentence makes clear his understanding of form as law.

tion, for the very understanding of agency itself was transformed. In the earlier ontological context, "to produce" meant "to communicate being" *(dare esse, influxus entis):* "A cause is that from whose being another being follows."[35] In the analysis in terms of quantitatively determined elements, however, productive causality came to mean an active force or impulse that initiated change by transference of energy to another, resulting in displacement of particles in a new configuration and with an accelerated or decelerated rate of motion among the particles.

The particles themselves came to be understood as the primary and rudimentary material components. This sense of "element" seems, at first glance, to be exactly equivalent to St. Thomas', but it is not in at least three very important respects. The elements according to St. Thomas were material, of course, and they were formed, so that they exhibited distinctive qualitative properties: "an element is not divisible into parts that differ in kind."[36] The first difference, then, between the old and the new sense of "element" is that the qualitative character of an element may be an important prelude to determining its difference from other elements, but it is not to be permitted to enter into the strict scientific account which sets forth its true and genuine constitution. That constitution must be determined by a set of numerically determinable values, such as mass, density, etc. In the older sense of element, on the contrary, the sensible qualities were constitutive of the physical nature of the element itself. It was this empirical dependence that led Kant to scold the older physicists, for keeping human reason in the "leading-strings" of nature.[37] Another way of expressing this first difference regarding the character of elements is to see the new mode of analysis as moving away from the previous primacy of the physical body towards the primacy of the mathematical body. Following in the wake of this shift, the earlier distinction between common sensibles and proper sensibles was transformed into the separation of primary qualities (the mathematically determinable and so-called "objective" properties) and the secondary qualities (which became "subjective"). In this way rational discourse withdrew from the immediacy of lived perceptual and sensible experience, to return to it only insofar as it was susceptible of numerically determinate values.

More fundamental yet, the first difference points beyond itself to a deeper difference. For the concept of "physical body" does not only stand for qualitatively formed material. It stands more deeply for a "natured" body, i.e., for a body possessed of active potency (powers) and

---

35. See notes 16 and 17 above.
36. See note 28 above.
37. *Critique of Pure Reason,* second preface, B xiii (trans. N. Kemp Smith, *Immanuel Kant's Critique of Pure Reason* [London: Macmillan, 1950], 20).

passive potency (matter). At its base lies that pure indeterminacy and utterly determinable capacity known as "prime matter." And so the very conception of material causality *(materia)* gives way, and a move of the scientific and philosophical intelligence towards the surface, towards phenomena is underway. It will reach a certain high point in Kant. but it is significant that even Hobbes makes much of "effects or appearances."[38]

The third and more general difference rests upon the absence of the act/potency relationship from the new mode of analysis. In the older analysis, an ontological composite unit existed as the composition of the incomplete *(imperfectus)* and the complete *(perfectus)*. Now, that ontological unit can be *really one* being *(ens per se et unum)*—and not two or more beings, not simply an organization or system of particles—only if the imperfect in the physical order must be traced back to and grounded in the radically passive and thoroughly determinable principle called "prime matter." For only such a radically determinable principle—a principle which has nothing in itself but the capacity to receive such a determination—can receive that determination from the other causes. Such a radically determinable principle can receive from them the determination to be *a* being, to be *radically* one; so that the ontological unit that results *(ens per se et unum)* is not merely a collection of relatively self-subsistent particles. In such an analysis of physical being, then, complexity and simplicity are not exclusive alternatives at war with one another; but rather, to be composite and to be one are reconciled and integrated in a really composite ontological unit. This comes about in the physical order only insofar as a principle of utter determinability (prime matter) receives the determinations of the other causes (of the agent and the end) by way of the determinative causality of the form. In other words, or rather, in the language of Aristotle and St. Thomas, this utterly indigent principle— for it would be too much to speak the language of Plato here and call it the "lover" of being and the forms—this utter capacity is indispensable for the analysis of physical nature in terms of ontological principles.

Nevertheless, at the center of the ontological analysis of physical nature in terms of the four causes, as set out in St. Thomas' *Principles*, there lies the properly *metaphysical* consideration of physical nature. For metaphysics alone can make explicit the ground and distinctive character of analysis in terms of ontological units.[39] Now, for such a task we need the recognition of *esse*, that principle which St. Thomas has shown in many of his works to be the most proper and explicit character of being. It

---

38. *De corpore*, 1.1.2 (Peters, *Body*, 24).
39. See Kenneth L. Schmitz, *The Gift: Creation*, The Aquinas Lecture (Milwaukee, WI: Marquette University Press, 1982), 111–18.

seems to me unlikely that a general ontological analysis in terms of the four causes can make much headway in the face of the brilliant success of the quantitative analysis of physical nature, unless such an ontological analysis deepens its discourse by turning to the leading principle of being understood as actuality, viz. existence *(esse)*. The primacy of such actuality rests—not upon its being the cause of all causal activity, though it is that as the principle of finality—but upon this: that *esse,* as the most determinative and actual of everything that is, is the supreme ontological principle, the principle of all the principles of being. It seems to me further that such a metaphysical analysis can situate and even enhance the unmistakable gains of analysis by elements, placing that analysis in a deeper and broader context. In his own philosophical work, as well as in his interpretation of St. Thomas, Aristotle, and others, Joseph Owens has lighted a path towards such a metaphysics and its future.[40]

40. See Joseph Owens, *St. Thomas and the Future of Metaphysics,* The Aquinas Lecture (Milwaukee, WI: Marquette University Press, 1957).

Chapter 3

FROM ANARCHY TO PRINCIPLES
Deconstruction and the Resources of Christian Philosophy

To domination, a Christian philosophy offers: giving; to hard unity: a unity charged with abundance; and to hiddenness: the mystery of presence.

One of the most influential movements among philosophers today is that of *Deconstruction*. It is the moving energy of thought at the center of much that has been called "postmodern." Its birthplace is Paris, but it has reached North America's universities through philosophy, linguistics, literary studies, sociology, political theory, and religious studies, and its influence among young teachers and scholars is already wide and diffuse. Its background was prepared by the hermeneutic work of German philosophers such as Heidegger, and by the work in linguistics and language by such thinkers as de Saussure and Wittgenstein. Deconstruction is part of a wider critical re-examination of nothing less than the nature and limits of rationality. Its importance may lie less in what it says than in what it attempts to "unsay." In its skepticism and, in more extreme instances, its nihilism, deconstruction strikes at the very core of long-held understandings of the philosophical enterprise, and has implications for law, politics, and social thought, as well as for theology. It subjects to criticism the basic modes of thought by which philosophy and theology have traditionally been developed, criticized, and defended. The very possibility of continuing the long conversation we call Western culture and Western civilization is, therefore, itself called into question. It is fair to ask, what resources are available in the more constructive traditions of Western thought, and specifically in Christian thought and experience, resources which we may bring to the wider contemporary dis-

Reprinted from *Communio* 16 (Spring 1989). © 1989 by *Communio: International Catholic Review*. An earlier version of this article was given as the 1988 Aquinas Medalist Lecture, University of Dallas.

cussion within which deconstruction forms a part? At the heart of the issues raised by its challenge lie the nature, status, and durability of the very principles by which reason has sought for a better understanding of what is true and good.

It is difficult for us nowadays to grasp what the ancients and medievals meant by principles, and in that degree we may be said to live in an age of anarchy. By that term, however, I do not mean to refer primarily to the violence and disrespect for the law of which we hear so much today, since there have been periods of great and continued violence during ancient and medieval times as well. I take the term, rather, in its original sense: to live, think, and act *without principles*. What is distinctive of our age, it seems to me, is that it has brought to a head a long-standing development in which the very conception of a principle—or, to speak Latin: *principium,* and to speak Greek: *archē*—has come under increasing challenge. What has become subject to criticism is, if I may so put it, the very "principle" of principle.

Now, if that is correct, then it is a matter of no little importance. For the very beginnings of our intellectual culture in ancient Greece may well be under challenge, and with it what we have known as reason and rational discourse, and especially philosophy. It is difficult to judge the import of one's own age, of course, because we cannot easily see through the smoke or hear through the din of the daily bustle of events which mix important and deeper issues with issues that hold interest only for the day. It may be that, when reading Richard Rorty's latest sigh of despair, we are merely seeing yet another of the recurrent descents into skepticism that have come and gone at various periods in our intellectual history. And yet there are signs that there may be deeper movement afoot.

Let me illustrate the confusion in which we find ourselves today when we try to read the signs of the times, empowered only with the knowledge of the history of our culture. Some twenty years ago there burst upon the intellectual scene a spate of books which argued that God is dead—not on the Cross, but in the mind of an abstract construction called "Modern Man." Now, that should have signaled a long and serious debate, since the reality of God has played such an important role in the development of European and American culture, whatever one might say of the present situation. And yet, within a matter of a very few years, the whole cycle of debate had been run through, with pros and cons and summations in plenty. And within five years of the first book on the topic, it had become a stale witticism that in the publishing business nothing was deader than the "death of God." Admittedly, one *did* get tired of the frantic pace of the discussion and of its topicality, i.e., its superficiality. And in the end nothing *was* settled; and everything returned more or less to the same state as before the outbreak. But it would be too easy to dismiss the controversy on these grounds, for there are deeper signs of a dismissal of God from the important problems of human existence. Thus, there is no diminution of the influence of two of the most powerful scriptures of contemporary intellectual atheism: the writings of Marx and of Nietzsche. If we attend to them, we may well dismiss the flurry of books that poured out twenty years ago, and yet not dismiss the serious nature of the *challenge* to theism represented, perhaps superficially, by the "death of God" controversy. Indeed, Nietzsche took a long view and looked towards the day when the very word "atheism" would be unused because the new age would have forgotten the very meaning of the word "God" *(theos)* which forms its root. And then there would be neither atheists nor theists, but the new Overman *(Übermensch)*, innocent even of the merest memory-trace of God. Now, I have appealed to the example of the "death of God" because I do not think atheism is separate from the question of principles and anarchy; and because it illustrates how difficult it is to assess the seriousness of the challenge to what I have already called the very "principle" of principles. The "death of God" controversy may not be as important as some thought it was at the time, but it points to a longer and deeper challenge to metaphysics and to religion itself.

We hear a good deal these days about *Deconstruction*, especially among certain French intellectuals, and increasingly among certain hermeneutists in America. What some of the philosophers among them are "deconstructing" is the heritage of philosophical understanding which has been built up according to principles and handed down over the centuries.[1] The Metaphysical Society of America has taken the challenge seriously enough to dedicate its 1988 annual meeting to the question of "Metaphysics, Deconstruction and the End of Philosophy?"[2] In the greater part of this article I propose to examine a current challenge to a philosophy of principles by providing a sketch of part of a recent important book on Heidegger which bears the subtitle: *From Principles to Anarchy*.[3] In the final section, however, I should like to suggest three topics that may

---

1. A good introduction and anthology of important texts may be found in *Deconstruction in Context: Literature and Philosophy*, ed. Mark C. Taylor (Chicago: University of Chicago Press, 1986). One of the key texts is Jacques Derrida, *Of Grammatology* (Baltimore: Johns Hopkins University Press, 1976).

2. Cf. K. Baynes, Jas. Bohman, and T. McCarthy, *After Philosophy: End or Transformation?* (Cambridge, MA: MIT Press, 1987). My own sense of the question is given in the opening paper of the conference, "Neither with nor without Foundations," which has appeared in the *Review of Metaphysics* 42, no. 1 (Sept. 1988): 3–25. See chapter 4 below.

3. Cf. Reiner Schürmann, *Heidegger on Being and Acting: From Principles to Anarchy*

lead us back from that criticism to a better understanding of traditional metaphysics, i.e., *from anarchy to principles.*

According to Reiner Schürmann, the author of the book mentioned above, Heidegger has come to think of Western culture as exhibiting a series of *epochs*. Thus, in modern intellectual history we can speak of the different epochs: the Renaissance with its emphasis upon cultural individuality, Rationalism with its emphasis upon reflective subjectivity, Critical Idealism with its emphasis upon transcendental subjectivity, and Ideology with its emphasis upon the practical subjectivity of the moral agent (*HOBA*, p. 46). Looking over the entire scope of Western thought, Heidegger paints a large canvas in three epochs: first, that of the pre-metaphysical age, the age of the Greek poets, dramatists, and early philosophers; secondly, the classical metaphysical age, whose influence has lasted well into modern times; and thirdly, the most recent epoch, in which (since Nietzsche) the reign of metaphysics has come to an end (*HOBA*, p. 122). In sum: metaphysics enjoyed an almost twenty-five-hundred-year hegemony in Western culture between an ancient pre-metaphysical and the present post-metaphysical epochs.

That reign began with Socrates' turn towards man in his philosophical inquiry, and it was initially presided over by the brilliance of Plato and Aristotle. Indeed, in large measure they gave to metaphysics its fixed shape and power. Heidegger holds that Aristotle's *Physics* has been the Basic Book *(Grundbuch)* of Western philosophy. Moreover, true to its older anthropocentric origins, metaphysics (in the philosophies of Descartes, Hume, Kant, and others) came to rest in and upon subjectivity as upon the *subjectum inconcussum* of thought and reality, its bedrock *(hypokeimenon)*. The turn to man was made complete, however, only

---

(Bloomington: Indiana University Press, 1987), translated by Christine-Marie Gros in collaboration with the author from *Le principe d'anarchie: Heidegger et la question de l'âgir* (Paris: Editions de Seuil, 1987) (cited in the text and notes hereafter as *HOBA*). Because I find Schürmann's interpretation of Heidegger *sometimes* a bit forced by the use of political metaphors, I will often refer to the interpretation as that of "Schürmann-Heidegger." Nevertheless, I think that Schürmann's interpretation is basically correct and that its slight simplification and exaggeration has the benefit of raising the issue of deconstruction more succinctly than did Heidegger himself. For another treatment, see G. Nicholson, "Camus and Heidegger: Anarchists," *University of Toronto Quarterly* 41 (1971): 14–23; and "The Commune in *Being and Time,*" *Dialogue* 10, no. 4 (1971): 708–26. The question of principles and its relation to discourse has been of concern to me for years. See, for example, "Analysis by Principles and Analysis by Elements," in *Graceful Reason: Essays in Ancient and Mediaeval Philosophy Presented to Joseph Owens, CSSR,* ed. Lloyd P. Gerson (Toronto: Pontifical Institute of Mediaeval Studies, 1983), 315–30; "Gibt es für Menschen Wichtigeres, als zu überleben? Das Erbe Griechenlands: Rationalität," in *Das europäische Erbe und seine christliche Zukunft,* ed. N. Lobkowicz (Cologne: Hans Martin Schleyer-Stiftung, 1985), 95–104 (English text: 348–56); and "Metaphysics: Radical, Comprehensive, Determinate Discourse," *Review of Metaphysics* 39, no. 4 (June 1986): 675–94. See chapters 1 and 2 above.

in modern metaphysics *(hypokeimenon* become *subjectum humanum).* Nor was this merely a matter of theoretical thought, for it bore practical fruit as well, and above all in the form of modern scientific technology, in whose grip the popular as well as much of the intellectual culture still lives *(HOBA,* pp. 34–35).

Now—still according to Schürmann-Heidegger—modern technology is the last product of metaphysics, and it is through technology that the long reign of metaphysics is brought to an end. The task of recognizing and realizing that end, however, demands a new kind of thinking, a new effort of *logos* which will pass beneath the very foundations of metaphysics and its last product, modern technology, in order to release us from its grip. Metaphysics is the long-standing thought-*construction* which has been produced by means of principles; and it can be brought to truth only through the task of *deconstruction,* the task of comprehending and overcoming *(Verwindung)* the way in which principles have sealed our thought in upon itself and away from the true disclosure of being.

Schürmann suggests that we may also call these large epochs "economies"—not in the restricted sense of commercial markets, nor even in its broader, more general meaning—but in the more original sense of any order of entities interrelated to one another by reference to a principle. These also constitute economies, i.e., social orders gathered about a single overriding idea or ideal; so that the various members and regions within the social order are principiates taking their direction, meaning, and value from the overriding principle. According to Schürmann-Heidegger, the vast economy of metaphysics just described exhibits a variety of smaller economies or epochs within it, such as the Greek order of things which is to be referred to substance or essence *(ousia),* or the medieval order of things referred to and centered upon God *(theos, Deus),* or the modern order of things referred to man *(Humanism),* and within the latter, the present order of things referred to technology *(Technik).*

Now, the words "economy" and "epoch" are closely associated in Heidegger's usage. For what marks each of these "epochs" or "economies" is that their order rests upon a *single* primary principle; and this foundation provides—for those who live, think, and act in terms of its order—first, a selective delimitation of open possibilities, in a word: *closure;* secondly, stability or regularity, in a word: *necessity;* and thirdly, credibility through repetitive confirmation, in a word: *certitude (HOBA,* pp. 1–25). The foundation prescribes an order that fixes the fundamental relations of the entities within the order to itself and to one another. Moreover, the primary principle provides a purpose for action and an explanation of events. It proscribes conduct and rules out inappropriate action by pre-empting more radical choice. Now, it is just this that brings together the economic and the epochal nature of such an order. For an epoch is taken by Heidegger in its original sense; that is, it suspends possibilities. The famous phenomenological *epochē* is just such a suspension. Among the ancient skeptics the *epochē* could mean a waiting until better evidence came to the fore;[4] but according to Schürmann-Heidegger the metaphysical *epochē* was meant to put an end to inquiry. It is in this sense that an epoch is an economy which, in selecting some possibilities for a culture or age, simultaneously closes off others. Moreover, it does this by means of principles, i.e., by referring the plurality of phenomena (things, actions, events) to a single overriding source *(archē)*. All members of the world of thought and reality are principiates which flow from and are directed to and justified by reference to the overriding first principle. Thus, all things in Aristotle's cosmos are referred to substance; all things in medieval thought and life, to God; all things in Cartesian philosophy, to human subjectivity; and all things *(pragmata)* in the modern world, to scientific technology.

When we turn to Aristotle's most formal discussion of the term[5] we find the following senses of *archē:* first, it may be taken as a starting point of anything from which a movement is *first* made; though the point of departure may be either from what is primary in the thing itself or from what provides easiest access for us. Second, *archē* may mean that which is first present in the coming-to-be of anything, as the initial part (e.g., a foundation) must be present as a primary constituent in the thing itself or as a generative cause must be present first at the coming-to-be of the thing, even though it is not present as an intrinsic and constituent part. Third, *archē* may mean that which is first as deliberately initiating the movement, or as providing it with a guiding principle, or finally as that from which something first comes to be knowable.

Heidegger reduces these related meanings to two important ones: the inceptive and the dominative meanings. Taking his lead from Heidegger, Schürmann suggests that the Greek word *archē* first meant in Homer: "to lead, to open up, e.g., a conversation, baffle, or action of some sort, and hence: 'to come first'"; and this is the *inceptive* meaning. A second meaning came to the fore with Herodotus and Pindar: viz., "to dominate," and this is the *dominative* meaning. Indeed, Heidegger himself[6] tells us that the Greeks heard two things in the word:

---

4. See Sextus Empiricus, *Outlines of Pyrrhonism*, 1.1, ed. R. C. Bury, Loeb Classical Library, vol. 273 (Cambridge, MA: Harvard University Press, 1976), 2–3: "*zetousi de hoi skeptikoi*: the Skeptics keep on searching." The "Dogmatists" stop searching because they have found the truth, whereas the "Academics" stop because it is inapprehensible.

5. *Metaphysics* 1012b34–1013a17.

6. "On the Being and Conception of *Physis* in Aristotle's *Physics* B, 1," *Man and World* 9 (1976): 227f.; *Wegmarken* (Frankfurt: Klostermann, 1967), 317 (cited from *HOBA*, 97).

On the one hand, *archē* means that from which something takes its egress and inception; on the other it means that which, *as* such egress and inception, at the same time reaches beyond whatever emerges from it, thereby dominating it. *Archē* means both inception and domination inseparably.

In Aristotle, then, according to Heidegger, "to begin" means "to dominate." Scholars generally agree that the term received its technical meaning from Aristotle, and that the latter's meaning overlays the famous interpretation of his earlier predecessors. Thus, Aristotle describes their attempts at natural philosophy as a search for principles in the form of causes (*aitiai* in his sense of the term), and mostly for the material cause of things.[7]

Schürmann remarks further that Aristotle's list of the several senses of the term[8]

is hardly more than a lexicographical enumeration. It mixes the two meanings. Aristotle defines *archē* as that out of which something is or becomes or is known. The term therefore designates a source of being, becoming and knowledge beyond which it is useless to try to investigate: the source is ultimate in that it both begins and commands.

And he concludes that such an *archē* is opaque, resistant to further analysis *(unhintergehbar)*.[9]

Moreover, Schürmann recognizes (*HOBA*, p. 99) that Heidegger's deconstruction of metaphysics must establish that the twofold technical meaning of the term does not occur before Plato and Aristotle; so that the conclusion may be drawn that "the metaphysical way of thinking . . .

---

7. John Burnet, *Early Greek Philosophy* (London: Adam and Charles Black, 1930), 54, supposes that the use of the word *archē* to describe Anaximander's *apeiron* is almost surely Aristotle's and that we cannot assume that the term itself occurred in Anaximander's writings. For another view (more reliant upon Aristotle), see F. E. Peters, *Greek Philosophical Terms: A Historical Lexicon* (New York: New York University Press, 1967), 23. Peters cites H. Diels, *Die Fragmente der Vorsokratiker*, ed. W. Kranz, 3 vols. (Berlin, 1934–54), and writes: "The pre-Socratic search for an *archē* in the sense of a material cause (Aristotle had located the investigation within his own categories of causality . . .) is described by Aristotle in *Metaphysics* 983–985b, and the word *archē* may have first been used in this technical sense by Anaximander (Diels 12A9)."

8. *HOBA*, 333–34, n. 5. Notice that the nuances fall away in favor of a reduction to two paramount senses. A similar simplification occurs in the reduction of *ousia* to sensible substance, and of a first principle into a sheer unity.

9. Indeed, cf., for example, the remarks of Etienne Gilson: "One does not explain *esse*, it is what explains everything else." (From Jacques Maritain, "Compagnons de route," in *Étienne Gilson: Philosophe de la Chrétienté* [Paris: Cerf, 1949], 291–92.) Cf. St. Thomas Aquinas' distinction between *esse* and "everything else" *(praeter esse)* in *Summa contra gentiles* (hereafter *SCG*) II, c. 52. There is implied here, of course, a criticism of the notion of self-evident principles. See Schürmann's discussion of Cicero on *energeia* and *evidential*, of the Vulgate on *te archen* and *principium*, and of Leibniz on *principium rationis sufficientis*, 106–7 and 336, nn. 1–7.)

begins only with Plato and [Aristotle]." Now that way of thinking—of which the original thinkers in Western philosophy supposedly were innocent—rests upon the amalgam of primacy and power, and proceeds by virtue of melding firstness (the inceptive meaning) with command (the dominative meaning). According to Schürmann, this "alliance between the notions of inception and domination is possible only once the metaphysics of the causes is constituted," for to cause means to initiate through command and domination.

Schürmann comes close to reducing principles *(archai)* to causes *(aitiai)* at the beginning of Attic metaphysics. The paradigm is allegedly natural motion *(physis)*, and the *telos* is: to render motion intelligible. The *archai*, then, become causes of motion *(aitiai)*, which render intelligible the regions of being, becoming, and knowing (*HOBA*, p. 99). Schürmann implies, without discussion and therefore somewhat gratuitously, that for the Attic philosophers the fundamental experience of cause-seeking rests upon "one very precise experience,—our own initiative as movers." He does, however, cite both Heidegger and Nietzsche, who denounce cause-seeking as derived from "the subjective conviction that *we* are causes" (*HOBA*, pp. 334f., fn. 25). Of course, this is meant to fit nicely with the anthropocentric turn from which metaphysics is alleged to have begun, i.e., the Socratic interest in human virtue. Finally, Schürmann maintains that "Aristotle's discovery of teleocracy [i.e., domination by that *archē* which is *telos*] is native to the field of fabrication [*technē*]." And he adds that "that is where it should stay" (*HOBA*, p. 103). It should stay there because, prior to Aristotle's amalgam of the two senses of *archē* as inception and domination, "the Greeks do not seem to have understood the origin as located in the phenomenal region of the maneuverable" (*HOBA*, p. 104). Now, this restriction has as its result the enclosure of thought within the realm of the operable, and even the theoretical sphere is infected by the practical conceived as the manipulable. Being is restricted to technique, and power now takes on the meaning of: "the capacity to dispose of," hence to dominate.[10]

Before we look more closely at this characterization of principle as coercive power, I will follow Schürmann-Heidegger a bit further as the account turns from the Greek *archē* to the Latin *principium*, from which our own word "principle" is so immediately derived. Schürmann-Heidegger discovers a shift from attention to the *archē* as the commanding origin of

---

10. Remember that St. Thomas distinguishes the theoretical from the practical on the basis of the inoperability of the one and the operability of the other (*In Boetii de Trinitate*, qq. 5–6). Also recall that St. Thomas traces the key term *actus* back to *agere* and suggests that its primacy derives initially from our observation of powerful human agents (cf. *princeps*).

becoming *(physis)* to *principium* as the commanding origin of order *(ordo)* (*HOBA*, pp. 108–10). The new concern, writes Schürmann,[11]

clearly stresses the element of domination over the element of inception, or [stresses] constant presence over time.

The influence of Heidegger's very formalistic understanding of John Duns Scotus is prominent in Schürmann's argument here. We have shifted from the sphere of becoming to the order of essences, to the "essential order" (*HOBA*, p. 111). The translation of Aristotle's *energeia* by *actualitas* represents a new epoch in which principles are more reified, more rigid and static than ever, and in which time and becoming give way to a hierarchical world governed by a supreme Prince *(princeps)*: God as *Gubernator mundi*. In modern times, according to Schürmann-Heidegger, the process of reification continues but shifts its center to human subjectivity, whose capacity for the representation of objects becomes the standard by which the truth of things is decided and their worth determined.[12]

The *locus* where the origin, understood in this way, obtains is the region of logical [mental] entities; the *locality* of that locus, the being of those entities, is [human] subjectivity; and the *foundation* through which logical entities, henceforth held as paradigmatic, are anchored in their being, the method of founding them, is representation.

The modern epoch with its economy of technical systems produces a hardening ("enframing": *Gestell*) of the order, a technical rigidity which reaches its apogee in contemporary technology and the social order framed by its demands. Nevertheless, it is important to recognize that, according to Heidegger, this humanization—which in a more important sense is a dehumanization—did not begin with modern technology; it began with Aristotle's turn to *technē* as paradigmatic. If we are to deconstruct metaphysics in order to release its grip, then, according to Schürmann-Heidegger, we must learn another way of thinking:

To say *Anfang* [beginning] or *Ursprung* [origin] instead of *archē* or *principium* is to abolish the patterns of command and rule that accompany the Classical Greek and Latin representations of origin. (*HOBA*, p. 120)

---

11. Schürmann adds (p. 110) that the origin comes to be understood as *thetic*, i.e., as will, command, Pantocrator (which is more than Creator), and as *princeps*.
12. Heidegger's development of the notion of philosophy as a kind of *topology* is discussed at length as a way of overcoming the tight rational systematic order of modern principles. The task of philosophy, then, is not to discover first principles, but rather to "locate" the region in which Being is to be heard.

It is not entirely facetious to sum up at this point by saying that philosophy must learn to speak German, or at least some deconstruction of it.

The coupling of inception with domination, and the alleged closure that fails to liberate us, is also a theme in neo-Marxist thought, especially among followers of the Frankfurt School. Perhaps the essay that most closely parallels the scope—though not the detail—of Heidegger's analysis of Western thought is the essay by Max Horkheimer and Theodor W. Adorno entitled *Dialectic of Enlightenment.*[13] The thesis is a sweeping one, and the term "Enlightenment" is by no means confined to the eighteenth century or even to the modern period. An *Excursus* to the principal essay takes us back to Homer, for—according to the authors—"enlightenment" is present even in the early struggle by which reason and rational discourse sought to extricate itself from myth. In the end, however, we are told that reason never quite freed itself from the old powers resident in the ancient myths, and before which our cultural ancestors quailed, and that these powers still live on throughout the entire development of Western philosophy, science, and society.[14] For the old fearful ghosts do not dwell only in thought, images, and ideas; they have exercised their malignant power over the very formation of social life. Indeed, the authors find the beginnings of bourgeois society itself in the Homeric epics.[15] And they trace the root of this entanglement of ra-

13. Trans. by J. Cumming (New York: Herder and Herder, 1972) from *Dialektik der Aufklärung* (1944) (Frankfurt am Main: Fischer, 1969). The essay proper, "The Concept of Enlightenment," should be read with the two excursus: "Odysseus or Myth and Enlightenment" and "Juliette or Enlightenment and Morality," as well as with the two additional essays: "The Culture Industry: Enlightenment as Mass Deception" and "Elements of Anti-Semitism: Limits of Enlightenment."

14. The reference is to the essentialities and powers—Cause *(Ursache)*, Substance and Quality, Action and Passion, Being and Determinate Being *(Dasein)*—which are alleged to be "rationalized precipitates of the mythical view." Moreover, "these categories, in which Western philosophy determined its eternal order of nature, marked the places in which Oknos and Persephone, Ariadne and Nereus had once dwelled" (T. W. Adorno, *Gesammelte Schriften*, vol. 3 [Frankfurt am Main: Suhrkamp, 1981], 21–22. References will hereafter be made to this edition. Translations are my own except where otherwise indicated.) The authors insist that the ghosts of the myths dwell there still; thus, for example, in the attempt to speak of the origin of things, enlightenment introduces the distinction between a manifest effect and its hidden cause. There is present in the concept of cause the primitive cry of terror before the unknown. Demythologization is the vain attempt to eradicate that fear (vol. 3, 31–32).

15. From the Preface (1944), vol. 3, 16: The first excursus pursues the dialectic of myth and enlightenment in the Odyssey "as one of the earliest representative witnesses of Western bourgeois civilization." Further: "Not merely the ideal, but also the practical tendency to self-annihilation belongs to rationality from its very beginning, and is in no way a mere phase . . . The 'irrationality' [here, precisely, of antisemitism, although the remark is meant to hold quite generally] is derived from the essence of domineering [*herrschenden*] reason itself and from the image [*Bild*] of its corresponding world" (vol. 3, 17). We are told that such thought "seals its own fate," if it does not reflect upon the presence of the seeds of its own destruction that lie within it. Without such reflection thought becomes pragmatic and blind, and loses its sublating character, and therewith its relation to truth

tionality and social reality to the technological determination to master nature. Eventually everything is submitted to calculation and utility, and number becomes canonical.[16] Moreover,[17]

> Myth passes over into enlightenment and nature into mere objectivity. Men count the increase of their power by their estrangement [*Entfremdungl*] from that over which they exercise their power. Enlightenment relates itself to things as a dictator does to men. He is acquainted [*kennt*] with them insofar as he can manipulate them. The man of science knows [*kennt*] things insofar as he can produce [*machen*] them. In the transformation [from myth to rationality] the essence of things always hides itself as ever the same, as substrate for dominion [*Herrschaft*]. This identity constitutes the unity of nature.

Adorno and Horkheimer insist that the development of discursive rationality is inseparable from the transition from a nomadic society to a stable social order in which possession of property becomes the mark of the social distance between the master and the laborer. The very distantiation which marks abstraction in thought confirms the social control of the owners and the stability of the power structure. The fragile success in controlling nature through technology produces a social elitism by which the powerful are able to command the services of the weak. Ultimately, however, mankind itself becomes the slave of the accumulated technological power, a power which knows *(Wissen, Erkenntnis)* no limitations *(Schranken)*. Such "knowledge" seeks neither the truth, nor happiness, but domination, eventually even over the dominators.[18]

What Adorno and Horkheimer present to us is what is known in oth-

---

(vol. 3, 13–14). Cf. Heidegger's remarks on closure; also his remarks on domination; and finally, his remarks on the way the epochal suspension hides being and truth. Nevertheless, Adorno and Horkheimer insist that there is a resistance to the liberating reflection, a resistance built within Western rationality itself and from its very inception. It is nothing less than the fear of truth and substitution of a false clarity for that truth. The fate of such rationality, then, is to lapse back into various mythologies, such as nationalism, Fascism, etc. (vol. 3, 14–15).

16. "The enlightenment holds in contempt whatever does not fit the measure of accountability [*Berechenbarkeit*] and utility [*Nützlichkeit*] ... Right from the beginning, enlightenment rationality had understood anthropomorphism to be the ground of myth, the projection of the subjective upon nature ... Whatever is not absorbed into numbers and finally into unity is turned into appearance ... Unity remains the solution from Parmenides to Russell" (vol. 3, 22–24). Indeed, the concept of law (both scientific and juridical) is traced back to the will to reduce differences to the same by means of "the power of repetition over reality" (*Dasein*, vol. 3, 27–29). Cf. Heidegger's remarks on the loss of the sense of becoming and of time.)

17. Vol. 3, 25. There follow further developments. "The substitution of a victim [for the king or the community in a religious sacrifice] indicates a step towards discursive logic ... Representability [*Vertretbarkeit*] turns about into functionability [*Fungibilität:* the sense is that of being a functionary, an agent in our sense of that word]" (vol. 3, 26). Cf. Heidegger's remarks on the closure that occurs in the process of "enframing." See also, "... representability is the measure of mastery..." (vol. 3, 52).

18. Vol. 3, 20–21.

er contexts as "instrumental reason," rationality used as an indifferent means to attaining an arbitrary end but unable itself to determine the true end of human life. "Representation," the authors tell us,[19] "is only an instrument... The concept is the ideal [*ideelle*] instrument." Indeed, we are told that the whole range of intellectual and spiritual thought is an exercise in domination of nature which, in the form of positive science and a supposedly "neutral" objectivity, really surrenders to nature and is mastered by it. But this, they further tell us, is still the ancient primitive fear of nature now transformed from the ghostly presence of mythical forces into a methodological submission to the given *(data)*. Western man masters nature only by being mastered by it out of a fear that he has never mastered; but in our own century that illusory mastery (driven by self-preservation) has laid bare before us the very essence of power: it is force as compulsion *(Zwang)*. In sum, then, the root of the entanglement of rationality and social life is the inseparable connection between technology and exploitation—it begins with the exploitation of nature, but it passes on to the domination over other human beings, and finally it subjects the true individuality of man himself to impersonal techniques and the contending forces of nature which they have unleashed.

We have been looking at two influential views of origins—of the origins of Western culture and philosophy, but also of the beginnings of man and things. Traditional metaphysics has produced a variety of differing views of origin; but to Schürmann-Heidegger and Adorno-Horkheimer they come to much the same result. Despite the apparent differences between realism, idealism, materialism, and the like, these epochs and economies are found to agree in that they couple the beginning with conquest, close off radical choice, hide the true nature of being, and reduce multiplicity and variety to a single uniform unity.

We have traced the deconstruction of metaphysics from principles to anarchy. Is there a way back from anarchy to principles? The most perennial of the traditional views is one that draws its support both from biblical religion and from what may be called Christian philosophy (which has its analogues in Jewish and Muslim forms). I cannot here enter into the discussion of whether there is or can be a *Christian* philosophy strictly so called. What I mean by the name, however, is that there has arisen among Christians who philosophize a tradition of thought—shared at least in part by many who are not Christian—that seeks to appropriate *by rational and properly philosophical* means certain insights first disclosed by Christian revelation. Nor need any apology be made for such a proceed-

---

19. Vol. 3, 56–60. From the English edition, on mastery: 57; on instrumentality of reason: 87.

ing, since philosophy has never been conceived exclusively from within pure reason itself. Thus, Russell developed certain of his philosophical views from insights disclosed by mathematics; Quine took experimental science as his paradigm; others have taken law or art or music or social interaction. Philosophers must draw from the totality of their experience, though the appropriation will be satisfactory only when it meets the canons of philosophical evidence and argument. A Christian philosophy, then, is neither of two extremes: on the one hand, it is not a philosophy that is done by someone who happens to be a Christian, but which could as easily have been done by someone who is not; on the other hand, it is not a philosophy that receives the vindication of its premises directly from religious faith, without its own work in accordance with the canons of rationality. We may speak of a Christian *philosophy*—and not merely of a Christian *philosopher*—when, in important ways and in addition to other sources, the philosophy itself responds with positive interest and follows out lines of inquiry first suggested by Christian experience. All philosophy begins in prior understanding, and Christian philosophy begins in a pre-understanding that is shaped in important ways by Christian faith, life, and action.

Now, such Christian philosophy has articulated an understanding of origin as creation, and precisely as *creatio ex nihilo*. Obviously such a philosophy is the target of the criticism of both Schürmann-Heidegger and Adorno-Horkheimer. Creation is understood by them to be a system of philosophy shaped by principles—and primarily and ultimately by one Principle—which fixes the beginning through domination. Now, my interest in the present article is not so much to defend Christian philosophy as to take the criticisms of Schürmann-Heidegger and of Adorno-Horkheimer as indications of pressure-points upon which these two contemporary philosophies have brought their weapons to bear; and to ask whether their attacks cannot be turned towards our own examination of Christian philosophy and thereby serve to clarify and even to advance the resources of traditional metaphysics.

I placed Schürmann-Heidegger alongside Adorno-Horkheimer, not only because they represent two of the most influential lines of contemporary thought regarding origins, but because they show lines of convergence that might also be found in some versions of other philosophies (such as process philosophy and philosophy of language). I must not be misunderstood at this point. I do not mean to suggest that Heidegger is a crypto-Marxist, or that Adorno and Horkheimer have cribbed Heidegger. One has only to read the scorn with which the Frankfurters treat Heidegger's writing to recognize the very considerable disagreement between them. Nevertheless, both place their critical fingers upon the same pressure-points in their criticism of what Schürmann-Heidegger calls a philosophy built by principles and what Adorno-Horkheimer calls a domineering bourgeois philosophy. These may be summed up as follows: Western philosophy in all of its forms, since Aristotle according to Schürmann-Heidegger, and even earlier according to Adorno-Horkheimer, has been basically metaphysical. It has understood the origin of things (whether as *archē* or *principium* or *subjectum humanum*) as both inception and domination, to be realized by means of representation and technology. As a result, the whole of reality has been understood as a closed order, whose principiates (things and men, actions and events, institutions and values) have been arranged into one or another economy, understood as having originated out of and being directed back to the one single overriding principle (be it substance, God, humanity, property, or technology itself). The result in modern times has been a humanism that is deeply dehumanizing, in which fixed practices and values suppress freedom and individuality. According to both critics, then, the only remedy is to find a new way of thinking about origins: either through deconstruction or through (at least in Adorno) negative dialectics.

Now, at each of these pressure-points there is a Christian disclosure that invites appropriation and interpretation by a Christian philosophy. Let me take up each of the three most important charges. They are: first, the inseparability of domination from inception; second, the reduction of all things within the *cosmos, ordo,* or *system* to a uniform principle; and third, the subjection of thought and action to the closure brought about by the origin. Each of these pressure-points invites us to re-examine our own understanding of origin in the light of a Christian philosophy.

There is, first of all, the characterization of principle as the opening up (either in time or in being, chronologically or ontologically, diachronically or synchronically) that dominates all that follows. There is here a pre-understanding of *power:* as force, command, conquest, subjection, domination. There is much evidence to support such an understanding of power, both from its proper base in nature and from its dubious presence in human affairs; but we need to ask (with Gabriel Marcel, for example) whether such an understanding of power is adequate to establish fully human relationships, inasmuch as it derives from and reflects the character of physical energy. We must ask whether it can sustain a social order appropriate for human persons. To the extent that we are not fully human, there will be the use of dominance—and, in our imperfect condition, there must needs be—but if we are trying to understand the way things are meant to be, and even more how they might be better, then we must ask whether the fault lies with the very notion of firstness as principle, or whether it is a faulty understanding of firstness that equates principle with dominance.

Again, we may well concede that aspects of domination are embedded in the various past metaphysical understandings of power, and that these must be sifted out and clarified by us; but this is a far cry from claiming that the very notion of principle is itself at fault and that every metaphysics of principles must be deconstructed. It is possible to retain the conception of principles as that which establishes a certain arrangement of consequents, but deny that the arrangement must be one of domination. Indeed, if we turn to St. Thomas' formal discussion of creation[20] we find that he arrives at it by a gradual deepening and broadening of the notion of cause as the communication of being. Now assuredly, the quality of the communication, and the character of the result, will flow from the quality of the being that is being communicated. Following Aristotle, St. Thomas tells us that the first philosophers, being confined to images, imagined reality in corporeal terms and sought the causes of coming-to-be in material causes, such as attraction and repulsion, condensation and rarefaction, seeds or elements, and the like. They were followed by others who were able to abstract from their imaginations in order to grasp by means of concepts the similarity among various sorts of things. This move was an important one, because the human intelligence came home to itself and was able to read in things more than the merely surface physical properties manifest in them. We find here in the origin of rational discourse a striking epiphany of the human spirit. But Thomas himself—in all modesty—takes us further. There were, he tells us, philosophers who asked after the very being of things, implying the question: Why anything at all, why not rather nothing? This question arose out of a freshly charged wonder, prompted no doubt by the Christian disclosure of the generosity of a Creator who sent his only Son to redeem a fallen humanity. So that a Christian philosophy is prompted to look for the primary form of power (and the ultimate meaning and worth of the term) not in domination, but in caring presence. Such a presence has the spiritual creative power to release us from those mythical fears of which Adorno-Horkheimer speaks. And, indeed, the term that St. Thomas uses to describe both the source of, and the first effect of, creation is not *vis;* it is *esse,* and finds its completion in a presence that is the source of everything else *(praeter esse).*[21]

20. Cf. St. Thomas Aquinas, *Summa theologiae* (hereafter *STh*) I, q. 44, especially a. 1 and 2. I have treated the topic at some length in *The Gift: Creation,* The Aquinas Lecture (Milwaukee, WI: Marquette University Press, 1982).

21. St. Thomas Aquinas, *SCG,* bk. I, c. 52. It is here, too, that the Christian disclosure of the beginning tempers the creative process of Genesis with the small and quiet beginnings of the Annunciation/Magnificat and the Nativity. This is an example of the way in which the Christian disclosure can invite a philosopher to rethink the first meaning of power. It is this, along with the recent studies in anthropology and the history of religions, that led me to explore creation under the category of the *gift.*

Domination gathers power into a unified center, and the understanding of the beginning as dominative power reduces the primary principle of any economy or order to a unity as bare and sheer as the order will permit. But here again, there stands a Christian disclosure that should give a Christian philosopher pause; for in the struggle to move within a belief in the one God, the early Christians arrived at the notion—not of Tritheism, three Gods—but of the Trinity, and the Tri-unity of the Godhead. Anyone who has followed the Fathers and the Councils on this matter realizes with what difficulty a new and richer sense of unity had to be forged: to retain the unity and simplicity of God, while enriching that unity and simplicity with a "plurification" that arose from the very abundance of the divine life. Now, that disclosure into the inherent "sociality" of the divine life has not yet been cultivated in philosophy to the degree that it needs to be done. The charge that a metaphysics of principles is a means of domination is strengthened by the reductionism of the many to a sheer, univocal unity. But, if the first principle is one, yet not hostile to inner distinction (as theologically and in respect of the Trinity, we speak of the distinct persons and their different processions and missions), then the charge of closure must be reopened for discussion. The unstinting generosity and infinite abundance of the first principle will give room for all possibilities within creation—even, it must be remarked, for the possibilities of evil.

Finally, to the charge that the hiddenness of being is brought about by the closure of each epochal economy, a Christian philosophy replies with the mystery of being. And here, too, there stands the Christian disclosure of the God who is so transcendent that he is not a part of the metaphysical order at all, indeed, so transcendent that he is more intimately present to his creatures than they are to themselves, precisely because he takes up no room in the world which he has created and continues to sustain by his transcendent immanent presence.[22] Yet this mystery is a mystery of presence rather than of absence, not a hiddenness brought about by domination and reductionism, but a light too bright for clear sight.

To domineering power such a philosophy offers caring presence; to sheer unity it expands into the primordial harmony of plurality within unity; and to the darkness of reductive closure it opens out onto the inexhaustible light of mystery. All of this, then, is implied in a metaphysics of principles which does not find the beginning in domination, nor the

---

22. Cf. R. Sokolowski, *The God of Faith and Reason* (Notre Dame, IN: University of Notre Dame Press, 1982), especially 1–11. Also my "La transcendance coincident: fondement de l'interrogation religieuse," in *Urgence de la philosophie*, ed. T. De Koninck and L. Morin (Quebec: University of Laval Press, 1986), 591–98.

end in reduction to unity and suppression of difference, nor in a hiddenness that withdraws from presence. Yet these are precisely the pressure-points at which new movements of thought and action press upon—not only Christian philosophy, nor even only upon the sphere of thought—but upon the very cultural and social traditions of the West. We must receive these criticisms with thanks, as tokens of the thought and work yet to be done—not in order to defend those traditions against all criticism—but in order to bring to light tendencies and confusions within those traditions, and even within Christian philosophy itself. For Christian philosophy has resources yet untapped. To domination, a Christian philosophy offers: giving; to hard unity: a unity charged with abundance; and to hiddenness: the mystery of presence. There is work yet to be done and thoughts yet to be thought, if we are to render a better account of the original creative power which is not domineering but generous, and of the richness of the primal unity which is no enemy of diversity, and of the mysterious nature of that which lies hidden in a great light.

Chapter 4

NEITHER WITH NOR WITHOUT FOUNDATIONS

This essay was originally prepared for the 1988 Metaphysical Society meeting, where I had been asked to speak out of what has been called "the great tradition," concerning the rumored "end of metaphysics." It is important, however, to notice what followed the colon in the chosen theme: "the question of foundations." For metaphysics has been pronounced dead several times already, according to different autopsies: by skepticism, nominalism, empiricism, and at least two versions of positivism, the one prescribed by Auguste Comte and the other more recently mandated by the Vienna Circle. Indeed, death notices of metaphysics have become traditional in "the great tradition" itself, so that these recurrent obituaries disclose something of the very nature of metaphysics. While several of these morbid diagnoses continue to play a role—since in these matters nothing ever seems to quite wholly die once it gets itself born—there is a new angel of death on the scene. It is Nietzsche, purged of the metaphysics that had allegedly infected him, a revisionist or at least a revised Nietzsche, a neo-Nietzsche who has rallied an impressive number of lively mourners to the wake. Should the notices prove premature, however, the question will then resolve itself into: "Who will bury whom?"

I have entitled my own modest reflections: "Neither with nor without Foundations," but I have a colon, and subjoin the qualifier: "Was entity dismissed without sufficient cause?" This is, of course, quite a different question from: "Was entity dismissed along with sufficient cause?" For that, indeed, has been done by many parties to the current philosophical discussion. Indeed, it has been done, on the one hand, as prelude to the *dismissal* of foundations and, on the other, as prelude to the *transfor-*

Reprinted from the *Review of Metaphysics* 42 (Sept. 1988): 3–25. Copyright © 1988 by the *Review of Metaphysics*.

mation of foundations.[1] Now, both the dismissal and the transformation of foundations by so many leading contemporary philosophers must point at the very least to some ambiguity in this "great tradition."

There is no doubt that the search for foundations of various sorts represents a certain line of thought in so-called Western philosophy, a line that goes all the way back to the origins of discourse, of *logos*. I suggest, however, that Western philosophy is ambiguous in this regard, and that foundationalism is not the only line the tradition offers. Moreover, I will argue that there are other lines that demand less sacrifice of the real world upon the altar of human knowledge, lines of thought more open, even mysterious. For the question *ti esti?* does not start with *ousia* in the sense of essence *(eidos)*, nor does it end with *System*—I deliberately leave the last word in the German. The question *ti esti?* begins in wonder *(thaumatzein)*.[2] But the suspect ambiguity has taken root in the very question itself, for even in Aristotle the specific wonder with which philosophy begins seems to all but evaporate with the arrival of *epistēmē*,[3] tempting the knower to replace the original entities with the explanatory account *(logos)*, given in terms of principles and causes *(archai kai aitiai)*. Now, by the term "entity" I mean "this being," or "these beings," or even "all beings," but I do not understand the term as equivalent to Heidegger's sense of *das Seiende*.

Some have caught from Heidegger the suspicion that the question of the meaning of Being (capital "B") has been forgotten in the metaphysical quest for entity (small "b"). But suppose that we take a different tack, and reverse the question: *Is it possible that entity has been forgotten in the question of Being?* Is it possible that the community of beings has been devalued in the search for Being? And may it not be time once again to let entity—whether it be a natural thing, a social community, or even the questioner himself—come forward and not be forgotten in the question *ti esti?* and in the answer to it? But, then, entities must not be relegated to a merely secondary, derivative status, as though they rest upon their principles and causes; for that is a perverse sort of foundationalism which places the only real things that *are*, at the mercy of the human formalisms by which we *think* them. Under that regime the foundations made up of universal principles co-opt the singulars, interpreting them as mere particular instantiations, or deride them as residual. What is more, in recent times and under the aegis of one or another variety

---

1. I have taken the distinction from K. Baynes, Jas. Bohman, and T. McCarthy, *After Philosophy: End or Transformation?* (Cambridge, MA: MIT Press, 1987).

2. Aristotle, *Metaphysics* 982b13; ed. W. Jaeger (Oxford: Oxford University Press, 1957).

3. Ibid., 982a13–21.

of idealism, universality in the form of fundamental principles has been replaced by universality in the form of totality—first as metaphysical system, then as horizon of experience, and lately as an organization of linguistic functions. We might well ask whether such foundations have come to obscure the proper object and subject matter of metaphysics.

The question is not easy to answer. For if we concede that a certain kind of knowledge, inherited from the Greeks *(logos* as *epistēmē)*, is not only *of* the universal but in the form of the universal as well, is it still possible to rescue the *individuality* of entity and yet preserve a discourse that is properly philosophical, and therefore in some sense universal? Suppose, then, that in its original being entity is neither universal or total, nor particular and instantive; suppose that it is *singular* and yet open to and constituted by *commonality;* I mean in the sense that natural things are inseparable from their ecology, and human beings from their community. Then it may be that a properly redefined conception of entity can survive the attacks upon it, and that metaphysics will also survive as the distinctive concern for such entity. We would then be able to ask that a metaphysics of entity once again be heard among the learned.

Such a metaphysics cannot be—to use Derrida's phrase—merely a new or old "economy of the evening guard," the last witness of a dying tradition. Instead, it must be the guardian of a distinctive and indispensable discourse—for yesterday, today, and tomorrow. Indeed, we must be careful not to foreclose too quickly on the past, since premature foreclosure may mortgage the future. Indeed, if there is a plurality of possibilities for the future, it is only because they are prepared for by a pluralism of the past. I mean not only a plurality of *present* understandings of the past, since they must always be narrow and selective, but of *past* understandings of the past as well. This, surely, is the principal justification for the *philosophical* study of the history of philosophy, and of the relevance of the "great tradition" to the contemporary discussion.

I

Suppose, then, that we direct our attention towards the conception of metaphysics as a distinctive discourse about entity. I must clarify further what I mean by these terms. I have already said that *entity* is not primarily and originally particular. The very word "particular" means: "part of —." And if we ask, part of what? the answer has been: part of a species or a class, part of something universal or total. But such answers found the particular upon the universal, the "this" *(tode, hoc)* upon the "whole" *(katholou)*. It is interesting that Aristotle has two meanings for the term that we translate usually as "the universal"; for, while *katholou* usually means a secondary substance, the species or genus, the abstract universal, it is occasionally used to denote "the sensible totality which includes its particulars."[4] This is the early latent ambiguity in the term "universal." And, as I have already remarked, in the "great tradition" the latter, more concrete meaning gradually freed itself from the first, more abstract meaning, eventually becoming (especially with Kant and Hegel) the concept of totality *(Totalitätsbegriff).*

There is a second, even more important ambiguity. For, while Aristotle (more than any other philosopher before him and many since) brought to philosophy the concern for the concrete individual entity *(tode ti),* and defended it as primary substance against various forms of Platonic ideality, when he came to formulate the essential meaning of the individual, he turned very quickly to the universal in the form of the specific nature—in a word, to the *ti.* To be sure, Aristotle did not mean that the "species" as such (*eidos* as definition) was primarily real, for the *ti* in the individual did not refer directly to the species as such but to the *form (eido)* of the individual. I recognize, therefore, that it would be an act of philosophical injustice and impiety to suggest that Aristotle ever lost the sense of the concrete individual. Still, the seeds of inversion are present in his philosophy, an inversion that—in minds less attuned to the concrete—threatens to place the universal at the foundation of the individual.

Nevertheless, in partial atonement for the unintended impiety, let me attempt to restore the concrete weight of the Aristotelian ontology by a closer examination of the individual—not as a strictly historical representation of Aristotle's view—but by an interpretation that takes advantage of the career of reflective thought since the Greeks, in order to enrich Aristotle's notion.[5] The question is, how, in the light of our present understanding, is the individual to be best understood? Among other formulas, Aristotle used the term: "this something of a certain kind," *tode ti* (cf. the Latin: *hoc aliquid*). This has been taken to mean that the individual is through and through individual, and so it is: *tode.* But equally, it is through and through communal: *ti.* For the factors that characterize the individual are not related as part to part, but as whole to whole; that is, the individual as a whole is singular *(tode)* and the individual as a whole is communal *(ti).* The factors of singularity *(tode)* and commonality *(ti)* are inseparable in reality. What is more, while they can and must

---

4. Aristotle, *Physics* 184a24; ed. Wicksteed and Cornford (Cambridge, MA: Harvard University Press, 1929), 10 and n.
5. For a fuller analysis see Kenneth L. Schmitz, "Community: The Elusive Unity," *Review of Metaphysics* 37 (Dec. 1983): 243–64; and "Metaphysics: Radical, Comprehensive, Determinate Discourse," *Review of Metaphysics* 39 (June 1986): 675–94. See chapter 1 above.

be thought of distinctly in discursive understanding, their *inseparability* itself must be brought back into thought if we are to think the *reality* of the individual. And so, the singularity cannot be thought of simply as a particular or an instance in the domain of real existence that is related externally to a type or universal in the mind. Nor ought we to identify real existence with isolated singulars (after the manner of nominalism), or identify reality with universal types (after the manner of a Platonism or a formalism). Rather, the individual is co-constituted through its singularity *and* its commonality. Now, to be "constituted" does not mean "to be made up out of previously existing parts," although individuals can be traced back to antecedent causes. But to be "constituted," in the sense that is relevant here, means "to possess certain factors as an intrinsic endowment." Thus, parents are causes of children, but the constitution of children as entities consists primarily of their singularity and their commonality. The commonality includes the individual's specific kind along with the ecology that envelops it. In the case of human beings, along with and out of the commonality of their natural constitution there also develops the commonality of community, culture, and social life.

It may be that the later Latin insistence upon *substantia* as *ens per se* (cf. *kath'auto*) put undue emphasis upon the primacy of separated individuatedness, more perhaps than the less insistent Greek *on, ousia*. And this emphasis may have contributed to the devaluation of the communal factor. Or perhaps, because the community was in ancient times more explicit in life, it could remain implicit in thought. Or more recently, because the individual has been so stressed in modern liberalism, utilitarianism, and existentialism, the commonality of the individual must now be made explicitly thematic. In any event, to correct the imbalance, I have come to recognize that the individual is a "contextualized singular," and that the adjective "contextualized" is equal to and inseparable from the singularity of the individual. Indeed, only the conventions of linguistic usage, the dangers of lapsing into a Platonism forgetful of singularity, and the intimate relation between existence and individuality— only these prevent me from suggesting that the individual is equally and inversely a "singularized context." For that context which is the world does not arise as a collection of secondary relations between radically isolated individuals; it is from the very beginning built into those individuals in and through what I have called the factor of commonality *(ti)*. The contextuality of the individual entity is indispensable to its very singularity; so that commonality (the *ti*) is a co-equal principle in the constitution of the individual. Through its commonality the individual expands beyond its singularity. Commonality *(ti)* is the factor that ensures the non-restriction of the individual to its singularity *(tode)*.

Now, human commonality or contextuality cannot be fully understood only in terms of an inherited nature. The commonality *(ti)* must also be understood in terms of the need for a whole range of other relations as well, and especially the call to be in space and time in distinctively human ways. For the call to be in human space is the call to human community and society, and the call to be in human time is the call to human history and tradition. What exists, then, are singulars-as-communal. The commonality expresses itself in a host of ways: through language, technology, art, religion, science, and philosophy. In respect to human individuals the context not only environs and even co-constitutes them: it awaits them. And it awaits them not only as a bare potentiality, but as an already developed context of actual, determinate institutions of language, techniques, beliefs, dispositions, and the like. Such commonalities *(ti)* are open to the contingencies of historical existence and shot through with natural forces, human aspirations, decisions, and desires. For human beings are entities whose enculturation, socialization, and historicity are as constitutive of them as is their natural endowment *(eidos)* and their singularity *(tode)*.

II

In the light of the foregoing account of entity, the very conception of foundations needs to be questioned, since it may carry with it presuppositions that are incompatible with the primacy of such contextualized and singular individuals. No doubt, these difficulties may not attend more special sciences, for we do speak of the foundations of algebra, of foundational logic, and of the fundamentals of engineering. But the question remains whether the notion of foundations is suitable for the trans-specific scope proper to a traditional metaphysics of entity. The conception of foundations may take one of several different forms. It may be thought of as a stable interlocking set of notions (self-evident, axiomatic, or postulational) that form the bedrock of human knowing and are accessible in themselves to conceptual and rational formulation prior to their application or employment. Such a foundation may also take form as a starting point for the methodical development of later knowledge, a starting point that is carried along with the development and provides the continuing justification for it.

The original purity and clarity of such a conception of foundation has come under criticism from many critics. They point to the pre-rational selectivity of our non-conceptual experience, the opacity of our sensory knowledge, the peculiarity of our images, the contingency of our cultural background, and the arbitrariness of our willed actions. In a word, if there are foundations, they do not seem to be self-evident, nor cut from the same cloth as our rational conceptualizations. At this point in the current discussion, some (such as Richard Rorty) abandon the concept of foundations, whereas others (such as Karl-Otto Apel) seek to transform the conception in order to take account of the opacity and complexity that has been brought at least partially to the surface. But, whether accepted, abandoned, or modified, the conception of foundations puts itself forward as a modern way of gathering together the presuppositions of intelligibility into a legitimizing conception.[6]

Now, it seems to me that at least some attempts at the deconstruction of metaphysics are not themselves sufficiently free of the metaphor of foundations, even when they equate the attack upon metaphysics with the attack upon foundations. A recent, important book by Reiner Schürmann has traced out the Heideggerian attack in detail, and while Schürmann has hardened some of the nuances of Heidegger's thought—so that I will refer to the interpretation as "Schürmann-Heidegger"—he has also brought to Heidegger's thought not only clarity but also the direction in which a good deal of contemporary discussion is moving.[7] According to Schürmann-Heidegger, the attack upon metaphysics and upon foundations takes shape as an attack upon the very conception of principle *(archē, principium)*. Since what is at stake is the very "principle" of principle, this issue is of no small importance to the self-understanding of "the great tradition." Indeed, we should be grateful for such critical service to philosophy, though I confess that it is not easy for a traditionally inclined metaphysician to offer thanks for what, after all, and despite the protestations of the undertakers, is yet another burial notice of the discipline.

The broad lines of Heidegger's deconstruction are familiar, and so I will only sketch it as Schürmann interprets it.[8] According to Schürmann-Heidegger, a fateful step was taken by Socrates when he turned away from nature towards man. That fate was sealed when Aristotle interpreted natural motion after the manner of human fabrication *(poiēsis, technē)*, and made human causality serve as the paradigm for physical causation. As Aristotle's *Physics* became the *Grundbuch* of Western thought, the translation of nature into the human project was further sealed and developed, so that the hidden primacy of man resurfaced in modern form as human subjectivity, the *subjectum inconcussum* of thought, reality,

---

6. See "Metaphysics: Radical," 683.
7. Reiner Schürmann, *Heidegger on Being and Acting: From Principles to Anarchy*, trans. Christine-Marie Gros and Reiner Schürmann (Bloomington: Indiana University Press, 1987). By "direction" I mean a certain proclivity to neo-Marxist analysis in terms of power.
8. The issue is treated in more detail in Kenneth L. Schmitz, "From Anarchy to Principles" (Aquinas Medalist Lecture, University of Dallas, 1988). See chapter 3 above.

and value, its bedrock and criterion. On the basis of such a humanism modern technology bound thought and imagination ever closer to the spirit of *technē*.

According to Schürmann-Heidegger, whereas Socrates stands (or sits) at the start of this history, its foundations are inaugurated and sustained by the conception of principle. And whereas its latest and last product is modern technology, its first was metaphysics. Now, according to Schürmann-Heidegger, metaphysics is the fundamental thought-construction produced by principles, and it can be overcome and recast *(Verwindung)* only by a deconstruction of the very notion of principle. For, in the Western tradition, it is by principle that each metaphysics rules. Each metaphysics creates and expresses its own epoch or economy by establishing an order that rests upon a primary, overriding principle. That principle provides a foundation for those who live, think, and act in terms of its order. Now, in providing that fundamental order, such an overriding principle selects, and thereby delimits, the open manifold of possibilities; it ensures stability and regularity; and it secures credibility for the established order. In a word, a principle brings about self-reference, regularity, and certitude; that is, closure, normativity, and conviction.

We are told further that, to the older meaning of principle as inception or beginning, Aristotle added the energy of domination so that a first principle (whether *ousia* among the Greeks, or God among the medievals, or human subjectivity among the moderns) has come to be an amalgam of primacy and power. This new meaning of principle is alleged to have resulted from Aristotle's hidden interpretation of physical motion as human fabrication. Moreover, the Latin *principium*, in close association with *princeps*, hardened the bias towards the primacy of the performable *(poiēsis, technē)*. It is all but inevitable, then, that the unshakeable foundation of reality, intelligibility, and value should eventually turn into human subjectivity expressed theoretically by certitude of method, and practically by technological control. In modern times, the mediation of theory and practice preserved the dominance of human subjectivity and the normativity of technical production by means of one or another theory of mental representation, fortified with epistemological criteria. Metaphysics has become more and more what it has been from its inception: agent of coercive power. What is called for, then, is not the destruction of metaphysics in favor of yet another metaphysics, but the deconstruction of the conception at the root of all metaphysical thinking, to wit, the very conception of principle. What is called for is a new mode of thinking that is without principle, thinking that is *anarchic*.

In response to such a deconstruction of all metaphysics of principles,

I should like to bring into play the metaphor of *firstness,* in order to re-examine the charges brought against the very concept of principle, whether understood as *archē* or *principium* or *principle.* By *firstness* I too understand a "source" from which consequences follow (as *principiata* from *principium*). Moreover, I too recognize that those consequences will bear some affinity with the character of the principle, and that the resultant order will bear its character. If the principle is a limited one, then the order will be limited (as when, if we are interested only in the design of a building, we need not consider its other features); if the principle is itself complex, the order that results will be complex as well. Every principle is a first principle in terms of its order, but the degree of "firstness" is made manifest by the character of the order that follows from it. There are many kinds of principles: real, mental, natural, social, moral, technical. Among them there are principles which inaugurate a distinctive and fundamental order of consequences that is not reducible without loss to another order, as the moral quality of an action is not reducible without loss to a consideration that is indifferent to good and evil, or as knowledge is not reducible without loss to brain-waves, or color without loss to light waves.

I readily concede that the conception of principles as "firstness"—which I am here articulating—resonates with the metaphor of fullness. For a principle (so understood) is a kind of plenitude, and it is generosity—not coercive power—that characterizes this understanding of principle. In this conception of principle as source, ancient *archē* is distinguished from the modern *Totalitätsbegriff.* In recent times the concept of totality has been conceived variously as context, or result, or both: it has taken shape as an unrealizable ideal in Kant's *conceptus cosmicus,* as a realized result in Hegel's *System,* as an experiential context in Husserl's *Horizont,* as an ontological environ in the early Heidegger's *Welt,* and as a system of symbolic differences in de Saussure's *langue.*

Now, the primordial sense of *archē* in Aristotle—or at the very least in my own rethinking of the conception of principle as source—is oriented towards actuality *(energeia)* though not in the sense of *Wirklichkeit.* And so, the first consequence of an effective principle is not inception, nor is it coercive power; it is rather the communication of actuality in some form. Of course, actuality can and often is a display of power, sometimes it is a display of coercive power, but sometimes it is not a display of power in any usual sense at all, as when a painter elicits an unprecedented and unexpected manifestation of beauty, or when an act of generous love infuses a banal situation with new energy, or when a brilliant insight illumines our understanding of a field of inquiry. Regarding these examples, it expresses the matter less adequately to speak of a hidden order enforced by a domineering principle than to speak of an open mystery that lies at once both within and beyond the routine limits of actuality.

Nothing prevents us from speaking of first principles as foundational, of course, but the term has acquired systemic and epistemic connotations that make it unsuitable for a philosophy of principles. The metaphor that is nearer the mark is that of *roots*. A metaphysics of principles is, therefore, radical—not in the curious recent sense of something one-sided and extreme—but in the proper sense of what is deep and axial. First principles are the roots of the orders which follow from them, and in themselves they are marked by a primacy of fullness, a firstness that need not be an amalgam of coercive power, and that is open to infusions of natural development, historical novelty, and human creativity.

Such a metaphysics is the study of the interlocking web of first principles. Now, if entity is such as I have set forth, then the most actual principles are actual entities (not quite in Whitehead's sense, but in the sense of contextualized individuals given above). Entities, as contextualized individuals, are the primary sources of actuality; they are properly "actuality-principles," direct sources for the actuation of any and every order that is actualized. As well, they are indirect sources of those orders that are embedded in and concomitant with actuality, such as orders of intention, meaning, and value. Individuals, then, are the principal agents, the principal principles: whether the order is a natural one or a human one, whether social, cultural, political, scientific, religious, or other. In summary, then, (1) there is a very general sense of the term "principle" as that unity to which an order of consequences is to be attributed; and further (2), among principles, there are first principles of distinctive orders (of being, knowledge, action); and finally (3), among first principles there are actual entities which are principles in the strongest sense, for they exist and initiate actual consequences by the direct communication of actuality.[9]

III

Among various kinds of principles, the *transcendentals*, associated with the medieval schoolmen, are unique and suggestive. Because they are trans-generic, they are of interest and importance to a traditional metaphysician, since metaphysics claims to be trans-generic knowledge. In his discussion of the nature of truth,[10] Thomas Aquinas sets out such very general terms as: "entity" *(ens)*, which expresses actuality; "thing"

---

9. See "Metaphysics: Radical," 685–88.
10. Thomas Aquinas, *De Veritate* I, 1 in *Quaestiones Disputatae et Quaestiones Duodecim Quodlibetales*, ed. 7, vol. 3 (Turin: Marietti, 1942), 1–4.

(res), which expresses reality; "unity" *(unum)*, which expresses the undividedness of entity; and "other" or "something else" *(aliquid)*, which expresses the negative relation of division. And then he comes upon an affirmative relation, which he calls one of "assembly" *(convenientia)*, the coming together of the human knower and lover with what is true and good. The relation is a concrete one, and the other—the known and the loved—is designated concretely as the true and the good *(verum et bonum)*. Now, this coming together of the knower and lover with the known and loved, this convention, requires a transcendental openness on the part of the knower and the lover, the capacity to enter into relationship with any and every being *(natum sit convenire cum omni ente)*. It is at this point that Thomas cites Aristotle's dictum that, for such collegiality, there must be a distinctive principle, and he calls that principle "soul" *(anima)* in the sense of "mind" *(nous)*, since mind alone is able "in its own way to be all things." What distinguishes the human entity, then, is its capacity to fit in with things, to "covenant with them."[11]

Indeed, St. Thomas uses several terms in *De Veritate* to interpret the truth-relation, each bringing the nuance of its original metaphor to the interpretation of the relation. The knower comes to be "disposed" towards the known. By likening itself, by taking on the character of the thing known, it "assimilates" to the thing known, more penetratingly even than in the manner of the chameleon which only displays the surface colors of its surroundings. This disposition is the "fit" that gives rise to knowledge *("per assimilationem cognoscentis ad rem cognitam, ita quod assimilatio dicta est causa cognitionis")*. But he speaks also of being "comparing" itself to the intellect. Now, by *comparatio* he means the power *(vis)* of making something equal to the intellect literally, of putting being and intellect on a par with each other. Indeed, he remarks that being "responds" along with the intellect to produce knowledge *("ens intellectui correspondeat")*, and this co-response attains to truth by bringing entity and intellect to the same level *("quidem correspondentia, adaequatio rei et intellectus dicitur")*. What the knower contributes to the situation through this transcendental relation of co-respondence, then, is a shared symmetry of thing and intellect *("conformitatem sive adaequationem rei et intellectus")*.

Now, we are prone today to think of knowledge as producing or bringing about truth, so that what Thomas next says may be somewhat surprising. For he tells us that the very nature of truth resides in this original concord between thing and intellect *"et in hoc* [i.e., *correspondentia*

---

11. Cf. Kenneth L. Schmitz, "Purity of Soul and Immortality," *The Monist* 69 (July 1986): 396–415. See chapter 12 below.

rei et intellectus] formaliter ratio veri perficitur." Truth *is* this resonant symmetry of knower and known, and is completed in it. Now, we must not let our modern preconceptions about truth mislead us as to his meaning here. To be sure, following Aristotle, Thomas insists that *expressed* truth comes about through the combination and separation of concepts in the judgment. But such propositional truth is not the original truth, whose very nature is completed in the ontological relationship just set forth. Indeed, Thomas makes the point forcefully, when he insists that the knowledge of things does not precede the attainment of truth; on the contrary, knowledge follows upon just such a conformity: *"ad quam conformitatem, ut dictum est, sequitur cognitio rei."* Moreover, he emphasizes the point again, saying that the being of the thing precedes its truth and its truth precedes knowledge of it. Knowledge, then, is the effect of truth, not its cause: *"Sic ergo entitas rei praecedit rationem veritatis, sed cognitio est quidam veritatis effectus."* Truth is first and foremost an ontological relationship; it is a relation between entities, between the knower and the known. Truth is not first and foremost a cognitive relation, and it certainly is not first and foremost a relation merely within the knower, or a relation between the knower and a representation. It is not primarily an epistemological relation. Rather, there is a distinctive sort of entity who can come into association with other beings in such a way as to enter into an ontological relation that releases their intelligibility and value. Out of such an entity there arises the transcendental relation of the true and the good.

IV

Nevertheless, traditional metaphysics is cognitive; it is the discursive cognition of entity by means of principles. I have indicated what I mean by entity and by principle; it remains to clarify what I mean by discourse. The term "discourse" can take several forms and bear a number of meanings. By *discourse in general* one can mean any sequential verbal expression ordered towards communication with others, whether to inform, exhort, command, praise, entreat, or request. As such, it is equivalent to any and every human language, including the primary languages of the so-called Western tradition of thought. The late Latin *discursus* means "a running to and fro" and, by extension, "a conversation," which may tell us something about a Roman colloquy (cf. Greek *dierchomai*, to narrate). The Greek *legō* (the verbal form of *logos*) can mean "to gather together into a chosen order," so that the centripetal energy of unification may be more strongly emphasized in the Greek than in the root meaning of the Latin *discursus,* which expresses a certain dispersal or centrifugal energy. Nevertheless both terms do indicate a verbal sequence, so that, despite important nuances, for my present purpose, the English term "discourse" may be used to cover the Greek, Latin, and vernacular developments of sequential expression.

Now, it seems to me possible to recognize two enduring features of discourse in general that have remained constant in the "great tradition" of Western thought. To indicate these features, I must briefly sketch out my understanding of the origin of discourse among the Greeks *(logos, dielthein, dialogos)*, since it is from them that "the great tradition" develops.[12] There is no doubt that the religious and poetic sense of order (apportionment: *moira, dikē, kosmos*) forms a background to the emergence of discourse. No doubt, too, the adoption and adaptation of written language from the Phoenicians played a role. So, too, the remarkable social organization, the *polis*—which is neither a city nor a state in our senses of these terms—became a place for the exchange of ideas as well as of goods. It formed a *locus* and a *topos* for conversation. Out of these and other elements—some of which we may never come to know—and in a way we may never be able to fully reconstruct, this fragile child of time and culture must have made its appearance as a sort of shift in the way in which the Greek addressed the world in which he lived. I suggest that two energies constituted that shift.

First, a certain *distantiation* from the things of the world took place. Given the current understanding of the term "object" as something set over *against* the modern subject, this distantiation is rather misleadingly understood as an "objectification." It consisted neither in the construction of an object, nor in the projection of a representation. It was, rather, an indwelling (immanent) activity that opened the knower out onto his situation by a distantiation from the things of the world but *within* the world, for it opened up a semantic space within which the speaker could relate to the things of the world without *in that relationship* disturbing them *(theōria)*. In this way the speaker gained a new sense of things through gaining a certain distance from them. Thus, a distinctive mode of freedom is the presupposition of such discourse. But the distantiation is also a distantiation within the speaker himself, so that he distanced himself from himself as well. Hegel tells us that before they could understand themselves as a historical people among other peoples, the Greeks first had to place themselves, so to speak, at a distance from themselves and relate to themselves as doers of deeds in the world.

---

12. For a more detailed consideration of the origins of discourse, as I understand them, see Kenneth L. Schmitz, "Gibt es für Menschen Wichtigeres, als zu überleben? Das Erbe Griechenlands: Rationalität," in *Das europäische Erbe und seine christliche Zukunft,* vol. 16, ed. N. Lobkowicz (Cologne: Hans Martin Schleyer-Stiftung, 1985), 95ff.

In this way "deeds" became "events," and historical discourse was born.

The second feature of discourse in general comprises the means by which this inner distantiation was brought about. It was by the energy of *conceptualization,* the process of concept formation in which, as part of the distantiation, the mind struggled to free itself from pictorial images (without fully succeeding). When Thales asserted the fundamental unity of all things, he did not invite his hearers to picture all things as variant images of water, but rather to grasp the unimaginable unity of things beneath and within their sensible forms. In sum, then, with the energies of what I have called distantiation and conceptualization, and out of their own wonder and experience, the Greeks strove to convert their mythical inheritance into rational values.

Four distinctive modes of discourse seem to have quickly arisen among them: philosophy, mathematics, history, and linguistics. In these modes, discourse takes on a more precise and disciplined form (from *discere:* to know), since it comes to signify modes of language ordered towards statements about the way things (i.e., entities, numbers, events, and words) are, and to the truth or falsity of other statements about the way things are. Such discourse comes under the discipline of the way things are for the sake of coming to know them. This is its veridical use. Now, *veridical discourse* takes two forms, which I will call "noetic" and "epistemic." *Noetic discourse* is a more or less open discourse that arises within the ontological truth-relation. It is an original, spontaneous yet receptive discourse under the influence of the concrete situation. Moreover, it has its own integrity, and can find expression in various ways: in ordinary conversation, in the "wisdom of experience" as well as the enthusiasm of the "songs of innocence." It can find its expression in poetry as well as in prose, in fiction as well as in fact, in wit as well as in wot. *Epistemic discourse,* on the other hand, is a special modification of noetic discourse. For, in addition to being *sequential* (discourse in general), and in addition to rendering a purportedly *true account* (veridical discourse), epistemic discourse performs such tasks *methodically*—by description, explanation, or interpretation. In this stricter sense, discourse proceeds along a determinate way—according to method *(meth-hodos)*—to describe, explain, or interpret the way matters stand. Now the theoretical use of a method is more than a commitment to consistency and coherence. It adopts, at least provisionally, a semantic context which includes (1) an explicit or implicit theory of what constitutes true knowledge, (2) some general canons regarding what passes as a valid argument, and (3) certain preconceptions respecting what counts as authentic evidence. In sum, epistemic discourse moves methodically within a semantic context of truth, argument, and evidence. Such learned speech—whether spoken or written—is a modification of noetic discourse, which is itself an expression of more general discourse (which in turn is a particular realization of a *matrix* language).[13]

Epistemic discourse, then, is a secondary modification of the discursive character of language, a modification which arises out of a methodical preoccupation with the conditions of truth and the systematic possibilities of cognition. It organizes language in the interests of definite cognitive ends and predetermines the horizon of what counts both as relevant and as valid speech.[14] Of course, validity and relevance are not determined solely by the objects of the discourse, but also by the objective which is intended by the community of discourse. The current discussion among foundationalists and anti-foundationalists has made ever more clear the degree to which the speech community itself, with its semantic past, preoccupations, interests, and possibilities, enters into the determination of the horizon of discourse. It sets limits of relevance and standards of validity within the various epistemic discourses, such as those of mathematics, the natural sciences, the social and human sciences, history, philosophy, and others in the shifting web of learned speech.

By *epistemic discourse,* then, I do not mean any and every form of verbal communication, nor even every locution meant to express what is true or false, since noetic discourse also aims at truth in its own ways. Epistemic discourse is methodically assertive language about some referent, however vague or elusive that referent may be. For the referent need not be taken as an object set over against the speaker and indifferent to him or her.[15] Such extreme "objectivism" is a rather recent and special modification of epistemic discourse. The opposition which it masks is breaking down presently under criticism from philosophers as diverse as hermeneutists, neo-Marxists, and other critics of "modernity." Nevertheless, even among them, epistemic discourse remains in the main conceptual and rational; that is, it is argumentative and seeks to state the way things are (or are not) in some specific context.

I say that epistemic discourse is conceptual and rational "in the main," because I do not discount the use of language ancillary to its princi-

13. For the latter term, see Kenneth L. Schmitz, "Restitution of Meaning in Religious Speech," *International Journal for Philosophy of Religion* 5 (Fall 1974): 134.
14. See Kenneth L. Schmitz, "Natural Imagery as Discriminatory Element in Religious Language," in *Experiences, Reason and God,* ed. E. T. Long, Studies in Philosophy and the History of Philosophy, vol. 8 (Washington, D.C.: The Catholic University of America Press, 1980), 161.
15. On the pre-modern sense of objectivity, see Kenneth L. Schmitz, "Another Look at Objectivity," in *Thomas and Bonaventure: A Septicentenary Commemoration Proceedings of the American Catholic Philosophical Association* 48 (1974): 86–98.

pal aim, that of methodical, argumentative veridical discourse. Nor do I mean to suggest that what counts as a concept, a rational judgment, or an argument, is something obvious and fully settled beforehand. One of the features of discourse is that just such matters are at issue. Thus, for example, what counts as an appropriate argumentative strategy in mathematics nowadays may not be what it was in Euclid's; and what counts nowadays as historical analysis in terms of social movements may differ considerably from the causal narration of individual actions that characterizes more traditional historical writing, and may differ even more from that moral history of which some ancient historians were able practitioners.

It is not surprising that the controversy regarding what constitutes discourse is more pronounced in philosophy than in other disciplines since philosophy is not only discourse about discourse—never more so than currently—but it is properly discourse about the ultimate status and significance of discourse. Compared with other forms of epistemic discourse, then, the criticism and transformation of the forms and scope of philosophical argument may well be more various and more radical. Thus, the classical modern fetish for constructing systems, which held sway for several centuries, has become increasingly problematic, and the explicit *systematic* ideal of knowledge has fallen out of favor. Nevertheless, the deeper *methodical, systemic* pressures are still at work in much of the discourse of hermeneutists and deconstructionists as well as among phenomenologists and ontologists, so that contemporary philosophical discussion falls within the horizon of what I have called epistemic discourse. But whereas other forms of epistemic discourse come to expression in formally definite contexts—for example, in history, mathematics, and linguistics—the distinctive, and perhaps tragicomic, character of metaphysical discourse is that it attempts to say what is true of the context of contexts. Nor does a metaphysics of entity escape such a fate, since it attempts to discourse about the order of orders (i.e., of *principia* and *principiata*).

V

I began by asking whether we could not once again raise the question of entity in such a way as to recommend metaphysics as principled discourse about entity. I have taken entity to be equally singular and communal. Moreover, I have understood the commonality of the individual to embrace not only the specific type, but even more the full range of relations within which the individual is freed from its singularity. In human individuals these relations include not only the inherited natural endowment, but also the heritage of culture, the institutions of society, and the open possibilities of historical decision. These coalesce in what I have called the ontological relation, and come to knowledge in the noetic strand embedded within that relation.

Now, the metaphor of foundations and the conception articulated from it seem to characterize an epistemological whole rather than the ontological milieu in which individual entities are source-principles for the institution of actual orders and indirect sources of concomitant orders. I say "principles" or "sources" rather than "foundations" because the metaphor of foundations has two biases. The first bias is towards inflation of the factor of commonality in favor of systemic totality. Such inflation may be understandable as a reaction against the isolated individualism of the recent liberal past, but an overemphasis upon commonality puts in jeopardy one of the distinctive insights towards which Western thought and life has labored, namely, the dignity of the individual. The sources for such an insight are manifold, but they include biblical religion, Hellenic skepticism, Roman jurisprudence, the Incarnation, and the Enlightenment insistence upon individual human rights. It seems to me that, even more remotely, the differentiation brought about by the distantiation and conceptualization constitutive of discourse also played a role. I have argued that individuals, properly understood as singular and communal, are radical ontological principles, sources of actuality and its concomitants. This insistence upon the individual is not "value-neutral." Indeed, in the discourse of the High Middle Ages the word *dignitas* was used as another name for "principle," a designation which, it seems to me, is especially fitting for those radical principles that are singular and communal entities.

The second bias is towards the epistemic. In its pursuit of methodic, systemic, justified cognition, epistemic discourse seeks foundations acceptable to its semantic context and standards. But to found reality, and the whole outreach of knowing, upon what is acceptable to epistemic foundations is to invert the proper relation between knowledge, truth, and reality. It seems to me that *both those who would transform foundations and those who would dismiss them still give too much to epistemology*—not, of course, in the classical modern sense of representational theory (for nowadays that is roundly condemned on all sides), but in the sense of carrying out the whole discussion in terms of the supposed primacy of epistemic discourse. It is these biases which have led me to find the metaphor of roots and the concept of firstness more illuminating to metaphysics than that of foundations.

Schürmann's interpretation of Heidegger's deconstruction of all metaphysics of principles identifies metaphysical thought too indiscriminately with that of coercive technical power. The metaphysical characterization of truth need be neither an unwitting nor a cynical endorsement of coercive power. Among the relations constitutive of the human individual, truth is a distinctive ontological relation which is not a relation of coercive power. Knowledge has its own character, though it may be put to various practical purposes, even dehumanizing ones. In its own character, however, it is a relation peculiar to and proper to a distinctive sort of entity. That entity is the root-principle of the veridical relation with other being. Out of the concrete relation of such an entity with other being and along with strands of physical interaction, feeling and perception, imagination and memory, attitude, interest and desire, there arises the strand of knowing. Within that ontological, noetic relationship, discourse in general is constituted by distantiation and conceptualization.

Within the ontological truth-relation and the discourse that arises within it, I have argued that a further distinction is to be made between noetic and epistemic discourse. I hope that it is clear by now that by non-epistemic, noetic discourse I do not mean opinion, *doxa*, since that is a name given to informal discourse measured by the standards of epistemic discourse. I do not accept such a depreciation of first-order knowing, because the source of truth is not epistemic discourse, but rather the transcendental ontological relation in which truth consists, and out of which cognition arises. Noetic discourse is genuine knowledge which moves within the transcendental ontological truth-relation. Far from being depreciated, it is, on the contrary, epistemic discourse that is a secondary modification of noetic discourse.[16]

The epistemic modification occurs on the basis of the presuppositions and restrictions mentioned previously. Epistemic discourse is instituted by a founding project that selects certain cognitive values as presuppositions, such as selective interest, methodical progress, limits of relevance, and criteria of evidence. Epistemic discourse is a semantic closure that rests upon those presuppositions and restrictions as upon a foundation, so that we can speak of epistemic discourse as having foundations. But those foundations are not noetic discourse. They are rather the implicit preferences or explicit epistemological decisions taken in favor of a project ordered towards methodically justified truth—a truth justified

---

16. The terms bear different shades of meaning in the Greek. Aristotle sometimes used the term *noēsis* in a general way to distinguish the intellectual mode of knowing from sensory perception, though he always connected intellection with sensible images *(phantasiai)*. But he also used the term *noēsis* to distinguish intuition proper *(nous)* from discursive reasoning *(dianoia)*. For him, then, knowing is constituted by immediacy, i.e., by intuition *(nous, noēsis, cf. intellectus)* and developed by mediation, i.e., by discourse *(dianoia, cf. ratio)*.

insofar as the method, horizon, canons, and relevant evidence permit. Noetic discourse does not provide such foundations, nor does it have them. They belong to epistemic discourse itself and are shot through with its project. But original knowing is the open, ongoing, living understanding, which can take many forms: metaphor, symbolism, narration, informal argument. If epistemic discourse requires discipline, noetic discourse is not without its asceticism as well. Indeed, there are certain requirements for greatness of noetic discourse—a self-disciplined openness, a kind of noetic wisdom, a *phronēsis* of the word.

Now the metaphysics of entity, as I have come to understand it, contains within itself a mode of epistemic discourse, but its own full discourse is of a distinctive character which is at once its misery and its glory. For its task is to mediate its own epistemic discourse by attentive association with noetic discourse, and through it with the values of being. Since epistemic discourse arises out of noetic discourse, one can speak of a continuum of discourse. Indeed, it is the task of metaphysics as first philosophy to monitor that continuum. To be sure, with regard to any given metaphysics it may be difficult to determine at what particular distance to place its discourse between noetic and epistemic poles, since in their purity they serve more as asymptotes whereas actual forms of discourse are always somewhat mixed. Nevertheless, there is an essential difference between noetic discourse, on the one hand, and the inception and direction of epistemic discourse, on the other. For what intervenes to modify noetic discourse and to constitute epistemic discourse is a founding project, which is usually not made explicit until its actual career is well underway. Indeed, for the most part, anticipatory manifestos succeed no better in science than in art.

I suggest, then, that one of the principal tasks of metaphysics is to keep open the traffic between these two polar modes of discourse. What has happened, especially in recent times, is that human subjectivity, defined over against a supposedly alien objectivity, has closed off the traffic. It is the task of a contemporary metaphysics to open that road again. Just because metaphysics as first philosophy is concerned with the context of contexts and with the ultimate status and significance of discourse, its proper task is to monitor the continuum between noetic and epistemic discourse. This requires it to pass back and forth among the modes of noetic and epistemic discourse, *including its own*. It must take up an inner distance from its own epistemic discourse in order to carry out that mediation. Thus, for example, it must be as concerned with Marcel's meandering metaphysics of the concrete as with its more abstract, systematic fellows.

It can be identified simply neither with ordinary noetic discourse nor with its own epistemic discourse. Metaphysical discourse is more self-consciously unified, integrated, and critical than noetic discourse. Noetic discourse is rooted in the openness of the transcendental truth-relation and its ontological character; it is buffeted by the contingencies of nature, the modulations of culture, and the winds of history. That is why metaphysics, which is open to noetic discourse, does develop, why it has a history and an endemic pluralism. On the other hand, metaphysics seeks radical, comprehensive, determinate knowing by way of methodical, conceptual argumentation. Nevertheless, it cannot be simply identified with its own epistemic discourse either, because that would give decisive primacy to an epistemological project rather than to the continuing ontological relationship. At any given time and in terms of its epistemic discourse, metaphysics is a discursive nomad; it has no settled speech. In the name of first philosophy, it will pitch its tent where it must. In its search for roots it will speak in one of the four basic modes of discourse: of being and entity, of event and temporality, of unity and measure, of word and language. It is my own view, however, that ontological discourse has a privileged role in this search for firstness, and I have developed that discourse as part of my own argument here, as well as by the use I have made of Aristotle, St. Thomas Aquinas, and Heidegger. More needs to be said on this score, but among the original modes of discourse I would argue that being and entity *(ousia, on, ens, esse)* can encompass reality more adequately than time, number, or word.

Metaphysics is constitutively open to noetic discourse, and this calls for its continuing development. It is called upon to nurture its understanding of firstness in and through the ontological truth-relation instituted by human entities seeking radical, comprehensive, determinate knowledge. In its bipolar nature such a metaphysics of entity neither takes upon itself foundations in the manner in which special sciences do, nor does it deny them to those sciences. It neither rests upon foundations nor condemns them, it is neither foundational nor anti-foundational. For the metaphysics of entity does not live with the support of foundations, nor is it buried in their ruins.

Chapter 5
ANOTHER LOOK AT OBJECTIVITY

In many philosophical quarters, and elsewhere, something called "objectivity" has come into low esteem. It seems to some to be a counterfeit goal and a hindrance to more worthwhile knowledge. We hear of "mere objectivity," of an approach which is "too objective," of the indignity of treating persons as though they are "nothing but objects," and of mistaking God as a "transcendent object." So much wrath must have some cause, and perhaps even some merit. On the other hand, the notion of objectivity has had a sturdy and influential career during the past three or four centuries. It arose explicitly at the beginning of modern philosophy. Indeed, it would not be too much to say that modern philosophy itself arose in the seventeenth century out of a concern for objectivity.

Nevertheless, objectivity did not spring up without antecedents. I find at its core the ancient concern for reason and truth to which St. Thomas Aquinas gave faithful service and brilliant witness. "Truth," he wrote, "is found in the intellect according as it apprehends a thing as it is."[1] Now objectivity is of value insofar as it is the adaptation of the human mind to the demands of truth. In taking another look at objectivity, then, I shall inquire into the factors which enter into the "apprehension of a thing as it is," without, however, attributing even remotely the approach, principles, or conclusions of this paper to the *doctor communis*.

CHARACTERIZATIONS OF OBJECTIVITY

Methodic: In the sixteenth and seventeenth centuries the revolution in the study of nature expressed itself as a demand for an objective meth-

---

Reprinted from *Thomas and Bonaventure: A Septicentenary Commemoration Proceedings of the American Catholic Philosophical Association* 48 (1974): 86–98. Copyright © 1974 by ACPA.

1. STh I, q. 16, a. 5. For an earlier and more extensive consideration of this factor, see Kenneth L. Schmitz, "Philosophical Pluralism and Philosophical Truth," *Philosophy Today* 10 (1966): 3–18.

od. Major philosophers, such as Galileo, Bacon, Descartes, Hobbes, and Spinoza, emphasized the need for disciplining our search into nature, man, and God. The methodical advantage of a certain restriction upon inquiry was evident to them. Knowledge could flourish only if an ascetic rigor avoided what seemed to them to be the ambush of final causes, substantial forms, prime matter, essential natures, mental faculties, and secondary qualities. According to some, advance was to be made only by the clarification of relationships to which a mathematical value could be assigned; according to others, by a controlled canon of observation; and according to many by both. The restriction permitted much to be said about nature which had not been said before, although in their minds natural things gave way to observable objects or representations, and entitative principles gave way to cosmic or psychic laws. To be sure, the demand for objectivity was also an expression of human subjectivity and was at least implicitly sensed to be such. Each of the major philosophers justified their new organon as an instrument which would bring the practical benefits of theoretical knowledge to men.

Exclusive: The most passionate denunciations of objective theories of knowledge are found today among those who accuse objective knowledge of leaving out just those values that are most vital to the knower, namely, his subjective and personal existence, without which he cannot make a creative and free response to his experience. An objective theory of knowledge is said to externalize that which is known, putting it outside of and over against the knower, and introducing into the relationship an indifference of the known to the knower. If the description of methodic objectivity given previously is correct, however, the flaw must be relocated. The division does not occur between the object and the subject, but is rather a self-division within the subject. The methodical restriction falls upon the goals of the knowing subject. The charge against methodic objectivity, then, is to be reformulated: it pre-empts the ontological shape of the known and restricts the knower to possibilities of meaning that are too narrow for the interests of both the known and the knower to be fully served.

Reductive: On the other hand, devotees of methodic objectivity sometimes carry the restriction one step further. They take the aims of the inquirer at the beginning of modern science to be the only legitimate aspirations. Sometimes they justify metaphysically the complete reduction of knowing to objective methods, criteria, and values by asserting that there is no more to things than their observable behavior, at other times they justify it positively by asserting that there is nothing of further interest to inquiry than what can be attained by these methods. Of course, this leads the critics of objectivity to think that the interests of human subjectivity are not well looked after by an objectivism which eliminates it.

Derivative: The most serious charge brought against the objective theory of knowledge arises, however, out of the life-philosophies of the past one hundred years. They charge that the pre-emption of the shape of the known and the restriction of the interests of the knower obscure the authentic character of knowledge. They insist that the pre-empted object and the restricted subject are merely abstractions which are detached from a more fundamental common situation. They maintain, therefore, that every theory of objectivity will inevitably fail to fulfill the responsibilities of a philosophical inquiry into knowledge, because it must assume its own presuppositions without any means for a critical self-investigation. They insist that an objective theory cannot account for its own criteria, which it must simply assert and use. It assumes that the knowledge relationship is between a subject and an object, resting primarily upon the subject (idealism) or upon the object (realism) or upon both (dualism). The life-philosophies, on the other hand, insist that the relationship itself is what is primary, and that the subject and object are merely functions which are founded in that relationship. The fault of objectivity, then, is that it disengages two factors of knowledge, shapes them into entities in their own right with the contours at external object-entities and internal subject-entities, and finally relates them in an external fashion. Such a procedure treats as fundamental what is merely derivative. According to the life-philosophies, in the beginning of knowledge there is neither object nor subject, but the world; in the beginning is the situation.

Nevertheless, it seems to me that the lure of objectivity is not tarnished under so many assaults, even if we accept a certain justice in the imputation that objectivity deflects knowledge from inward subjectivity and that it introduces a certain altereity and even externality into the relationship. What is important is that there is preserved in the sense of objective validity a certain transcendence, which is not to be discounted simply as the attempt to attain certitude by fixing this or that knowledge-claim with the abstract values of universality and necessity. It seems to me, rather, that objectivity is the keystone of theoretical knowledge just because it discloses a trans-cognitional terminus which is the source of the cognitive value, truth. Objectivity thus manifests a trans-cognitional value within cognition itself. To see this, we must look again at objectivity.

FACTORS OF OBJECTIVITY: COMPREHENSION

The situation in which knowledge comes about has been neglected or left implicit in some theories of knowledge. They focus narrowly upon the relation between the knower and the determinate objects of his knowledge, which they take to be either ideas, impressions, or representations of some sort. Other theories of knowledge have made this important factor explicit, although they have understood it in very different ways. Thus, according to St. Thomas Aquinas, the situation in which knowledge comes about is to be understood as the community of beings, and into this *(ad rem)* all knowledge claims are to be resolved. For Leibniz, the situation within which knowledge comes about is the pre-established monadic harmony within which God's wisdom and benevolence are realized. For Kant, the original situation is not the manifold of sensory data, but the *conceptus cosmicus (Weltbegriff)* by which pure reason apprehends *a priori* the totality of its interests in a rational life of speculative knowledge and practical freedom. For Hegel, situation takes definite form in the ontological category of the true infinite by which spirit acquires the explicit shape of totality. For Husserl, the situation is the open horizon within which the knowledge of objects advances. For Heidegger, it is the existential being-in-the-world in which *Dasein* pursues its possibilities.

In these very diverse conceptions the situation of knowledge has already been defined in some basic way. Thus, if the term "situation" is to be used of all the conceptions mentioned, it will have to bear an equivocal meaning. Unlike the word "bark" said of dogs and trees, however, the equivocation is interesting. What is interesting in this analogous equivocation is the similar meaning which, however, cannot be disengaged to form an identical meaning that is realized in the same way in each. Here the meaning of "situation" is not that of a type or class abstracted from individual differences, or of a genus drawn from types. The meaning is irreducible to types, since it expresses in each conception a first principle prior to all types. Nevertheless, we can discern a thread of meaning which, except in a merely formal way, is inseparable from the conceptions themselves. Thus, each of these conceptions exhibits the interplay of two features: depth and scope, origin and horizon, foundation and universality. But if we try to say in what the depth or scope consists, we must revert to each of the various conceptions and simply point to them and to the way they function within each of the different philosophies. What I have called "situation," then, is a first principle, that is, an original and underived factor within knowledge.

The latent character of the situation and the manner in which it functions will determine the way in which knower and known come into union with one another. I shall attempt to clarify the conception of situation in such a way that it helps to exhibit the primary value of objectivity. The previous reference to other philosophies pointed out two indispensable characteristics of the situation of knowledge: universality and fundamentality. Together they constitute the comprehension required for objectivity.

The universality is not that which permits us to add to propositions the quantifier "all" or "always," though it is the basis for such quantifiers. It is instead the singular universal, that within which all human knowledge is situated and resolved. Thus, for example, the Thomistic values of knowledge are resolved into the universe of beings and its creative source. Leibnizian values are secured by God's actualized pre-cognition of the best set of compossible adequate concepts of individuals. Kantian interests are served by a primitive concept of totality—distinct from the category of totality—which provides reason with the *a priori* architectonic it needs for the systematic unity within which it pursues those interests. In the Hegelian category of the true infinite, spirit first makes the universality of its claim explicit, viz., that all being and knowledge must be reconciled within its integrity. In the phenomenological horizon, consciousness first lies open as an indeterminate field, out of which and within which the perspectives and horizons that constitute objects may arise. In the existential horizon of the world, the assemblage at human purposes and interests is to be organized and interpreted.

It is obvious, then, that it would be rather too simple to conceive the situation of knowledge merely as a spatio-temporal field. A reference to Kant will illustrate the point well enough. It is correct to say that Kantian data become a manifold by being received according to the *a priori* forms at space and time. It is also correct to say that Kantian judgments of existence are resolved back into the manifold wherein they receive a spatio-temporal index through the schematism and the postulates of empirical thought. But the origin of knowledge and its determining limits, and its final validation are to be found purely *a priori* in the concept of the total life of reason *(conceptus cosmicus)*. Or again, in Husserl the consciousness of horizon includes not merely the unintuited sides of the perceptual object but also the expectations, validity alterations, and the idealizations open to the transcendental ego. The situation of knowledge, then, is the singular, circumambient universal.

The second feature at the situation is its fundamentality. The various conceptions of situation point to that out of which and into which knowledge moves as into its ground. The ground does not function as a material substrate, however, but in cooperation with the feature of universality it functions as the principle of inclusion. The situation is not inclusive in the way in which a spatial container includes its contents, nor even as a collectivity includes its members. It is inclusive as a principle of affinity. A certain not wholly indeterminate compatibility must hold as the condition for the universe of beings, the compossible monads, the moments of spirit, and the like. It seems to me, however, that the affinity is not the rather too tightly logical compossibility of Leibniz' monadology, nor even any systematic unity, whether architectonic, categorical, phenomenological, or existential. What is operative here is not a predetermined totality, but the transcendental demand for mutuality.

It is just this demand for mutuality that is the basis of the more determinate interconnections without which human discourse could not move. It is the fundamental inclusion which excludes nothing that is or can be, that is or can be known. It is not a fixed set of determinate relations, but only that tolerance which must be shared even between beings which destroy one another, or between theories which contradict one another. Conflict, after all, presupposes mutuality. Nevertheless, if all were tolerated, nothing would be tolerable; where there is no order, there cannot even be disorder. It is the task of first philosophy to attempt to render our knowledge of this transcendental tolerance more determinate. It is in just this task, with its attendant risks, that first philosophy reaches for comprehension.

The first factor operative in an adequate conception of objectivity is then its comprehensive situation. The situation itself is neither fixed nor variable because it is not determinate. It is rather that out of which, within which, and into which determinate possibilities and actual knowledge move. We have here, then, a fundamental universality—out of, within, and into—which provides knowledge with its origin, *discursus*, and resolution, for the situation functions as a pervasive mediator. It is neither a third thing which interposes itself between knower and known, nor a relation sustained by them. Nor is it a determinate medium through which the union of knower and known is achieved. It is that transcendental demand for affinity which secures the compatibility within which the union takes place. In describing the situation of knowledge as one of comprehension, then, we mean to mark its basic, inclusive, and unitive character.

It is necessary to insist upon such comprehension, if we are to develop a theory of objectivity beyond that which identifies objectivity with the meeting of epistemic criteria, such as clear, distinct, or determinate ideas, primary impressions, or measurable patterns. I have deliberately used the term "comprehension" in order to emphasize that the situation we are examining here is the circumambience of knowledge. The earlier illustrations were mentioned as contributions to a theory of knowledge. Though the universe of beings or the system of monads, for example, may be characterized in other ways, our present interest in them is in their role as providing the situation for knowledge. Being, after all, is simply being, not the situation of being; nor is pure reason its own situation, or the world the situation of the world. Yet each has been taken as the situation of knowledge. It is necessary to stress the point, because if the situation is to help secure the values of objectivity it must function in and for knowledge. If the situation is to ground noetic values for consciousness, it must be "known" in some fashion. We must not, therefore, identify knowledge exclusively with the actually and determinately known. The situation, too, is "known"—not by unconscious motivations, but by a unique sense of the integrity that is inseparable from knowledge itself. This circumambient sense of comprehension gives rise to determinate descriptions of itself, as we have seen. There are even more definite modifications of circumambience in knowledge, such as background and figure which divide attention into periphery and focus. The meaning that I assign to the term "situation" here, however, is the most radical principle of comprehension required for knowledge.

To describe the circumambient foundation of knowledge as its "comprehension" is not to describe it as "comprehensible" in the manner in which a determinate object is knowable. A comprehensible object is potentially known before it is actually known. It may appear too paradoxical to say that the situation is known but unknowable. It is clearer to say that the situation is and must be apprehended by the knower in his knowing, but that it is neither knowable nor known in the manner of an object. Indeed, it has a neither-nor status which is not unlike other curious transcendental principles, such as, for example, active potency which is neither passive potentiality nor actual operation. Comprehension is an active noetic structure which must be sustained by the knower if there is to be human knowledge. It is always and necessarily apprehended in any actual determinate knowledge. Neither knowable nor actually known, neither indeterminate nor determinate, it is the transcendental constituent of integrity which is mandatory for objective knowledge. Indeed, it is just this, with the other factors, that makes the structure of objectivity at once the height and center of knowledge, from which theoretical and practical modifications of knowledge take their essential nature.

FACTORS OF OBJECTIVITY: THE IMPERATIVE

But there is more to objectivity than comprehension; there is also transcendence. The history of philosophy shows forth this transcendence in a tradition of inquiry. Now a tradition arises only where there has been some sense of development and achievement. I do not consider the history of philosophy to be a pointless tale. Nor do other philosophers who continually go back to some unexploited possibility latent within it. It is, I think, the record of often solid achievements of lasting value, accompanied by a development of critical acumen and the deepening of many problems.

It is not surprising, then, that philosophical inquiry does not respect the attempt of any one philosopher to fix human knowledge with certitude in a determinate statement. For the inquiring intelligence, no actual determinate statement is ever the last word to be said. The history of philosophy teaches us that philosophy transcends its philosophies. The spirit of criticism impels philosophical inquiry towards new, unexploited, or forgotten possibilities of meaning and truth. Anaximander criticized his teacher, and philosophy took a step forward. Socrates attempted to sting his fellows into thought, and philosophy acquired a new sense of responsibility. In the tradition of inquiring intelligence whose beginnings we credit to the Greeks, we reserve the title "first philosophy" for the questioning which is most radical and sweeping. Put with a critical spirit and pursued in a methodical manner, the questioning is carried to the deepest stratum of known meaning on the borders of our ignorance. A mandate draws such questioners on, for there are questions still to be asked, and answers still to be found. Any definite synthesis of knowledge does not break down of its own weight. It is dismantled. Sometimes there are rather curious occasions for rejecting a philosophical or scientific position. It may seem irrelevant to new interests, mistaken in an important but not fatal point, or inadequate in some other way.

Nevertheless, the only reasons which justify the rejection, modification, or contraction of its claim are those which conform to the demand placed by truth upon the inquiring intelligence. Thus, philosophy not only transcends its philosophies, but it does so in the name of the very same values which the philosophies themselves are thought to serve. In answer to an impelling call, the spirit of criticism keeps human knowing open to further demands. However, the spirit of criticism does not nourish itself, nor is it a value in and for itself. Behind it stands the spirit of truth which makes its presence felt as an imperative. Its authority alone counts, and grounds both subjectivity as the exigency for further inquiry and objectivity as the measure of its results.

FACTORS OF OBJECTIVITY: DISCLOSURE

The imperative which authorizes inquiry is deeply rooted in the very character of knowledge itself. To see this we must turn to a different factor: human knowing needs an other. In the long run, however, the recent insistence upon intentionality is not important because it repudiates Cartesian immanence. To be sure, it permits much of modern philosophy to extricate itself from insoluble problems associated with the privacy of a solitary ego. But the lasting importance of intentionality is not that it is directional, a "getting out of towards . . . ," a pointing of consciousness towards the object. It is important because it points up the character of consciousness as disclosure. The intentional relatedness of consciousness breaks open possibilities that stand in contrast to the pre-cognitive ingathering of our organism. The latter's dynamic immersion in itself still lingers in the diffuse feelings that make up our primitive awareness of the situatedness of our knowing. Knowledge takes definite cognitive form when the need for another is converted into the disclosure of situation and object, field and figure, periphery and attention.

In disclosure, knowledge realizes itself to the extent to which it "lets the other be as other." There are advantages to this formula. To say instead that the knower "becomes the other" is at best to describe the process of learning rather than the act of knowing, and at worst to reduce disclosure to appropriation. We began by noticing that the early modern conception of objectivity insisted upon the methodic control of the known by the knower. Whatever noetic advantages there are in such methodic control—and they are many and important—nonetheless objectivity at its deepest must ultimately renounce any restriction upon the object.

Even the formula that knowing is "being the other as other" must make this renunciation explicit. In its primary character as disclosure, knowledge announces the presence of the knowing subject even as it renounces the control of the subject over the known object. In the formula, knowledge is "letting the other be as other," the words "letting" and "other" concede the imperative to which the knower must submit. In "letting," he comprehends the situation and thereby provides the context for the disclosure. In calling the thing known the "other" the formula expresses the presence of the knower in the disclosure. Since the thing known is not in itself an "other," the formula expresses the position from which the other is to be considered, that is, as a participant within a double disclosure of itself as object and of the knower as subject. The "othering" of the thing in knowledge is inseparable from the "selving" of the knower.

The presence of the thing as known and knowable points up the curious poverty and riches of the human way of knowing, which cannot function without the other and yet is able to be open to it. The knowability of the thing consists in the mutual affinity of knower and thing by which, in different ways, they can enter into a transcendental dimension of the thing's own being. It is in relation to the knower that the thing is intelligible, but intelligibility is the awakening in the thing of possibilities of its being-in-situation and of its cooperating with the imperative in a disclosure of its own being. In so doing, the thing participates in the realization of its own truth.

In the disclosure the thing inasmuch as it is known undergoes neither material nor formal transmutation. It does not become something other than it is, some other thing. What it is constituted of and the manner in which it is constituted must not be altered or it will not be known. This does not mean that the object must be static, but rather that if it is continually changing it must be known as such. In being known, it must remain somehow untouched in its own being while yet being somehow in touch with the knower. The disclosure is proportionate to a distinctive kind of respect for the thing, even a peculiar sort of acknowledgment of its rights within the new relationship. It may seem extravagant to talk of objectivity in almost intimate terms, but even methodic objectivity attains knowledge only to the degree that it proceeds, not as the desire to control the thing known, but by a sort of love of friendship, a benevolence which is concerned for the integrity of the thing within the new relationship. Now for the knower to wish the other well is to wish the other its being by providing it with an appropriate context in which it can be just as it is. This context is the comprehensive situation, for truth demands of knowledge that it be a disclosure of the thing known in its being, just as it is, whatever more it also thereby discloses. Lines from Wallace Stevens express the ideal in its uncompromising absoluteness:

All approaches gone, being completely there.

He evokes it again in a winter landscape:

One must have a mind of winter . . .
And have been cold a long time
To behold the junipers shagged with ice.
. . . and not to think
Of any misery in the sound of the wind,

Which is the sound of the land
Full of the same wind
That is blowing in the same bare place
For the listener, who listens in the snow,
And, nothing himself, beholds
Nothing that is not there and the nothing that is.[2]

---

2. The first line is from "Arrival at the Waldorf," the remainder are from "The Snow Man." *Poems,* selected by S. F. Morse (New York: Vintage, 1959), 101, 123.

We must not forget that disclosure of the object is also disclosure of the subject. Though the ideal of objectivity is never realized in its absoluteness, it does not remain a mere formality. It is already effectively present in the exigency of the knower and in the other as bearer of meaning. Objectivity is an ought which already functions as imperfectly embodied.

FACTORS OF OBJECTIVITY: SELECTIVITY

Inquiry and knowledge entail risk, because there is tension and the possibility of conflict among the constituents of disclosure. In order to know the object, the knower must let it be itself; but it may seem that the more completely the knower lets the thing be, the more he releases it from the relationship. To know may be "to let the thing be just as it is"; but what, then, is the thing just as it is? The thing is involved in innumerable actual and possible relationships with other things. Among these relationships are relations with the thingly aspects of the human knower. There is, however, another order of relationships which are grounded in the knowability of the thing. These are actualized in disclosure.

"To know the thing just as it is," therefore, expresses the thing with all its relationships translated into this order of knowability. "To know the thing just as it is" does not mean to represent it as though it were in itself and apart from knowledge. This would be Kant's thing-in-itself, which is neither known nor knowable. Instead, "to know the thing as it is in itself" means first of all to apprehend it as having a transcendental order of relations with a knower. It means knowing the thing as a whole (this is the integrity of the object), within a whole (this is the comprehension of the situation), in some actual determinate manner (this is the actual knowledge of it), and with further possibilities of disclosure (this is the further intelligibility of the object). It is to know the thing as co-habitant in the same universe with the knower, as sharing in the same comprehensive situation, and as participating in the same noetic values, though in quite diverse ways.

Now to know the integrity of the object does not mean to exhaust its knowability. To know it as whole is not to wholly know it. For the human knower, the actuality of the disclosure is always perspectival; our actual knowledge is itself always from a point of view. Disclosure is always limited and selective. The nature of any limitation is determined, however, by the order to which it belongs. A point of view is a noetic limitation. It is not limited as is a piece of pie, but in a sense which Leibniz understood well. In a point of view the whole (this is the comprehensive situation) is present, yet with a determinate modification or emphasis (this is the perspective taken upon the object and its features). The selection is also noetic. It is not a slice taken out of the object, but the whole object (its integrity in situation) apprehended in a way which gives prominence to a profile, schema, or outline. This is the mien or demeanor of the object as it is taken or as it presents itself to the knower.

The noetic character of perspective does not consist only in its cofunction in disclosure with comprehension and imperative. In addition to focused attention, perspective is a point of view built up by the retrospect of past meanings and the prospect of future ones. Finally, it is constituted also by introspect, that is, by the disclosure of the knower as in situation with the known. Now it is in just such an introspect that the knower both recognizes his limitation and overcomes it, for he recognizes the determinate, limited, selective nature of his knowledge. He knows that he knows completely neither the object, nor the situation, nor even himself. Nevertheless, he apprehends the totality of his situation, that is, he comprehends it as the indefinitely open basis of disclosure. He thereby frees himself from the perspectivity of his actual knowledge in the very openness through which he recognizes it as perspectival.

He completes his knowledge in principle in comprehending its actual incompleteness. He never achieves complete and absolute actual knowledge of anything; but in comprehending the situation as situation for determination, limitation, and selection, he encompasses all that is and can be. The comprehension invites the knower to further determinate knowledge, to further limitation and selection, even as the imperative draws him on to other features of the object and to other objects.

The perspectivity of human meaning is poised in tension with the absolute inclusion of the comprehension and the absolute authority of the imperative. Objectivity is not an automatic achievement. The degree of dedication required from the knower differs with the difficulty and importance of the knowledge. But when the knower holds himself open to comprehension, respectful of the imperative and careful of the perspective, he moves towards objectivity in letting the other be just as it is. In so doing, meaning moves towards a participation in the transcendental value of truth in which knowers, knowns, and knowables all share in their different ways.

CONCLUSION

What has another look at objectivity shown us? First, that objectivity is not a mere formalism, but the embodied demand for truth. Second, that it requires the structure of disclosure, comprised of situation, imperative, and perspective. We have the comprehension of the whole, and the knowledge that we don't know it fully. We have the imperative which measures the truth of our limited and selective achievements. We have the intelligibility of the thing as the bearer of its meaning, and we have the energy to inquire. The cognitivity of the knower and the cognoscibility of the object both bear the imperative: the one as exigence, the other as intelligibility. The imperative does not confine its authority to the inquiring knower, and certainly not exclusively to the spirit of criticism. The imperative is effectually present also in the thing to be known. There is in the thing its unrealized meanings and the demand of those meanings to be actualized. This is the demand for truth on the part of the thing, which in inviting the knower also lays upon him the claim and responsibility of truth. The demand is disciplined by the character of the thing in accordance with the law of the thing.[3] Disclosure, then, is an existential relationship between knower and known in which the situation for the relationship is provided by the knower, but in accordance with respect for the thing.

We began with the notion of methodic objectivity and its search for objective validity in certified knowledge. We then probed to find the vital center of objectivity, and found it in the disclosure of a thing as it is. This required the laying bare of a structure: comprehension (situation), imperative (truth as demand), and perspective (limitation of meaning). The present account does not give warranties such as clear and distinct ideas, lively and forceful impressions, or formal logical frameworks as criteria to validate this or that determinate knowledge-claim. What it does attempt to set forth is the pattern of disclosure in which such criteria may be grounded for limited purposes. But more, it seeks to ground knowledge in the disclosure of meaning, the actualization of the intelligibility of the thing, and the self-realization of the knower. Objectivity as *theoria* is a dynamic structure of human knowing, which also centers *praxis*, for things must be disclosed in being done. Indeed, there is no human knowledge without comprehension, imperative, and perspective; so that this structure is the very essence and spirit of knowing. It is self-and-other disclosure.

Objectivity is never common or cheap. At its best it is contemplation. Its value does not consist only in rare minds rarely achieving it, but in the pervasive quality that—even when, as usual, it is but barely glimpsed—it gives to a mind which would be faithful to it, a quality that leads to the liberation of the mind. Objectivity can vitalize a philosophy, theory, judgment, discovery, or conversation. It is the concession to the

---

3. For an ampler consideration of the role of the thing as other, see "Enriching the Copula," *Review of Metaphysics* 27 (1974): 492–512. See chapter 6 below.

other in truth; which in turn, brings realization to the self as knower. The concession may cost pain or give joy to the man who makes it, but it unfailingly brings light.

What, then, is objective knowledge? It is not the exhaustive knowledge of the whole truth, nor an exhaustive knowledge of part of it. To know with objectivity is to apprehend the entire structure of disclosure: comprehension, imperative, and perspective, in the meeting of knower and knowable thing, and to apprehend by and in that structure the thing which offers itself as object to be known.

Chapter 6

ENRICHING THE COPULA

It is a commonplace among students of St. Thomas Aquinas that in his view a judgment does not come to rest in its truth until it reaches the thing being judged about. For him the judgment in its fundamental nature is not simply a union of subject and predicate, but is rather the surge of the mind itself towards rest in the being of things *(esse rerum)*. The judgment terminates not in a mental construction but in the thing itself *(ad rem)*. This has led many Thomists to salute the judgment as the cash value of knowledge. Usually our attention is directed emphatically to what is said in a judgment, and therefore to the terms which express its first-blush meaning. Ordinary attention takes the copula of the judgment more or less for granted. Like a familiar shy companion it is seldom noticed and barely audible. The historical study of St. Thomas' writings in this century, and the Thomism which has grown up with that study, has shifted attention to the copula and urged its importance. Under the influence of an "existential" interpretation of St. Thomas the central disclosure of his thought is held to be the radical value of *esse* (to be, be-ing). It is not surprising, then, that some Thomists have placed the key to the truth of the judgment in the copula rather than in a correspondence between the terms and the reality signified by them. Accordingly, *adequatio* of mind with reality is brought about in and through the copula.[1]

Reprinted from the *Review of Metaphysics, A Commemorative Issue: Thomas Aquinas 1224–1274* 27 (1974): 492–512. Copyright © by the ACPA.

1. I do not intend in this commemorative essay to contribute to the recovery of the sense of St. Thomas Aquinas' writings, although that continues to be an exacting and significant task. My purpose is neither to restate nor to continue his doctrine, but to find in it suggestions for another line of thought, a line which St. Thomas may never have intended even remotely, and which in the end may even be incompatible with his intention. To a student of St. Thomas the differences will be obvious. Nevertheless, I hope that my indebtedness will not remain too obscure.

I

The history of philosophy provides examples of attempts to vindicate the adequation of thought with being. Thought has sometimes armed itself in the Cartesian manner with criteria for measuring its own conformity with being. But such an immediate and direct appeal to "pure" thought rests inescapably upon a tacit appeal to a human experience, which includes sensible factors; and so it begs the question. Moreover, it seems to me that all attempts fail which try to join the knower and the known by putting the idea or judgment between them. For whether the intervention is by criterion, instrument, or method, it merely complicates the problem of their union by adding a useless intermediary. Indeed, in the face of the idealism of Descartes and Locke, and within the presuppositions of a theory of noetic species, modern scholastics were right to insist upon the "non-entity" of ideas and judgments. They insisted that a noetic principle, such as an idea or judgment, is nothing in itself but a pure sign *(medium quo),* and that it is not an object which, while signifying something else, also exists in its own right as a mental entity *(medium quod).* In trying to account for the concrete unity of language and cognition—which I may be forgiven for calling "linguo-knowledge"—there is much to recommend a theory of signs which differentiates knowledge-signs from all other kinds. It is an attempt to do justice to the quasi-instrumental features of linguo-knowledge, while at the same time keeping before us its radical ontological openness. Nothing *intervenes* between knowing and being, least of all the "equipment" of knowing, its ideas and judgments. The relationship between language and knowledge, however, would have to be determined more precisely since linguistic signs lend themselves to being considered as odd sorts of instruments, and by some linguists even as entities. Nevertheless, although linguistic signs are inseparable *in concreto* from noetic signs, it remains true that noetic signs are non-entitative, for there is a fundamental sense in which knowing is not an affair of entities or instruments at all. The essential possibility of knowledge lies in what has traditionally been called its immateriality and even its spirituality.

In much of current philosophical speculation, however, the duplicity inherent in linguo-knowledge seems to have split up into two theories which are for the most part indifferent or even opposed to one another. The instrumental theory, instanced by its cybernetic versions, treats knowing as an affair of signals, codes, and receptors. The revelatory theory of ontologists such as Heidegger, on the other hand, considers knowing to be an opening or clearing. Now it seems to me that in its roots, knowing is not instrumental and that scholastics and ontologists in their different ways are right on this score. Of course, the factors that constitute knowledge can be disengaged and looked at in themselves. Indeed, it is important to remark that such a disengagement is not practiced only by theorists, for it is done by knowing itself. Thus, a natural reflection upon the act of remembering what I had previously seen or said innocently posits "a something which remains for recall," the remembered image. This is almost inevitably taken to stand in place of the original perception, by a kind of substitution. Some theorists, coming upon this rudimentary separation of image from object, sharpen the self-subsistence of the various factors in order to analyze them abstractly in and for themselves. When, at the end of their analysis, they integrate them once again in their unity, they may easily re-shape them instead within a synthetic context brought about by their own analysis. The original unity of experience may easily be lost. The factors, a term or a proposition, may then become a sort of thing which operates in itself, and the whole account of knowing may be surrendered to a set of instrumentalities and entities. The task of an ontology of knowledge, on the contrary, is to recover the original integrity of knowledge and to reinstate the recognition of the non-instrumental openness of language and its thought to the world in which it is situated.

It is not enough, however, to vindicate the truth of the judgment by simply pointing to the coincidence of the copula with the thing affirmed or denied by it. This would replace vindication by mere indication. Hegel's objections to Kant may not reflect nuances important to the older philosopher, but they are an instructive objection in principle regarding this very point. Hegel considered the Kantian account of the synthetic a priori judgment to be deficient because it posited no more than a "happy coincidence" between subject and predicate, and therefore failed to establish subjective thought in objective being. Indeed, the synthetic a priori judgment eventually fell apart, according to Hegel, into empty analytic forms of thought (categories) and unjustified syntheses of sense (intuitions). The Kantian theory of judgment complacently let the copula merely *assert* the union of subject and predicate under the indeterminate concept of an object. The result was a bare mindless assertion without any title authenticated in terms of thought, and based merely upon inspection of the sensible manifold and the "lucky find" of a given content submissive to the forms of thought. Kant's radical dualism forbade a transformative principle which could authenticate the claims of experience in terms of thought. To be sure, he subordinated the sensible content to the a priori forms of thought, but he did it as a master imposes his own conditions upon a slave. And he got what a master gets from a slave, not his genuine being but something less—an appearance.[2]

2. G. W. F. Hegel, *Glauben und Wissen*, ed. G. Lasson (Hamburg: F. Meiner, 1962), 1–40.

A Thomist presumably is not plagued by the radical dualism of Kant. Nevertheless, although it must avoid a Cartesian criteriology, a philosophy must provide more than a Kantian critique. For any philosophical account of judgment must recover the validity of the connective in terms of thought. And so, while a philosophy may recognize that real being is reached in and through the sensible, still it cannot rest content with an *immediate* concession to it, but must appeal to the sensible on grounds that also lie within thought itself. For thought, after all, must institute the sensible in its own thoughtful mode of being. St. Thomas provides an example of an attempt to meet this need with respect to the simple apprehension of universals. For he taught that, in abstracting the species in the phantasm, the agent intellect actualizes it in the possible intellect, and thereby proceeds to recover in thought that very meaning towards which the mind directs itself. Moreover, his theory of participative causality provides a principle of transformation common to both being and thought.

The transcendental turn and the empiricist demand have more recently brought new pressures to bear upon the efficacy of the judgment. The union of thought and being in the judgment, therefore, must be thought through in terms of these pressures. Failure to secure the grounds for the truth of the judgment in the face of these pressures threatens to impede the drive of the mind towards that objectivity in which thought seeks to become more itself by letting the thing be more and more in its own being. There is here a striking similitude between cognition and the love of friendship, for both must let the other be in its appropriate being—the known in its, the friend in his—while sustaining that being in their own. But in going out to and reaching the thing, knowing in that very activity of assertion returns also into itself and becomes more itself. So that, in returning to itself, it seals its discovery with the transcendental completeness of truth.

It may seem that the judgment promises more than it can deliver. For the asserted statement is but one wedge in a larger intelligible pie, the act of asserting is but one attestation in a life of thought, and what is asserted to is but one item in an ontological network. Hegel's strictures upon the judgment, therefore, run deeper than his dissatisfaction with any previous theory of judgment. To him the weak point of the judgment is the undeveloped meaning of the copula, for it never attains to a fully articulated meaning. Under the traditional logical forms of judgment, in which a predicate is attributed to a subject, there lies according to Hegel an ontological process. It begins with immediate empirical judgments in which a predicate is simply posited as inhering in a subject. The copula is unenriched, an abstract "is," a bare assertion. More developed forms of judgment achieve greater universality and necessity until the most perfect form is reached in the apodeictic judgment. Thus, a movement of mutual interpenetration binds the terms through the integrative power of the copula. For the copula is the energy of the mediation. It is also, for Hegel, the reconciling presence of speculative reason and the promise of absolute spirit. Indeed, the whole story of the judgment for Hegel lies in the gradual "coming of age" of the copula. Still, it fails to reach full maturity in the judgment, for in its very fulfillment it passes over into the middle term of the syllogism in search of a more adequate and expanded vehicle of expression.[3] Undoubtedly the Kantian deficiency, as well as his own conception of the ultimate aims of philosophy, lies behind Hegel's depreciation of the copula. The judgment is, for him, a partial attempt to reconcile the dualism of ought and is, of ideal and real, of fact and value. Without accepting his dual problematic, however, or his dissatisfaction over the allegedly abstract and indeterminate form of the copula, it is still possible to take seriously his suggestion that the copula must be understood through a process of concretion and fulfillment. Lacking such a process, a philosophical theory, whether criteriology or criticism, whether empiricism or realism, must leave the copula as an immediate and merely asserted conjunction without a ground in an intelligible structure, a mere complacency of the mind in the opportune "fit" of the judgment with actual states of being. Of course, Hegel is right that the judgment must pass over into and become part of a larger discourse, with other kinds of connectives. Before it does, however, more can be said on behalf of the copula than Hegel thought. For the copula shows itself to be the *actual* unity of thought and being. In the present essay its features are condensed into a theory, but they are the very power which moves speech from one statement to another.

II

Any attempt to "make metaphysics" out of the copula as the actual unity of thought and being must face charges of cultural and linguistic provincialism. It will be said that the copula is merely a logical-linguistic device, that many languages do nicely without one, and that the copula distributes the understanding of reality into subjects and attributes. This is undoubtedly true. It is also true that the full meaning of a philosophy is affected by the language within which it is conceived and expressed. Otherwise translations could be substitutions. No doubt, too, philoso-

3. G. W. F. Hegel, *Wissenschaft der Logik,* ed. G. Lasson, 2 vols. (Hamburg: F. Meiner, 1967), 264–308. (In English: *Hegel's Science of Logic,* trans. A. V. Miller [New York: Humanities Press, 1969], 623–63).

phies written in non-copulative or non-attributive languages would disclose different aspects and emphases about reality. To admit this, however, is not to concede to what is suggested, viz., that distinctions properly drawn in one language must be essentially incommunicable in another and even false in reality. There is nothing in the generalized attacks upon the particularity of a linguistic structure which shows why the distinctions drawn within it must be null and void. There is nothing in the attempts to discredit Greek and Indo-European languages generally that aborts distinctions carefully drawn in and through them. Thus, for example, the most sweeping attacks upon "Hellenistic" modes of thought seem to be promoted by an assumption that is as uncritical in the twentieth century as was a similar shock at the discovery of non-European cultures in the seventeenth. Both share the assumption that radical difference means error somewhere, and that differing conceptions render each other relative, subjective, and imaginary. Linguistic self-criticism is valuable when it is directed against one or another false extrapolation of a linguistic feature into a metaphysical structure. These failures, of course, are not strictly failures of language as such, but are rather the user's failure to understand the scope and import of the locution he uses. In extending the attack to a whole cast of mind and to an entire language or family of languages, however, the critique comes into danger of a self-referential inconsistency. For the more extreme "anti-Hellenists" argue in an attributive language to undermine the possibility of attributive modes of expression. The possibility, not only of philosophy, but of discourse itself comes into question, and with it thought itself. For philosophy requires some particular language, just because thought itself requires such a particularity. If we are forbidden to philosophize in some particular language—in our own, in German, Latin, Greek, or some other—then philosophy becomes impossible for us. And if this stricture were extended without discrimination to all languages in principle, then not only philosophy but thought itself would perish, including that of the "anti-Hellenists."

I shall make two suppositions about language, therefore, which at least some critics may not share with me. 1) Language as such, and therefore any language—even the Greek, it may be necessary to add—is an aid to thought, however uncertain. Language is not the enemy of thought. It is not its trap. 2) On the contrary, thought is the energy of language and outstrips the forms of language. Such transcendence is a quite general characteristic of other human activities, such as technology, but in language it proceeds in accordance with the heritage of a particular speech community. The transcendence of thought, however, does not mean that language is simply its external shell. It means rather that, while language is the embodiment of thought, the latter is not so identified with language that it simply *is* linguistic behavior. A thought entrapped by language would deserve its fate, for it would be dead thought, unable to enliven its own body. The expression of meaning demands an embodiment of thought in language in such a way that neither language nor thought remains indifferent to the other. Nor can the two together, linguo-thought, remain indifferent to the demands and possibilities of life. There arise in thought and speech, therefore, non-cognitive as well as cognitive modes of expression, and no theory of judgment can be adequate which disregards them. Nevertheless, the focus of judgment is cognition. The cognitive structure of language manifests itself in the sentences of language, the propositions of logic, and the judgmental activities of thought. Of these three, the sentence is the most conditioned by the particularity of its language. The proposition is a formalization, which comes under more universal conditions of thought. The judgment is the cognitive act by which thought, seeking its ends within human life, seeks them precisely in and through the sentence and the proposition.

In its cognitive aspirations, thought seeks to know things *as they are,* and so it is a transcendental necessity of thought that every language be *assertive.* The assertion that such and such is so and so may be either a descriptive or, more generally, a declarative utterance. The linguistic means available for such utterances will vary from one linguistic family to another. But the need to assert, to describe or to declare, and to judge is written into the nature of human thought, action, and life. The concrete demands of human life require all men to recognize and express the difference between saying and doing and between thinking and being. These distinctions are not exclusions, of course, for saying is a manner of doing, and thinking is a way of being. Still, there is an important difference between speech or thought informed by a presence other than itself, and speech or thought that is empty of it

> [a mere] speech of the self that must sustain itself on speech.[4]

Speech is untruthful when it is empty, and false when it is misguided. These basic distinctions between saying and doing and between thinking and being are the fabric out of which the truth or falsity of assertions is cut, and each language must preserve them in its own way. Assertions may be brought about in some language without a copula, but not without some intended copulation. The copulative function may be

---

4. From "The Well Dressed Man with a Beard," by Wallace Stevens in *Poems,* ed. S. F. Morse (New York: Vintage, 1959), 104. I have taken the phrase, but not the full sense it has in the poem.

discharged without using an onto-existential family of verbs. In our own and cognate languages, however, the linguistic incarnation of the assertive force takes the form of a copula, and precisely some form of the verb "to be." Moreover, the reality which calls forth "is" and "is not" to service in the judgment also calls forth philosophy to an onto-existential reflection.

III

The first step in reducing the copula from its apparent brute immediacy is to distinguish the *esse* of the copula proper from the *esse* of the being in which the judgment terminates *(ad rem)*. The former may be called a mental construct or being of reason *(ens rationis)* to distinguish it from a real being *(ens naturae)*. The aim of the reduction, however, is not simply the disengagement of mental from real being and the separation of two modes of *esse*. Quite the contrary, it is a liberation, which allows reflection to study the being of the copula and to unfold its capacity for bringing meaning to truth. The self-realization of thought is a very peculiar opening out on to the thing *(processus ad rem)*. For it is both an advance of thought into being, and a trial to determine the objectivity of thought. Thus, the copula discloses itself as a linguistic function, which is sponsored by thought in the name of the truth of what is being judged. It takes its sense from the being, which, in being brought to judgment by thought, provides the norm for that judgment. This interchange constitutes the paradox of objectivity: that the judger judging is brought to judgment by the necessity of submitting his judgment to the terms of the one being judged. And so, the thing which utters no word determines the deciding word *(krisis)*, or rather settles the appropriate range of words that can be spoken within the terms of the language. The primary distribution of the thing in terms of thought *(Ur-teil)* is a process which arises from the speaker who pronounces judgment, but it joins thought to being under the law of being *(jus, judicium)*. The dictionary etymologies of both *res* (cf. reality) and *thing* are tantalizing, even if doubtful. *Res* may have been derived from *reor*, which means "to reckon, think, judge," making *res* that which is thought about, as in the term "public affairs" *(res publica)*. So, too, *thing* may be the object of *think* (as *Ding* of *Denken*), making *thing* that which thought is about. In any event, both terms can indicate the correlative of thought, which is then a *processus ad rem*.

Nevertheless, it is easy to misunderstand the law of the thing *(jus rerum)*, in accordance with which the decisive word is taken from the thing. We must, therefore, redress a possible imbalance by restoring the rights of thought *(jus rationis)*, its freedom and integrity. For the decisive word, though spoken according to the thing, is uttered by the speaker in his judgment. To avoid misunderstanding the meaning intended by the term *thing* here, we must broaden and lighten the too restrictive and solid sense often given to the term today. A similar emendation must be made for other terms used to designate the focus of judgment. Such terms as "entity" and "being" need not exclusively designate a subsistent being, but may mean only that ultimate and decisive situation which is resolved by the judgment into terms of being and non-being. Thus a judgment may terminate in *anything:* in Hamlet as *dramatis persona*, just as well as in a natural thing; or it may terminate in a well-formed idea as a "good thing," or in our present purpose as a "thing of some difficulty"; or again, a judgment may refer to a lost childhood or a lost leg. Language and examples usually favor affirmative judgments which terminate in real things, the familiar trees and tables, but it must be remembered that negative as well as affirmative judgments can terminate in situations of existence, and that affirmative as well as negative judgments can terminate truthfully in situations of non-existence. Thus, the attributive form of a judgment which discloses a privation may be similar in its linguistic form to other judgments, but its full onto-existential intention is privative, for it does not simply deny a real childhood or a real leg, it marks the lost thing precisely *as lost.* The judgment, then, is the surge of the mind as it resolves something into its ontological character and mode, but the thing may be in an order of real beings, of fictions, projects, or privations, or in some other manner or condition of being and non-being. Indeed, it is in a variety of ontological modes. When a guide refers to the solid thing before him as "Churchill's writing desk," he discloses an object constituted of past, present, and future modes of being, including ones of fact and value.

It should be clear, then, that the thing in which the judgment terminates need not be static or even completed. Sometimes the thing being judged comes about because of the judgment, or even in and through the very judgment being made about it. Such a judgment does not terminate in an already finished thing, for it discloses not only the emergence of the thing, but sometimes also the dependence of the thing upon the judgment itself. This is especially true of the practical judgments which swarm into being around our purposes, for performative utterances are the very stuff out of which personal lives and social institutions make further meaning. Such judgments are true if they disclose just what and how the thing is in its appropriate way of being. So great is the freedom of thought that it may even utter its protest in the face of the very being which it discloses in its judgment; but then it passes over into a judgment of value, for "it is" becomes "it ought." This continually happens with situations in social time and space which are still underway and which are partially constituted by the very judgments rendered upon the developing situation from within it. So too, the present essay addresses itself to a component of judgment, the copula, which itself comes into being only in and through the judgment. For the copula is a thing only in its coming alive in and through the judgment which employs it. Our present reflection, then, is about just such a strangely broad and unsolid *thing*. When we insist upon the law of the thing, we merely insist that human thought cannot confer truth simply and solely upon itself, but that it can come into its truth only by resolving the thing into its ontological situation by judging it in terms of the value of being and non-being. Thought submits itself to the full range of being and non-being in a way that preserves its own integrity by disengaging itself from being submerged by real subsistent being. It identifies the thing judged about within the context of being and non-being, but with all the shades and modes which various ontological situations embody, whether subsistent or insubstantial, finished or in process, real or ideal.

The distinction of the *esse* of the copula from the *esse* of the thing, then, is not meant to throw the judgment back upon purely mental structures *(entia rationis)*. Indeed, the copula is just that which, in uniting the subject and predicate, intends the *esse* of the thing, and has no other justification for that conjunction than the *esse* of the thing. The distinction is made, rather, in order to break the unqualified identity of copulative and real being, and to replace it with an intended identification. Unless the distinction is made, the *esse* of the copula and the *esse* of the thing will remain immediate values whose coincidence may be accepted as a happy accident which cannot, however, be grounded intelligibly in the necessity of thought. This would be the defect of any philosophy which remained satisfied with merely asserting the confrontation of the mind with sensible being under the law of the thing and in an intellectual intuition. For such satisfaction confuses an assertion with an account. It recognizes the role of perception in knowledge and the law of the thing, but it provides no explanation of how the conjunction is possible. In order to ground the judgment intelligibly, that is, in the necessities of thought, we must give an account of it not only in terms of the law of the thing *(jus rerum)*, but also in terms of the grounds for the possibility of truth *(jus rationis)*. And this carries us further into the significance of the copula.

IV

In bringing about the union of thought and being the copula functions as a limit. Our initial sense of a limit is of that which stops and excludes, but a limit also joins. Moreover, it belongs to the beings limited by it. Does the copula belong to the knower? Yes, for it is a judgmental device, although we do not fall back through it upon an empty subjective thought. On the contrary, it thrusts us towards the objective of thought under the law of the thing. Does it belong, then, to the thing? Yes, for it discloses the thing in its being, although it remains an expression of linguo-thought.

Before we plunge into the ambiguity of the copula taken as connecting limit, we ought to clarify three senses of the term *being* as it is used here. 1) The expression "the thing in its being" means the thing resolved into its ontological situation. It designates the thing understood in terms of its mode or modes of being and its ontological relations with other beings, including knowers. 2) Since thought *is,* it too is a version of being, for it is the activity or process of opening out onto the thing and of returning to itself. Thought as active process *is* in some sense, even when it is mistaken; but 3) we may speak of thought coming into its truth as a coming into a fullness of being appropriate to it. Here it realizes itself by bringing about the context in which it joins the being of the thing and surrenders to it, while also recovering itself and illuminating the being which they share with each other: that is, the unitive being which is the thing in its being known by the knower in his. Thought (2), then, has a double ontological relation: to the being of the thing (1) and to the being of its union with the thing (3). These are not simply identical; they are an identification, for they both are and are not the same being. *The relation to the being of the thing* (1): if the copula does not join thought and being, the identification needed for truth is absent. *The relation to the being of their union* (3): but the copula must also distinguish thought and thing in order that there might be knowledge, for only in this distinction can thought return to itself to recover its own being. In so doing it seals itself with its native quality, the transcendental consummation we call *truth*.

The double-nature of the copula as limit is, of course, the source of the ambiguity in its connective function. In affirmative and negative judgments, the copula combines or divides the predicate and the subject: and this is its attributive function. But it also identifies and distinguishes thought and being: and this is its onto-existential function. The degree to which such an identification and distinction becomes explicit will vary from one utterance to another. Nevertheless, since the copula uses some form of the verb "to be," its onto-existentialist force is at least implicit in all judgments. It is not confined to the controverted judgments of existence ("X is"), nor to judgments which attribute real existence to a subject ("There exists an X such that . . ."). The index of the onto-existential function may be carried by the context within which the judgment is uttered or understood, but it still belongs to the total intention of the judgment. The onto-existential function of the copula, then, is a dense and undeveloped intention to recover the being of things in truth and for thought, an intention launched by thought itself and directing itself to determine the appropriate ontological contexts of the objects of its interest. It belongs to philosophical reflection, however, to render explicit the nature of that function and the interrelation of the modes of being involved.

The attributive and onto-existential functions differ. For the copula *either* combines *or* divides, whereas it must in the very same act *both* identify *and* distinguish. Indeed, even in the negative judgment in which it divides a predicate from a subject, the truthful copula thereby identifies thought with being. It is not enough, however, to simply distinguish the attributive function of the copula, by which it either combines or divides subject and predicate, from its onto-existential weight, by which it both identifies and distinguishes thought and being. If we are to recapture the full sense of the judgment, we must also relate these two functions. Since the copula retains its verbal memory, it functions at least implicitly with its ontological heritage of participles and nouns. And so, the combination and division done in its attributive role finds its ultimate justification in the onto-existential function, by which thought identifies the thing as a disclosure of being. But the disclosure is brought about by assertive thought through its affirmations and denials, and so it also discloses the ontological difference between the being of things (1) and the being of thought (2, 3).

It is, of course, possible and even advantageous sometimes to hold in abeyance the ontological power of the copula, and to consider the attributive function in and for itself as a pure connective of terms within a proposition. The non-consideration of the ontological weight of the copula can be carried out in many ways. It can be partial as in traditional logic; or the ontological weight can be formally excluded as in some modern logics. Along such a path of reflection logic can move beyond the simple attributive function to logics based upon other logical relations. Moreover, modal logics are not a straightforward return to the ontological weight of the copula, but an amplification of the modes of attribution. For the "may be" and "must be" of modal logics are considered as possibilities for proposition-formation, and are equivalent to "may be said" and "must be said." Furthermore, other modes of reflective analysis may put some aspect of the ontological weight of the copula out of play, as does the *epochē* which initiates Husserlian phenomenology. So too, in a quite different sense, do the objectives and methods usually employed in the natural and social sciences. In such reductions of the onto-existential force of the copula, thought frees itself to explore structures and processes in and for themselves without having to explicate their relation to their ontological foundations. This dispensation is especially beneficial because the articulation of those foundations in a definite philosophical formulation, such as in the present essay, is not only difficult; since it is a determinate statement, it will inevitably have limitations and defects. Nevertheless, the plethora of possible approaches to the judgment, including its phenomenology, psychology, sociology, and logic, must not be allowed to obscure the need for an ontology of judgment. From different perspectives, the present emphasis upon the copula may seem irrelevant, secondary, or even mistaken, but it is an important task of philosophical reflection to revitalize our understanding of the metaphysical and ontological foundations of the judgment. When we put into play the full onto-existential weight of the copula, we commit language and things, thought and being, to a nexus with each other. That association brings about an actual double double-presence within a linguistic and ontological totality.

V

The copula discloses a linguistic totality. The word uttered by a judgment—that something is so and not otherwise—is not the only or the last word. For the copula does not arise out of the mind as a solitary connective, any more than the whole judgment presents itself as an isolated unit. On the contrary, the judgment is an individual and actualized utterance which presupposes a linguistic totality for its ground. It can take form only within such a comprehensive unity. The comprehension is not actual, however, for the totality of actual and possible speech acts is, of course, never present to any speaker. All the possibilities of a language are not at hand at any given moment. Neither is its past wholly recoverable, nor its future wholly predictable. Nevertheless, the "whole" language is "there" in the sense that its forms and functions are available to any skilled speaker. They are not so much *all* there, as they are there in their *allness*, or better, the linguistic possibilities are present in their unity and as a totality which can be drawn upon in determinate ways. If we do not restrict the process of habituation to conscious assimilation or restrict it too closely to acquired habits of particular usage, we might say that language is there as a totality somewhat in the manner of a habit. For it is present with a readiness that is not a fully actual presence, since we are not always speaking, nor is it a mere potentiality for speech, since we are not always learning anew how to speak. Linguists insist that the process of acquiring the structure of a language is a complex one, largely unconscious and appropriated somewhat in the way in which we assimilate other systems and social institutions through enculturation. We come into possession of our native language by a set of processes which bring into play the adoption of motor rhythms and the response to sensory values as well as to meanings. Language, then, is not simply a totality of meaningful sounds. It is an organic adaptation to patterns and possibilities of a distinctive form of behavior, that of the communication of meaning. Never appearing in itself, the linguistic totality is embedded in the speaker's motor and perceptual systems and in his social institutions. Within these possibilities of behavior and by means of assimilated patterns, human consciousness strives for the comprehension and communication of meaning. Language is the availability to the speaker of a totality of communicability in a historically conditioned system of verbal signs and forms of expression. Like a diaphanous medium, this totality is both lit up and shadowed forth through individual acts of speech. Language gathers itself up as a structured totality which breaks forth into concrete and actual expression in individual acts of speech. When the locution is assertive and cognitive, it expresses itself in judgment. When that judgment uses an onto-existential copula, it rises out of a totality of language and thought in order to manifest the quality of truth through a disclosure of being.

VI

The copula discloses an ontological totality, the comprehensive ultimacy of being and non-being. The vigorous verb, "to be" or "not to be," moves easily throughout the language, coupling and uncoupling terms with its discriminatory power of affirmation and denial. Its onto-existential force can, as we have already suggested, be suspended in the interests of exploring factors of language or reality in and for themselves. And it moves so unobtrusively that its onto-existential force and its own intended meaning can be ignored, as when the copula is taken as a mere place holder which is supposed merely to make room for the union of terms or for preventing their union. It can be all but rendered invisible and ineffective by assigning even its unifying function to the other parts of the judgment. Thus Bosanquet agrees with Mill's view that we really need nothing but the subject and predicate, and that the copula is a mere sign of their connection *as* subject and predicate.[5]

---

5. B. Bosanquet, *The Essentials of Logic* (London: Macmillan, 1895), 99, referring to J. S. Mill, *Logic*, bk. 1, c. iv, #1.

The unobtrusiveness which permits the copula to insinuate itself modestly between the terms can easily be mistaken for barren impotence. But the ubiquity, which makes it so obvious that it can be overlooked, arises out of its comprehensive intention. For the copula means to submit the subject and predicate in their relationship to the measure of being and non-being. Indeed, the copula breaks open into its unrestricted universality just because, in breaking open into "is" and "is not," it breaks open into a transcendental value, a value which pervades both speech and things, which counts both in truth and in being. For in asserting the relatedness or non-relatedness of a subject and predicate an ontological measure is elicited through the copula by thought in order to apprehend and appraise the relationship. The disjunct, "is" or "is not," releases the decisive value into which all affirmation and denial is to be ultimately resolved. Within the totality of language, then, the copula discloses itself as the density of all possible affirmations and denials. The totality of assertive speech is gathered together and rooted in the distinction of being and non-being.

Such an onto-existential copula reveals its capacity to be more than a mere place holder. For the intention of the copula is not only comprehensive, it is also radical and ultimate. With assertive force it carries through a probe which reaches down to the fundamental value associated with truth, to a probity which exceeds the bare coupling and uncoupling of terms, and which authorizes and authenticates the attributive function. As a component of linguo-thought, the onto-existential copula does not forget its primitive verbal meaning, nor the familial associations of "is," "exists," and "being." And so it arises out of linguo-thought with the intention to measure and declare what is and is not, was and was not, will and will not, can and cannot, must and must not, ought and ought not.[6] Taken with its ontological weight the copula expresses something which neither the subject alone nor the predicate alone nor both together can say: that their unity or disunity is grounded ultimately neither in an analytic implication nor in a synthetic coincidence of thought and sensible being, but in some appropriate condominium of being and truth. Taken in its assertive sense—that this *is* so and not otherwise—the copula expresses the thrust of the mind towards a true statement which is intended to disclose whatever mode of being is warranted and proper for the declared relationship. Consider these assertions: "The *physical* components of Lear are the markings on a page and the voice and movements of an actor." "He played Lear well *tonight*."

---

6. Each of these needs further analysis in order to disclose the interplay of being and non-being, presence and absence, temporality and atemporality, and ideality that constitutes the fully concrete intensions of the copula. The present essay is only one step in the attempt to enrich the copula through reflection.

"Lear, after all, is a *dramatic character.*" What is such speech about? It directs itself towards a grand vague unity which gathers to itself printed page, voice and gesture, a tradition of acting, a history of performances, a context of scholarship, the reflections of critics, a theatrical community, and more. This in its unfinished totality is Lear, and is the measure of what can truly be said of it—past, present, and future. The copula is the energy of the judgment just because it is suffused with the assertive force of the mind's activity as it strives to associate itself and its concepts with whatever regions, modes, and contexts of being are appropriate for them. The copula is the very presence of the mind itself in the act of identifying and distinguishing thought and being. In this activity both being and truth disclose themselves as comprehensive and radical values. For the copula is the achievement of truth just because it is the assertive force of the mind under the discipline of the thing. And it is the disclosure of being just because it reaches the ontological terminus intended *(ad rem)* inasmuch as the thing referred to is or is not in just the way it is signified in the judgment.

VII

The copula discloses a double double-presence. Judgment establishes a unity of thought and being, while preserving their distinctness. The meeting of thought and being is, then, a kind of twosome; but what kind? Judgment does not result in two entities, such as a being in knowledge and a being outside knowledge, for that sacrifices their union to a dualism of known and unknowable, against which Berkeley protested. Nor can judgment result in two entities of which one is an original and the other a copy, for this presupposes knowledge rather than explains it, as Sartre and others have shown. For similar reasons I do not think that knowledge consists in the acquisition of a property or state, although human knowing may involve both. The division into "is" and "is not" which is intrinsic to judgment provides a better clue to the character of knowledge, for it arises out of the needs of linguo-thought. The division exhibits a decisive tension within thought itself in the face of being. Hegel takes the division to be self-negation and seeks the reconciliation of thought with itself through the medium of being. The resultant dialectic throws a brilliant light upon many aspects of thought and being. To be sure, thought is not indifferent to its intrinsic division, but the secret power of thought does not lie in its self-division and self-negation alone. It is rooted even more basically in its complicity with being, and in the onto-existential function by which it both identifies and distinguishes itself and being.

Moreover, its complicity with being is rooted not only in the being of the thing, but just as basically in its own being. The complicity shows that thought is not autonomous. From the side of the thing, thought is governed by a capacity which the thing holds within itself: the intelligibility of its being. If thought must serve under the law of the thing, then, without the intelligibility which the thing has in virtue of the intelligibility of its being, thought could not itself be intelligent, that is, could not be thought. But this intelligibility rises up from within thought, too. For, because being is intelligible in the thing, and because thought is itself a manner of being, thought contains a similar capacity within itself: viz., the possibility of disclosing its own intelligibility to itself in virtue of the intelligibility of its being. Such a possibility is the promise of truth. For in realizing the truth of something else, thought vindicates the mutual intelligibility of the being of the thing and the being of thought itself *(ens et verum convertuntur)*. This is the first double-presence: the mutual presence of the being of thought and the being of the thing.

Even more fundamental to thought than its intrinsic self-division by which it declares either-or, then, is the doubling of presence by which it establishes both-and. For thought brings together what is in some sense two: knower and known, thought and thing (the first double-presence). It can do this, however, only out of a more original possibility, by which it brings about the doubling of what remains one. When a thing is known, it *is* both in its own being and in its being known. Now being known is not simply being, or everything that is would be known; and yet it is one and the same being that both is and is known, or nothing would ever be known. This second double-presence is the peculiar consummation of the wedding of thought and being. (It is *being* in the third sense noticed above.) Thought opens out onto the thing *(adesse)*, even as the thing opens out in the presence of thought *(adesse)*. The intelligence of thought realizes itself as the actual intelligibility of being. In doubling what remains one, thought arrives at the truth of something, both distinguishing itself from the thing and identifying itself with it.

The decisive word which being utters in the doubling brought about by judgment is a sort of excess. It is not, however, the excess of a remainder or a redundancy, the superfluity which the early Sartre found absurd and irrational. To call cognition an "excess" may shock some philosophers who secure the respectability of thought by appealing to its economy and necessity, for it seems to make thought unnecessary, useless, and trifling. What "excess" means here, however, is that the possibility of intelligence is rooted in the intelligibility of being, and that the intelligibility of being is a certain propensity for self-transcendence by which a thing both holds itself in its own being while it yields that being to another. Intelligibility is a certain abundance and generosity written into being, its capacity for making a gift of itself to thought. Such ontological gifts are not always easily received, of course, for they do not yield themselves indiscriminately. Yet it is the peculiar capability of thought that it can coax a thing out of itself, at least to some degree. It can do this, undoubtedly, because in being known the thing does not really go out of itself but only enters upon an enlargement of its possibilities. For as it becomes grounded in the being of thought, it remains itself and also remains within a context of being, although that context is a modulation of its being. The possibility of cognition is rooted in this ontological generosity, and in a vicariosity which permits one being to bear the presence and meaning of another.

The copula provides the principle of limit for such a double double-presence. From the side of the thing, and in accordance with the law of the thing, there can be no two entities present, but only the one and same being being known. For the truth arrived at is the truth of *that* being, and not of some other. But there is also duality, because simply being is not actually being known. The presence is double, then, yet a single thing is present. The copula is the limit and focal point of this ontological double-presence. The thing loans its being, but in the loan it does not detach its being from itself. Rather, it offers up its being to a modulation, an enlargement of its horizon, so that it can be in association with another of a peculiar sort, a knower. From the side of thought, this double-presence of the thing known is grounded in the co-presence of thought and being. For in the judgment and through the copula, thought sustains itself and the thing in their union. Indeed, thought makes itself present as receiving the loan which the thing makes of its own being. Thought loans its being, too, then, for it is present to the thing as sustaining it in a relation which lies beyond the power of the thing itself. This community of thought and thing is for the sake of the truth of being. Cognition, then, is brought about by a reciprocity of loaned modes of being, in which thought brings the energy of its active attention and the thing brings the intelligibility of its being. Cognition is a double double-presence, in which both thought and the original being of the thing form a new actuality, the actual community of knower and thing known. The copula functions as the ontological limit for thought and for the being to which the truth must gravitate as to its objective measure: *pondus cognoscentis rei cognoscendae pondus.*

Chapter 7

CREATED RECEPTIVITY AND THE PHILOSOPHY OF THE CONCRETE

Gabriel Marcel gave his phenomenological inquiries the name "Philosophy of the Concrete,"[1] and he made no bones about the distance between his philosophy and that of Thomism.[2] Between these philosophies there can be no question of an *approchement* of tone, nor even of manner, but at most a convergence of truths shared differently. Moreover, there can be no doubt that the two philosophies differ in their relation to experience. Within the broad sense of "Christian experience," Thomas drew upon *experientia (empiria)* in the narrower sense in order to derive by way of conceptual abstraction the principles of his philosophy, including those of act and potency. Marcel's relation to experience was more immediate, more deliberate, and more explicit. Yet his philosophy has provided an articulate basis in contemporary experience for many of the ideas that underlie St. Thomas' thought in a very different way.

There may not have been a need in the society and culture of thirteenth-century Europe to make explicit in a methodical, *descriptive* manner the direct experiential underpinnings of such notions as mystery, fidelity, vocation, and community. They were in the cultural air and

---

Reprinted from *The Thomist* 61, no. 3 (July 1977): 339–71. Copyright © 1977 by *The Thomist*.

1. Actually, he usually referred to "concrete philosophy" and preferred "approaches to the concrete." See the "Author's Preface to the English Edition" of the *Metaphysical Journal* (Paris: Gallimard, 1927; London: Rockliff, 1952), viiif.

2. In his "Autobiography" (in *The Philosophy of Gabriel Marcel*, ed. A. Schilpp and L. E. Hahn [La Salle, IL.: Open Court, 1984], 3–68) he writes: "the essentially Thomist dogmatism I found in Abbott Altermann aroused my unalterable protest. At the time, I made several attempts to understand St. Thomas's thinking better and to read some of his contemporary disciples. But I am obliged to acknowledge that this effort was not crowned with success, and the most elementary fairness forces me to add that I did not carry it out with the requisite earnestness and tenacity. It was at this time that Charles Du Bos and I had weekly meetings with Jacques Maritain, who took great pains to help us understand Thomist thought better and to appreciate it more. All three of us showed good will, but the result was meager indeed" (30). Nonetheless, he showed a certain reservation in his criticism of St. Thomas without, however, much sympathy.

had taken institutional form as dogmas, vows, art and architecture, religious orders, and a sense of the transcendent in everyday life in and through the visible presence of the Church. These notions were accessible to lived experience and were given realistic expression in the public speech in a way that they are not in the more secularized contemporary society in which we live and think. With us they have, for the most part, taken refuge in the private sphere.

I. INTRODUCING RECEPTIVITY

Especially important in Marcel's approach to the concrete are the concepts of availability *(disponibilité)*, recognition (*reconnâitre*, reconnaissance) (cf. reconnoiter), and receptivity *(recevoir)* (cf. *accueillir:* to welcome). Originating from quite different considerations, receptivity has recently been brought into relation with the thought of St. Thomas, through further philosophical reflection upon his texts and through reflection upon the theology of the Trinity.[3]

In an article entitled "The First Principle of Personal Becoming,"[4] I had sought to identify the mark of spirit in a thought-world that, for the most part, rejects the metaphysical understanding of the person as spirit. I had pointed to the capacity of the human spirit to "communicate without loss," as when we do not unlearn what we have known in teaching it to others. This was meant to indicate the traditional sphere of immanent activity as distinct from transitive (productive) physical action.[5] The correlate of communication without loss is reception without (physical) mutation: receptivity. Both together point to a distinctive mode of existence. I had taken the term *receptivity* in Marcel's sense and had used the term *non-passive receptivity* to designate this feature of the human spirit.

The critique of my own writing on the person by Mr. Steve Long has brought the issue of the relation between these two philosophies to a head. I might formulate the question thus: Are the principles of act and potency (so central to the metaphysics of St. Thomas) adequate to interpret the contemporary experience of the person?[6] Mr. Long finds the

---

3. This is particularly true for David Schindler. See Norris Clarke, *Person and Being* (Milwaukee, WI: Marquette University Press, 1993); and David Schindler, "Norris Clarke on Person, Being and St. Thomas," *Communio* 20 (Fall 1993): 580ff.

4. *Review of Metaphysics* 47 (June 1994): 757–74.

5. Cf. Marcel's notion of "meta-problematical" or "secondary reflection": "The Ontological Mystery," in *The Philosophy of Existentialism*, 6th ed. (New York: Citadel, 1966), 16, 22; and in more detail, *The Mystery of Being*, vol. 1: *Reflection and Mystery*, trans. G. S. Fraser (Chicago: Henry Regnery, 1960).

6. See Steven A. Long, "Personal Receptivity and Act: A Thomistic Critique," *The Thomist* 61 (1997): 1–31. Mr. Long has rendered a service to all who are interested in

aforesaid notion of *receptivity* to be in conflict with the thought of St. Thomas, and he charges me with three faults: (1) I am alleged to find the principles of act and potency inadequate to account for the personal mode of being; (2) I make of receptivity a third principle that is neither act nor potency; and (3) the error derives from a too-active view of the person as *causa sui*. I am further alleged to have unwittingly accepted the modern divorce between person and nature and the consequent abandonment of analogy.[7]

What comes in for trenchant criticism is the double term *non-passive receptivity*, which I used to describe the way the human person relates to others, insofar as he or she is a *spiritual* being. I must confess that the double term is a new term for me, but it is not a new concept.[8] The choice of the adjective *non-passive* was determined in large part by the context, background, and audience in which I first employed the term. In its original version the essay on personal becoming was read to a meeting of the Metaphysical Society of America, whose conference theme was that of "Becoming" in its several senses. I anticipated that the audience would be made up very significantly of American naturalists, pragmatists, and process philosophers. I thought there was a need to disengage the notion of "spirit" from the general view of becoming as process, change, alteration, and mutation, without however losing the sense of the dynamism of spirit. For that reason I spelled out what I meant by *non-passive receptivity*, stressing the distinctive character of becoming without mutation. The term was meant to be correlative with "communication without loss," which I took to be a clear if initial sign of the spiritual order. The passivity that the term *non-passive* was meant to reject, then, is precisely *material*, mutable passivity.

---

the philosophy of the person and in St. Thomas' thought. With characteristic thoroughness he has amassed an impressive set of texts from the saint's works. His argument deserves careful consideration. As to his critique of my own writing on the person, I can only thank him for pointing up the ambiguities that may well dog not only my style but my thought as well. I should make it clear, however, that, while I have always acknowledged my debt to the great saint, I have always avoided claiming the honorific "Thomist" for my own thought. Still, I must confess that I experience a certain uneasiness whenever my own thought seems to be in contradiction with the balanced and profound thought of St. Thomas. Now it is just such uneasiness that arises as I read Steve Long's criticism of my own essay on the person, for he clearly finds me delinquent in fidelity to the principles of Thomistic thought, and precisely in regard to the principles of act and potency.

7. Norris Clarke's Aquinas lecture, *Person and Being*, also comes in for criticism as well as his "Person, Being, and St. Thomas," *Communio* 19 (Winter 1992): 601–18.

8. Mr. Long's criticism makes me aware of the term's potential for misunderstanding. His criticism would have been more telling, however, had he taken into consideration both parts of the combined term. Instead he has fastened upon the adjective *non-passive* to the neglect of the verbal substantive *receptivity*, and has transferred to the combined term a rejection of all potency. Hence the charge that I have invented a new third principle that is neither act nor potency and have divorced the person from nature as entirely active *causa sui*.

I did not reject the quasi-passivity to which Mr. Long refers in quoting St. Thomas.[9] That so-called passivity *(potest dici pati)* is the very sense of passivity in which there is no loss.[10] The translator renders *pati communiter* as "passive in a wide sense." That is fair enough, but the condition is better served by understanding it to mean "analogously passive," remembering with the Fourth Lateran Council that analogy emphasizes the diversity of meanings rather than the identity.[11] Far from departing from St. Thomas on this score, the burden of my essay was to recover precisely that sense of non-deprivation proper to personal becoming and to the order of spiritual being. Belatedly, I must admit that with suitable nuances the term *non-privative* would have fit my intent better. Still, the sense of "communication without loss" fits well with St. Thomas' clause, *absque hoc quod aliquid abiiciatur.* It seems to me that the phrase "communication without loss" is a contemporary metaphysical term for distinguishing the spiritual mode of personal being and immanent activity from the sub-personal modes of physical nature with their alteration and generation. It seems to me, too, that the correlative terms "non-passive [or better, non-privative] receptivity" and "communication without loss" carry the weight of St. Thomas' *absque . . . abiiciatur.*

II. THE NEED FOR A METAPHYSICAL GROUNDING OF PERSONALISM

Personalist philosophies are a feature of twentieth-century thought. Many have taken non-traditional form through one or another variant of idealism,[12] or by way of phenomenology.[13] But it seems to me that many forms of personalism in this century are rather "free-floating," using a notion of spirit that would benefit by being situated in the context of a more traditional metaphysics of being.[14] What is more, the absence

---

9. *STh* I, q. 79, a. 2: "Tertio (modo), dicitur aliqui pati communiter, ex hoc solo quod id quod est in potentia ad aliquid, recipit illud ad quod erat in potentia, absque hoc quod aliquid abiiciatur. Secundum quem modum, omne quod exit de potentia in actum, *potest dici pati,* etiam cum perficitur. Et sic intelligere nostrum est pati" (emphasis added).

10. Towards the close of the article (see n. 4 above) I do recognize certain forms of loss that afflict an incarnate spirit, such as the loss of memory due to its physical basis and the deliberate spiritual loss entailed in moral evil. But the proper mode of spiritual being is communication without loss.

11. Denzinger, *Enchiridion Symbolorum,* no. 806 (32nd ed.; Freiburg: Herder, 1963), 262: "quia inter creatorem et creaturam non potest similtudo notari, quin inter eos maior sit dissimilitude notanda."

12. For example, the philosophy of Josiah Royce or of Ralph Flewelling Tyler.

13. Cf. also Maurice Nédoncelle's existential personalism and the sociological personalism of Emmanuel Mounier.

14. An outstanding exception is the metaphysical personalism of Jacques Maritain, which owes its originating principles to St. Thomas. See, for example, *The Person and the Common Good,* trans. John J. Fitzgerald (Notre Dame, IN: University of Notre Dame Press,

of such a contemporary resolution favors the modern tendency to reduce personal modes of being and acting to a dynamic network of physical forces.[15] Thus, for example, there is the tendency among popularizers of the natural sciences to reduce knowing to brain chemistry or to computers. And, what amounts to the same reductionism in reverse, the absence of an adequately contemporary notion of spirit encourages the modern tendency to inflate the notion of physical energy and physical process, so that a vague notion of matter is called upon to explain properly spiritual activities.[16] There is need, then, to recover a properly metaphysical sense of spirit in order to meet the present situation, and it is fitting to ask, given the objection of Mr. Long, whether the principles of act and potency (indispensable to the metaphysics of St. Thomas) are adequate to articulate a contemporary metaphysics of the person.

The last great attempt to restore the concept of spirit to philosophical discourse was made by Hegel with his notion of cosmic self-determination *(der absolute Geist)*. There was, however, no role for potency in the system, since instead of a movement from potency to act the determinate was drawn forth from the indeterminate which already *somehow* contained its determinations. Without dismissing the thought of this great philosopher, yet without detailing my own particular criticisms here,[17] I may be excused in saying that the attempt failed through its immodesty. Nevertheless, to its credit, it did try to take into account modern developments and to reconcile the *being* of the ancients with the *subjectivity* of the moderns. Unfortunately, its widespread rejection (along with the present rejection of all "grand narratives")[18] has seemed to discredit further the very notion of spirit itself in many quarters of contemporary philosophy. The roots for this incomprehension lie, however, not simply in the rejection of Hegel's philosophy but in the career of modern thought.

1966). An interesting use of the metaphysics of St. Thomas and phenomenology is found in Karol Wojtyla, *The Acting Person* (Dordrecht: Reidel, 1979).

15. Examples are numerous, especially among the materialists, positivists, and naturalists.

16. I have in mind a work such as that of James K. Feiblemann, *The Pious Scientist: Nature, God and Man in Religion* (New York: Bookman Associates, 1958): "All matter is divine, because it constitutes the world and thus serves the reason for the world; and the higher forms are only its complications . . . If matter in the old sense is gone, so is the concept of spirit, which lived largely on its opposition to matter . . . Matter is far more complex than we had supposed . . . The old materialism was insufficient, but the new is capacious" (70f.).

17. See "On a Resistant Strain within the Hegelian Dialectic," *The Owl of Minerva* 25 (Spring 1994): 147–54. The strain is a full-fledged nominalism without which the dialectic will not work.

18. See Jean-Francois Lyotard, *The Postmodern Condition: A Report on Knowledge* (French original, 1979; Minneapolis: University of Minnesota Press, 1984), 31–41 and passim.

III. TAKING THE RECENT HISTORY OF BEING INTO ACCOUNT

In attempting to recover a metaphysical understanding of spirit it is important to take the modern background into account, given that things have happened in the seven hundred years since St. Thomas reinterpreted Aristotle; not even being itself has stood still. Nor has everything that has happened been a falling away from being. If being is truly universal, then modern developments must have occurred *within* being and be in some sense connected with the *history of being*.[19] The more so if Marcel's maxim is true—that being is precisely that which withstands every assault upon it.[20]

It is important for those who value the great tradition, and who are acutely aware of the deficiencies in modern thought, to appreciate the great advance in self-understanding that has been brought about—as a by-product, so to speak[21]—through an admittedly exaggerated emphasis upon self-identity and self-reference.[22] The human person has become more prominent, even as its full spiritual nature has been obscured by the parade of terms used during the modern period to disguise its specificity: mind, *ego*, self, receptacle of sensory impressions, consciousness,

---

19. Cf. the oft-quoted text from *De Potentia Dei* q. 7, a. 2, ad 9: "Ad nonum dicendum, quod hoc quod dico esse est inter omnia perfectissimum: quod ex hoc patet quia actus est semper perfectior potential ... Unde patet quod hoc quod dico esse est actualitas omnium actuum, et propter hoc est perfectio omnium perfectionum. Nec intelligendum est, quod ei quod dico esse, aliquid additur quod sit eo formalius, ipsum determinans, sicut actus potentiam: esse enim quod hujusmodi est, est aliud secundum essentiam ab eo cui additur determinandum. Nihil autem potest addi ad esse quod sit extraneum ab ipso, cum ab eo nihil sit extraneum nisi non ens, quod non potest esse nec forma nec materia. Unde non sic determinatur esse per aliud sicut potentia per actum, sed magis sicut actus per potentiam."

20. "The Ontological Mystery" (1933), in *The Philosophy of Existentialism*, 14. In fact, Marcel says that "Being is that which is—or should be—necessary," and "what withstands—or would withstand—an exhaustive analysis bearing upon the data of experience." That "should" and "would" indicate that there is no sure guarantee of the continuing presence of being *(bene esse)* but that there are grounds for the hope that it will survive even the most reductionist onslaught. The "should/would" reminds us that Marcel's thought concentrates not on *esse simpliciter* so much as upon *bene esse* in keeping with his emphasis on being as full.

21. Or, to speak providentially, by the mysterious process in which God draws truth out of error, good out of evil, and unity out of disunity. We human beings do not seem capable of advancing in a straight line, so that He makes our crooked paths somehow straight and our wanderings reach an often unexpected goal; for hope, as Marcel tells us, consists in lending "credit" to being, whereas despair declares its bankruptcy. Is this not a rational act of faith in the ultimate intelligibility of being without which there would be no philosophy?

22. Jacques Maritain serves as a guide in this. For critical as he was of modern developments, he nonetheless was able to see the positive results as well as the negative. For example, in *Religion and Culture* (London: Sheed and Ward, 1931), 84f., he writes: "To de-

will, *Dasein*, and subjectivity. Literature has done better.[23] There can be no doubt that modern novels and poems, along with modern psychology, present a heightened portrait of the distinctive character of the human person, sometimes in the darkest colors. At the same time, a metaphysical understanding of the person has been all but lost. Admittedly, many of these presentations still follow from the modern sense of self as wholly self-determining *(causa sui)*. Either they still presuppose the confident assurance of the primacy of the self or they react against the shadow of self that still fascinates more recent critics of modernity. Or yet again, they are filled with the reductionist tendencies already mentioned.

There can be no doubt that the classical modern period, from the sixteenth to the nineteenth century, from Descartes to Kant, exaggerated the relation of self-reference, and presented a relatively closed sense of subjectivity. This was so, even as I began my own studies fifty years ago, though the criticism was already underway. This primacy of self-reference obscured the role of the other in knowing and willing, turning the other into the pale shadow of the self in the form of ideas (Descartes), sensations (Hume), or phenomena (Kant). Nowadays, the deficiencies of the emphasis upon the self-same are familiar to all who have read contemporary philosophers from Heidegger on. And though it had long been criticized by scholastic philosophers on other grounds, this subjectivist tendency has recently come in for further criticism by postmodern thinkers. Indeed, the current effort seems to be to restore some sense of otherness beyond the horizon of the human subject.[24]

---

nounce a fundamental spiritual deviation in a period of culture is not to condemn that period. During the same [modern] period there is an evolution in human affairs, an expansion of history; there are, conjoined to certain evils, gains and achievements of mankind that have an almost sacred value since they are produced in the order of divine providence; we must acknowledge these attainments and these gains." And, in *True Humanism*, trans. Margot Adamson (London: Geoffrey Bles, 1946), 18f., he writes: "Much progress has thus been made, above all in the world of reflection and self-consciousness, revealing often by lowly means, in science, in art, in poetry, in the very passions and even the vices of man, his proper spirituality. Science has undertaken the conquest of created nature, the human soul has made a universe of its subjectivity, the secular world has been differentiated according to its own proper law, the creature has come to know itself. And such progress taken in itself was entirely normal."

23. Milan Kundera in *The Art of the Novel* (New York: Harper and Row, 1993) argues that while the philosophers (chiefly Husserl and Heidegger) have underscored the loss of the sense of being (cf. Marcel also), the tradition of the European novel, beginning with Cervantes, has preserved the sense of being. For all that, Kundera's own sense of being seems "unbearably light."

24. Cf. Emmanuel Levinas, *Totality and Infinity: An Essay on Exteriority* (Pittsburgh: Duquesne University Press, 1969), 212f.; and in a quite different sense the effort of Derrida and others to equate otherness with linguistic heterogeneity, but offering us little more than equivocity and a reduction of meaning to non-meaning. See, for example, Jacques Derrida, "Differance," in *Margins of Philosophy* (Chicago: University of Chicago Press, 1982), 3–27.

Nevertheless, the exaggeration of self-same subjectivity ought not to prevent us from recognizing a genuine increase in the appreciation of the distinctiveness of being human. What is more, even though this modern recognition is distorted, it must be conceded that it does lodge the distinctiveness, if not exactly in the classical *differentia* (the *rationale*), at least in the region of consciousness. This modern development has yielded a more intensive appreciation of the (sometimes dangerous) constructive energies of the person, which express themselves in an expansion of freedom of choice and a recognition of a certain dizzying depth of human freedom which is not simply a matter of thought but of life as well.

Given the climate of latter-day nominalism and the loss of contact with nature in favor of an urban technical environment, the distinctiveness of the human person has led to a quite general sense of divorce between person and nature. The prevalent alternatives seem to be either a materialist reductionism or an anti-metaphysical historicism. Both alternatives dismiss the metaphysics of being and its understanding of the spiritual dimension of the person. Moreover, these alternatives are often coupled with a dialectical tendency that turns otherness into conflict.[25]

IV. THE RECENT SHIFT TO THE CONCRETE AMONG THOMISTS

Reflecting these developments, there has been a rather wide-ranging shift in the understanding of rationality and the expectation of meaning, and this shift finds its expression in a somewhat different emphasis regarding the task of philosophy. Among contemporary philosophers from a number of traditions—including dialectics, pragmatics, existential analysis, ordinary language analysis, phenomenological description, hermeneutic interpretation, and deconstructive criticism—there has been an engagement with the concrete order and a general avoidance of strong systematic claims. It seems to me that this recent approach to the concrete has been fed not so much by the general empirical emphasis of modern science, which considers the instance rather than the singular, as by the recognition of the more historical mode of being and meaning that has engaged modern thought, from Dilthey on, especially in aspects of the social, cultural, and historical disciplines.[26] In philoso-

---

25. Echoing Nietzsche's "Homer's Contest," Lyotard places speech not in the category of communication but in that of the *agon*, with the slogan "to speak is to fight," softening Nietzsche's "noisy philosophical hammer," however, by adding, "in the sense of playing" (*Report on Knowledge*, 10, nn. 34, 35). A common objection by German Catholic philosophers in the second quarter of this century (Romano Guardini, Gustav Siewerth, Eric Przywara, and others) was that, in the wake of Hegel, difference was turned into dialectical conflict instead of into analogous diversity.

26. Within the broad uniformity of logical reasoning, a different epistemology is more

phy, it seems likely that the shift to the concrete has been in response to the inadequacies in evidential practice and theory that have brought about the rise of phenomenology, not only of the Husserlian variety but of the broader type according to which Marcel might be said to be a phenomenologist of the concrete.[27]

Now, it seems to me that the charge that "receptivity" introduces a new principle which is neither act nor potency fails to take account of the shift in the level of philosophical reflection. Receptivity is not to be understood simply at the general and abstract level of act and potency. My argument is that receptivity is a principle of personal being at the concrete level. Far from being a principle that is neither act nor potency, I mean by it an *integral mode* constituted of both act and potency.[28]

Nor has this trend towards the concrete left recent interpreters of St. Thomas unaffected. Indeed, the shift is observable over the past sixty years, as witnessed by, among others, the works of Aimé Forest (1931),[29] Cornelio Fabro (1938),[30] Joseph de Finance (1938),[31] L.-B. Geiger, O.P. (1941),[32] Etienne Gilson (1942),[33] Thomas Gilby, O.P.,[34] the later work

---

suitable to the properly historical aspect of the human disciplines insofar as they do not attempt to model themselves upon the natural sciences. The reason is that the empirical practice in the natural sciences can be accommodated to, though not identified with, the classical division of terms into universal and particular, in the form of class and member or law and instance, whereas historicity calls for the recognition that the human person in his or her freedom is more than a particular instance of a law or member of a class, and that concrete meaning is more than an instantiation of a general law or class, just because, as we shall see, the concrete incorporates these abstract divisions within its sense of the singular.

27. I have in mind the circle in Munich around Pfänder. See Herbert Spiegelberg, *The Phenomenological Movement: A Historical Introduction*, 2 vols. (2nd ed.; The Hague: Nijhoff, 1969).

28. Mr. Long seems to recognize this when he attributes to me a "symbiosis" of act and potency; but he dismisses the value of such analysis by discounting its results as "merely" symbiotic. In so doing he fails to take into account the transformation of the principles at the concrete level as they are operative in the human person.

29. *La structure métaphysique du concret selon S. Thomas d'Aquin* (Paris: Vrin, 1931): "Ainsi la réalité de l'essence n'est veritablement pas indépendante du rapport qu'elle soutient avec existence" (164). And more succinctly in his summary: "L'être de l'essence est d'être relative á l'existence" (376).

30. *La nozione metafisica de partecipazione* (3rd ed.; Turin: Marietti, 1963).

31. *Etre et agir dans la philosophie de saint Thomas* (Paris: Beauchesne, 1945).

32. *La participation dans la philosophie de St. Thomas* (2nd ed.; Paris: Vrin, 1953). What I have called the shift to the concrete has come about in association with the retrieval of the modified Platonic elements in St. Thomas' thought. Platonic exemplarism is integrated into existential causality.

33. *Le Thomisme* (4th ed.; Paris, 1942). A comparison with the earlier editions shows that the shift came gradually. See my Gilson Lecture, "What Has Clio to Do with Athena?" in *Etienne Gilson: Historian and Philosopher* (Toronto: Pontifical Institute of Mediaeval Studies, 1988).

34. *The Phoenix and the Turtle* (London: Longmans Green, 1950; mostly written, however, during the war years).

of Jacques Maritain (1947),[35] and the essays of Josef Pieper.[36] It seems to me, then, that the recent development of existential Thomism finds its tendencies realized in a metaphysics of the concrete singular.

Providing one recognizes that this shift to the concrete incorporates the recent history of being, and therefore provides a selective interpretation of St. Thomas, this seems to me to be a legitimate and consequential reading of the saint. There are solid grounds in the study of St. Thomas for such an emphasis, even though the emphasis has been brought about by the modern history of being, providing that the end result stands in continuity with St. Thomas as the source of the development, and providing that continuity does not mean simply the repetition but rather the development of his thought.

There can be no doubt, however, that a comparison with St. Thomas' sense of *concretum* and its variants discloses a certain difference of weight or emphasis within the term as it is now reflected in the tendencies of the above-mentioned Thomists. For St. Thomas, the primary signification of the term in creatures is composition.[37] Nevertheless, he tells us that the term contains two elements: composition and perfection (i.e., completeness or subsistence, *per se existens*).[38] The present shift to the concrete is already signaled by the recognition of the primacy of judgment in the metaphysics of St. Thomas.[39] Indeed, the development is

---

35. *Existence and the Existent* (New York: Pantheon, 1948; Doubleday/Image, 1957).

36. In *Guide to Thomas Aquinas* (Notre Dame, IN: University of Notre Dame Press, 1987), Pieper introduces a further level of concreteness without obliterating the distinction between philosophy and theology: "If Thomas' theological interpretation of this divine name [He Who Is] is a whole dimension deeper than St. Augustine's interpretation, is Thomas indebted to philosophy (or even to Aristotle)? Or is it the philosophical conception of Being which here profits by the experience of theology? Must we not say that what takes place is a unitary act, or *a compound of acts which is no longer separable* into its philosophical and theological 'components'? Of course the philosophical element can still be distinguished theoretically from the theological element. But *concretely* the situation is that a living man, confronted with the Whole of reality—one Thomas Aquinas—as believer and thinker (and experiencer of sense perceptions), as a man reflecting upon his belief and at the same time observing man and the universe with all his powers of natural cognition, asks himself: 'What is all this about?'" (152; emphasis added). The word "separable" should draw attention to the fact that philosophy and theology can be distinguished without being separated in a thinker. Such theoretical distinction is not only possible; it is necessary and provides the charter for the traditional metaphysics of being.

37. *Expositio in Libros Sententiarum I* (hereafter *Sent.* I), d. 1, q. 4, a. 2, expositio textus: "concreta [nomina] autem significant quid compositum."

38. *Sent. I*, d. 33, q. 1, a. 2: "In concreto autem est duo considerare in rebus creatis: scilicet compositionem, et perfectionem, quia quod significatur concretive significat ut per se existens."

39. Benoit Garceau, *Judicium: Vocabulaire, sources, doctrine de saint Thomas d'Aquin* (Paris: Vrin, 2002). Despite the earlier controversy over certain insufficiently thought through expressions in the first edition of Gilson's *L'être et l'essence*, the primacy of judgment need not threaten the importance of conceptual knowledge; rather it completes conceptualization.

called for by St. Thomas' own understanding of act *(esse)* which is *at once both comprehensive and intimate*,[40] for it recognizes being in its actuality as the ultimate horizon of all reality, truth, and goodness, and at the same time also recognizes *esse* as most inward within being, as the intensive excellence of being itself.[41] And it is this paradox of utter comprehensiveness and radical inner presence that calls for an epistemology and a metaphysics that attend to the concrete singular and its tensions.

Closely allied with this sensitivity to the singularity of the human person is the modern recognition of the historical mode of being, an awareness that has been fostered in modern life as well as in modern thought. This has prompted essays among recent Thomists regarding the tension between being and history in the attempt to accommodate the properly historical mode of being within a metaphysics of being.[42] And, indeed, there are sources within Thomism for the recognition of the historical mode of being. The intimacy of act *(esse)* in St. Thomas' thought has drawn interpreters towards the not always explicit concreteness in his Aristotelian vocabulary, a concreteness that does not simply belong to its empirical character. To be sure, the abstract nature of thought is rooted in the human condition, for the grandeur and the misery of metaphysics is that it always has to speak in limping syllables of abstraction even as it has always intended—at least for St. Thomas—the most concrete of realities.[43] This disproportion takes ultimate form in St. Thomas' own thought as the distinction between our *modus significandi* and the *res significata* in our predication to and about God.

If the foregoing is true, then the translation of reflection from the general principles of act and potency to the concrete order of integral modes is far from a "mere" shift. Neither need it be an abandonment of those principles. Still, in keeping with the general tendencies of St. Thomas' thought, the shift to the concrete does call for a further deepening of the sense of act and potency constitutive of all creatures as well

---

40. *STh* I, q. 8, a. 1: "Esse autem est illud quod est magis intimum cuilibet, et quod profundius omnibus inest. . . . Unde oportet quod Deus sit in omnibus, et intime."

41. Cf. Marcel's insistence on the global character of being and the intimacy of its presence.

42. See, for example, M. D. Chenu, O.P., "Création et Histoire," in *St. Thomas Aquinas: 1274–1974 Commemorative Studies*, vol. 2 (Toronto: Pontifical Institute of Mediaeval Studies, 1974), 391–99.

43. *STh* I, q. 12, a. 4, ad 3: "intellectus creatus per suam naturam natus sit apprehendere formam concretam et esse concretum in abstractione," And in the *In Boethium De hebdomadibus* 2: "ipsum esse significatur ut abstractum, id quod est ut concretum." Cf. *STh* I, q. 13, a. 1, ad 2: We apply to God abstract names to indicate his simplicity and concrete names to indicate his subsistence, and so "attribuimus ei [i.e., to God] . . . nomma concreta ad significandum subsistentiam et perfectionem ipsius, quamvis utraque nomina [i.e., concrete as well as abstract names] dificiant a modo ipsius." Also *STh* I, q. 3, a. 3, ad 1.

as a refinement of the properly personal sense of these terms. But, first, we need to take into account the implications of such a shift to the concrete, for it transforms the nature of the subject of metaphysics and calls for a different epistemology from the familiar one. It is not easy to set forth this difference.

V. TOWARDS AN EPISTEMOLOGY OF THE SINGULAR

As the natural sciences broke away from philosophy during the late medieval period, the shift began to alter the character of the methodology associated with the study of nature, giving an increasingly mathematical character to what was already an evolving empirical study.[44] But, while this changed the "coloration" of the method, it left the received distribution of meaning basically intact. That is, while it moved away from the ontological understanding of universal and particular, it kept the generic basis for the distribution of meaning intact. It modified the understanding of universal and particular into that of generality and instance, class and member, and eventually into law and case, where law as repetitive regularity eventually replaced causality in explanatory power.

Although the basic distribution of meaning into a modified version of the universal and the particular remained in play, the way meaning was distributed in the natural sciences was modified. The result was to displace natural philosophy as the study that resolved motion into the principles of being *(ens mobile)* in favor of the natural sciences, which took motion itself as the basis of resolution. The unexpected result, only slowly and fitfully realized, indeed only during the past two centuries, was the recognition that there is another, more concrete mode of thought open to philosophy. For as the continuum of meaning which subordinated the particular to the general drew away more and more from traditional philosophy in order to assert its own autonomy in the form, for example, of covering laws, a new possibility for philosophy emerged, the possibility of addressing, not the empirical order of tested knowledge, but the concrete order of being. No doubt, the general turn to history in our own time also favored this recognition of a distinctive

---

44. Olaf Pedersen, *Early Physics and Astronomy* (rev. ed.; Cambridge: Cambridge University Press, 1993), 182–213, remarks that "the history of scholastic mechanics is thus not only an account of how Aristotelian theory was repeated again and again, it is also the history of a critical movement gaining more and more strength until Galileo and the physics of the Renaissance administered its deathblow" (191). And he traces in some detail the separation of motion *quo ad causam* (dynamics) from motion *quoad effectum* (kinematics), remarking that "at the beginning of the fourteenth century the emerging nominalist movement in philosophy had attempted to give the problem of motion a new basis" (193).

mode of thought, since history does not rest easy with the view that its particular figures or events are instantiations of a general law or even of a universal category.[45]

It is as though the search for the intelligibility of being has urged metaphysics on towards the singular, an exigency brought about by the history of being itself. But if most personalisms are in need of an adequate metaphysics of being, a Thomism that moves towards the concrete singular needs to think through to a modified epistemology in keeping with that metaphysics. Now, a finite being is more than an individual *(ens indivisum)* though not thereby a simple unit *(ens indivisibile)*. A concrete finite being is, as Thomas acknowledges, a composite; but we have seen that he also asserted that it is complete. It is this completeness that, it seems to me, is the real terminus and attraction for the shift towards a metaphysics that seeks the intelligibility of the concrete. It is, as we will see, an open completeness.[46]

Now, the concrete singular is not the empirical particular, and certainly not an isolated atom. Insofar as it is composite, the singular includes within its constitution all manner of relations to others. So did Leibniz's monads; but the concrete metaphysical singular differs from Leibniz's monads in two very important ways. First, it is not without "windows," that is, real relations; indeed it is constituted by its relations to others, including relations of causality and participation.[47] Second, the Leibnizian monad mirrors the whole universe uniquely by way of exemplarity as its *exemplans*, whereas the metaphysical singular participates in a manifold of causalities. Nevertheless, each being is an ingathering *(esse-in)* of the principal causal energies, principles, and transcendentals of being as such. Unlike the monad, the singular does not mirror the

---

45. This realization may have contributed to the importance given by some Thomists to the autograph terminology of St. Thomas' *In librum Boethii de Trinitate. Quaestiones Quinta et Sexta*, ed. P. Wyser (Fribourg, 1948); ed. B. Decker (Leiden, 1955). Stress is laid upon the move of St. Thomas away from the language of degrees of abstraction to recognition of a break between the natural and mathematical modes of thought, on the one hand, and, on the other, the metaphysical, which takes as its proper mode neither *abstractio totius* nor *abstraction formae* but *separatio*. See A. Maurer, *The Division and Methods of the Sciences* (Toronto: Pontifical Institute of Mediaeval Studies, 1963).

46. Lest the notion of an open completeness seem too paradoxical for St. Thomas, we may recall his understanding of the human soul as an incomplete substance. *STh* I, q. 75, a. 2, ad 1: In contrast to a complete substance (pro subsistente completo in natura alicuius speciei), "potest dici [of the human soul] quod hoc aliquid ... quasi subsistens." Also *Q. D. de Anima*, a. 1, ad 3: "anima humana non est hoc aliquid sicut substantia completiva [or completa]."

47. I have earlier ("Is Liberalism Good Enough?" in *Liberalism and the Good*, ed. Bruce Douglass et al. [London: Routledge, 1990], 86–104) used the term "constitutive individual," but that remains too much within the orbit of the traditional theory of meaning, and too close to Hegel's concrete universal which operates within that traditional theory. See chapter 13 below.

universe, except insofar as it actualizes the requirements of being. This means that the singular incorporates within itself those requirements without which no created being can be.

What are these requirements? Thomas sums them up with the words *esse et praeter esse*, existence and everything else.[48] *Praeter:* For that reason there should be no fear that the ontological ground of natural law is destroyed, since the requirement of finite being is to have a determinate nature. Nor are the principles of strict demonstration rendered ineffective, since they too are grounded in the causalities that are constitutive of the singular being. Finally, to assert that the inclination of metaphysical reflection terminates, not in the empirical, but ultimately in the singular, does not require a Scotistic intellectual intuition of the singular, but only a recognition of the singular character of being in a judgment that terminates in the actual existence of things.[49] All the principles remain in play.

We may well ask, then, what difference does this drive to the concrete singular make? First of all, metaphysics no longer hankers after a systematization of objective knowledge, even as an ideal, but rather attends to the gathering of the principles of being insofar as they terminate in the community of beings. *Ens commune* is understood principally as the community of beings and not merely as an *ens rationis*. Language is reopened to the concrete and reverses the modern penchant which places second-order language in a position of dominance over first-order language.[50] Such a metaphysics of the singular becomes more descriptive of

---

48. *SCG* II, cc. 52–54. See the remarks of Serge-Thomas Bonino, O.P., in *Revue Thomiste* 95 (1995): 495, regarding my own emphasis, to the effect that it risks rejecting the "by no means negligible" other aspects of St. Thomas' thought. It seems to me, however, that the risk must be undertaken to bring out the radically metaphysical character of his thought, especially now that the philosophical viability of the notion of creation is at stake. But an existential reading need not abandon these "by no means negligible" aspects (*praeter esse*), once the nature and status of essence is secured within its relation to existential act.

49. Maurer, *Division and Methods*, xxi: "For judgment is primarily pointed to the act of existing of things, whereas simple apprehension has to do rather with their essences or natures. As a result, the subject of metaphysics will have an existential character not found in those of the other two speculative sciences." It may help to distinguish the real as extramental (objective), which the natural sciences address, from the real as existential, which is the domain of metaphysics.

50. I have made the distinction between *epistemic* and *noetic* discourse in several essays. The former proceeds with a more or less definitive prior demand for what counts as evidence (e.g., only quantified data), for proof (e.g., verification or falsification), and for truth (e.g., what is fruitful for further experimental research), whereas the latter approaches reality with a more open yet not less rigorous expectation of meaning in search of the concrete. See "Metaphysics: Radical, Comprehensive, Determinate Discourse," *Review of Metaphysics* 39 (June 1986): 675–94. See chapter 1 above. Again, compare Marcel's distinction between primary and secondary reflection, or between problematic and metaproblematic discourse.

actual situations than abstracted from them. It recognizes contingent relations not only as accidental to a substance, but even more as historical developments within concrete beings. The principal difference is this: *esse*, since it is *formalissime* in each singular being, since it is the superabundance of act within the limits of the received nature of the singular, thereby *opens up from within each being the intelligibility of its singularity*,[51] opens to its circumstances and contingencies, in a word, to its history—properly to human history, but in an extended sense to the recognition that all created beings have a "history." *Esse*, more formal, indeed transformal, and so more actual than anything else in the being, charges the other principles with a kind of hyper-determinacy that realizes itself only in the concrete order of being, in a certain fullness or completeness.[52]

VI. FURTHER REFLECTION ON ACT AND POTENCY IN CREATURES

The charge that I have introduced a third principle forces the issue, then, of whether act and potency are adequate to provide a basic account of personal being. But before that, it raises the issue of whether these principles are universally adequate to account for created being; for if the real composition of act and potency fails to account for the constitution of created personal being, then such a composition cannot lay claim to complete universality in the order of created being. Moreover, we cannot resolve the relation of act and potency within created persons without first determining the character of that relation as it holds for all creatures. It remains, therefore, to probe the precise character of the transformation in the meaning of act and potency that occurs in the shift to the concrete, as it discloses first the general condition of the creature and then that of the created person.

A brief, if well-known and no doubt unneeded, reminder of the history of these principles illustrates the radical nature of the transformation in the understanding of act and potency brought about by the recogni-

---

51. Cf. de Finance, *Etre et agir*, 321: "Mais si la forme n'est pas l'actualité la plus profonde de l'être, la vision des essences ne peut plus combler un esprit dont l'ambition est de posséder *l'être* dans ses profondeurs. La connaissance de la réalité concrète présente pour moi un double intéret: un intérêt pratique, puisque ce monde réel forme le cadre de ma vie et l'ensemble des moyens qui me serviront á conquérir ma fin;—mais aussi, semble-t-il un intérêt spéculatif. Fondement de l'intelligibilité, se peut-il que l'existence n'ait aucune valeur intelligible? Le concret, dans une métaphysique de *l'esse* doit-il pas être la pature par excellence de l'esprit?" The passage brings out the integration of praxis and theoria in the concern for the concrete.

52. Marcel remarks ("The Ontological Mystery," 12): "Providing it is taken in its metaphysical and not its physical sense, the distinction between the *full* and the *empty* seems to me more fundamental than that between the *one* and the *many*."

tion of being *qua* created. The insight into *potency (dunamis)* had initially come about through Aristotle's reflection upon change and the principles needed to resolve the apparent impasse of the Eleatics. His distinction (already anticipated by Plato) within the unanalyzed notion of non-being between what we might call the simple privative meaning (the absolute negation, *ouk on*) and the qualified or relative negation *(mê on)* released the notion of qualified non-being to indicate a potential principle in the explanation of change:[53] for the potential is the able-but-not-yet of the subject in accidental change and analogously the able-but-not-yet of primary matter in substantial change. With his sense of creation *ex nihilo*, St. Thomas interprets the distinction by situating potency within a more radical context of being.[54]

With the entry of the doctrine of creation, however, comes a deeper sense of potentiality: for the potential is not potentiality to the reception of form *(eidos)* on the part of matter *(hyle)* or subject *(hypokeimenon)*, but the reception of being where there had been none at all *(esse absolute seu simpliciter)*.[55] In this sense, one might say, not without a touch of paradox, that the recognition of creation gives new meaning to the notion of absolute non-being without returning the notion to the dead-end *ouk on*.[56] God's creative act is so powerful that, after the fact, it throws light

---

53. *Metaphysics* XII (L), 2, 1069b15–20; also VII (Z), 7–9, 1032a12–1034b19. Cf. the many senses of potency in St. Thomas, V *Metaphysics*, lect. 13. It is characteristic of St. Thomas' project of commenting upon Aristotle that (as far as I can tell) he entirely avoids discussion of the principle of potency in relation to creation, not only in this work but in all of the Aristotelian commentaries.

54. See St. Thomas, XIII *Metaphysics*, Parma ed. (1868), lect. 2, 624: "Solvit autem hanc dubitationem antiquorum naturalium philosophorum, qui removebant generationem propter hoc, quod non credebant quod posset aliqui fieri ex non ente, quia ex nihilo fit nihil; nec etiam ex ente, quia sic esset antequam fieret. Hanc ergo dubitationem Philosophus solvit, ostendendo qualiter aliquid fit ex ente et ex non ente; dicens, quod duplex est ens, scilicet ens actu, et ens potentia." I am aware of a certain difference in emphasis between Thomas' account and my own, insofar as mine places an emphasis upon non-being that is absent from St. Thomas', though the emphasis, I believe, is compatible with his understanding of creation *ex nihilo*.

55. *STh* I, q. 44, a. 2, ad 1: "Dicendum quod Philosophus in I *Phys.* (190b1) *loquitur* de fieri particulari, quod est de forma in formam, sive accidentalem sive substantialem; nunc autem *loquimur* de rebus secundum emanationem earum ab universali principio essendi" (emphasis added).

56. For the insightful texts of St. Anselm on the new sense of "nothing," see *Monologium* 8–9 (*S. Anselmi Opera Omnia*, ed. F. S. Schmitt [Stuttgart: Frommann, 1968], vol. 1, 22–24; English translation, ed. J. Hopkins and H. W. Richardson [Toronto: Edwin Mellen, 1975], 15–18). See also my reflection upon these texts in *The Gift: Creation* (Milwaukee, WI: Marquette University Press, 1982), 28–34, esp. 32: "The term [*de nihilo*] denotes *after the fact* the state of affairs before the endowment. It makes no strict sense to say, before I have received a gift, that I am giftless, as though there is a lack in me in the way that a painting lacks the right colour.... Certainly, before I have received a gift, I am without a gift; I simply do not have one. But I do not lack something due me. And yet, viewed after the fact, after the endowment, the lack of that endowment is more than a simple nega-

even upon absolute non-being, and endows the very contingency of the creature (its always present non-being that constitutes its contingency) with the abundance of the Creator's own gift. And it draws our attention to the fragility and utter gratuity of any and all created existence, so that in a mysterious way we draw fresh meaning from the contrast of being with that dark region of absolute non-being. It is as though the very gift of being does not leave the creature's non-being untouched; its very non-being is gifted too.

This is not to give some pseudo-positive reality to non-being; quite the opposite, it is to highlight its utter negativity by deepening the sense of contingency. The early Fathers of the Church were conscious of the distinctive character of God's creative act. They insisted that creation *ex nihilo* is not a motion, neither an alteration nor a generation, because these require a pre-existent subject. Even more, they insisted that creation is not a labor at all,[57] and that it is an effortless actuation at the most fundamental level of reality: divine "communication without loss."

What, then, has happened to potency? We must look to act, in keeping with its primacy, in order to determine the character of the indeterminacy and otherness that is characteristic of potency. For the Aristotelian understanding of potency posits a pre-existent recipient (ultimately, underived matter) whereas potency to being simultaneously demands that there can be no recipient before the reception itself has been achieved.[58] And so creation *ex nihilo* is to be understood as the endowment of the capacity to receive being in the very communication in which that actuality is being received. Nature, or properly the essence *(essentia)*, functions

---

tion.... We have more here than a simple negation, but we have it only after the fact, not before. The gift is not as such a remedy for some lack, but is rather an unexpected surplus that comes without prior conditions set by the recipient. The element of gratuity indicates that there is no ground in the recipient for this gift, so that the gift is strictly uncalled for. It is not compensation for anything.... Creation is to be understood as the reception of a good not due in any way, so that there cannot be even a [pre-existent] subject of that reception. It is absolute reception, there is not something which receives, but rather sheer receiving." Incidentally, this new sense of non-being is also the condition for the modern sense of dialectics; though, because it repudiates a notion of creation, dialectics gives too much to the power of the negative within non-being.

57. Cf. St. Athanasius, *Contra Arianos* 2, c. 17, n. 1 (Oxford, 1844), 315f., (*Patrologiae graeca* [hereafter *PG*] 26:197), writes, "For God is not wearied by commanding... but he willed only; and all things subsisted." Also Hyppolytus, *Against Noetus*, c. 10 (*PG* 10:818), insists that "the divine will in moving all things is itself without motion." Then, too, St. John Damascene, *On the Orthodox Faith* 2, c. 29 (*PG* 94:964) remarks, "He wills all things to come to be and they are made." Cf. Judith 16:17: "You spoke and things came into being."

58. Without in any way suggesting that Marcel thinks in terms of act and potency, it is perhaps worth noticing his remark that I must already be and be within being before I can question being. That is the basic feature of ontological mystery, that it encroaches upon its own data; "The Ontological Mystery," 19–20 and passim.

as the potential principle that marks the finitude (receptive dependency, radical contingency) of created being and ensures its limited integrity (*per essentiam/naturam*). A creature, then, is nothing but the relation of dependence upon the proper cause of its being: *tantum esse ad Deum*. But that "nothing but" is everything for the creature!

VII. THE CREATURE AS SUBSISTING RELATION

It is in this sense that I dare to say that a creature is a subsisting relation, knowing full well the privileged use of the term for the persons of the Trinity.[59] The inequality and limitation inherent in the relation of dependence is such as to ensure the distinction between God and creatures. The advantage of the term is that it removes all suggestion of *absolute* autonomy from the creature at the originating level of its being. The foregoing reflection on the creature as subsisting (yet dependent) relation is meant to remove all traces of potency as in any way a *prius* to God's creative act. For His is the act which, with the touch of eternity, endows the being of the creature simultaneously with essence and existence.

Once again, as with the turn to the concrete singular and its historicity, it is noteworthy that this emphasis upon the primacy of relation parallels the emphasis on relationality which has become a basic theme—one might well say, a preoccupation—of twentieth-century thought. Not surprisingly, the shift to relationality in contemporary thought arises from different considerations and has taken forms other than the metaphysical relation of creation. Thus, for example, in first philosophy there is Hei-

---

59. I recognize that this term is privileged by St. Thomas for the divine persons of the Trinity and that it is one of his keenest and most fruitful insights (*STh* I, q. 29, a. 4: "Persona igitur divina significat relationem ut subsistentem"). I also recognize that in his argument he refers the designation *human person* to the individual substance and with the impeccable logic of genus and specific difference excludes subsistent relation from the term *person* when applied to man. It is only the identity of the relations with the divine essence itself that permits him to conclude that the divine persons are subsistent relations, or more precisely, distinct relations subsisting in the divine essence. Of course, the term *relation* in the two denominations is analogously diverse. Moreover, there are sufficient ways of avoiding confusion with created beings. Ian Ramsey (*Religious Language* [New York: Macmillan, 1957], 182ff.) has indicated the linguistic ways in which such a distinction is made: the divine person of Christ is Son of the Father, but He is *begotten not made, only* Son of the Father, *eternally* begotten, *one in being* with the Father, etc. These are "qualifiers" of the original model (father-son). The Father and the Spirit can be differentiated from creatures in similar ways through relations of origin. Or we can phrase the difference expressed by many of the Fathers of the Church in terms of Christ's being equal to the Father in essence and His Son by nature *(kata physin)*, whereas we are sons by the grace of adoption *(kata charin)* (cf. St. Athanasius, *De Decretis*, in *The Nicene and Post-Nicene Fathers*, 2d ser., vol. 4 [repr.; Grand Rapids, MI: Eerdmans, 1987], 156). The value of the term *subsistent relation* as applied to creatures is that it manifests the radical dependence for all that is in them through participation in the *communicatio entis* flowing from the First Being.

degger's *In-der-Welt-Sein;* in philosophy of science, Ernst Cassirer's notice of the withering away of substance in favor of function and law; in philosophy of religion, Buber's relation of I-Thou and I-It; and most recently, in the philosophy of language, the postmodern stress on intertextuality.

In much of the thought of the past two centuries, however, otherness has been understood in terms of conflict (dialectics) or equivocity (deconstruction). It is as though nominalism has turned twice upon itself: first in modernity which, having given the primacy to self-identity in the form of self-reference, yet re-established unity as totality through a comprehensive system of external relations among utterly simple self-identical units.[60] Then, the first post-Kantian attempts to overcome the restrictive self-reference understood otherness in terms of conflict (dialectics), whereas the full-blown rejection of self-reference and totality has given primacy to otherness in the form of a modified equivocity (deconstruction). In rejecting the modern fascination with totality, postmodernism seeks to prolong nominalism by reinstating the reign—not so much of the other, and certainly not of the Other—but, of otherness in the form of relations of contrast. It seems that nominalism eats its own children. It will undoubtedly produce further variations, but what seems likely is that it will turn all relations into features that are arbitrary and quasi-external.[61]

Not unaffected by the widespread promotion of relationality, Thomists of the concrete have followed their own path, drawing however upon the thought of St. Thomas. All Thomists agree that the creature exists in total dependence upon the Giver of being, and that dependence is to be understood in terms of the category of primary cause and effect. This is to look at the ontological relation from the point of view of the communication of being. What is it to look at it from the point of view of the reception of being? Since the dependence is total, everything in the creature is *gifted*, so that even act itself is included in that reception; *created esse* is itself receptive.[62] The meaning of all the causes and principles within the being are thereby transformed.

What, then, is the inner content of that relation? Certainly the po-

---

60. Newton's *Principles of Natural Philosophy* gives us the paradigm, but Kant's architectonic system provides its philosophical justification by moving towards an incomplete internalization of relations determined by the "needs of reason."

61. The root of much linguistic theory is, of course, de Saussure, who sought a theory of language in which meaning played a minimal part, if at all, and who found in language "only [arbitrary] differences" (*Course in General Linguistics* [La Salle, IL: Open Court, 1986], 118; cf. 67–69, 115).

62. See the exchange between David Schindler and Norris Clarke regarding Clarke's Aquinas lecture, *Person and Being,* and in particular Schindler's insistence upon a three-fold moment within the relation of creation: *esse-ab, esse-in,* and *esse-ad,* in which the latter two have as their *prius* the first, so that the *esse* of the creature is through and through receptive (Schindler, "Norris Clarke on Person, Being and St. Thomas," 586–88).

tentiality of the creature (*essentia* in the broad sense)[63] is included within that ontological relation, and it plays its role as a co-principle of "ontological reception"; essence is the principle within the created being that is the intrinsic "receptor" of being.[64] But it is not only potency that is received; the act is received as well, because the whole being (essence and existence) is received. God creates beings whole and entire, singular beings in community. He does not put together principles of act and potency that are antecedent in any sense. The ontological relation determines the act at its very core as a *received* act. We must, then, include created act within the notion of ontological reception.[65] Created act is a received act. Moreover, everything in the created being is penetrated by this receptive relation. Since act determines everything within the being, it follows that the meaning of all the causes and principles of the being reflect this reception.

It is not only the agency of the creature (its secondary activity) that is affected by its participation. All the causes are affected. Matter is not uncaused nor out of itself but is *ex nihilo*;[66] finality, as the first of causes, is no longer understood as only an immanent principle specifying the end, but is also simultaneously that immanent/transcendent principle by which the being is called forth into existence;[67] and form participates in *esse* as the first formal perfection of finite[68] substantial being. When the seventeenth-century philosophers threw out the four causes, they

63. What, as we have seen, in a felicitous phrase St. Thomas calls *praeter esse*. SCG 2, c. 52: "Esse autem, inquantum est esse, non potest esse diversum: potest autem diversificari per aliquid quod est praeter esse."

64. At first glance, the terms *receptus* and *receptio* are not very suitable, for they mean the "re-taking" of something, "taking again." But the "re-" also functions as a reflexive intensifier, and there are usages in which the term means "taking upon oneself" (cf. *ens per se*) and even "taking up an obligation" (cf. Marcel's "answering a call"). This is surely the basis for the "re-sponse" to which all created beings, and in a special way, personal beings are called. The term can also mean "to accept" and "to preserve," and these latter senses are more suitable in the present context.

65. David Schindler puts the question well in pressing Norris Clarke's fine analysis further: "How can relationality... be said to be ... 'an equally primordial dimension of being' ... if relationality begins not in first but in second act," that is, not in *esse* but in *agere* (Schindler, "Norris Clarke on Person, Being and St. Thomas," 582). Clarke replies that the *agere* is an expression of *esse*, thus seeming to endorse a Thomistic version of the Dionysian principle that *esse* is expansive, as though to say: *esse est diffusivum sui* (ibid., 593). I find the invocation of the expansive principle an interesting opening to further reflection, but at the same time I agree with Schindler that we must press home the *received* character of created act in the most explicit and intensive manner, finding its receptive character not simply in the expression of the creature's activity or its tendency towards expression but in the very character of the instituting act itself.

66. *STh* I, q. 44, a. 2: "Utrum materia prima sit creata a deo."

67. See the analysis of finality by Gerard Smith, S.J., *The Philosophy of Being* (New York: Macmillan, 1961), ch. 8, esp. 109, which brings out the double determinant in final causality, its formal and its existential role. The whole book considers the transformed meanings of act, potency, and the causes in the light of existential act.

68. See Hegel's acute discussion of the difference between the mere limit (*die Grenze*,

not only cast aside Aristotle, they also disavowed the transformed senses of these principles and thereby began the elimination of intelligibility from the very notion of creation, which ceased to play a role in the modern understanding of reality.

So far, then, through its total dependence upon God, we have understood the creature as a subsisting relation. The creature is an effect of God's communication of being and stands in causal dependence upon God as upon the Cause of its being. The absolute nature of ontological dependence entitles us to use the category of gift to articulate the implications of the relation, since it belongs to a gift to be uncalled for, to be given without prior conditions. Now reception is integral to the very character of a gift, for a gift refused is an unfinished gift. At this absolute level of the reception of being the refusal can only occur within the primordial reception, even as the non-being of privation can arise only on the supposit of finite being. And just as non-being threatens the destruction of being, so too the refusal can penetrate to the depths of a received being, distorting it in the most radical way.[69] On the other hand, the acceptance completes the gift, fulfills it. This creaturely acceptance takes the form of ontological self-affirmation *(ens per se subsistens)*.[70] And, since it is first act that is being received, it is received *as act* at a level deeper and more original than secondary activity which is grounded in and expressive of first act. It follows, then, that both first act and secondary activity are re-sponses.

At the level of first act, however paradoxical it sounds, the creature accepts its being in the very reception of it *(esse-ab)*. How are we to understand this, since the creature does not stand outside the relation so as to receive being before it even exists? We must understand the acceptance as expressed by its subsistent self-reference *(autos, per se)* and within its primordial ordination towards the Source of the being communicated to it without which there would be no self *(autos)*, so that its original reception is communicated to it in its very institution. This relation to self and Source is the tension—one might say, paradox—of finite being.

Aristotle) and the positive finite (*das Endliche,* Christianity) in *The Science of Logic,* book 1, sect. 1, ch. 2, B.

69. Cf. Gabriel Marcel, *Du refus à l'invocation* (Paris: Editions Gallimard, 1940). And so, at the personal level, there can be loss through generosity refused, or through abuse of freedom (moral evil), but this spiritual loss does not of itself entail physical mutation. Cf. St. Thomas' *"absque ... abiiciatur"* (above, n. 9). At the subpersonal level the "refusal" is manifest in the privations endemic to the rule of finitude (ontological evil), which God freely respects for the good of the finite.

70. Cf. Schindler's *esse-in* ("Norris Clarke on Person, Being and St. Thomas," 582–86). I find this acceptance recognized in the popular and subsequently the learned sense of *ousia* and *substantia* which take the form of an ontological self-reference *(autos).* See my "Selves and Persons," *Communio* 18, no. 2 (1991), esp. 184–96.

Metaphorically, the flow from God *(influxus entis, esse-ab)* is such that it is completed only in a flow back towards the source *(reditus entis, esse-ad)*. This means that the created "self" of each being is preserved only through reference to the Creative Other. This communication and response is the initial generosity, the initial deposit of being, that is inseparable from the creative endowment and that weights created being towards the actual good (i.e., the good of its own being and the Good that is its Source). And this is the meaning of final causality in the ontological relation, that is, insofar as final causality bears first of all on created being and only then on its agency. For there is more than passivity in reception; there is also self-possession and ordination to the good. *Esse* as the supposit of secondary activity already possesses the integral mode of potency and act in the form of an integral ordination towards *(esse-ad)*.

The notion of an integral mode of act and potency is not entirely alien to Thomistic metaphysics. If one considers the elusive concept of active potency,[71] we recognize here a principle that is not simply that of passive potency. Created active potency needs initiation in order to be actuated and in that aspect may be said to be passive, but the power itself *(potentia activa)* is not simply a mutable subject, a capacity awaiting in-formation; it is a *capability*, the ability to respond to the initiative that first institutes it. The notion of active potency is usually considered at the level of secondary activity, insofar as it is the potency of specific powers; but if it is deepened to mean the re-sponse to the primary institution of created being, its primordial reception, such active potency is enfolded within the integral mode of non-privative receptivity.

Now, this endowment and reception of being is constitutive of the created being and cannot, therefore, be understood as an external relation. It is the very inner constitution of the being itself. It is imperative, therefore, to release interiority from its modern prison in human subjectivity and to restore to natural things *(res)* the appropriate kind of interiority which they have in a metaphysics of being, where they are not mere objects standing before the human subject. For the principles that constitute a created being comprise the complex depth appropriate to the things we have not made. Indeed, they lead us back to the Source of being, so that the depth in created things is without measure. It is not only human subjectivity that has an interior, then; things do too.[72] Once

---

71. Cf. the many senses of the term *potency (dunamis)* considered by Aristotle, *Metaphysics* 1019a15ff. The privileged sense is the active, in keeping with the primacy of act over passivity. Nevertheless, the distinction is between *poiein* and *paschein* within the analysis of change and not within that of creation. Compare St. Thomas on the many senses of potency in note 53.

72. On natural interiority, see Schmitz, "The First Principle of Personal Becoming," *Review of Metaphysics* 47 (June 1994): esp. 763–68. See chapter 11 below.

that interiority is recognized, things receive the name of "subject" *(suppositum entis)*, the privileged name we give to primary centers. And this ontological interiority lends its character to all interior relations, including the spiritual interiority encountered in personal beings.

If, however, the very subsistence of a creature is relational, then the understanding of the reality of created substance is thereby transformed. For substance is now understood to rest ultimately not on uncreated matter, nor does it have the ambiguous status of an *ens possibile*. Instead, substance is determined in and through its radical participation in and relation to the Source of its existence. The supposit of the creature does not stand in any way "outside" of or "prior" to the ontological relation, not even as a possibility, but is brought into being within that relation. "Before" the world came to be it was not "possible" for it to be *(potentia passiva)*, except in the actual power *(potentia activa)* of God.

The primacy of the ontological relation may seem to threaten the reality of substance by undercutting it. That would be so only if the notion of created substance were thought somehow to retain a sort of quasi-independence apart from the ontological relation. Nonetheless, given the proven effectiveness of the logic of substantive predication and its prominent use by St. Thomas the concern is legitimate and more needs to be said in order to offset the charge that substance itself is being dissolved in this radical relation. Such a defense is especially important today, if only because the metaphysical sense of substance is not readily understood or tolerated in the contemporary thought-world.

A full defense of the pre-eminence of relation needs to show that the integrity of created substance is not dissolved in the relation.[73] This requires an adequate notion of spirit which brings forward the intransitive character of spiritual relations. Creation is the effect of Perfect Intelligence, but it is not a motion. The relations of intelligence and love, with their spiritual nature, are the specific ways in which God communicates being to his creatures. The traditional first way names him the First Mover, but it adds, Unmoved, meaning that He "moves" without moving. Now, even human intelligence can enter into relation with its objects without mutating them; so too human love. Indeed the search for truth demands that the knower respect the integrity of the known, even when (as in experiments) the search for knowledge calls for the manipulation of the knowable. But if even the incarnate human spirit can enter into such relations imperfectly, how much more can the divine intelligence and love communicate, institute, and preserve the integrity and actual existence of its creatures?

---

73. I have indicated the basic outlines of the argument in *The Gift: Creation*, 81–86.

Indeed, *at the level of creative causality and existential effect* there is no mutation: creation is not a motion. And so the "law" of creative causality may be stated thus: the non-invasive yet creative activity of (divine) spirit brings about its correlate in the non-privative receptivity of the creature.[74] Created spirit communicates without loss just because it is known (and with God this "knowing" is a creative knowing) without the creature being mutated, and is loved by a (divine) love which respects the beloved (which the Creator's free act brings into being). Spiritual relations are not transitive; the knowledge and love that sustains creatures, far from being a threat to their existence and integrity, is the very ground of their being, nature, and substance.

The ontological relation as understood in creation not only rejects the primacy of external relations; it also introduces a new sense of internality that transcends the spatially restricted set of "inside-outside." In the order of constitution or creation there is nothing "outside" such a primordial relation, for the simple reason that there is literally nothing outside being. What there is is finitude, formal difference among purely spiritual creatures and formal and spatio-temporal diversity among physical beings. The immanence of the principles provides the basis for understanding relations of interiority. And, just as the transcendental ontological relation comes to prominence, so too there comes to prominence the interior character of all fundamental relations, both in the Creator and in the creature.

How are we to understand an interiority that is not merely an internality correlative with an externality (inside-outside)? What we are dealing with is the notion of incomplete principles,[75] not simply correlative or reciprocal, but radically open to each other in the constitution of a *single* entity. They do not achieve this unity by themselves. If God's creative act is left out of the picture, it is impossible to explain how a non-existent and merely possible essence can determine the creature's act of existence. Once the co-determination of principles is situated within God's creative activity, however, these two incomplete principles play the role assigned to them by their Agent-Creator. Each principle taken in itself is incomplete; but even more, taken together they constitute a being that is no being except in relation to its primordial cause. Each principle is inherently implicated in the other through the causal activity of the First Cause, and by a subordination of the one (potency) to the other (act) rather than by a reciprocity of two complete principles.

74. In physical creatures this receptivity is the mark of the presence of the Creator within them. In created persons the receptivity is the mark of their spiritual nature and the image of the creative presence within them.

75. See n. 46.

VIII. TRANSFORMATION OF THE PRINCIPLES IN CREATED PERSONS

Nonetheless, the reception that is common to all creatures must be refined further, if it is to fit the analogical modes of being, and if it is to be of use in determining the proper character of spiritual being. For while there is a general sense of receptivity appropriate to all creatures, there is a special sense, a proper sense, in which human beings as spiritual creatures are receptive. What marks a created spirit from other created beings is that it has been endowed with an ability to respond in accordance with the "law" of spirit, that is, the capacity for freedom. It is here that the integral concept of non-privative receptivity seems especially appropriate, for it illuminates the distinctive relation between God and spiritual creatures. The human creature receives along with its very capacity to exist *(essentia)* the capability of responding *(actus essendi)* in a way that, insofar as it is spiritual, does not involve mutation or loss.[76] The evidence for this is just the normal operations of association proper to human beings: love and knowledge, understanding and communication, which rise from the creature's primordial receptivity.

In the creation of a human person, the otherness *(praeter esse)* is proportionate to the act that is communicated; and being proportionate it follows along lines of (incarnate) spiritual being, in which there is communication without loss and non-privative receptivity. At the level of personal being this is more adequately expressed by receptivity than by pure passive potency. In personal beings, the receptivity takes the form of a specific response. The response is in no way a *causa sui*, it is a *re-sponse;* that is, it is the primordial acknowledgment of a gift received and is expressed in the "acceptance" (i.e., the subsistence and ordination) of the creature. At the level of secondary activity this receptivity is expressed in a variety of individual and cultural ways as a seeking out of the Giver, in the search for the true and the good in the community of beings.

The consequence of such an intrinsic relation is a higher degree of unity of the constitutive principles than in sub-personal beings. Here lies the ontological ground for the proper immanence of spiritual being, whereby the unity of personal being is a conscious, deliberate integrity. From this ground there follows at the level of activity the non-privative nature of personal dynamism, first manifested in communication without

---

76. I add the qualifier "insofar as it is spiritual" in order to acknowledge the incarnate nature of human spirituality, which is itself a sort of integral mode of being, so that human spirituality operates within the larger context in which there is physical mutation. The physical order is given over to mutation. In created persons, on the other hand, the creature itself is properly endowed with non-privative receptivity and response in accordance with the "law" of spiritual existence.

loss. The absence of loss is coordinate with the power of retrieval. This is seen in the distinctive relation to temporality that is characteristic of personal being. Memory, and even more the *memoria* of which St. Augustine wrote, is the retrieval of past time, even as anticipation perfected in hope is the appropriation of the structure of future time. The indefinite scope of the time-scale at the root of human culture and human history is made possible by the capability of cognition, which liberates the universal in abstract form but within the horizon of being.

And so, there is a special sense in which the created person responds, for he responds in his very being through intelligence and freedom, and this response is constituted of an appropriate and proportionate act and potency, both in the constitution of its being and the overflow of its activity.[77]

Here we approach once again one of the prominent themes of Marcel's philosophy of the concrete, that the fortunes of being depend in some significant way upon the use we make of our freedom. Marcel's distance from Thomism seems to have arisen from a view that it was too "objective" a mode of thinking to be sensitive to the most profound truths and realities of human existence. Moreover, his opposition was heightened by the modern dichotomy between passivity and activity, which he attributed to Kant, and which he thought approximated most closely to inanimate objects, as when the wax is utterly passive to receiving the imprint of the wholly active seal. He countered the reduction of receptivity to passivity by invoking the experience of the host who welcomes (i.e., receives) a guest into his home. This reception is no mere metaphor, nor is it mere passivity;[78] it is a genuine receptivity that transcends the gulf between activity and passivity without destroying their real distinction. It does this by including them within what I have called an integral mode of being. The sense of receptivity has deeper ontological roots than either created act or potency considered in themselves. These roots are opened up to the light of a metaphysics of the concrete, a light that situates the human person and all created beings within the community as gift.

---

77. It is this recognition that is so prominent among many German Catholic philosophers, who make of freedom a primary ontological principle.

78. Reflecting upon the nature of feeling (*sentir*), Marcel remarks that it is not only a passive submitting to sensory impulses (sensation), but also an active opening out onto . . . (*s'ouvrir a . . .*). This is precisely the transition from the empirical to the concrete. Cf. Marcel, *Du refus à l'invocation*, 43: "Dès le moment ou nous avons clairement reconnu que sentir ne se réduit pas à subir, tout en maintentant que c'est en quelque façon recevoir, nous sommes en mesure de déceler en son centre la présence d'un élément actif, quelque chose comme le pouvoir d'assumer, ou mieux encore, de s'ouvrir à . . ." Now one "opens out onto" what is able to receive one, and that cannot be an object in the modern sense, for the objectivity of the object reflects back to the knowing subject the criteria already brought to it by the subject. (See the canonical expression of this view in Kant, *Critique of Pure Reason*, second preface, vii–xii.)

Chapter 8

THE SOLIDARITY OF PERSONALISM AND THE METAPHYSICS OF EXISTENTIAL ACT

There have been human persons since Adam delved and Eve span. And the word *persona, prosopon*—thickened and deepened by the revelation of the God-man Jesus Christ—has been with us since the great Councils of the Church. Is it not surprising, then, that we have had to wait until the twentieth century to hear of philosophies that bear the name "personalism"? Emmanuel Mounier suggests that the neo-Kantian idealist Charles-Bernard Renouvier first used the term to describe his own philosophy in 1903,[1] before it was rescued from idealism for Catholic thinkers by Max Scheler.[2] No doubt, the thing, the reality—the person and the name—played an important part in the thought of earlier thinkers: referring to the Godhead, Tertullian wrote of *una essentia, tres personae;* turning to man, St. Augustine sang of the restless spirit; Boethius drew from the reality a classical definition; Richard of St. Victor stressed the existential spirituality of the person; Thomas Aquinas saw in the person the most perfect reality in all of creation; Pascal celebrated its ambiguity; and more recently, Kierkegaard proposed the drama of religious existence. On the philosophical plane, Immanuel Kant insisted that the person was to be treated as an end of all moral action.

Reprinted from *Fides Quaerens Intellectum* 1, no. 1 (Summer 2001): 183–99. Copyright © 2001 by *Fides Quaerens Intellectum*.

1. *Le personnalisme*, 1950; English translation by Philip Mairet, *Personalism* (Notre Dame, IN: Notre Dame University Press, 1952), xv, also xxvi.

2. Inasmuch as Kant meant by "person" a fully autonomous self-reflective reason, his use posed difficulties for a Catholic philosopher, so that its use was generally avoided until Scheler rescued the term from such radical immanent individualism with his phenomenology of the realism of values. For this reason, Scheler can be counted among the "fathers of the so-called theological and Christian personalism." Heinrich M. Schmidinger, "Max Scheler (1874–1928) und sein Einfluss auf das katholische Denken," in *Christliche Philosophie*, vol. 3, ed. E. Coreth et al. (Graz/Vienna: Styria, 1990), 89–111, in particular 103–105.

Yet, on the other hand, one may read the development of modern philosophy in the past four centuries as a series of attempts to redefine man in terms other than person: as the *adunatio* of mind and body (Descartes), the vessel of impressions and dynamo of passions (Hume), a material machine (de la Mettrie), pure and practical reason (Kant), the speculative determination of Absolute Spirit (Schelling, Hegel), transcendental subjectivity (Husserl), *Dasein* as Being-in-the World (Heidegger)—until more than one postmodernist (Derrida, Foucault) has put a stop to all such attempts at defining the human reality. For all that, during the preceding centuries, conditions arose which disposed a wide and varied group of thinkers to tread a path that has led in this past century to the person as a focus for philosophical reflection. These preconditions are operative in the constitution of the thought of personalist philosophers.

It is readily agreed that the variety of personalisms does not admit of any easy unification or categorization, but rather, precludes their being gathered together into anything resembling a school or even a well-defined movement; it is enough to call it a "turn."[3] Nevertheless, they share more than a name, so that it is fruitful to look briefly at some of the more important features that are constitutive of this "turn." Now, in such a perilous undertaking as that of speaking of shared dispositions among such a varied group of thinkers, one may still discern mutual features and themes, while respecting the different ways in which they are conceived and expressed. An old usage was wont to call the profusion of birds in song a "charm," and the word serves well to recall the resonant diversity of present-day personalisms.[4]

---

3. I borrow the term from Richard Rorty who used it to express the "linguistic turn" that defied any easy uniform description of ordinary language philosophers.

4. Mounier briefly mentions philosophers who have contributed to the emergence of personalism (*Personalism*, xv–xxviii). Among those he names: Lotze, Scheler, Buber, Berdyaev, Bergson, Laberthonniére, Blondel, Peguy (who greatly influenced Mounier), Maritain, Marcel, and Jaspers. As he conceives it, such thought has remote affinities with Pascal, Leibniz, Kant, Rousseau. He also acknowledges the role that Nietzsche and Marx have played in his own personalist development, and distinguishing "an existentialist tangent of personalism (comprising Berdyaev, Landsberg, Ricoeur, Nédoncelle), a Marxian tangent often concurrent with this one, and another tangent, more classical in the French philosophic tradition (Lachièse-Rey, Nabert, LaSenne, Madinier, H. J. Lacroix)." In the United States he mentions Royce, Flewelling, and Brightman, and in Great Britain, Macmurray among others (xxvii–xxviii). While the movement has been especially strong in France, it has shown itself vital in other European countries as well: In Germany, one would have to mention Peter Wust, Ferdinand Ebener, Dietrich von Hildebrand, Romano Guardini, and Theodor Haecker. In Italy personalism developed in relation to neo-idealism with Armando Carlini, and to existentialism with Luigi Stefanini in the context of the history of philosophy; mention would have to be made of Augusto Guzzo, Felice Battaglia, Renato Lazzarini, Giuseppe Bozzetti, and Michele Federico Sciacca, and more recently of Luigi Pareyson, Armando Rigobello, and Carlo Arata. (See Osvaldo Rossi, "Der christliche Per-

From this rich texture of thought, I should like to draw upon aspects that are of signal importance in understanding, not only human reality, but *all* reality; in effect to realize the universal aim of philosophy that a traditional metaphysics accomplished in a more abstract conceptual manner, but which one might call the aspiration for wisdom as distinct from science.[5]

Such an ambitious aim draws us into the question of the relation of this philosophical turn to the rest of philosophy,[6] and to ask about the contribution of personalism to philosophical thought more broadly considered. Nevertheless, nothing short of a full-blown history of this turn, written with philosophical insight, could do justice to the rich analogous plurality. To simplify such an undertaking, and because of my own indebtedness to his thought, I will more modestly reflect upon certain themes in Gabriel Marcel within this broader scope, leaving others to deal with the issue in terms of other personalists, should they wish.

The question I should like to introduce is the question of what precisely the personalist turn contributes to philosophical understanding. For some time now I have held the view that, given the lingering positivist climate hostile to metaphysics, the personalism of a thinker such as Gabriel Marcel has played the part of a sort of "holding operation" for the values formerly associated with a traditional metaphysics of being and resonant with the Christian faith: hence, a Christian personalism.[7] I still hold that view. One need think only of Marcel's meditation on being and truth, and his reflections on the appropriate response to transcendent ontological values in hope, fidelity, and metatechnical reflection. But I have lately come to see that such a personalist philosophy surpasses its role as keeper of the treasury of traditional values, and that it realizes an *advance* in the progressive unfolding of being—mark this well: an advance, not only in our *understanding* of being, but a forwarding of the unfolding of *being itself* in its history.

---

sonalismus," *Christliche Philosophie*, vol. 3, ed. E. Coreth et al. [Graz/Vienna: Verlag Styria, 1990], 550–63). In Poland see S. Kowalczyk, "Personnalisme polonais contemporain," *Divus Thomas* 88 (1985): 1–3, 58–76. Nevertheless, the foregoing scarcely does justice to the various philosophies that can be termed "personalist" in other countries, languages, and cultures, but it may indicate its breadth.

5. See Gabriel Marcel's reflections on the personal meaning of truth in *The Mystery of Being*, vol. 1, *Reflection and Mystery*, trans. G. S. Fraser (Chicago: Henry Regnery, 1960).

6. Marcel addresses the question of universality in philosophy in the context of the personal quest for truth, shaping the appropriate form of universality after the exemplar of great art which, in its singular excellence, nonetheless exhibits a truth that holds for all those prepared to acknowledge it. Nowhere does Marcel's early study of Schelling manifest itself more than in this effort to articulate a form of meaning that is not narrowly rational, abstract, and conceptual.

7. See, for example, his closing remarks to the essay "On the Ontological Mystery," in the English edition entitled (somewhat inappropriately) *The Philosophy of Existentialism* (New York: Citadel Press, 1966), 45–46.

And so, I have come to the conclusion that the philosophy of the person and the history of the person—the former a development in thought, the latter a development in actuality—disclose something about all being, and thereby attain a genuine universality, indispensable for any thought that merits the name "philosophy," albeit in a form other than that of traditional metaphysics. There is more here, too, than a difference in method or approach, the one proceeding from conceptual principles, the other by way of phenomenological description. For that difference in approach arises out of and moves towards a different grasp of the actual condition of philosophical thought. Given the resistance of a thinker such as Marcel to any mere restatement of traditional metaphysics,[8] and more generally, acknowledging a distinctive atmosphere shared by personalists—this advance is expressed in personalism, not as a return to a metaphysics of beings in the traditional fashion, but as an ontology of being in the contemporary fashion: I mean, as an understanding of being that has passed through the twin fires of modern idealism and twentieth-century positivism. That is why a phenomenological personalism, such as Marcel's, does not speak of a metaphysics of beings but rather of an ontology of Being.

If the preceding reflection is at all justified, it remains to ask whether one might consolidate the pre-modern, pre-objective understanding of being with the post-idealist and post-positivist understanding of modern times; and further, to ask what mutual transformation might be required by such an undertaking. This may require passing from the more obvious features to their deeper significance, much as waves wash surface patterns upon a shore, each brought there by a deeper current. If the consolidation is to prosper, neither traditional metaphysics of existential act nor the ontology of personalism can be expected to surrender what is central to them.

On the one hand, the consolidation will not require of traditional metaphysics an alteration in the very sources *(archai, principia)* of being as articulated in a metaphysics of existential act. Nevertheless, the consolidation will manifest in concrete fashion a radical development in our understanding of the modern modalities of being, such as: a detailed sense of the contingency of the world of nature, a contingency that in modern science has called for a recognition of nature's historicity and development and the consequent need to have recourse to experiment in probing its inner secrets; secondly, what can almost be described as a transformation in the very nature of the power and control available to human action; then, too, a heightened sense of the particu-

---

8. See his amusing account in the biographical essay in *The Philosophy of Gabriel Marcel*, Library of Living Philosophers, vol. 17, ed. Paul Schilpp and Lewis Hahn (La Salle, IL: Open Court Press), 29–31.

larity of individual experience and the expanded range of options for free activity; and by no means least, an expanded *finesse* of the creative imagination in the arts of the novel, music, and painting. On the darker side, there is the unprecedented accumulation and exercise of destructive power. On the side of personalism, the consolidation calls for situating the person among things in the community of beings (understood as *res*)—things which, along with the person, participate each in its own way in the dignity that is proper to all and every being in the exercise of their actuality.

An obvious theme in the personalism of Marcel and others is the nature and use of power.[9] What first strikes one among these thinkers is a certain discretion in the face of modern technology. I say a discretion or circumspection, not an unqualified disapproval or opposition in the manner of the Luddites. More precisely, there is a critical assessment of the ways in which modern technology has expanded into spheres in which it is not competent; to create what Marcel has called a change in the "weather" of modern man.[10] We see this every day. The effects of an indiscriminate use of power come under scrutiny inasmuch as they contribute to the depersonalization of human life, and more generally to the impoverishment of being; for if being itself—in its supreme Exemplar *(Ipsum esse subsistens)*—does not suffer diminution, created being can and does.

What is at stake in these actual conditions is nothing less than the gain or loss of being. Recall Marcel's critique: through the irresponsible exercise of power, human agency is reduced to technical function with the resultant uniformity and deadening conformity of much of contemporary social existence. This brings about a radical modification in a specific modality of being (technology) that encapsulates the *bonum honestum* of personal existence. Instead of a community in which personal integrity respects what is unique about each person, there results a collectivity driven by general, impersonal forces.[11] Access to personal interiority and intimacy is obstructed, not only in relation to others but to oneself as well, whose unique reality is dissolved into membership in

---

9. For example, including Mounier and Maritain, but also those whom we would not call "personalists," such as Ortega y Gasset and Unamuno, as well as Heidegger and Jean-Francois Lyotard.

10. Or, as he puts it in *Man against Mass Society* (Chicago: Henry Regnery, 1951), 27ff., it is difficult for us to register the meteorological change that distances us from pretechnological man.

11. See also the critique by Maritain at the close of *The Person and the Common Good* (Notre Dame, IN: University of Notre Dame Press, 1966), 90–105; and by Karol Wojtyla, *The Acting Person* (Dordrecht: Reidel, 1979), chap. 7; as well as Wojtyla's essay on the person and subjectivity in *Person and Community*, ed. T. Sandok, OSM (New York: Peter Lang, 1993), 219–58.

the collective—whether according to the deliberate manner of a communist or fascist ideology or in the unreflecting manner of mass democracy in disarray.

It should be noted, here, that such a personalism is not to be confused with liberal individualism, but is as much opposed to individualism as it is to collectivism. What it seeks is the realization of a mutually fulfilling participation of person and community. The accepted and prevailing conflict between individual and collective is the result of a false logic of culture promoted by forces antithetical to the person.

Now, this criticism of an indiscriminately expansive technology is not directed at technology as such, but probes more deeply; for it is directed to habits of the mind that arise out of an attitude which surrenders human and personal values to an objective and systematic order. So that the critique directs one's reflection to the very nature of thought. Personalist thought refuses to identify the intellectual life with objective cognition. In subordinating objectivity to human subjectivity, it does not so much deny the limited role of objective thinking as it places it in a context of subjective, interpersonal relations.

What is most fruitful, then, is not the denial of the exclusive primacy of objective cognition, utilized in science and technology, but the recovery of the fuller context of knowing—of what (in *Fides et Ratio*) John Paul points to as wisdom.[12] What personalism can receive from the resources of a metaphysics of existential act is a more expansive appreciation of the interiority constitutive of *all* beings, and not only—as in the standard modern view—the psychological introspection associated with human subjects *(subjecta mentis)*. In a metaphysics of existential act ontological interiority is proper to all beings *(subjecta entis)*. What is of benefit to personalism through association with such a metaphysics is an express recognition—admittedly already intuitively implicit but relatively inarticulate in Marcel, whose approach does not permit its explicitation—the express articulation of a trans-objective dignity and depth ingredient in non-human things *(res)* as well as in persons.

To be sure, the appreciation of interiority is heightened in personalist thought. The disengagement of thought from the primacy of systematic objectivity gives to personalist philosophies an aura of drama. For it stresses that the human person is not in assured control of his or her life and destiny. I have mentioned that personalism has emerged from the testing fires of idealism and positivism, but it has also passed through the fires of voluntarism. One need only recall such figures as Ockham, Pico della Mirandola, and Luther, and more recently Nietzsche and Sar-

---

12. See especially section 32.

tre. There can be no doubt that a heightened sense of the arbitrary, cultivated by the modern current of voluntarism, forms a background condition to a modern appreciation of freedom as of paramount value in personalist thought.

But personalist philosophy also draws upon what in the past was known as the logic of the heart, and embodies a call to inner conversion, along with the dramatic possibility of refusal. Such "vital insecurity" is not to be confused with the dull metaphysical unease of one who has surrendered his existential issues and crises to technical problem-solving. For, in Marcel's view, this existential openness calls upon our freedom, not to sink into despair but to take up a renewed confidence and hope.

There can be no doubt that personalism emerged, if not out of, certainly concomitant with modern idealism with its emphasis upon consciousness and experience, in one or another thinker often as a not entirely convinced fellow-traveler. The principle of my thesis is that, in and through the distortions of modern idealism, *an advance in the understanding of being has come about*. The generally accepted primacy of the distinction between external objectivity and internal subjectivity sets up a condition in which the opposition—not so much to the distinction itself, as to the claim on behalf of its primacy—brings forth a more intensive recognition of the person which transcends that distinction. In the company of a widely accepted idealism, and following out the *actual* career of philosophy during the four centuries of idealism, not only has knowledge been affected, but *being has disclosed aspects of itself that had not been disclosed in such explicit and emphatic ways in earlier centuries*. What is astonishing to me is that, on the whole, personalism has emerged out of idealism into a robust realism.

Now here we must be precise regarding the nature of that realism. If, in contradistinction to idealism, one can speak of the *realism* of values in Marcel and other (especially Christian) personalists, this realism is not intended in the post-Cartesian and objectivist sense. That excludes the subject of experience in the interest of modern objective criteria, and is one side of the Cartesian and post-Cartesian dualism of subject and object.

On the other hand—and here I register not so much a criticism as a certain weakness—such personalism defines itself in direct reaction to just such criteria of objectivity. It is here that a fresh look at the pre-objective transcendental *res* proves helpful; for, unlike modern realism which—in the form of materialism or functionalism or other objectivisms—suppresses the full role of the subject, the transcendental "property" (*proprium*) of all being in a metaphysics of being does not stand in opposition to the emergent modern sense of subjectivity. Rather, in generous embrace, the transcendental *res* situates the human subject within the community of beings. In so doing, it provides the path to the subject's own interiority which it shares analogously with all other beings, as it opens up a co-existent intimacy with other beings in the broadest actual community of beings.

One of the shortcomings of the way in which the personalism of Gabriel Marcel has developed—and at the same time the source of much of its vitality and relevance—is its direct engagement with the modern understanding of realism. For—and here one must be precise—one might almost say that this direct confrontation, on the one hand, concedes to modern objectivity a negative yet defining role in establishing the character of secondary reflection with its precious positive qualities, but which, on the other, also prohibits an equally rigorous articulation of non-personal being. I have been impressed by Marcel's generous sensibility, which has led him to acknowledge the rich qualities of being in both nature and art; his telling essays on Rainer Maria Rilke[13] alone are enough to confirm an appreciation that reaches beyond the personal to the mysterious heart of Being itself. But his approach does not permit a fully articulated account of non-personal reality.[14]

In justice, however, it must be said that Marcel's advance, and that of personalism generally, lies not simply in responding to the modern turn by a critique of the non-subjective and impersonal objective modes of thought which leave the issue of their full Being untouched. The advance consists, rather, in recognizing the need in the very movement of transcendence to ground even those modes in a greater depth and interiority through the recognition of, and response to, the understanding of being as primordial fullness. Still, while Marcel himself acknowledges the depth of being in the non-personal forms of nature, he scarcely articulates it with the care that he gives to the way in which being manifests itself in personal experience. Nor does his approach permit him to do so. Marcel quite rightly rejects the modern methodical objectivity that excludes the interiority properly resident in non-personal beings.

---

13. *Homo Viator: Introduction to a Metaphysics of Hope* (Chicago: Henry Regnery, 1951), the last two essays. Moreover, he often remarks upon the beauty and peace of the pre-technological environment, without however the slightest concession to sentimentality or nostalgia.

14. This is true even of his rescue of the human body from the techniques of objective problem-solving as in *Man against Mass Society*. His refreshing insistence that "I am my body," I do not simply "have my body," *Being and Having: An Existential Diary* (New York: Harper and Row, 1965), recognizes the truth of the incarnate character of the body, too easily lost in objective techniques. But Marcel's phenomenology interprets the body in terms of personal existence and not in terms of the wider community of beings.

He sees clearly that such methodical objectivity posits the objective *over against* the person, literally as that which stands in front of the person as a barrier and which thereby turns human consciousness from its native community and back onto and into itself, culminating in a modern form of subjective idealism—methodical in Descartes, critical in Kant.[15] In short, while he overcomes the functionalist claim to the primacy of a supposedly objective world, he equally rejects the idealist claim to the primacy of a self that recoils from that world. It is remarkable with how much clarity and vigor he rejects a Cartesian-like *ego* that turns away from the external cast of an objectively construed world in an attempt to "save" itself by "the beautiful rule" of *the* method. For such an objectivity places upon the supposedly autonomous self the unrealizable burden of validating both the certitude of knowledge and the value of freedom. Marcel is fully aware of this situation and supplies his own corrective in his call for a "secondary," meta-objective reflection that transcends this fixed dualism. He thereby frees the person from a grip which simultaneously forces the self towards isolated autonomy and, contrariwise, pulls it to manifest itself in the external form of objectively measurable behavior.

Without in any way denigrating his remarkable achievement, is it possible to take a further step and implant his brilliant insights in a larger and deeper soil? No doubt, it is in this modern crucible—of the mutual repulsion of the objective and subjective—that an adequate personal consciousness has been tested and has emerged in clearer, more decisive fashion. In Marcel, as well as in the more metaphysical personalists, this purgation has yielded a rich harvest through concentrating and intensifying the sense of the personal. For it has brought new appreciation of that precious mode of being whose distinctive character is its interiority and capacity for intimacy. It is in the light of this heightened awareness that we can now read the Fathers and the medieval Doctors—even St. Augustine's intimate *Confessions*[16]—with a fresh appreciation of their understanding of the person; so that when Thomas Aquinas tells us that the person is the most perfect being in the created world, and that as such the name is fittingly attributed—with all its shortcomings—to the Blessed Trinity, a whole world of interiority, human and divine, opens up to us. It is just this modern world of interiority and creative imagina-

---

15. This lies at the root of Marcel's severed rejection of the dualism of activity and passivity which he finds pronounced in Kant.

16. This remarkable work anticipates the concentration upon the self but without erecting a system upon such a principle as Descartes did. A similar anticipation is evident in the relation of Augustine's *si fallor sum* and Descartes' *cogito ergo sum*. The former was a particular argument directed against the skeptics, whereas the latter became a first principle for the erection of an entire system.

tion that Jacques Maritain acknowledges as the proper fruit of modernity, celebrated in its literature, art, and music.[17]

At the center of the focus on the person, Marcel's phenomenology seizes upon the modern sense of transcendence as the movement of the human spirit, a movement that obeys other laws than those of physical motion.[18] Furthermore, instead of the "progressive" or linear sense of transcendence, associated with Sartre and originally promoted by the Encyclopaedists of the Enlightenment through the ideal of progress, Marcel takes the word in the Kierkegaardian sense of "vertical" or upward "ex-sistence."[19] And this usage marks a difference in the outlook of modern personalism and the metaphysics of being. Anyone who has tried to find a vocabulary that bridges the epochal difference between St. Thomas' *esse actu (actus essendi)* as primary source or principle *(archē)* and the modern use of the term "existence" has faced the difficulty of rendering the meaning of being-as-actuality with the term "existence." For, at least since Kierkegaard, modern usage has been true to the etymology of the word. And although it is often used in the positivist sense of mere fact,[20] of merely being there in space and time, to "exist in the personal sense" means to be in the process of "standing outside one's previous state," and to be moving towards a new state.[21] In this movement the person discloses the distinctive character of spirit.

The person, in his or her existence, "transcends" when moving freely towards the realization of a fullness of being that is expectant in the person and towards which he or she is called to become. Conversely, he or she "descends" when that movement diminishes being. What is up-

---

17. See his *Antimoderne* (Paris: Editions de la Revue des jeunes, 1922) as well as his *Three Reformers: Luther-Descartes-Rousseau* (New York: Scribner's, 1929), as well as his writings on poetry and art, for example, *Creative Intuition in Art and Poetry* (New York: Meridian, 1957), and elsewhere.

18. Marcel, of course, protested against describing his own philosophy as an "existentialism," a term he thought best consigned to Jean-Paul Sartre. As a designation of his own philosophy, Marcel preferred "philosophy of the concrete."

19. As expressed by Kierkegaard with his notion of "existence" as moving from one personal state to another.

20. An early formulation of this view is found in Turgot's definition in the *Encyclopédie Dictionnaire raisonné des sciences, des arts, et des métiers,* ed. Denis Diderot and Jean Le Rond d'Alembert (Lausanne: Sociétéé typographique, 1751–80), republished (Stuttgart: Frommann, 1966–67), article: *existence.*

21. Recall Kierkegaard's three stages: aesthetic, moral, and religious. Interestingly, Suarez provides a sort of bridge to this meaning when he takes created being to exist *"extra causas."* More generally, the difficulty in translating medieval Latin terms into modern German is subtle but real; e.g., *actualitas* in the late Latin stems from the verb *ago* (Sansk. *ag*) which refers back to the originating agent, whereas *Wirklichkeit* stems from the verb *wirken* which points rather to the effect produced. This represents an important shift away from the sense of principle *(principium, archē)* as source. Thus, for St. Thomas, *esse* in the sense of act is the intrinsic source of all that is in a being, and leads back to that "pure act" *(Ipsum esse)* that is the source of all that is and the proper philosophical name of God.

permost in this transcendence, however, is the dramatic tissue of human life with its invitation to freedom and responsibility. For Marcel recognizes an intrinsic relation between freedom and being.

Here, I would dare to say, we come upon the most crucial development in contemporary personalism. It consists in the importance given to freedom. While in no way a personalist, it is small wonder that Jean-Paul Sartre elevated this aspect of existence to the primary character of his own kind of humanism; that is, he exalted freedom, though he took it to be exclusively realized in the exercise of value-conferring choice. Personalism, on the other hand, in its metaphysical and Christian version, moves more deeply and more truly towards the signal relation between freedom and being. Here again, we must acknowledge the contribution of idealism, especially in the German tradition of speculative thought, which has shown forth the inextricable relation between freedom and being.

For that tradition—despite its later distortion and unfortunate military adventures—gave to the full meaning of being the accolade of freedom. This did not mean, however, merely the restricted movement of choice between given alternatives, but a more primordial, creative movement. Among the conditions in which this insight emerged, we know of the relative ineffectuality of political power in the plethora of eighteenth-century German principalities, before the unification of the German states under Prussian and National Liberal hegemony. And it may be that this dispersal of political power gave rise, not only to a remarkably rich musical tradition, but that it also contributed to a deep sense of creative freedom. No doubt, Nietzsche's influential concept of the will to power gave a dubious expression to this deeper insight during the nineteenth century. At any rate, this sense of freedom is at once more diffuse and unformed than the politically defined British and French concept of liberty as freedom of choice.[22]

But, if the German development differed from the Anglo-French, it also took a step beyond the classical and medieval understanding of *liberum arbitrium* as well, though not necessarily in conflict with it.[23] After Kant, in its understanding of being as *Geist* (Schelling, Hegel) or will (Nietzsche) or being-in-the-world (Heidegger), this speculative tradition gave to freedom the overarching character of the movement of being itself.

This relatively modern understanding of freedom became prevalent

22. It is no accident, then, that the first academic chair in aesthetics was founded in Germany in the early eighteenth century.

23. I say "not in conflict" because one can discern in the medieval understanding a distinction between a certain spontaneous movement towards the ultimate good with which each and every being is endowed by the Creator and the deliberative choice that is proper to rational and intellectual beings.

in nineteenth-century German thought as resistance to the formal stability of substance and in favor of becoming and historicity *(Werden* and *Geschichte)* as the proper modality of Being *(Sein)*. Not surprisingly, however, this understanding of freedom also arose in the modern context of the distinction between the objective and subjective. It was thereby still conditioned by that distinction, expressed, for example, by Heidegger's distinction between the ontic and the ontological, or the *existentiel* and the *existential*. And as with Marcel, so too here, the full possibility of this ontological freedom has not yet been fully articulated.

In view of this close association of freedom with being, is it too daring to ask whether freedom itself may be considered a transcendental property of being as such? Or, if that is too rash, then if not as a transcendental, certainly as a new insight into the nature of *unum*. For the unity of each being is no longer to be understood simply as *ens indivisum*, but as *conatus*, that is, as the drive for self-expression. Each being *in-sists, re-sists*, and *ex-sists* in relation to others, enjoying an integrity which each being receives from its Source, namely, the "freedom" to be itself *(ens per se)*. This does not close beings into themselves, since the metaphysics of being confirms that no caused being owns its own being; on the contrary, the fundamental character of receptivity resonates throughout each created being *(recevoir* now extended to non-personal things as well as to personal beings).

If this expansion of freedom seems extravagant, we might reflect that the Source of all being is the absolute Freedom, Who is God, and that, if His handiwork does not belie His nature, surely some residue of freedom in its analogous modes is present in all creation and not only explicitly in the intellectual and spiritual modes of personal being.[24] Assuredly, the natural world of things (understood as *res*) is not free as persons are free, but it still remains for thought to integrate the freedom of persons into a broader horizon and a deeper soil if the universal aspiration of philosophy is to be realized. It is here that the trans-formal metaphysics of being as existential act provides both the root and the branch, the depth and the horizon, for such an integration without denigrating the precious values that personalism so jealously guards.

But the new insights into the interiority of the person that are the capital harvest of modernity suggest that the truth of personalism cannot be simply integrated into the classical and medieval understanding of being without recognizing an advance in our understanding of being. And it is in the consolidation of being and freedom that the transforma-

---

24. One can see prefigurements of such an emphasis upon freedom as primary in voluntarist thinkers, but also in more complex thinkers such as Pico della Mirandola, Valla, and Vico.

tion in our understanding of being must come about. And to this advance, personalism makes an indispensable contribution.

To see how such a consolidation might be carried out, we can begin with the classical medieval understanding of the person among the world of created beings as a special kind of being. According to this view, everything above the world of matter, everything that transcends the physical in any way, is free; that is, all are free in the realm of spiritual being. Freedom is the transcendental character of being ingredient in the intellectual and spiritual factor in man, and present throughout the hierarchy of created spiritual substances, and perfectly actual in the very center of divine life. Nor is this a denial of received natures on the part of created beings; indeed, it is in the denial of received natures that voluntarism distorted the truth of its insight into the primacy of freedom. To be sure, among created spiritual substances, including the incarnate spirit man, the dynamic structures of being are themselves in place; that is the meaning of natural law, given that freedom is not license, though it contains that possibility. Still, being in its historical unfolding moves in mysterious ways its character to affirm. It is perhaps paradoxical that the withdrawal of natural law from the mind of the age, leading to the modern recasting of natural law in physicalist and determinist terms has been one of the conditions that has made possible the personalist rediscovery of a lawful responsiveness and responsibility that is not opposed to but is the compatriot of the freedom of being.[25]

As idealism has taught us, if in exemplary fashion we read the whole of reality from its highest peak down,[26] then the first character of being par excellence is freedom. It is, minimally, the freedom of each being to be itself and to develop in accord with the received potential for its fullness. Indeed, if one surrenders to the Source of being and the Providential Governance of Being—what Marcel expresses as being in connivance with Being—then contingent events themselves are seen as occurring within the context of freedom and not unintelligent chance. In the strictly physical domain, this freedom to be expresses itself in the simple spontaneity of developmental activity, each being possessing its own dynamism; for we now know that even the smallest particle is possessed of its own pattern of activity, so that a certain self-affirmation lies at the root of existence.[27] This is the affirmation to be and to act in ac-

---

25. Maritain's attention to the role of "inclination" in the ethical life points towards a reconciliation of personal freedom and received law.

26. I say "idealism has taught us," but in truth St. Bonaventure had already shown the way theologically in his exemplary Trinitarianism.

27. This affirmation of being stands in contrast to the conflictual dynamics of modern dialectic which raises the negative to a first principle (after the manner of Hegel and Marx), and to which Catholic thinkers (such as Guardini and Przywara) proposed the complementary principle of *Polarität*.

cord with its received nature: this is the minimal expression of the transcendental *unum* or better said: *integrity*. In the organic realm, it is the impulse to self-directed growth and maturation; in the animal domain, it is sense-directed activity in accord with a given species *(voluntarium)*; and in man, it is the call to the exercise of a responsible freedom *(deliberative)*. The call to transcendence, then, is the call to a specific mode of becoming for man. That, in turn, calls for a developed and contemporary understanding of spirit in the context of the community of beings; it calls for an understanding of spirit that is free from its reaction to objectivity and that penetrates beyond controlled objectivity to the deeper level of the generosity of being itself.

Marcel provides a key to this progress when he remarks upon the fullness of being as that which cannot be dismembered by the most exhaustive analysis—a plenitude that survives every attempt to control it and subordinate it to arbitrary and partial aims. Here Marcel's secondary reflection joins with the metaphysical notion of being as horizon and root of all that is. For the consolidation of personalist philosophy with the metaphysics of existential act must be a mutually beneficial engagement, in which each is transformed in a way that perfects both. If the genius of the traditional metaphysics of being is its universal comprehension and its radical depth, by which it provides for an ultimate context of understanding and judgment, the genius of contemporary personalism is that, once it is grounded in a community with all beings, it can show forth in new ways—through receptivity, fidelity, vocation, and *reconnaissance*—the concrete and historical drama of being itself.

PART II

MAN

Chapter 9

THE GEOGRAPHY OF THE HUMAN PERSON

It is upon the uniqueness of each person and the diversity of all that human dignity rests.

If an inquisitive acquaintance gets uncomfortably close to what we don't want broadcast to others, we are likely to demur with the excuse: "I really don't want to talk about that, it's very personal." If the questioner has any sensitivity at all, that should warn him or her off any further inquisition, since to cry "Personal" is one of our acceptable informal social ways of preserving our privacy. In another sense of the term, however, we may credit a person (sometimes a figure in authority) with treating us "as a person." By that, we mean that he or she respects us and accords us a particular dignity and value; he or she shows interest in us, not out of curiosity, but intrinsically "for ourselves." Some commercial interests have caught on to this, availing themselves of something from which they can profit. And so, not infrequently the mail delivers "personalized" letters, embossed with our names, not excluding degrees of familiarity, ranging from the formal to the informal. This trick—aided by electronic devices nowadays—while itself a fraud, plays upon something genuine in the meaning of the term *person*, viz., that a person is a unique center and that access to a person is access to a certain privileged intimacy. In flattering us, the advertiser plays upon three facets of the term: he accords us the innate dignity of a unique status and claims a certain insider's knowledge of us, a kind of intimacy. *Dignity, uniqueness, and intimacy:* these cling to the meaning of the term *person,* and to the adjective *personal* today, even in such clichés as the sign-off "Personally yours."

Paradoxically, however, the term *personality* as we often use it lends itself to the opposite meaning. For if we say that he or she "has person-

---

Reprinted from *Communio* 13 (Spring 1986): 27–48. Copyright © by *Communio: International Catholic Review.*

ality," that may pass as a compliment, meaning that he or she creates a pleasing or striking impression upon first meeting; but such "personal charm" stands to intimacy as surface to depth. And if we say that someone "is a personality," we usually mean that he manages to project a public image and is even well-known for it. The suspicion can never quite be banished that the image may not correspond to the private reality underneath. So that the term *personality* seems to suggest anything but intimacy, since it refers primarily to the surface impression. Nor does the term *personality* suggest dignity; if anything it carries the notion of a marketable asset. Finally, the distinctiveness of an image or personality often seems to be a product. As such, it stands in contrast to what we mean when we say that someone treats us "as a person," since by that we mean that he or she appreciates us as we are and values us—not for our public appearance or fame or wealth or talent or connections to power and privilege—but in and for ourselves alone. Now, this ambivalence, between the hidden depth implied in the term *person* and the manifest display exhibited by the term *personality*, has been attached to the network of meanings associated with the terms from the beginning. It seems to me enlightening, therefore, to trace out the geography of the term *person* and its associates, and to note both the development of meaning and the constancy that preserves the original double sense of the terms.

ANCIENT AND MEDIEVAL UNDERSTANDING OF "PERSON"

Following the most probable account,[1] we begin our tour more than two thousand years ago in the region of Etruria, which lies north of Rome on the way to Florence. The Etruscans observed a cult to the goddess Persephone, and they called the mask used in the religious rites by a name derived from the goddess: *phersu*. The Etruscans were influential in the development of the Roman theater, and so Persephone's mask came to be known among the Romans by the adjective: *persona*, which later came to signify any mask, especially those used in the theater. In taking up the Etruscan word, the Romans fused it with one of their own

---

1. In addition to the standard etymological dictionaries, I take much of this from Alois Grillimeier, *Jesus der Christus im Glauben der Kircle*, vol. 1: *Von der Apostolischen Zeit bis zum Konzil von Chalcedon (451)* (Freiburg: Herder, 1981), 250–55. An earlier version of the second edition exists in English (London: Oxford University Press, 1975). He cites among others: M. Nédoncelle, "Prosopon et person dans l'antiquité classique," *Revue des Sciences Religieuse* 22 (1948): 277–99; H. Rheinfelder, *Das Wort "Persona"*... (Halle: M. Niemeyer, 1928); Cornelia J. de Vogel, "The Concept of Personality in Greek and Christian Thought," in *Studies in Philosophy and the History of Philosophy*, vol. 2 (Washington, DC: The Catholic University of America Press, 1963), 20–60.

words, which means "sounding or speaking through" *(personus* from *personare)*, because the mask was that through which the sounds of the goddess or the character were heard. The word *persona* was on its way. From the beginning, however, the mask had not only visual and acoustic functions or properties; it was also used to represent a personage, and so the term was easily transferred from the wooden or clay device to the theatrical role or dramatic character represented through it. One can imagine a stage play with characters speaking to one another and about one another through the masks. As a result, about the time of the Second Punic War (third century B.C.) it is likely that the grammarians borrowed the word to signify the different forms of address: the first, second, and third persons. Then about the time of Cicero (first century B.C.), the word expanded rapidly and took on several related meanings: it was used to indicate the concrete character of a real personage and not merely of a dramatic role; it was also used in the law courts to distinguish the juridical person, with its legal rights and duties, from mere things of property. Finally, it came to be used in the philosophical sense of a human substance in its properly and distinctively human individuality. We have now arrived at the sense of the real and the unique that has clung to the term *person* ever since. Given the cultic origin of the term, we might say that it comes to its human application "trailing clouds of glory"! And it is interesting that a Gothic word belonging to the network of meanings associated with the term *person* means "glory" *(vulthus)*.

Meanwhile, in Greece, a word with a very different etymology began a career that would merge with that of the Latin *persona*, and thereby reinforce a meaning not entirely absent from the Latin word. It is the word *prósopon*, which is formed from three parts *(pró-, óps-,* and *-on);* and its central part is taken from the verb: to see and to be seen. It is one of those words associated with the process of manifestation, and brings with it the implicit distinction between light and shadow, foreground and background, surface and depth, between what is unveiled and what remains hidden. This is the root of the ambivalence between the senses of *person* and *personality* previously mentioned. The Greek term easily passes over into the "look" or "countenance" of someone, which is also ambiguous. But here the notion of difference comes forward, for we recognize each other most easily by our countenances or faces. That is why police sketches of suspects are portraits. This distinctiveness points towards the uniqueness already associated with the Latin notion of a dramatic character *(dramatis personae);* and indeed, a variant of the Greek word *(prosopéion)* means "mask"!

Even more important, however, the Greeks used the word *prósopon* periphrastically *(tò sòn prósopon)*, i.e., as a roundabout way of speaking in the second person: so that to say "person" is to say: "thou"! It is to use the direct form of address, for it means "I and thou," "you and me." It does not mean: he or she or they, or even I. It means: "face to face" *(katà prósopon)*, a direct encounter with nothing between. And of course, the usual setting for intimacy is a *tête-à-tête*, one-on-one, a twosome. The old saying "Three's a crowd" expresses the infrequency of expecting intimacy between more than two persons. As Shakespeare's dying Caesar turns to Brutus, his murmured: "Et tu, Brute," "even you, my Brutus," whispers the betrayal of a long and trusted intimacy.

"Face to face." The Latin words for "face" *(vultus, facies)* are related to the term *person;* and the Greeks often used their word *(prósopon)* to mean someone's face. Now, the Greeks were very jealous of the human face, for they took it to be not simply a physical structure: the front part of the head. It is not equivalent to its physiognomy. Aristotle remarked (in his *Historia animalium*, 491 b9–11) that the "part below the skull is named the face *(prósopon)*, but only in man, and in no other animal; we do not speak of the face of a fish or of an ox!" So that we are entitled to say that hidden within the Greek term for "person" *(prósopon)* is the sense that only human beings have faces. This is because a face is a structure that shows forth meaning. It is transparent with the innocent, concealing with the devious, glowing with the joyful, grieving with the sad, indifferent with the bored. It is just this expressiveness upon which the actor and film star capitalize, that the portraitist and photographer record, and towards which the clown directs our attention. A person's face is meant to be the signature of the character within; one cannot disengage the face from a certain interiority. A face has depth; it is not all surface. And yet that depth is not a *thing* at all; it does not yield to a scalpel. It is not the muscles or bones or brain, but a depth that plays upon the surface of the countenance. In philosophical terms, the face displays a spiritual reality. Indeed, when we are misled by surface appearances to find ugliness of character beneath the beauty of the surface, to find evil purpose beneath a seeming good, we are all the more shocked by what we take to be a betrayal on the part of nature itself. And bewildered, we ask: How could something have seemed so contrary to what it really is?

I have so far combined the Greek and Latin senses of *person* with the meaning of *face:* both terms indicate the manifestation of meaningful depth, the distinctiveness of the individual, the intimacy of direct personal encounter, and the dignity associated with the divine and with the specifically human. And indeed, the term *person*, as we have come to use it today, is haunted by uniqueness, intimacy, and dignity. Despite the initial independence of the words *(phersu, personare, prósopon)*, it seems to me that a reality has been at work calling upon their affinity and drawing them together into a rich and complex term. I further suggest that the reality that convokes the term is nothing short of personhood itself—both divine and human.

It is appropriate, then, to continue our tour, passing now to Alexandria in Egypt, and from pagan to biblical culture.[2] Biblical exegetes (such as Philo Judaeus) used the figure of *personification* (prosopographic exegesis) extensively to explain passages in the Bible, especially those speaking of "Wisdom." Even more importantly the Septuagint translators of the Bible from Hebrew into Greek used the word *prósopon* to express such phrases as "out of the mouth of the Lord," meaning by the term a mouthpiece or mask. And the early translators of the Bible into Latin translated the Septuagint Greek *prósopon* by the Latin *persona (ex persona domini,* or *persona patris),* thereby helping to establish the equivalence of the Greek and Latin technical meanings.

This usage was much favored by Christians, and during the first four centuries of reflection the term came to be defined by the great Church Councils that laid down the Christian Creed still accepted by all but a small number of those churches which go by the name of Christian. Now, it is well to remember that the whole Christian discussion took place as an effort to bring to speech the mysterious "unveiling" of the Godhead (which we call "revelation"). The question before them was: Who is this Christ whom we acknowledge as sent by the Father and Who with the Father sends the guiding Spirit of the Church? The term *person* eventually recommended itself above all others for talking in a special way about God, even though it was generally held that all terms were inadequate to express the eternal mystery of the Godhead, and even though Eastern Christians tended to emphasize the mysterious play of visible and invisible ingredient in the term, while Western Christians tended to emphasize the reality and uniqueness that is also inseparable from the term. This was, however, a matter of emphasis and not of contradiction. Thus, the term was used to call Christ the visible display (*species,* i.e., mirror) of God in the world, the face *(prósopon)* of the Father, the image *(eikón)* that discloses God. But it was also used to express the distinctive though inseparable realities *(hypostáseis, supposita)* of the one triune Godhead with its identical nature *(ousia essentia, natura:* "one in

---

2. For what follows, in addition to the writings of the Church Fathers—particularly of Hippolytus *(prosopa:* C. Noet.) and Tertullian *(persona:* Adversus Praxeam), as well as the Alexandrian and Cappadocian Fathers—the following are helpful and available: J. N. D. Kelly, *Early Christian Doctrines* (San Francisco: Harper and Row, 1960; rev. ed., 1978); and J. Pelikan, *The Christian Tradition; A History of the Development of Doctrine,* vol. 1, *The Emergence of the Catholic Tradition (100–600);* vol. 2, *The Spirit of Eastern Christendom (600–1700);* and vol. 3, *The Growth of Medieval Theology (600–1300)* (Chicago: University of Chicago Press, 1971–78).

being, substance, or nature"). Boethius[3] stressed the distinctive reality of both the human and divine personhood, with his classical definition of the person as "an individual substance of a rational [we might rather say "intellectual"] nature," to which Thomas Aquinas added: that such a term was fittingly applied to God because it designated "what is most perfect in all nature," viz., a substance capable of knowledge, love, and freedom.[4]

Now, there are at least three advantages to talking about the Godhead in personal terms, and they all bring a new sense of intimacy with them. First of all, the term *person* is used to dramatize the inner life of the Godhead. For, it provides believers—if not with a clear window—then at least with a mirror that reflects, no matter how darkly, the otherwise hidden and inexpressible life of the High Godhead. The seemingly dry talk about the "eternal processions" of the Persons of the Trinity can still bristle with excitement if one takes the trouble to recapture the original freshness of discovery; for these processions are nothing less than the loving communication within the life of God, that divine community of friendship which is more united than any unity we can conceive of, and that divine mutual unity whose life is richer than any community we can imagine.

Secondly, in acknowledging Christ to be the Lord, fully human and fully divine, the orthodox formula confesses Him to be the personal union of two distinct natures (human and divine), natures which are taken up into the unitary personal life of the eternally begotten Son of God (hypostatic union). Once again, however, we need to break the crust that hardens over the formula, if we are to recover its deeper significance. For it means, not simply that this or that particular human individual (Jesus of Nazareth) is assumed into the divine person, but that the very meaning and reality of what it is to be human has been drawn up in the closest way into a personal union with the divinity, to become part of the very being of a divine Person. God not only loved the world

---

3. *Contra Eutychen,* also known as *De persona et duabus naturis in Christo,* especially secs. 2 and 3. The famous definition is "naturae rationabilis individua substantia," to which Boethius immediately adds: "Now by this definition we Latins have described what the Greeks call *hypostasis.* For the word person *(nomen persona)* seems to be borrowed from a different source . . ." The whole tractate is worth reading. A convenient edition (with translation by H. F. Stewart and E. K. Rand) exists in the Loeb Classical Library (Harvard University Press, 1962).

4. *STh* I, q. 29, a. 3. The quotation was used to set the theme of the 1985 Crispo Memorial Lectures at Gannon College, and the first version of this paper was delivered as one of those lectures. See also *STh* I, q. 29, a. 1 and ad 1m, for St. Thomas' discussion of Boethius' definition; and a. 3, ad 2m, for reference to Alain of Lille's remark in *Theological Reg.* 32, *Patrologiae latina* 210:637, that "Some define person as an *hypostasis* distinct by reason of dignity."

so much that He gave up His only Son to suffering and death for it, but in the Incarnation that very world in the form of humanity gained new access to, and unprecedented intimacy with, God. Only the intimacy of the divine Persons with one another in the Trinitarian Godhead can be closer than this hypostatic (personal) intimacy of humanity and divinity within Christ.

Now, and only now, can we speak of a third intimacy. Israel already enjoys a certain intimacy with God as His chosen people, and the Covenant is celebrated in the love-song of Solomon, the pleadings of Hosea, and elsewhere. But the Christians received an invitation to an unprecedented intimacy, sealed within the very person and being of Christ. It is the invitation to all who believe in Christ to live their lives within a new community of friendship *(ecclesia)*. This call to a new access to God and to a new intimacy with Him and among one another rests upon the two prior intimacies. All of this, then—the mystery of the Trinity, the birth, death, and resurrection of Christ, and the fellowship of the Church— amounted to an unprecedented call to access to and intimacy with persons, both divine and human.[5] And the articulation of that call contributed new meaning to the dignity, uniqueness, and intimacy associated with the term *person*.

THE MODERN UNDERSTANDING OF "PERSON"

So far I have gathered up the ancient elements that have gone into the meaning of the term *person* and its related terms. It is especially interesting that the term *person* is an amalgam of three initially quite different words, drawn from quite different aspects of reality and experience, and quite different cultural regions. Moreover, unlike many words whose origins are lost in the mists of our various linguistic memories, the history of the term *person* has been recovered with considerable plausibility. It has come about through the coalescence of independent words and the emergence of the term out of them; so that its career is thoroughly historical. More important still, however, the reality designated by the term is itself immersed in historical existence. Indeed, I am not concerned here only with a recondite reconstruction of the term. In addition and principally, I am tracing out the story of *a human reality in search of its appropriate name*. The name did not spring up directly out of nature, but in keeping with the historical character of human reality it emerged from quite distinct meanings in answer to the historical and cultural career

---

5. I have treated the theme of an unprecedented expectation of intimacy elsewhere, in "The Roots of Catholic Intellectuality," in *CCICA* (Catholic Commission on Intellectual and Cultural Affairs) *Annual* (1984): 1–18.

of that reality as it developed in the context of Mediterranean cultures.

This does not mean at all that the term *person* finds its only application within Mediterranean cultures, since the human reality which receives that name receives it in virtue of characteristics that are deeply and universally shared by all of mankind, and exhibited in all eras and cultures. There are elements that seem to be as ancient as man himself. Thus, it would be difficult to call that "human" which was not in any way subject to feelings of tenderness and compassion, feelings which are closely associated with what we now call "personal." Indeed, the first evidences of such feelings are the endearments placed by grieving parents tens of thousands of years ago in their children's graves. Moreover, building upon these affective tendencies within the human heart, the ancients celebrated the special attraction that one particular human being comes to feel for another particular human being. Often erotic passion sustained these feelings, if it did not destroy them. They are celebrated in the love songs of Sappho and Catullus, and in the more symbolic lays of medieval courtly love. There is no doubt that this perennially human inclination has been raised to a very high value in "Western" society. One thinks of the Romantic novels of the previous two centuries;[6] and today's popular ballads sing of little else. But *eros* alone does not rule the human heart. One thinks, too, of the praise of friendship between persons of differing states, ages, backgrounds, and even interests. Such friendship arises as an inexplicable bond attaching two persons to each other, and affording a mutual recognition of the special worth of each. This friendship *(amor benevolentiae et amicitiae)* consists of affection towards another for that other's own true good. Such affection is often called "disinterested," but it is the highest interest in another just because it is not interested in what advantage can be gained from the relationship. The experience of such "elective affinity," and the poetry, theater, and literature that extols it, has undoubtedly intensified the sense of interpersonal relationships among us; so much so that such relationships have become a sort of wished-for ideal of human togetherness, and add their meanings to the network of terms that speak of the personal.[7]

In addition to such perennial inclinations calling humans towards the recognition of the personal nature of their being, the cultural and historical character of that being contributes to further development of

---

6. For example, Samuel Richardson's *Pamela,* J. J. Rousseau's *The New Heloise,* Goethe's *Werther,* and Fr. Schlegel's *Lucinde* are expressions of intimacy and feeling, each in its own way.

7. While it is an important element in a vibrant community, such interpersonal fellowship alone is not enough to make a community. For full community institutions are also needed. See "Community: The Elusive Unity," *Review of Metaphysics* 37, no. 2 (1983): 243–64, esp. 247–48.

the meaning of the term. Nor is there much doubt that the term and its network of related terms lies open even today to further developments of which we are ignorant: we do not, after all, possess perfect self-knowledge, nor are we even in perfect possession of the promise of full personhood. In view of the historical character of the reality and the term, then, it is not surprising that some characteristics often associated with the meaning of *person* and *personal* today are of recent origin. They find that origin in the Europe of about five hundred years ago. Wherever what has been called "modern" culture comes on the scene—in Europe during the past several centuries, in North and South America from their beginnings, and now (with the spread of industrial technology, urbanization, and mass media) almost everywhere—a high degree of *self-consciousness of a certain introverted sort* also arrives with it. Now, self-consciousness as such is very ancient and has found various forms in different cultures. Thus, for example, in "Western" culture, a religious form found expression in the *Confessions* of St. Augustine and his equally beautiful *Soliloquies*, and in the mystical writings of St. Bernard of Clairvaux and others.

But that religious self-consciousness has also undergone various changes. Thus towards the end of the Middle Ages a sort of profound depression seemed to seize upon Europe: induced in part perhaps by the Great Plague which weakened and decimated the population, and in part perhaps because of apparently insoluble conflicts between Church and Empire, wars between nation-states, and conflicts among groups within society as well. For whatever reasons, the old order began to change more rapidly and more deeply, bringing with it many desirable changes, but also a certain instability in the dominant institutions. One of the first to fall under attack was the Church itself. A division arose within Christianity that issued forth as the Protestant Reformation, followed by interreligious wars. For these and other reasons, a long and intense meditation upon the sinfulness of the individual spread widely throughout Catholic as well as Protestant Christianity, and deepened the introspective bent already nourished in earlier ages. In its first phase, this constituted an often powerful negative intimacy with God, stressing the depravity and unworthiness of humanity.

No doubt, this religious introversion helped to bring about a climate within which there came into play a sort of secular retreat within the self, an introspection that helped to bring about attitudes and values which have been influential ever since. The seventeenth-century philosophers Descartes and Locke led the attempt to anchor knowledge within the human self as a sort of foundation of whatever certitude we could achieve *(subjectum fundamentum inconcussum)*. Subsequently, as part of an attack upon the dominant institutions of eighteenth-century European society—at first directed against the Church and later against the Monarchy—there arose a new leadership, a literary intelligentsia which wielded the pen rather than the sword, and who—as Enlightenment philosophers and writers—for the most part promoted secular and republican ideas. In some writings the attack seems bent upon the abolition of the existing institutions (e.g., Voltaire), but in others upon the erection of new ones (e.g., Rousseau). In any event, these Enlightenment thinkers had at best only tangential relations with the existing institutions, and for the most part held no official status in the older institutions of society, i.e., in the state, the church, or the universities. As a result, they addressed their appeal to the rational element within each individual, so that a new kind of individualism arose.[8]

By the eighteenth century, then, there had emerged a more defined sense of human individuality. The economic and political orders came to be thought of as the network of fundamentally independent individuals (economic liberalism), who came into political union through a social contract (political liberalism). Moreover, in ethics the fully moral agent was considered to be the absolutely autonomous individual; and the cultivated intelligence was supposed to belong to the fully self-conscious individual. There are many aspects of the new individualism that are still present in our society today, but I will attend only to the character of self-consciousness that is a primary aspect of the new individualism. The older medieval interiority with its immediacy and passion gave way before a more deliberate and reflective modern sense of *privacy*. For *qua* individual, the human being was now understood to be materially individuated and—far more important—*psychologically isolated*. Indeed, the modern individual was so enclosed in privacy that it even had to find a method or criterion with which to gain access to the everyday world that had been taken previously as simply there.[9] Descartes sought to "get out" of the self by rational demonstration; more skeptical empiricists doubt-

---

8. See Kenneth L. Schmitz, "The Authority of Institutions: Meddling or Middling?" *Communio* 12, no. 2 (1985): 5–24.

9. Of course, skeptics—both ancient and modern—had doubted the validity of knowledge claims that rested upon sensory perception of the world of nature. Hegel remarks more than once that the difference between ancient and modern skepticism is that the former lodged their complaint against the untrustworthy instability of nature, whereas the latter (in contrast to the rationalists and idealists) placed their mistrust in the self and in the inadequacy of its powers. Doubt about the *knowability* of the physical world had been expressed ever since Plato, and in a certain way earlier by Parmenides. It is interesting to notice that Matthew of Aquasparta at the end of the thirteenth century had posed the question, whether we could ever know by natural rational means that the world existed. Berkeley is also said to have raised this question with Malebranche, who fell back upon the revelation of the creation of the world in Genesis to justify our belief in its existence. In all of these positions, human powers alone were thought to be unable to maintain veridical association with the real world.

ed they could do so even by direct appeal to the senses. Of course, common sense may object that these abstruse problems troubled only a few overly subtle philosophers. But such philosophers were influential just because they gave expression to a widely held and deep-seated misgiving about the "shape of things." A kind of private darkness was widely perceived to lie at the heart of human life. There was among the leaders of thought, especially those who helped to promote "enlightened ideas," an overwhelming sense of private inwardness which needed "a way out" to the public world of tested reality. Moreover, variants of this desperate isolation are with us still.

Indeed, the very principle of *subjectivity*—the subjective consciousness about which the idealists, empiricists, and existentialists have said so much over the past two centuries or more—takes its origin out of this sense of inner individual solitariness. The scientific canons of objectivity had won admirable success in gaining knowledge about physical nature, and in developing modern scientific technology; and so, it is not surprising that this sense of human inwardness should also seek outward expression by translation into scientifically objective language. It was to receive that translation in modern psychology and psychoanalysis. Largely through these disciplines and techniques, human inwardness came to outward expression, but it did so in the form of objective language; that is, the psyche is treated in these disciplines as a special sort of object. It seems to me, then, that what is distinctive about the modern principle of subjectivity is the process of *inward uniqueness outwardizing itself*.[10] In contrast to this modern sense of privacy, the older theological *interiority* arises out of an open intimacy with God. The modern psychological *subjectivity* emerges out of the desperate conviction that the human *psyche* is a private enclosure.[11] The term *subjectivity* is intellectual shorthand for the modern history of the unique inwardness of individual human beings insofar as they feel themselves threatened by an objectified—and largely material, quantified, and reified—world. It is a defense of human inwardness in a world of objects. For that reason, it is also a holding operation for the older sense of human interiority that is latent within it.

To turn the new sense of self-conscious individuality to advantage, however, we need to distinguish between intimacy and privacy.[12] Intimacy is a kind of communication between persons, but it is far removed

10. For another context from which the following has been drawn, see note 8.
11. Cf. Humean empiricist skepticism and its development into positivism; Kantian critical idealism which can only reach objective knowledge of things as they appear to us (phenomena); and Husserlian phenomenology with its emphasis upon the intentionality of consciousness.
12. For an earlier consideration of intimacy, see "Intimacy and the Knowledge of Persons," *Filosofia e Comunicação* (1981): 87–90.

from "information theory" and does not depend upon being broadcast over a telecommunications network. A computer hook-up can carry information in overwhelming detail, and can contribute to knowing a great deal *about* someone. That is, it can lead to familiarity; but familiarity does not necessarily lead to intimacy, as anyone knows who has lived in a barracks or college dorm. Indeed, intimacy cannot be ensured by means of tools and devices of any type, as the pathetic stories of the patrons of sex-shops seem to indicate. For intimacy differs from familiarity, as well as from privacy. Let us look briefly, then, at these three terms: intimacy, familiarity, and privacy, because although they are often used interchangeably in ordinary speech, a closer look at their nuances discovers important differences.

Privacy is the effort to block another from knowing something about us. It is essentially a negative term, deriving from Latin words *(privo, privatus)* used in such expressions as "withdrawn from public life," "stripped of office," and "delivered from something or someone." Today it has taken on a somewhat more positive, if still defensive, meaning. More precisely, familiarity and privacy are related to one another today more as opposites.

Familiarity designates knowledge that comes about gradually through the accumulation of details about a thing or person, leading us to expect a pattern of behavior. The Latin words from which it derives *(famulus* or *familiaris* meaning "servant," and *familia* meaning "a household," but unlike our present word "family," excluding wife and children) carries with it the notions of subordination and of the ordinary or commonplace, which are still adumbrated in the term today. In its tendency to refer to what is ordinary and everyday knowledge, the term *familiarity* shares that reference to surface previously noticed in respect of the term *personality*. Thus, we may become familiar with a person's behavior without coming to know him or her intimately.

Intimacy, on the other hand, designates a relation of some depth between persons. The term derives from Latin words that associate inwardness with depth: the adverbs *intus, inter,* meaning "in the midst of" and "within," carry connotations of depth (cf. the English *under*). The inward depth is built up through the comparative *interior,* meaning "inner, nearer, more deeply," and the superlative *intimus,* meaning "inmost, most profound, most hidden and secret." Intimacy is not gained, however, through just any penetration directed by one person to another, such as a look that indecently strips away those safeguards that protect another's vulnerability. That is why the philosophy of the existentialist Sartre, despite its intense concentration upon self-consciousness, has no inkling of intimacy. Instead, it has room only for intense introspection and violated privacy, the familiarity that so often breeds contempt. Intimacy cannot be expected to be present in a relation of domineering and dominated. It is not to be found within the search for an absolute freedom (autonomy) whose only alternative is a humiliating submission to another (heteronomy). Genuine intimacy cannot be forced. It is offered by a person in the trust that the offer will be received by another with respect, and on the basis of a certain mutual integrity and openness. Intimacy arises within the circle of giving and receiving, and so it is not without a certain risk, the risk of self-rejection that is inseparable from the generosity of the gift of self.[13] Intimacy is possible only through self-disclosure, and full intimacy calls for shared self-disclosure. Our intimate knowledge of a person is grounded in this act of mutual self-disclosure.

But this self-disclosure brings persons together in a closeness that reaches beyond formalities. For although individual features and social roles usually play a part in setting the tone and character of the relationship, and continue to be recognized within it, nevertheless, intimacy transcends these forms. So that intimacy is not rooted ultimately in the formal features we can identify about persons: their charm or intelligence, their culture or learning, their physical strength and looks, their achievements, social status, or influence. Intimacy is rooted rather in the unique *being present* of a person; and the principal mark of intimacy is *attentiveness to the presence of another*. Intimacy is the sustained wonder in the sheer presence of another, a wonder that is not unrelated to what Aristotle describes as the beginning of philosophy itself. This wonder at sheer presence is why we may sometimes experience a kind of intimacy of the moment, whenever we are surprised by another person who manifests his or her presence, and who (to use Marcel's word) shares with us a secret, "the hidden depth of our co-presence."[14]

The trans-formal character of intimacy is the reason why it is not unconditionally necessary for intimates to communicate the meaning of their association to one another in ordinary words, although they may often do so, and often feel the need to confirm it through non-verbal signs of intimacy. But it is not easy to find adequate words, for intimacy may surprise us too deeply for anything but wordless joy or grief, or

---

13. For a further development of the theme, see *The Gift: Creation*, Aquinas Lecture 46 (Milwaukee, WI: Marquette University Press, 1982), sec. 2, 34–63.

14. The indebtedness to Gabriel Marcel (in such works as *The Mystery of Being* and *Presence and Immortality*) is considerable in what follows, though my own use of the term "presence," while it is meant to include Marcel's phenomenological and experiential sense, is meant to be primarily metaphysical, i.e., to characterize the constitutive actuality of the person within the varied context of being.

it may consist of a felt shared presence that is all but ineffable. Moreover, even when it is appropriate to communicate intimate knowledge of someone to others who do not share the intimacy, the trans-formal character of intimacy makes that communication difficult. For the intimate knowledge we have of another person requires for its expression meaning that is scarcely formulable, and evidence that is usually inaccessible to public forums. This is why religious revelation requires self-disclosure in faith before access can be gained to participation in the inner life of God.[15] And analogously, trust is also required for intimacy between human persons. Once again, we come upon that play of the manifest and the hidden, of what is public and what is secret. And just because intimacy is a shared secret, if (when it is appropriate to share it with others) I urge, for example, that my friend is to be trusted, and am challenged to offer reasons for my trust, I may be able to say only: "It is because I *know* him, and I know that he will never betray us." This is a quite distinct and ancient sense of "know" which gives expression to more than merely mental associations; it signifies real relations with their consequences, as in the biblical phrase for sexual union: "to know a woman." This "real knowledge" has wider application, however, than to relations between the sexes, and is applicable to all awareness that is attuned to a certain depth of personal reality in existing concrete situations. Indeed, contrary to the current widely accepted view, gender difference and sexuality are expressions of the whole person rather than the other way round. Indeed, when such concrete, integral awareness reached the highest and purest order the ancients called it "wisdom." Such "knowing" does not fare well in a world of increasing information networks in which the persuasive power of a claim lies chiefly in the ease by which it can be communicated. Nevertheless, it would be shallow and wrongheaded to lightly discount intimate knowledge as merely subjective and private, "just one person's opinion," on the grounds that it is not accessible to public scrutiny or objective facts; for matters of great import may hang upon such personal witness.[16]

Strictly speaking, we do not *learn* anything *about* another person through intimacy; or rather, if we do (and we often do), the information gleaned is incidental to the central gain. Rather, we simply acknowledge our attunement with another personal presence; and the self we come to know in and through intimacy is just this *presencing*. In knowing

---

15. "And even self-disclosure in and through religious action." See "Faith and Practice: The Nature and Importance of Religious Activities," in *The Life of Religion: A Marquette University Symposium on the Nature of Religious Belief*, ed. Stanley H. Harrison and Richard C. Taylor (Lanham, MD: University Press of America, 1986), 39–60.

16. See Ian Ramsey, *Religious Language* (London: SCM, 1957), 20–30.

this presencing we come to the root of the person, to *personal existence* as such.

I have already remarked that this self-presencing is not formless, since its presence is interwoven with features that express the character of the person and are grounded in that self-presence. Indeed, as with all finite things, each individual human person is "this something of a certain kind" *(tode ti)*.[17] In its singularity the individual has both peculiar and common features. Now, such an individual cannot be grasped in its integrity and its unity through the formation of concepts alone, since concept formation attends to the common aspects at the expense of the peculiar. Nor, if we are trying to understand the individual and not merely to observe it, is it enough simply to hand the particularity over to sensory perception. The original integrity of the singular can be reached, however, through the existential force of the judgment—I do not use the term here in the current sense of "judgmental," i.e., of assigning praise and blame, but as characterizing the way in which we recover the actual singularity of things in their existential context. The standard theories of meaning lose the integrity of the individual, inasmuch as they introduce a division between the universal and the particular, or between generality and instance, law and case, or class and member.

The existential force of the judgment, on the other hand, is the medium for reaching the singular in order to recover its original unity; but this recovery is only the prelude to an account of the uniqueness of the human person and the trans-formal character of its self-disclosure. The trans-formality can be indicated by speaking of metaphysics (theory of reality) instead of epistemology (theory of meaning). Metaphysically speaking, intimacy is not grounded in the recognition of this or that characteristic a person has, but rather in the simple unqualified presence the person is. That is to say, the ontological constitution of the human person does not consist merely of a thing which possesses certain distinctive traits (properties); for that is to understand a person in terms of what the person possesses (has). Such a metaphysics of things and their properties corresponds to the previously mentioned theories of meaning (which distribute meaning into particular and universal, instance and generality, case and law, or member and class); whereas the recognition of the unique individual in the integrity of its singular existence requires both a different metaphysics and a different theory of knowledge. Only such a transformed metaphysics and its epistemology can provide a prelude to an understanding of what it means to say that

---

17. The point is developed in "Community: The Elusive Unity," esp. 250–54 (see note 7).

intimacy is the self-disclosure of a personal presence that transcends its formalities even while it retains them.[18]

Indeed, it seems to me that the presence in which intimacy is rooted is nothing short of the unique act of existing of each person. Presence is but another name for the being of something insofar as it is actual, and in intimacy we come upon and are received into the very act of existing of another. We are, then, at the heart, not only of another person, but at the heart of the texture of being itself. No doubt it is true that the person is incommunicable in objective terms insofar as he or she is existentially unique. But in intimacy, as we approach the very act of self-disclosure, we approach the center of all communicability. It is this "secret" that we share with the other person. It is the sense of being with another at the foundation not only of our personal existence, but of being with each other in the most fundamental texture of being itself. Put in the most general terms—though we must not forget that each intimacy is through and through singular—the "secret" that we discover through intimacy is this: that *reality is not indifferent to the presence of persons.*

Intimacy is the ontological *locus* out of which all other personal values take their rise, for this unique presence is the root of personal and therefore of distinctively human dignity. Just as the human person is not formless, so too, the human dignity that finds its source in the uniqueness of personal presence also contains the dignity of the human form. The formal dignity of human individuals rests upon their instantiation of the human type. The medieval schoolmen spoke of "human nature," and framed that dignity in terms of Natural Law. In quite different circumstances, Enlightenment philosophers spoke of "Humanity as such," and framed the dignity in terms of the Rights of Man. Personal dignity incorporates these formal directives, but these formal human values arise out of the concrete individual's unique presence, a presence whose peculiar value is situated within the context of the non-specific values (what the schoolmen called "Transcendentals") inherent within being itself.[19] To speak metaphysically, form is rooted in act—understanding

---

18. I cannot enter into such a discussion here, of course, but I have indicated its lines in "Enriching the Copula," and in "Metaphysics: Radical, Comprehensive, Determinate Discourse." See chapters 1 and 6 above.

19. In "Natural Imagery as a Discriminatory Element in Religious Language," in *Experience, Reason and God,* ed. E. T. Long, Studies in Philosophy and the History of Philosophy, vol. 8 (Washington, DC: The Catholic University of America Press, 1980), 159–76, esp. 175–76, I have indicated how non-specific terms can provide access to an understanding of religious texts in ontological terms, precisely because they are not abstracted from the specific meanings inseparable from particular religious revelations, and because they have an integral relation to *presence.* I have also touched upon their metaphysical role briefly. See chapter 1 above.

by *act* what Aristotle meant in *enérgeia,* and even more, what Thomas Aquinas meant more radically by *esse.* Personal dignity is specified by the formal dignity appropriate to human nature, but that formal dignity is itself rooted in the dignity of actual personal existence.

The insistence upon rooting the commonality of human nature in the singularity of personal existence does not return us to a state of isolated privacy. To be sure, intimate relations often include privacy, and intimate secrets are often private; but the "secret" which is shared in intimacy differs from knowledge held in a condition of privacy. First of all, knowledge held in privacy may be of the kind of factual information that is all too easily communicable, and must be hedged about with promises of confidentiality between the parties; or, in the case of state papers, such knowledge may receive the designation of "top secret" and the protection of counter-intelligence. The "secret" shared in intimacy, on the other hand, is an open secret, in the sense in which the shared meaning of a Gospel parable is genuinely accessible (though only through faith), and is by no means merely private. A secular analogy can also serve to illustrate the point: a popular song of the Great Depression, "The Best Things in Life Are Free," broadcast a secret in something like this sense of the word, for although these "best things" are available to anyone who appreciates them, their value remains a secret to those who can or will see no deeper than the shallows of life.

Despite its relative inaccessibility, intimacy builds ontological bridges. We have seen that Christian faith inclines to it as a pathway to the divine: first of all, it takes intimacy to be expressive of the very life of the Godhead; secondly, the intimacy of man and God come "face to face" in the divine person of Christ; finally, this twofold disclosure of the divine issues in the call to a new assembly *(ecclesia),* the fellowship of Christians in the Church. These are religious and theological bridges, of course. Nevertheless, they can teach us something about ourselves and the human community that always needs to be built up in the world at large.

As we turn to suggest the importance of leaving room for intimacy in a healthy human society, we need to acknowledge the difference between the religious intimacy that involves God or God and man, and the intimacy between human persons. There is no privacy in relation to God, there is only more or less perfect intimacy. Among humans, on the other hand, privacy often has a legitimate role to play. That role can be indicated by drawing a contrast within the singular human being between his or her individual aspect and its privacy, on the one hand, and his or her person and its capacity for intimacy, on the other. The contrast may be made clearer by considering first, whether we can be intimate with ourselves alone. We may mean by self-intimacy: "being alone," in the sense of "getting away from others," "communing with nature," "meditating upon the sacred," or "praying in the presence of God." But, if we mean by self-intimacy such utter privacy that we would be without God or other things or persons, then that privacy would itself be the darkness at the heart of human life which, it seems to me, is the distinctively modern source of isolation, alienation, and abandonment. In contrast, intimacy gives access to ourselves as well as to others, and always implicates others, either God or other human persons. This is in keeping with Thomas Aquinas' insistence that we come to self-knowledge in and through the knowledge of others, with Hegel's presentation of self-consciousness as the mutual recognition between persons, and with Husserl's insistence upon the intentional character of consciousness.

Nevertheless, even though complete privacy is incompatible with the very nature of human consciousness, a healthy intimacy between human persons is shot through with a dialectic of privacy and intimacy. So that perfect intimacy between humans without any privacy at all is, like perfect privacy, an asymptote rather than a reality. In interpersonal relationships privacy has a role to play in safeguarding the limits of one human being in relation to another. Privacy serves to mark the possibility of our transgressions towards one another. In the present condition of humankind, exposed as we are to the terrible powers that we can wield against each other, privacy can serve as a fragile protective barrier, a refuge of last resort against Big Brother or Sister Snoop; but only as long as a civil will supports it. The mark of modern totalitarianism is the destruction of the possibility of the will both to privacy and to intimacy.

Nevertheless, important as it is, privacy must cease to be the ruling consideration in our relations with others. The individualism that protects its subjectivity by means of privacy is the price we have paid for our uncertain conquest of nature and its forces; but as long as it is taken as primary in our relationships, it seems increasingly liable to produce fragmentation, isolation, and alienation from one another and the disintegration of society itself. It is time, then, to look anew at the concept of *person* to see whether it holds out some promise for a reformation of social relationships. We learn from the concept of *person* that interiority is not the same as privacy, since interiority does not exclude others. Its career shows its capacity for opening out to God, to Christ, and to Christian fellowship. It seems to me that it can lead to a new sense of mutual association in society at large, and without prejudice to those who are not Christian. It is not without precedent for a society to adapt concepts and values without necessarily accepting them in their original setting and with their original premises. Given the assaults upon human dignity in the contemporary world, and the pressing problems of population and resources, it is not clear that a sufficiently strong conviction of personal dignity can be maintained without the religious beliefs out of which it has for the most part arisen, but it seems clear that individualism and its sense of privacy is too fragile and ambivalent in its effects to be an ultimate safeguard of human values. The concept of *person*, on the other hand, holds promise because it expresses distinctiveness without separation. It nourishes uniqueness, not by way of privacy with its inclusiveness and alienation, but by way of distinctness with its variety and abundance. It is upon the uniqueness of each person, then, and the diversity of all that human dignity and the rights and responsibilities of human persons rest: the dignity of all rests upon the original dignity of each.

Chapter 10

IMMATERIALITY PAST AND PRESENT

The medieval conception of immateriality was prominent in discussions of God, man, and nature, of causality, activity, and order, of knowledge, freedom, and immortality. Yet this once noble conception seems absent from most present-day discussions of similar topics. Terms such as consciousness, subjectivity, *Existenz* and *Dasein,* temporality, historicity, and language have taken its place, and even current talk about spirituality does not seem quite the same.

Has the conception remained unscathed, braving the gauntlet of misdirected blows? Has this grand weapon of the philosophical armory merely become blunt from too much wear? Has it been displaced instead by a paradigm shift in the manner of Kuhn's scientific revolutions? Or, Dionysus-like, has it suffered the fate of dismemberment, passing over into a scattered existence among its very executioners? Has the ongoing search for the philosopher's stone transmuted it, perhaps, in alchemical fashion, into better or baser metal? Or finally, has this once indispensable conception simply evaporated under the heat of critical inquiry and the pressure of new interests?

In less metaphorical terms, has the conception of immateriality disappeared entirely from effective philosophical use? Has it lost its explanatory power, if it ever had any? And has the alleged reality to which it referred become so obscured as to render the use of the term obscurantist? Worse still, has its referent been exposed as non-existent? Even a brief answer to these questions must begin by recalling the chief features of the classical conception of immateriality, especially as it was generally understood in the High Middle Ages within a received Aristotelianism that in its turn had been shaped at critical points by a received Platonism.

Reprinted from *Proceedings of the American Catholic Philosophical Association* 52 (1978): 1–15. Copyright © 1978 by the ACPA.

THE CLASSICAL CONCEPTION OF IMMATERIALITY

Initially considered, immateriality is a negative term set over against materiality. The couplet, materiality-immateriality, provides a flexible correlation between the determinable and the determinative in any order of analysis or reality. Etymologically, immateriality carries the mind to the conception of matter itself. For our present purpose we can set aside the problem of the relation of the medieval conception of matter to various modern scientific conceptions.[1] We can also set aside the medieval controversies over whether matter is an odd sort of primitive positive entity or an absolutely formless potential principle. It is enough for our purpose to recall the very general medieval meaning of matter. It refers to an underlying passive potentiality that, when coupled with form, is the root of features that attend any composite into whose constitution matter has entered. Insofar as anything manifests these features materiality is attributed to it.

The "properties" of matter, according to medieval thought, are three. (1) The passive potentiality of material things renders them subject to, and subjects of, change. (2) They are subject to the transitive power of agents which transmute them, so that they are more or less radically altered by the new relationships into which they are brought by the transitive, transmutant power. They undergo rearrangement of their parts, qualitative changes of shape and disposition, as well as displacement by other adjoining things. (3) These processes take time, so that the whole movement together with its subject is indexible in reference to some determinate space and time. Indeed, a material thing insists upon its simple primary location at some definite place and time. Material things, then, are characterized by their (1) *passivity*, (2) *transitivity*, and (3) *indexicity*.

Immateriality in medieval thought receives its first positive meaning as the formal principle in any composite into which materiality has entered. In medieval philosophies there are many modes, kinds, and degrees of immateriality, beginning with the simplest forms of primitive material composites and building in complexity, unity, and power towards the human intellectual form and beyond it. It is tempting to pass over the medieval conception of form, as though its meaning is obvious. Moreover, it is risky to say anything about it, lest we introduce modern constructivist tendencies into it. Nevertheless, when we reflect upon how formal principles function in medieval philosophies, it is correct to point to three features that are explicit characteristics of form, even if only indirectly.

---

1. See William Wallace, "Immateriality and Its Surrogates in Modern Science," *Proceedings of the American Catholic Philosophical Association* 52 (1978): 28–83.

(1) Contrary to the principle of material passivity, which is other-directed, medieval formal principles manifest a sort of eidetic autonomy: they are what it is they are, and the composites of which they are forms are what they are by virtue of their formal principles. This initial positive meaning of immateriality in medieval thought derives, of course, from classical Greek philosophy, especially from Plato and Aristotle, but not without development. Whatever was held about the eternity of species or the fixity of biological species, there is a much more important character inseparable from the very conception of form in traditional philosophy: its self-identity. The first positive sense of immateriality, then, is inseparable from a sort of self-possession and self-definition. Form discloses itself by a sort of self-declaration and self-display. If we could speak of a movement interior to form, we might say that it is self-coincident: it agrees with itself. Hegel later advanced this radical self-coherence as the formal basis for possibility.[2]

(2) In medieval philosophy form is a principle of activity, either as itself pure form or as the formal principle of a material composite. When form translates itself into activity in and through the composite, it manifests its radical self-determinateness as self-determination. It carries out its self-determination by a certain reflexivity that is rooted in the very nature of form and its self-determinateness. This primitive reflexivity lies deeper than self-conscious reflection, deeper even than the great cycle of organic activity. It is inseparable from all action. Indeed, the concept of purely transitive action is a limit-concept that is most closely approximated only by minute particles that dissolve themselves in their own ephemeral activity. In the transitivity of a material thing the formal element demands that the outgoing (transitive) action "flow back" in some manner upon the agent, like the backwash of an outgoing tide; both transitive agent and material patient are affected and together carry out a bonded exchange. Primitive reflexivity is the active basis upon which the principle of reciprocity is built, and Kant saw that the reciprocity of action was necessary for a rational system of natural action. Hegel went beyond reciprocity to recover in a richer sense the self-directedness inherent in all activity.[3] In those activities, of course, in which the agent itself is its own primary term, the formal element may then be said to dwell within the sphere of power originating from its own activity *(immanens)*. Instead of determining others, the activity is primarily self-determining. In such an activity medieval thought recognized the feature of immanence as contrasted with transience.

---

2. *Hegel's Science of Logic,* vol. I, bk. 2. sec. 3, c. 2A: "Contingency or Formal Actuality, Possibility and Necessity," trans. A. V. Miller (New York: Humanities Press, 1969), 542–46.
3. Ibid., vol. I, bk. 2, sec. 3, c. 3: "The Absolute Relation," 554–71.

(3) Medieval thought also attributed a certain "generosity" to form. The forms of material things (precisely in their formal character) escape the strict circumscription of space and time and outstrip determinate indexing. They are trans-indexical just because they are principles of order that are replicable in the many spatially and temporally distinct individuals that instantiate them. The trans-indexicity of form does not prove a Platonic priority of the universal over the individual; it can be maintained just as well on an Aristotelian basis of the primacy of the individual. The point shared by both is that the formal principles, even of material things, are not exhausted in their formation of a single spatially and temporally distinct individual. Form, if we may so speak, radiates beyond any determinately indexed instance of it. To sum up, then: the "properties" of immateriality, as understood in medieval philosophy, are (1) *self-determinateness*, (2) *self-determination*, and (3) *trans-indexicity*.

Immateriality in the strongest sense of the term manifests itself, according to medieval thought, as spirituality, that being in which actuality and its activity is independent of matter and its conditions free of its passivity, transitivity, and indexicity. Medieval thinkers learned from St. Augustine and others to place subsistent immateriality at the center of spiritual life. In it self-determinateness is self-actual, self-determination is immanent, and trans-indexicity is transcendent. The characteristics of knowing and being known provided medieval philosophers with an illustration of the strong sense of immateriality. The same material thing that manifests passivity, transitivity, and indexicity in its own being can also be known; and when it is actually known it manifests different features. These distinctive features are due to the intrusion of an immaterial principle in some strong sense, for when it is known, a material thing is not thereby reconstituted in its parts like a can of frozen orange juice, as though analysis were an actual physical separation; nor is it decreased in its size or altered in its shape or diminished in its power; it is not even transported from one space-time index to another. Yet it is "converted" (if I may use this logical and religious word in its intransitive, immaterial sense) into a known fact that can fly from every gossip's tongue or flow from a historian's pen into a printed medium that can be read everywhere and anytime.

This conversion gives the material thing a sort of second and immaterial "nature," a *meta-physics* which the ancients called an intelligible nature or species. They understood it to be an immaterial, intelligible mode of being because it was a second nature through and in which the thing could be present to the knower.[4] In sum, immateriality in its

---

4. "Enriching the Copula," *Review of Metaphysics, A Commemorative Issue: Thomas Aquinas 1224–1274* 27 (1974): 492–512. See chapter 6 above.

traditional strong sense is characterized by self-originating activity over against the radical passivity of matter, by an absence of transitivity in favor of a corresponding intransitivity, and by a freedom from simple space-time location in favor of a distinctive manner of presence. The "properties" of immateriality, explicit in the strong sense as spirituality, are, then, (1) *self-actuation*, (2) *immanence*, and (3) *transcendence*.

THE CURRENT CONCEPTION OF IMMATERIALITY

Having indicated the traditional understanding of immateriality in general as formal, and maximally as spiritual, the original question returns: What import, if any, does this traditional understanding have for present philosophical inquiry? The traditional "properties" of matter may still be recognized, although the meaning of matter has changed in modern thought.[5] So, too, we might well expect the meaning of immateriality, that is, of "something other than matter," to have paralleled that change. We cannot assume that it has. Still, it is significant that important meanings of a formerly durable philosophical vocabulary, meanings such as those of traditional matter and immateriality, seem to be largely absent from the mainstream of current philosophical discussion. This silence is especially difficult for those of us—often, but not exclusively, Catholic—who wish to draw upon earlier traditions in our own philosophical reflection. It is a philosophical wonder and not simply a religious piety that moves us to reconsider Plato, Plotinus or St. Augustine, Aristotle, St. Thomas Aquinas or Meister Eckhart, St. Bonaventure, Duns Scotus or Ockham. We think that there are important things yet to be said with the help of one or another past intellectual tradition; yet we want to philosophize in a serious, and therefore in a genuinely current, sense. We are not just interested in phenomenology or language analysis or transcendental philosophy, and then incidentally also interested in Platonism, or Augustinianism, or Thomism. Rather, we bring these traditional and contemporary interests together so that they might make up one single philosophical life and bear upon the whole of our intellectual tradition and its present needs.

Instead, however, we often enough find a division—not so much between one school and another, or even between one of our interests and another—but a flaw within ourselves, a disjunct that pulls us now one way, now another. Moreover, the solution is not so easy as shaping clear current phrases in which to expound either old traditions or new philos-

---

5. See E. McMullin, ed., *The Concept of Matter*, 2nd ed. (Notre Dame, IN: University of Notre Dame Press, 1977).

ophies. It requires us to confront the pervasive shift that has thrown the traditional discussion somehow off balance and out of phase with the current philosophical discussions. It is not surprising that the readjustment is difficult, in view of the massive shift that has intervened between us and medieval thought. Indeed, I chose the conception of immateriality for the theme of this meeting just because I thought that it would highlight the shift and the division.[6] It need not be emphasized that other conceptions basic to the medieval thought-world would serve as well.

If I were to come upon a conversation today whose theme was immateriality, whether so named or not, what might I expect to hear? If I were to ask for directions towards immateriality in the medieval world, I would be directed towards form and away from matter. But if, bewildered, I were to ask for direction in our own world, towards what should I be pointed? If I have correctly understood the shift, I should expect the apex and paradigm of immateriality in the medieval world to be the spirituality of God, and in the contemporary world to be the spirituality of man, if such there be. Indeed, the unforgivable crime in our world does not seem to be the sin against the Holy Spirit or even lesé majesté, but the de-humanization of man. This suggests that there has not only been a change of direction, but to use Gabriel Marcel's expression there has also been a change of weather. It seems to me, then, that we are not simply to search for a new place at which to draw the line between spirit and non-spirit, as though we might draw it between man and things, or even between man and God, instead of between man and animals as it has been traditionally drawn. Rather, we need a new way of apprehending immateriality and its paradigmatic spirituality, a way that reflects the more systemic expectations of modern thought and life, with its greater sensitivity to the structures of human history than to the order of nature.

In discerning the marks of the spirit in our times, I intend, therefore, to emphasize its formal-ontological features, hopefully striking path lights along the way and not—like Abelard's teacher—simply setting off smoke bombs. It would be a quite different task to describe the concrete signs of the human spirit in our day, and would touch upon the intensely tragic mix of fidelity and despair that is often enough taken to be its present inheritance. That task is being continually attempted today, and the concrete expression of it is best left to poets, novelists, and saints, unless Athena and the Muses consort in some blessed philosopher as they did in Plato. Nevertheless, the formal-ontological features are shorthand for, and receive their validity from, just such a

---

6. A number of papers in the APCA volume 52 reflect this shift.

concrete milieu, so that they ought to be recognizably consistent with it, even when they constitute a criticism of that concrete milieu.

Three formal-ontological features of twentieth-century spirituality are pre-eminent: they are openness, totality, and limit. The first two are already more or less discernible in the medieval conception of immateriality, and the third is present in its creaturely forms. The spirit is *openness:* much present-day writing presents man as an opening. One thinks of Heidegger, of course, but the feature is much more pervasive. Even the despairing anti-heroes of the early Sartre cry out for a sort of dark light, for a freshet of chill air. In other philosophies it may be world-constitution, syntactical structure, social imperative, or interpersonal encounter. As *Existenz* man stands forth from the natural and social capital with which he has been endowed in order to repudiate or reappropriate it. Intentionality itself is the intransitive movement of the human spirit out of its subjective (even its biological) origins towards the disclosure of another as other, and as an opening to the world of experienced objects. Intentionality is a transcendence that can be understood either in a so-called "horizontal" manner as the movement of consciousness from one situation to another, or in a so-called "vertical" manner as the reaching out for that which is in principle beyond human initiative and which must wait upon another in order to receive a gift. In this latter sense, which Gabriel Marcel has so thoughtfully articulated, transcendence is not the act of constituting an object of experience, but the receiving of light and life from a transcendent source.

This spiritual *receptivity* is not to be confused with the passivity of matter,[7] for the matter of wax must first be disposed in order to submit to the imprint of the seal by being rendered passive to the determinative activity of the seal. On the other hand, a host in receiving a guest into his home must rally all his resources in order to receive him well. He will be available to his guest, attending to, and even anticipating, his wants. The clear and distinct line between activity and passivity has itself been transcended here, and the host is both active and passive, or rather simply neither. An unwilling and sullen house owner is no host, though he may passively permit a stranger to enter his house. Nor does the frantic activity of a salesman bent upon closing a deal ensure that there will be a genuine reception of another. Neither passivity nor activity is the essential feature of a host, who now active, now passive, serves the paramount intention of making himself available for a more fully human

---

7. G. Marcel, *The Mystery of Being,* vol. 1: *Reflection and Mystery* (Chicago: Henry Regnery, 1960), 54–56; also 117–18; to receive is "to receive in one's own prepared place of reception . . . not in a wasteland." Cf. in the ACPA volume 52, T. Busch, "Gabriel Marcel on Existence, Being and Immortality."

relationship, for the encounter with another person, and for the disclosure that attends such receptivity.

The test of the authenticity of such receptivity is whether the host is appropriately present, so that *presence* is the measure of the relationship. Now it is just such presence, a being to and with, that is anticipated by the medieval understanding of the intelligible co-presence of knower and known.[8] This spiritual union *(idem est intellectus et res)* is recognized in their different ways by theories of participation and exemplarity developed from Plato as well as by theories of abstraction taking their start from Aristotle. The same transcendental demand also reigns in our affective relationships, so that to love in a spiritual manner is to accept the beloved as he or she is. So far: openness, leading through receptivity to co-presence.

The second formal-ontological feature of twentieth-century spirituality is *totality*, which is itself a sort of openness. It is the aspiration for comprehension, and its modern predecessor is the seventeenth-century conception of system that was further developed by Kant in the "Architectonic of Pure Reason" in accordance with what he called the eternal and essential needs of reason.[9] This *conceptus cosmicus (Weltbegriff)* was still further transformed by the post-Kantians into some form of absolute system. Yet even after absolute systems lose favor the concept of totality lives on in the non-systematic philosophies of phenomenology, existentialism, linguistic and hermeneutic philosophy. It lives on, it seems to me, because it is an indispensable feature of contemporary spirituality, and is expressed in such conceptions as being-in-the-world, Jasper's *Umgreifende*, Husserl's horizon, and even as *langue* (distinct from *parole*). It is important to notice, however, that it has survived insofar as it has become background to a foreground that displays the finitude of human spirituality.

I have arrived at the third formal-ontological feature of contemporary spirit. Spirit is openness and totality, but it is also *limit*.[10] The term "limit" is a quite general term applicable to everything except the absolutely limitless. The latter term can be taken in a quasi-negative sense in cosmological discourse as *apeiron*. The term finite, however, strictly presupposes an affirmative conception of the infinite (as *Ipsum esse*, Unity, Divine Light, etc.) and carries us over into theological discourse. The term finite is properly not to be said of unwitting things, because they are not said to be finite strictly out of themselves. Although they are truly finite, they do not have within themselves the capacity to so manifest themselves, for finitude arises properly only with the recognition of the

---

8. "Enriching the Copula," 510–12.
9. *The Critique of Pure Reason*, A832B860–A851B879; also Axii.
10. For a different, but perhaps not ultimately incompatible emphasis, see J. Robb, *Man as Infinite Spirit*, Aquinas Lecture (Milwaukee, WI: Marquette University Press, 1974).

true nature of limit; and that requires the co-recognition of something affirmative that lies beyond the limit.[11] Unwitting things indicate the true nature of what lies beyond them only in an obscure way that does not justify either the term finite being given to them nor the name creature. That is why the *quinque viae,* for example, start with the limitedness of things and not with their finitude, and why the finitude of things is discovered only in the very conclusion that also establishes the infinite source of their limitation.

In addition, the term *situation* adds to finitude the specifically immaterial way in which human beings are limited. The literary emphasis upon "the human condition" is matched in contemporary philosophical writing by its emphasis upon the category of situation. What is more, man's situatedness is rooted in his embodiment, in his incarnate way of being in the world. Situation, then, is a sort of anthropological equivalent of the material limitation spoken of in cosmological discourse, since both situation and matter play distinctive but analogous limiting roles. Nevertheless, it is necessary to insist that individuality of a spiritual sort is radically diverse from the individuation of matter. The properly human mode of limitation is not one of spatial confinement or material individuation, though human beings are so confined and individuated. Still, human limitation is brought about by and through perspective. It is not only man's perception that is perspectival. Rather, he takes a position (and so is situated) in all of his knowing, willing, and acting. Perspective is a pervasive and transcendental feature of the human spirit. Thus, the category of situation is not simply a contraction of the conception of totality, as though a situation is simply a part of space related externally to the rest. The limitation that operates as human perspective rests somehow upon the comprehension of totality.

Moreover, the tension between situation and totality gives rise, not only to an ambivalence whose alternatives are separable, but also to an ambiguity whose sides are not. Man is faced with the problems that arise from this recognition of his own limitedness. Thus, in our own time, just because the human spirit is seen to be perspectival and situated, contemporary hermeneutics has altered direct explanations into indirect interpretations and is haunted by the danger of historical relativism. The ambiguity does not arise, therefore, simply because man is limited, but because he is also aware of being limited, and in being aware he already comprehends, in some vague way at least, the totality that lies beyond the limits.

What is more, this comprehension of the beyond counts in his thinking, for it is always present as meaning that he has not yet penetrated,

---

11. Cf. *Hegel's Science of Logic,* vol. I, bk. 1, c. 2BC: "Finitude" and "Infinity," 122–50.

as a depth that may prove inexhaustible. It is present in myths of the beginning and the end, in values that remain fresh no matter how often they are imperfectly realized; but it is also present in our ignorance, in the shadow of death, in the quickening of hope, and in other apprehensions of ultimacy. Ambiguity, then, is spiritual finitude that arises out of the tension generated by totality and situation, by comprehension and perspective. Faced with the need to select, yet aware of the totality from which the selection is made, man is faced with problems of choice, freedom, and self-determination. This self-determination is the contemporary analogue of that self-actuation already met with in medieval immateriality. Insofar as the form of a composite functions as principle of its nature and activity, it realizes itself in the composite in terms of its own formal actuation.

So, too, insofar as contemporary self-determination realizes and expresses its own spirituality through open receptivity and totality, it rises towards its ontological foundations out of its situation. Spirit in the present century, although it does not comport itself explicitly as *capax dei*, is nevertheless self-determining *capax fundamenti*. The human spirit today seeks origins not only in philosophy, but also in physics, geology, and astronomy, in anthropology, linguistics, and history, and in the study of religion itself. The waste of time and trivial motion that we lament so much in our own age is a profound search for origins that is pressed forward on all fronts today.

The contemporary spirit exhibits an intransitive fluidity which realizes itself in an active transcendence and a receptivity that leads to the co-presence of the human spirit with others. The comprehension of that totality founds a disclosure of mutual presence within a limiting situation. The marks of twentieth-century spirituality, then, are the formal-ontological moments of comprehension or totality, of situation or perspective, and of receptive openness or presence. In this comprehending situated disclosure the spiritual value of truth operates, not only as a theoretical standard, but also as an imperative that, beyond theory and practice, calls the spirit to its origins and to ultimacy.[12]

THE AFFINITY OF MEDIEVAL "IMMATERIALITY" AND CONTEMPORARY "SPIRITUALITY"

What, finally and today, are we to make of the conception of immateriality that derives from classical and especially from medieval thought?

---

12. For development of the factors of comprehension, disclosure, selectivity, and the imperative, see "Another Look at Objectivity," *Thomas and Bonaventure: A Septicentenary Commemoration Proceedings of the American Catholic Philosophical Association* 48 (1974): 86–98. See chapter 5 above.

Having tried to indicate the so-called "properties" of medieval and current conceptions and the shift that separates them, I return in conclusion to put the question with which I began: Is there an important affinity between the medieval sense of immateriality and the current sense of spirituality? An answer must draw upon the features of the two conceptions already set forth. These features crystallize into two distinctive versions of rational discourse. *Dis-cursus* is to run to and fro: the inseparable prefix is perhaps intensive, but certainly divisive and partitive. To discourse, then, is to move from part to part, to proceed from place to place, to run through step by step; and *cursus verborum* is the flow of conversation. *Rational* discourse[13] is an intransitive movement of human thought and speech, organized for cognitive purposes and sustained by a more or less explicit theory of truth, criteria of evidence, and canons of argumentation. Rational discourse is the appropriate mode of human intelligence in theology and philosophy, in the natural and social sciences, in history, literary criticism, and wherever understanding is sought out.

According to medieval thought, man is an embodied spirit, and according to contemporary thought he is situated in the world; both medieval and contemporary theories of discourse root themselves in man's embodiment or situatedness. Embodiment is an entitative principle, and situation is a systemic description; yet each in its distinctive way grounds the discursive nature of human intelligence. For the most part later medieval thinkers explained the discursive nature of human thought by some theory of abstraction, since that accounts for the relatively partial and empty character of human concepts and necessitates an accumulative development of meaning in syllogistic or other form. So, too, aware of the selectivity of human thought and language, rational discourse today demands more or less explicit reference to the "position" of the speaker and to the limitations of the context, along with continual empirical confirmation and enrichment.

The medieval conception of discourse recognizes the tension between the intuitive grasp of principles and conclusions *(intellectus)* and the progressive development of meaning *(ratio)*. So that we have a sort of parallel: As medieval *incarnatio* is the ground of the tension between *ratio* and *intellectus*, so the contemporary *situation* is the ground of the tension between *totality* and *presence*. Medieval theological discourse about embodiment is not simply equivocal to contemporary anthropological discourse

---

13. I have discussed this meaning of discourse somewhat more fully in "Restitution of Meaning in Religious Speech," *International Journal for Philosophy of Religion* 5 (1974): 131–51; see 134–36.

about situation. Medieval thought is aware of the profound spiritualization of man's embodiment; the psychological and subjective emphasis in modern thought is a recognition of the spirituality of the conditions of human existence. Indeed, there are similarities of role between *incarnatio* and *situation*, between *ratio* and *totality*, and between *intellectus* and *presence*. Nevertheless, there is no exact correspondence between the pairs. Instead there is an affinity and resonance between the triadic structures each taken as a whole with respect to the other. Both present the process of spiritualization, but somewhat differently. In medieval cognitional theory, for example, the forms of the imagination are sublimated into conceptual elements, and in ethical theory sensory appetites are put in the service of the will. In contemporary thought, on the other hand, spiritualization is manifest in the roles played by the features of totality and presence. It remains to indicate just how.

The contemporary category of totality is the conceptual recognition that human meanings bear the marks of spatiality. Moreover, this spatiality is never wholly absent even from the mind's most sublime conceptions. All human speech and thought is inseparably bi-valent, reaching down into the situation and thereby transcending it. To mean, for the human spirit, is to move; but the movement, although it is genuine, is not transitive. There is intellectual movement to and fro (and not merely qualitative change from same to other), but the movement is transphysical and intransitive, since it does not alter the physical being of the things known and loved through it. Thought and love do not, precisely as thought and love, alter the things known and loved. The human intelligence does not move in the heavy materiality of the natural space of things; it is not indexed in the sense in which we have already used the term. Nor is its proper medium the particulate and relative atmosphere of sensory perception. Its movement traverses the possibilities of thought and speech; it does not move in among the potential parts of primary space or remain with the particulars of sensory perception. It moves intransitively towards objectivity and truth in the intellectual medium of conceptual discourse. Its terminus is the "represence" of things as they actually are in their own being; its term is the thing as known, its goal is the thing in its truth. Nevertheless, wherever there is movement to and fro, there must be an enabling space. This immaterial kind of movement rests upon an immaterial mode of space.

The concept of totality holds within itself the contextuality which more limited contexts of meaning demand and which makes human meanings possible. The comprehension of totality breaks open dimensions of order: meanings are profound, sublime, commonplace, superficial. It lays open directions of movement: thought advances, withdraws, infers, sums up, reflects. It indicates references to objects: knowing signifies now this, now that, refers, relates, judges. Such a "making room" for meaning is more than a "mere" metaphor, at least as that term is often understood. On the contrary, these are the very dynamics of a situated thought, and discursive thought is inextricable from them. The human spirit in its search for the true and the good transcends, not simply this or that place, but primary space itself. It does this, however, not simply by fleeing, but rather by breaking out the spatiality that is appropriate to meaningfulness. That spatiality is expressed through the comprehensive factor of totality. This factor functions in contemporary philosophies as some more or less explicit version of the concept of totality. But it has always been available to the human spirit, since without it that spirit could not be receptive of the co-presence of others and itself.

Genuine transcendence, however, is not achieved by the systemic order of meanings alone. Whether or not totality takes form as a comprehensive system, totality is not enough. Meanings break out into truth only with disclosure, and that requires presence. In a medieval thought-world, meaning comes into truth only when it transcends form and reaches some trans-formal principle of actuality, such as *actus essendi*, the light of the divine Exemplars, Unity, or *Dator formarum*. Where, under the influence of Aristotle, metaphysics is the science of being as being, it is understood to be the science of whatever is inasmuch as it actually is. All potentiality for being is resolved into actual being of some sort. Metaphysics is the science of that which is because it is actual, and because any principle of being, such as matter, form, finality, accident, or any result of these, such as motion or activity, is related to and reducible to something actual, that is, to one or more entities and ultimately to God. The reduction is accomplished by appeal to necessary causes, participation, exemplarity, teleology, and so forth.

On the side of the metaphysician, this metaphysical "is" declares the intent of the science to resolve all factors of being—material and formal—and all states of being—past, present, and future—into the actuality of present being. Metaphysical discourse, then, is in terms of what *must be*, of what *always is;* and it grounds all finite being ultimately in uncreated *omnipresent* necessary and eternal being. Such a medieval metaphysics is the science of ontological presence. It is intent upon saying something true about all being by relating its meanings to the presence of *supposita*, essences, and natures: entitative presence.

In contemporary thought the formal-ontological feature of openness invites a presence that discloses itself as a temporal principle of meaning and value. A contemporary metaphysics of presence would relate its meanings to presence grasped within the fuller context of temporality.

Such a metaphysics would center not simply upon *supposita*, essences, or natures, but would include the actuality of historical existence itself. To do that, however, it would first have to recognize the temporal origins of its central conception. Now, metaphysical presence can be understood as arising through a modification of the time-structure, in which the metaphysical intention expands the ordinary conception of the temporal present so that it draws the actuality in the other moments of time towards it, thereby condensing all actuality within what becomes a transcendental conception of presence.

If the principle of actuality in both medieval and contemporary metaphysics is transcendental presence, then the contemporary sense of presence recovers, deepens, and expands the medieval sense of actuality. It does this by redefining it in appropriately temporal and historical terms. In so doing, it also defines immateriality in those terms. The immateriality of contemporary presence converts actuality from its older context of formal entitative principles to a historical systemic context: systemic presence. The formal principles of medieval immateriality remain as directives of the more or less stable arrangement of nature, but the world of natural things is now understood to be subject to natural historical development and its reverse. This immateriality of historical presence is the source of a new order, able to be congenial to the career of natural things, sensitive to the historical existence of men and their societies, and able also to disclose the spiritual resources that live at the origin of men and things.

This redefined immateriality may be called "historical consciousness," but the term is misleading, since it should not be taken in a merely subjective sense. Rather, the re-definition of immateriality discloses the real historicity of all finite things, human and non-human. Far from collapsing into subjectivism, this contemporary metaphysical insight demands an objectivity free from radical historical relativism, and can achieve it. Natural things really do have temporal and spatial relations without the intervention of the human mind, and nothing said so far should even appear to deny that. Things have sides, are near to or far from each other, are large or small with respect to one another. Moreover, they are temporal, constituted of a just-having-been which is now tending towards an immediately future state. Of course, some of the meaning which things have is theirs, but theirs only by a curious association with the immaterial presence of the finite human spirit.[14]

When a thing is timed in its movement, new "properties" emerge which "belong" to the thing in virtue of a principle that is not the thing's. The

---

14. "Enriching the Copula," 511–12.

thing becomes a memory and an expectation. It acquires a past and a future as well as a present that is constituted in part through them. But the past *as past* is not in the thing; only determinate states of being are there, and the future is there only as present tendencies. Prior states of being are not present *as past*. In a sedimentary deposit one layer is lower than another, and in a tree one circle of growth is inside another, but they are not related as past to present, nor even strictly speaking as causes, though it remains true that they are earlier, that they did exist before and "have" a past, and true also that they were causes.

The "property" of pastness belongs to the domain of intransitivity, transcendence, and truth; in a word, it is an immaterial "property" which springs up through the loan of a principle that is not in the thing itself. We may say that there are grounds in the thing in itself for a certain "expansion" of its being whenever it comes into association with a spiritual receptive presence. These "properties" which are true of the thing become manifest in the thing, however, only through association with the temporal cadence and spatial perspective of situated intelligence.

What has been theologically expressed in medieval thought—that actuality is formal without being form, that it is trans-formal—is expressed anthropologically in contemporary thought when it recognizes actuality in historical presence. Indeed, presence is the immaterial coin of human spirituality, and perhaps the medium through which the anthropological circle itself can be enriched by being broken.

Chapter 11

THE FIRST PRINCIPLE OF PERSONAL BECOMING

I

Personal development has two broad phases: the first is that of infancy, childhood, and adolescence; the second is that of our continuing development as adults. Without excluding the former, I wish to concentrate upon the latter in order to describe what I will argue is a spiritual form of life in the individual human being. Becoming in the order of human personhood arises out of a dynamic source that is not easy to name with accuracy. It has been called the "psyche," or "subjectivity," or "personality," and sometimes "the human spirit," though the latter term often remains rather too vague for philosophical purposes. Aristotle has said that the fruits of understanding come with getting the name right. What, then, is the proper name with which to designate the dynamic principle at the center of the movement of life that is appropriate to the human person?

Hegel insisted that the answer to such a question required an adequate concept of spirit *(Geist)*, though he extended the notion of spirit to what he called the Absolute. Under the rubric of spirit he sought to integrate what he took to be the restriction of ancient philosophy with what he took to be the contribution of modern philosophy. He thought that ancient philosophy had understood being as objectivity, while modern philosophy had given primacy to consciousness as subjectivity. My aim is more modest and more traditional, but not less difficult: Is it possible that contemporary philosophies stand in need of a more or less traditional metaphysical concept of spirit? Is it possible that a closer look at such a notion might contribute to what I sense is a growing tendency to

---

Reprinted from the *Review of Metaphysics* 47 (June 1994): 757–74. Copyright © 1994 by the *Review of Metaphysics*. I should like to express my appreciation for the helpful comments made by James Felt (Santa Clara University).

understand human reality less mechanistically and less materialistically?

When we speak of spirit, however, a certain ambiguity comes to the fore, an ambiguity that needs to be clarified before my present project can get off the ground. There is first the memory of the long Latin metaphysical tradition of *spiritus,* and second, the newer German postmetaphysical tradition of *Geist.* The terms are by no means identical, even though translators think themselves forced to treat them as equivalent. In fact, however, the two terms draw about themselves curtains of differing connotation, including different resonances of meaning and assonances of sound. For that reason they function in semantically different ways. To be sure, both indicate an internal dynamic and both secure a certain unity, but the terminus of their efficacy is not the same, nor is the context within which they operate. At present, the Germanic sense of "spirit" dominates those discussions in which the notion of spirit plays a role. It will serve a purpose, then, to compare the Germanic with the Latin sense, and even to see whether the Latin notion has any relevance to a contemporary discussion of personal becoming.

At the center of the technical use of *spiritus* in the Latin philosophical traditions there is the Greek heritage proclaimed by the term *eidos.* The Greek is not incorrectly translated by, and thereby converted into, the Latin term *forma. Forma* functions in traditional metaphysics as an immanent *specifying* principle; it is the constituent factor within a complex entity that gives to the entity a unity of a certain kind.[1] *Geist,* on the other hand, tends to perform as a *totality* principle: it brings unity to an even wider context, to a system, horizon, or world. It is a kind of organizing form that brings diverse factors into a complex and more or less internally related arrangement; in a word, *Geist* provides systemic configuration *(Gestalt).*

To clarify the ambiguity in the use of the two terms, it is fair enough to reduce the consideration of the Latin *spiritus* to the principle of specificity, and to reduce the German *Geist* to the principle of totality.[2] In contrast to the specific unity of a metaphysical composite, the unity that results from the dynamism of *Geist* is an organized totality. If Aristotle gives a definitive meaning to form *(eidos)* as specifying the unity of a substance

---

1. When as with St. Thomas Aquinas, the formal principle is expanded to include non-specific aspects of a being, the broader specific principle becomes known as the immanent formal principle, *essentia.* See *SCG* II, 52. The adjustment is made necessary by Thomas' recognition of God's pure act of existing *(esse),* and the consequent presence of the transformal principle of *actus essendi* within each creature, since that principle throws everything else *(praeter esse)* into the formal order.

2. Whereas in the Latin tradition totality (world) tends to be reduced to the order among interrelated entities, in the German tradition entities tend to be reduced to items in a system, functions within a context, or the collectivity of "mere" beings (as in *das Seiende*).

or entity ("this something of a certain kind," *tode ti*), Kant (though he uses the term *Vernunft*) gives definitive meaning to the term *Geist* when he defines the architectonic system that crowns his philosophical undertaking.[3] Both Schelling and Hegel provide the notion of *Geist* with the content of the Absolute System. The architectonic sense survives even in the thought of thinkers who reject the classical modern notion of system, however. The systemic sense remains as the dynamic inner expression of unity in the configuration of a totality; and it takes shape as a dialectical movement or a symphonic orchestration or as the horizon of an open historicity.[4] This is not surprising, since, if spirit—whether understood as *Geist* or as *spiritus*—is in fact central to the human person, it must be found at work wherever persons are found, even under one or another assumed name.[5]

The upshot of the difference between spirit as *forma* and spirit as *Geist* is that two sets of subordinate onto-logic cluster about this semantic difference. It is important, however, to recognize that the Germanic sense of spirit did not arise in direct conflict with the Latin sense, and therefore that the two notions may prove to be complementary. An interval of two to three centuries has occurred in the mainline of European culture between the disappearance of the Latin sense in the late sixteenth century and the first half of the seventeenth century, and the philosophical appearance of the Germanic notion at the end of the eighteenth century and during the first quarter of the nineteenth century. What is even more important is to recall that this interval stretches from the emergence of the modern natural sciences (under the tutelage of mechanics) to the emergence of the newly empowered historical disciplines (ranging from the earth sciences to biblical exegesis). It is not unreasonable to suggest that the German sense of spirit came to prominence with the newer appreciation of historicality and in view of the insufficiency of the classical modern sense of interiority. Such a suggestion needs a word of

---

3. See the penultimate chapter of the *Critique of Pure Reason* (B860–79).

4. I would say that this totality principle is at work unwittingly and against itself even in the deconstructed linguistic system of differential signs, and negatively in those postmoderns who wish to make war upon totality.

5. It seems to me that this explains the attempt to include the effects of spirit within a concept of matter, such as the notion of dialectical or historical materialism. There have been other expansionist attempts to accommodate the effects of spirit within a materialistic analysis. Thus, the mechanistic notions of matter and energy have been opened up to include some of the features of spirit, but this seems to me to verge upon verbal magic, not unlike some of the more fine-spun measures of late medieval scholasticism. The attempt does, however, indicate a growing recognition of the need for a proper concept of spirit. On the other hand, personalist philosophies explicitly invoke the name of spirit, but often a reluctance on the part to endorse a more traditional metaphysical notion of spirit seems to leave the reality of spirit still in need of adequate metaphysical grounding.

explanation, however. Let me very briefly set out the process by which spirit as *forma* went to its death in the main intellectual currents of our culture, while spirit as *Geist* latterly arose to take its place.

II

To tell that story we need to go back to the early modern era. The story is familiar enough that I can omit the more detailed citations to particular philosophers, in order to isolate a certain strain of mainline philosophical thought in the modern era, a strain which is central to the present issue. It is important to remark, however, that I do not pretend to describe the entire process of modernization, and that I distinguish the *process* of modernization with its bewildering plethora of factors from its various *interpretations,* such as Enlightenment liberalism or its partial reaction in dialectical materialism.

The well-known seventeenth-century attack upon scholastic principles exhibits several pressure-points relevant to the notion of spirit. The most obvious target of that attack is the principle of finality, which was either reduced to human purpose (as in Francis Bacon) or abolished *tout court* (as in Spinoza). More than finality fell, however, with the fall of final causality. Thus, there are no metaphysical natures in Descartes, and for that matter in most influential philosophies to this day. Moreover, since the principle of *forma* played the constitutive role in the metaphysical concept of *natura,* one should not expect to find forms functioning as immanent constituent specifying principles. The notion of form did not lose its formality entirely, but it did lose its metaphysical energy (by which form was act in the order of essence), so that form resurfaced as figure, structure, or design.

The concept of matter as pure potentiality-to-form fared no better. Its residue crystallized into matter formed by the so-called primary qualities of mass, size, and dimension. This was what the schoolmen had been wont to call "secondary matter." Indeed, the exploration of this secondary matter became the search for ultimate particles, the elements of modern physics and chemistry whose progressive isolation fuelled more than three centuries of intensive experimentation.

Finally, with the modern adoption of the postulate of the primacy of motion, motion assumed the role of explaining everything else without itself standing in need of explanation; supposedly, it needed only description.[6] As a result, the need for a source of motion gradually lost its

---

6. In the late Middle Ages the study of kinematics (motion *quo ad effectum,* by description) had been distinguished from the study of dynamics (motion *quo ad causam*) and was the forerunner to the new physics of the seventeenth century. Kinematics was furthered by

meaning, so that efficient (that is, effecting) causality, and especially *creation ex nihilo*, lost credibility in the proportion to which a transcendent cause of motion lost its *raison d'être*. What in traditional metaphysics had been the primary source for the communication of existence (God as *causa prima*) was replaced by the various forces that initiate motion and rest. Whereas in the metaphysical view motion received its intelligibility through our setting forth its causes, in early modern physics the intelligibility of causes gave way to the governance of general laws.

What may not be so easily noticed is that in the collapse of the famous four causes of Aristotelian philosophy, the traditional metaphysical sense of being was lost as well. With that loss a shift occurred in the distribution of explanatory terms. To see what the shift entailed we need only look at the transformation in the meaning and function of the terms *subject* and *object*.

In the metaphysics of the High Middle Ages, the term *object* stood for the way in which something other than the knower made itself present to the knower. The actual tree in the garden was not in itself an object; but it became an object insofar as it made its presence seen, heard, or understood by the conformation of the visual, auditory, or intellectual power to the tree's causal action. The actual tree as it stood there in the garden in its own being was not as such an object; on the contrary, it was a subject. So that the relation of knower to known was a relation of subject to subject, that is, a relation between two subjects of being. This observation places us at the great shift, one might even say the decisive reversal, that differentiates the modern outlook from the ancient and medieval understanding. The shift can be seen in the altered role of the term *subject*. According to the traditional metaphysics the tree in the garden was a subject of being *(suppositum entis)*, whereas in the modern outlook the term subject came to mean the subject of consciousness *(subjectum mentis)*.[7]

Before we leave the story of the demise of the older metaphysics, a most important observation must be made. There is more to be noticed about that metaphysics than the lumber of the four causes and the entitative meaning of being. Metaphysical causes are not observable; this was the complaint against them. But it can be claimed on their behalf that they operate beneath the surface of things. Each constituent principle and cause—form, matter, finality, and agency—gave to each and ev-

---

nominalism in philosophy and developments in mechanics. Cf. Olaf Pedersen, *Early Physics and Astronomy*, rev. ed. (Cambridge: Cambridge University Press, 1993), chaps. 16–17, esp. 194, 203.

7. The term "subject-matter" still retains the old meaning, but with the passivity associated with the notion of matter.

ery being an interiority and depth that wove the web of a certain natural mystery. Paradoxically, it was a mystery of intelligible light that shrouded each and every thing. What is more, at the very root of each being the mind was led to the originating cause of the existence of all created beings, and to the *communicatio entis* that made up the drama of that ontological mystery.

If in the traditional metaphysics each thing was a subject of being, in the modern outlook each thing became an object standing over against the inquisitiveness of consciousness. On the side of the known, the ideal of scientific objectivity spelled out the immediate aim of modern scientific inquiry. The key to the modern shift is to be found even more pronounced, however, in the changed meaning of the term *subject*, for that term came to be restricted to human consciousness. Consciousness has received various names and has been identified in various ways in the course of modern philosophy.[8] Insofar as it is the field of objects that is worthy of being known, however, it is consciousness alone under whatever name that is the subject facing that field.

Indeed, the term *subjectivity* condenses within it the history of modern consciousness as it faces what it dubs the world of objects. To see this more clearly, it helps to recall the origins of subjectivity in the early classical modern period. The success of mechanics in the late sixteenth century and the seventeenth century led to a widespread conviction that nature must be read mechanistically as the domain of particles in collision with one another in accordance with the general laws of motion. Instead of the study of nature as the realm of *ens mobile*, science turned to the study of *motion as such;* it turned from the study of motion translated into the terms of being to the study of motion in its own terms. The older philosophy of nature had led motion back to being and its inner constituent principles and ultimately back to the originating cause of the being of motion. The new study of motion, on the other hand, looked for intelligibility, not in the intrinsic ontological constitution of motion, but rather in the general laws that describe its empirical and observable manifestations. Such an approach made no pretense at attributing a constituent and inobservable interiority to what it took to be the external objects standing before the mind in the world of nature.

The sense of natural interiority dried up within the operative sphere

---

8. To wit, the *ego cogito* of Descartes with its method and criteria, the *substantia sive natura sive Deus* of Spinoza with its adequate idea, the "self" of Locke and the sensory receptacle of Hume, or the transcendental unity of apperception and its outreach in Kant, or the finite ego of Fichte, or the absolute spirit of Schelling and Hegel. Even the reactions to idealism center about this meaning of subject—to wit, Marx's revolutionary proletariat, August Comte's humanity-writ-large, or Nietzsche's will to power, even Husserl's transcendental subjectivity—each of these move within the horizon of a sublimated consciousness.

of scientific intelligence. To be sure, a certain metaphorical interiority was rescued and retained in some measure by poetry, but the latter tended to be reduced to fantasy, at least until the imagination received new philosophical power from Kant onward.[9] Of course, religion retains an ancient purchase upon interiority, but however effective it is in its own domain, theological speculation became more and more removed from the mainstream of the methodical study of the natural world. The sense of the sacramental character of the things of nature is tied to a recognition of transcendence, and that sense more and more seemed to lose intellectual relevance and respectability.

Despite the demise of natural interiority—that is, the interiority that traditional metaphysics attributed to all things—nevertheless, interiority itself survived. Its survival, however, was not without cost; for the remnant interiority was reduced to the confines of human subjectivity. Interiority retreated from a natural world that had lost its own interiority and could no longer share a common though analogous interiority with the human person. To be sure, what I have called the reduction of interiority to merely human dimensions was hailed by Enlightenment protagonists as the new dawn of secular humanism. From the standpoint of the traditional metaphysics, however, a once generous interiority had been sent into exile: "By the waters of Babylon . . ." In losing its interiority, nature also lost its integrity. Indeed, it seems that integrity requires interiority.

Descartes is justifiedly emblematic of modernity just because he found new power in the modern retreat within. The emphasis upon the control of and mastery over nature animates the early modern philosophers. If the restriction of subject-status and interiority to human consciousness may be called a retreat, it was nevertheless a calculated and methodical withdrawal that retained and confirmed its control over the natural world by reducing it to the status of objectivity. The natural world came to be viewed as a field for the deployment of technological power. Whereas the object stood over against consciousness, the newly fortified subject played a double role. On the one hand, it was a party to the new relation of subject and object; but, on the other hand, and much more importantly, the subject also underwrote the conditions that were to be satisfied if something other than the subject was to qualify as an object worthy of consideration. It is this turnabout that has given status to the

---

9. I see in Kant's third *Critique* a growing determination to rescue some kind of interiority from the blatant mechanism of the earlier modern period. Something similar might be said of the twentieth-century efforts of certain theoretical physicists to overcome the inheritance of mechanism. While these indications are promising, they do not break out beyond the horizon of subjectivity in the modern sense. Nothing short of an intellectual *reprise* of genuine transcendence can break through that horizon.

concept of experience far beyond what ancient and medieval thought gave to it. Experience has become the common currency into which all meaning is to be exchanged.

This new and unprecedented power came to the subject not in the old form of a power to create being but as an authoritative warranty. It was no longer ontology but epistemology that was to legitimate the course of philosophy for two centuries and was to awaken the reactions to that self-warranty that continue to this day. If Descartes is emblematic of the modern primacy of consciousness, Kant provides its charter when he appoints Reason to the status of an active and suspicious judge vis-à-vis nature. He compels it to answer questions drawn up by reason beforehand according to a schema fashioned from its own transcendental needs. One may well ask postmodernists whether that modern horizon has undergone as fundamental a change as they claim, or whether instead one or another facet of human subjectivity still continues to set the rules of evidence and to appoint itself the final court of appeal, as having either epistemic authority (in the guise of rationality), decisive authority (in the guise of will), affective authority (in the guise of feeling), or expressive authority (in the guise of the linguistic system of differential signs).[10]

Hegel quite rightly found the modern contribution to philosophy to consist in the inner exploration of human subjectivity. It is an exploration that has lasted even into our own day, and it has involved not only philosophers but also psychologists, novelists, and religionists.[11] There is no question of detracting from the value of this development; my only wish is to understand it more clearly and to situate it within a fuller and deeper context. The motive of the Cartesian withdrawal was to reach certitude, and the initial yet fundamental resting place to which all knowledge was to be brought was the human subject, *subjectum fundamentum inconcussum*. St. Augustine had used the argument *si fallor sum* to ward off dogmatic skepticism by an *argumentum ad hominem*, but he did

---

10. These alternatives are eminently understandable within the primacy of subjectivity in retreat from the externality of particles in motion. I have begun a reflection upon how we might break out of this circle through a reversal of what I have called epistemic and noetic discourse in my "Neither with nor without Foundations," *Review of Metaphysics* 42, no. 1 (Sept. 1988): 3–25. See chapter 4 above.

11. No doubt the Lutheran emphasis upon the inward grace of salvation, as well as other developments of Reformation Protestantism such as Pietism, played a formative role in this exploration even before the philosophers took over. Hegel dubbed this modern inward turn "the Protestant Principle." On the Catholic side one also sees a certain exploitation of this modern turn in Ignatian spirituality. It remains only to add that the Reformation and Counter-Reformation contained a mix of other factors within them, such as properly religious concerns, as well as institutional issues in the economic and political spheres.

not use it to construct an entire philosophy as Descartes did with his *dubito, cogito ergo sum*.

Nevertheless, withdrawal from the external world was not new. It is therefore important to distinguish the ancient religious path within, such as Augustine followed, from the modern epistemological path followed by Descartes and successors. Consider the religious interiority of someone, such as St. Bernard of Clairvaux, for whom the interior path led first to self-examination and purgation, then to prayer for forgiveness, and finally to the elevation of the soul beyond itself; so that under the power of grace it would be lifted into the broad uplands of the divine presence, placing itself before God in all humility and exaltation.

That path is not the route taken by what I have called modern subjectivity.[12] Modern subjectivity was initiated as the retreat from a mechanistic world of objects with which it could not identify except through technological mastery. Criticism has been made of the biblical influence upon modern technology regarding the command to master the world. Much of the criticism is misplaced, since it is often forgotten that the biblical command was to a conditional stewardship under God and not to a technological assertion of absolute human power over nature. There is, however, a similarity—more equivocal perhaps than real—in point of departure: both the biblical mandate and the modern project originate out of the recognition of a certain insufficiency in the world. The religious retreat within seeks a greater good (communion with God) than the created world can supply, so that it is an absolute retreat that recovers the world within a relationship with God. The modern retreat, on the other hand, is a relative retreat that withdraws from the world as insufficient for certain human purposes, and from an objective world that—as the sphere of exteriority—has no room for interiority, either natural or human. Indeed there was no interiority in that modern world of objects, nor was there any place for those aspects of human existence that were now classified as non-objective.[13]

I have spent some time in describing the loss of a more general and more generous metaphysical interiority and the reduction of the residue of interiority to the confines of the human consciousness. It is time to link the interiority of natural things with the immateriality resident within them. As I have already remarked, the constituent factors touted by the traditional metaphysics were not perceptible. They were intelligi-

---

12. The most interesting attempts to use modern interiority for religious and philosophical purposes include those of Malebranche, Kierkegaard, and Blondel.

13. One has merely to look at the distinction between primary and secondary qualities as they functioned in the modern period, whereby the latter were driven from the world of objects to seek refuge at the fringes of subjective awareness.

ble factors open to intellectual analysis, so that every caused being was comprised of perceptible surface and intelligible depth, of outer show and interior reality.

The story of lost interiority is intended, therefore, to reawaken consideration of the more general notion of *immateriality*, since I think that a better understanding of spirit must await the recovery of the broader notion of immateriality. This is so because interiority is not exclusively psychological. There is a certain immateriality that is to be found in all things, even physical things. The traditional metaphysics attributed a non-materiality to physical things by virtue of their complex constitution, since, in addition to the passive and potential factor within them that was dubbed primary matter, there were the factors of form, finality, and participation in the cosmic web of existence. These non-material factors were held to be the forms of immateriality proper to physical things, but they were also held to be the physical analogues of the immateriality that was held to be inseparable from the depth and interiority constitutive of every caused being. In sum, the traditional metaphysics held that some kind of immateriality was inseparable from every being by virtue of its being.[14]

To be sure, the interiority of natural things is not the same as the interiority of spirit. It is important, therefore, to distinguish the general notion of immateriality from the specific form of immateriality that is appropriate to spiritual being. It is also important to distinguish both the general and the specific notions of immateriality from the false modern notion that immateriality is opposed to physicality. If we oppose the immaterial to the physical we fall into some version of Cartesian dualism, a fate worth avoiding as the insoluble attendant problems show. If, on the contrary, by material is meant whatever in a thing is sub-formal[15]—that is, whatever in a thing is its fundamental capacity to undergo in-formation and transformation—then we can recognize that everything physical is constituted in part by formal factors that are neither material nor perceptible and that constitute a dimension of interiority within each physical individual. Considered in itself *qua* form, the very structure and design of a physical thing is immaterial yet physical. What is required is recogni-

---

14. I have developed the general notion at more length in "Immateriality Past and Present," *Proceedings of the American Catholic Philosophical Association* 52 (1978): 1–15. See also chapter 10 above. The basis in St. Thomas for such general immateriality derives from the nature of being as indicated by the role of *separatio* in the science of metaphysics. See *Expositio super Librum Boethii de Trinitate*, q. 5, a. 3, trans. Armand Maurer, in *The Division and Methods of the Sciences*, 4th ed. (Toronto: Pontifical Institute of Mediaeval Studies, 1986), 32–46. See also Maurer's Introduction, xxvi–xxvii.

15. I use the term "sub-formal" to indicate the plasticity present in mutable things, a plasticity that is the capacity within things to receive formation and re-formation; what the ancients termed primary matter. I say "sub-formal" in order to distinguish it both from the formal factors in things, as well as from the trans-formal factor of the act of existing *(esse)*.

tion of the physical as containing non-conscious modes of immateriality. In every physical thing these non-conscious immaterial modalities are received in the plasticity of the material principle, but they enter along with the material principle into the constitution of the physical thing itself.[16]

It is important to secure a notion of immateriality in physical things in order to come out from under the shadow of a contemporary analysis that draws all communication into the vortex of an objectivity that is the external projection of modern subjectivity. Once we have secured the recognition of immaterial factors within physical reality, we are in a better disposition to recognize the proper mode of immateriality that is constitutive of each human person. Such immateriality is spirit and is the principle of personal becoming.

III

What, then, are the marks of spirit operative within each human person? Philosophers have usually pointed to two indicators: knowledge and love. The spiritual factor in the human person lives by its own law, and both its nature and its modality are disclosed by this law. Reflection upon these two relationships has led me to describe the movement of spirit as *communication without loss*. But it is in just such a formulation that we encounter a roadblock. Conventional wisdom holds that every action is transitive—that it brings about a reaction—and that every movement entails an exchange that must be understood as a material transfer or a mutual give and take of some form of mass or energy such that the contributors suffer a loss, though new energy may be acquired in the transaction from the other party or from some other source. The conventional wisdom has it that all communication consists in such traffic. Hegel remarks concerning the concept of utility that each hand washes the other. On the other hand, it is well known that conventional wisdom often acts as a blinder, obscuring the most obvious facts, setting them aside without due consideration. Such a conventional mind-set can even put aside an obvious aspect of experience in the interest of what Karol Wojtyla has called a "methodological reservation," that is, the exclusion of obvious facts for the sake of the presuppositions of a method and its aims.[17]

---

16. Communications theory (by using the language of consciousness metaphorically, with such terms as "codification," "information," and "message") seems to grope towards the articulation of something like pre-conscious modes of immateriality. It is characteristic of the modern shift, however, to draw its vocabulary from within the primacy of consciousness, whereas the designation "non-conscious" does not impose the metaphor of consciousness upon things, but rather lets them be in their own way of being.

17. It is worth noting, however, that postclassical physics has tended to move away from this mechanistic view in favor of more formal (and in my sense non-material) concepts.

Inasmuch as the method that defines so much of modernity entails the primacy of motion, rest is taken to be a negative term, since it indicates the absence of what is primary. It is comparable to non-being in the traditional metaphysics. Rest is depreciated as merely static.[18] From the point of view of kinematics, rest is a privative condition, the lack of motion. The term "rest" is ambiguous, however. It indicates two very different conditions: they are, respectively, a *state* and a *modality*. To be sure, the Greeks also recognized rest as a state, as the absence of motion. Far more important to them, however, was the modality of rest that they identified with being at leisure. The essence of leisure is not the mere lack of physical motion, but rather the enjoyment of free activity. It is the emergence of activity that is not governed intrinsically by the laws that govern physical motion. It is in this domain that the human spirit lives at its peak, with a life more actual than that of the traffic of gain and loss.

Indeed, even in Aristotle's analysis of change the terminus is not rest as the simple lack of motion, but the possession of new actuality (form). When he spoke of properly human activity, he recognized within the human agent a realm of activity that is not governed by the laws of physical motion and yet that is not simply the absence of such motion. Far from being static, he thought this realm to be the most intense of living actuality, realized variously in the effort to understand, in the bliss of friendship, in the energy of artistic creation, and in the acknowledgment of the divine.[19]

It is among these activities that we need to look for the human spirit, and precisely in the activities that engage the human spirit so intensively: those of inquiry and friendship. Consider inquiry. In the Preface to the *Phenomenology of Spirit* Hegel describes the movement of consciousness: it goes out to the object, identifies with it, loses itself in the object, and yet returns to itself surviving in the result, knowledge. This going

---

18. I use the term here in its root sense and not in the sense of the science of statics, which is the study of the equilibrium of forces that sustain a body at rest. I should add that even the tendencies of postclassical physics to move away from mechanism do not question the primacy of motion.

19. Several versions of process philosophy have recovered some of the features of spirit. Thus, for example, some process philosophers assign to God the role of preserver of genuine value. More generally, however, within process philosophy the only alternative category to becoming is the static. Aristotle's analysis of change (*Physics* 1-3) offers two further categories: those of permanence and actuality. Underlying change Aristotle saw what is neither process nor stasis but the permanent, that which abides throughout the change and that, without losing its fundamental identity, is yet permeated by the change. Kant (*Critique of Pure Reason*, first analogy of experience, A182-9/B224-32) saw the importance of the notion of permanence, but his critical idealism forbade him to attribute metaphysical significance to the notion. Second, the "rest" in which change terminates is for Aristotle actuality *(energeia/eidos)* which is neither *kinesis* nor stasis.

and coming that results in knowledge, this *exitus* and *reditus,* is no mere metaphor; it is a real movement. But it is not a natural movement in the sense of a physical transaction; it is the movement of the human spirit.

To be sure, physical transactions of light and sound and the mutations of the sensory organs are the necessary conditions within which the movement of consciousness occurs; but, precisely speaking, they are not that in which knowing as such consists. Knowing does not relate the world to us so much as it relates us to the world in an irreducibly distinctive way. All attempts to translate this distinctive relation into material or physical terms, and into transactions of loss and gain, at best catch at only the outer shell of the relationship. Knowing does not put the world inside us; if it did we would have no way of speaking of the reality of the world. Rather, knowing puts us in the world in a non-physical immaterial way. I mean that precisely as knowing, consciousness does not disturb the world, though the world is constantly being disturbed on the basis of knowing. If we were to disturb the world in our knowing it, then we should have to get rid of the word "know" and substitute for it the word "construct." No matter how complex the physical conditions, no matter how perspectival the relationship, the discursus that is human knowing is the distinctive modality of the life of personal embodied spirit in the world.

What evidence do we have of communication without loss? A most obvious fact is that which many of us have at hand: it is the evidence of teaching, whether formally in a classroom setting or informally in a conversation among friends. For when we bring someone to understand what we have come to understand, or when they bring us to that point, neither we nor they lose the knowledge communicated. Yet there has been genuine sharing, an insight has been born in a receptive mind. While there has been the transfer of waves of sound or shapes of print, those account only for the physical means of transfer. They are the necessary conditions for a spirit that is embodied, but they are not the inner being and law of communication.

In this communication we meet another indicator of the human spirit and its proper law. In order to receive the communication we must be properly disposed. We must listen to what is being said or be attentive to the printed page. Gabriel Marcel has remarked upon the need to distinguish the notion of receptivity from that of passivity. In receiving a guest or a gift, the recipient is not simply passive. It makes no sense to say that the host has been mutated. He or she is called to conform to the disposition of a certain gracious activity that transcends any merely physical mode of passivity or activity, though the entire performance contains elements of both. The climate of the Enlightenment is very much with us still, and so the notion of receptivity is not easy to understand in a non-passive sense. The insistence upon the identification of human dignity with autonomy and choice understood as individual independence makes reception something less than a transcendental value that is compatible with and even ennobling to our humanity. Yet non-passive receptivity is as much a mark of the human spirit as is its activity, and the laws of such receptivity and activity are the laws that govern scientific understanding, artistic creativity, social civility, moral respect, and religious life.

Something similar occurs in the deepest form of giving. True giving may mean a sharing that is not a losing, as in teaching, but it may also mean a certain giving up, as when one gives up something of great value to another, even perhaps one's own life. But ineradicable from the notion of the gift—I say the gift, as distinct from the present, for we often give each other presents in a mutual transaction—there is the notion that all is not lost, that a great value has been originated in and through such giving. We recognize that a freely given gift—and there is none other—increases the value of both giver and receiver, so that we honor the increase of value and the person who has originated it.

To be sure, we must not look to the human person for an exhibition of pure spirit, for the obvious reason that, although the human person is spiritual, integral to the human person are the material and immaterial modalities of a physical being. Even when we speak of spiritual activities, such as knowing and loving, we must bear in mind that it is the whole human being who knows and who loves. It follows that in any actual exercise of knowing there will be found physical movements that are both the necessary conditions and the constant companions of what is the spiritual factor in such activities. The kind of becoming that is proper to the human person, then, is a becoming that is mixed with mutations to eye and ear and body, but the becoming is not to be identified simply with those mutations. The human spirit gives evidence, rather, of a distinctive principle operating within an ever-changing physical totality.

IV

Once we have secured the sphere of spirit and its law as communication without physical loss, we must acknowledge a kind of movement, a "quasi-mutation" of the spirit. In the life of the human spirit we recognize instances of a distinctively non-physical gain and loss. These are, however, properly spiritual mutations. There can be no doubt that we are changed personally in and through our spiritual modality. Thus, we can be increased in our being through the things we come to know, and enhanced in our being through what we love. There can be loss, too: for there can be distorted love, irresponsibility in our relationships, unwanted forgetfulness, repression in our knowing, and unrequited affection. The literature of the confessional, the poetry of the elegy, the music of the requiem, the tragedy of the stage, and the casebooks of the psychiatrist's couch all speak of spiritual anguish. We need, then, to look more closely at what it means to communicate without loss.

There are three kinds of quasi-mutation that enter into the movement of the human spirit. The first is properly spiritual enhancement or gain, the second is loss brought about by non-spiritual conditions, and the third is properly spiritual loss. There is enhancement: Teaching has already been instanced as an example of enhancement or gain, since effective teaching usually leads the teacher to better understand what he or she has already understood in some measure but without the loss of the prior understanding. Again, the mutual love of friends can only be acknowledged as a gain without loss. Then, too, we speak of many challenges as opportunities for personal growth, thus implying a sort of change. Such growth in personal maturity follows its own path. It occurs in time, and yet the character of temporality for the human spirit is not simply identical with the time that measures bodily changes. The temporal measure of the human spirit is not identical with the measurement of physical motion. The prevalence of myths regarding the time of origins and of the end-time indicates a capacity for transcending ordinary time by gathering it up into a totality, well beyond any possible actual experience of the limits of time.

There are other evidences of transcendence of ordinary time through a modality of duration that is distinctive of the human spirit. Thus, the capacity for conceptual thought lies at the base of the ability to frame descriptive statements about the nature and condition of things, even to designating definite past times. Such conceptualization has been described as abstract, timeless, and static—as though it is merely derivative—but in truth such chronometry marks stages in the ongoing life of spirit. It lies beyond this modest paper to further articulate a kind of duration that is not the measure of spatio-temporal motion, a kind of duration that much of human culture witnesses to. There is a duration that is more appropriate to the measure of the movement of the human spirit as it projects forward into the unknown by way of expectation and backward through past times in order to understand them and its own situatedness better. Once again, such a spiritual duration operates within the broad course of the temporality of the whole human person and is carried along by the inevitable course of physical time, but the initiatives of the human spirit do not follow its inevitable course. Indeed, the spirit redirects the processes of ordinary time in many surprising ways. If it did not, neither technology, nor art, nor fiction, nor metaphor would be possible, nor would conceptual understanding.

The second quasi-mutation is brought about by physical loss: We are not pure spirits, and we require the bodily functions in order to live spiritually, if only because we require them to live at all. Aging, forgetfulness, brain damage, dreaded Alzheimer's, and other mental illnesses—all impact upon the fragility of the human spirit, and remind us that the spiritual factor in us operates in a most intimate involvement with our bodily existence. The spiritual factor both penetrates and is penetrated through and through by the bodily conditions of our existence as persons. It is neither the eye that sees nor the mind that knows but it is the entire human being who both sees and knows. This fusion does not necessarily point to confusion; rather it points to distinction within unity, so that the human person is a complex of differing factors, each bound to operate in accordance with its own specific nature. Among these factors—nay, what we most properly call human and personal among these factors—is that which operates in its own distinctive way: it is the modality of the spirit in the human individual.

Finally, there is the possibility of spiritual loss: indeed, the most disturbing of the quasi-mutations are those to which the spirit is prey. They are such as moral failures, the loss of the sense of meaning, indifference and apathy, and more mysterious than all, the enactment of evil. It is the element of freedom at work in these forms of spiritual loss that differentiate these losses from the pitiable losses due to the physical conditions within which the spiritual factor operates. For these losses can be laid at the door of spirit itself. Perhaps we ought not to speak too quickly of deliberate choice as the only or even the deepest aspect of our freedom. We must speak also of a kind of lethargy that can arise within spirit and that allows the spirit to drift along lines that worsen it, even to a kind of self-abandonment of its calling.

We ought neither to think of that abandonment solely as submission to non-spiritual forces, to the line of least physical resistance, to the elevation of the pleasure principle, and the like. The gravest spiritual loss is the surrender, not to non-spiritual dis-values, but to anti-spiritual dis-values. Marcel pointed to these in his analysis of despair. He distinguished optimism and pessimism from hope and despair, on the grounds that the former couplet was predicated on the estimation of future outcomes. Thus, we might be optimistic about recovering from the present economic depression, or pessimistic that economic standards will ever revert to their former level. On the other hand, hope and despair do not depend upon such anticipated results. Perhaps you have tried to show someone in despair that the prospects are not so bleak as imagined, and yet have failed to change the painful disposition to nihilism. Despair gathers up the whole of reality, everywhere and at all times, and declares its bankruptcy. Hope is exactly the opposite outreach; it lends credit to reality, even to the reality that lies beyond our ken.

This realm of spiritual values and dis-values is a realm of contradictory possibilities that is given actuality by the self-determination of spiritual freedom. Personalist philosophies have recognized this realm and some have used the notion of spirit to describe it. I have tried to locate it within the context of reality by attempting to see the relevance of a more traditional metaphysical sense of spirit, so that the movement of the mature life of the human person is to be seen as centered in a spiritual factor that is primary within the life of the human person. Personal becoming, then, is the coming-to-be of spirit in the flesh.

Chapter 12
PURITY OF SOUL AND IMMORTALITY

It is said of St. Thomas Aquinas' teacher, St. Albert the Great, that he grew forgetful towards the end of his life and began to say mass for himself as though he were dead: *quasi defunctus est.* The fact that he was one of the most learned persons of Western Europe during his lifetime did not save him from a pathetic loss of memory. The story illustrates a bitter knowledge known from time immemorial: that age may steal away one's innermost possessions. Of course, it has always been known too that a blow upon the head in the prime of life may rob a person of consciousness and leave him or her permanently impaired. To this general wisdom about the fragility of conscious life, researchers have lately added an increasingly complex and precise knowledge of just how the brain and its various regions participate in our conscious life. So that this new detailed knowledge fills out the ancient recognition of the soul's reliance upon its physical base; it gives new weight to that dependence, and confirms the human spirit's immersion in matter. And if it does not quite overwhelm us with the intimacy of the alliance between soul and body, it bids fair to change the tone and degree of our awareness of that connection, so that the claim to the soul's immortality is likely nowadays to fall upon less receptive ears. Indeed, talk about the soul sounds strange to the ears of many present-day psychologists and philosophers. And even Christian theologians write copiously today about the resurrection of Christ and of the dead, but little about the immortality of the soul.

On the other hand, in the face of the frailty of human knowing, yet buoyed up by an ancient intuition of survival after death, Thomas Aquinas has formulated what seems to me to be one of the strongest arguments yet presented in support of the immortality of the human soul.[1]

Reprinted from *The Monist* 69, no. 3 (1986): 396–415. Copyright © 1986 by *The Monist.*

1. I have in mind *STh* I, q. 75, esp. a, 1, 2, and 6; and q. 76, a. 1. But from among a variety of texts in other works, see also *Quaestiones disputatae de anima,* esp. qq. 1, 2, and 14; and *SCG* II, cc. 79, 80–81.

Of course, a complex of metaphysical principles and prior conclusions underlies the proof, for he drew upon the Aristotelian principles of causality, form, and matter, even while he transformed them by situating them within a deeper and broader context of analysis. That context permitted him to arrive at a more definitive conclusion regarding the soul's immortality than his master seems to have.[2] The metaphysical basis is broader, because to the question: Is it? Thomas responded with a distinct constitutive principle of actual existence *(esse,* sometimes designated *actus essendi).* It is not enough, he thought, then, to determine the various principles (the factors and causes) that enter into the definition of a thing and that determine what it is; it is also necessary, in any metaphysical or ontological analysis, to acknowledge that the thing contains within its constitution a distinctive principle of existence which is its own but which it has received through a web of causes from the primary source of existence, and without which the thing would quite simply not be at all.

This broader, more complete analysis is, therefore, also deeper because it reaches to the very origin of the being of things, and takes seriously the philosophical pertinence of the absolute question: Why anything at all, why not rather nothing? In more technical terms: to the four causes that accounted for the generation of things and which he had learned from Aristotle (matter, form, agent, and end), Thomas joined a doctrine of *creatio ex nihilo* and recognized a principle *(esse)* which not only plays the primary role in the coming to be of things but sustains them in their very being. The things in the world including ourselves are not merely the limited things of a certain kind (after the manner of Aristotle's primary substances, which are composites of matter and form within an unbegotten cosmos), but are rather *creatures.* That is to say, taken in themselves and apart from the ultimate source of their being, they (along with their Aristotelian principles and factors) are, quite simply: nothing. The shift from Aristotelian limited substances to Thomistic finite creatures is the shift from the recognition of the primacy of limit

---

2. At least if we are to judge by the centuries-long controversy over whether Aristotle concluded to the immortality of the soul. See his *De anima,* bk. III, cc. 4–5 (429a10–430a25), including: "The thinking part of the soul must therefore be, while impassible, capable of receiving the form of an object; that is, must be potentially identical in character with its object without being the object . . . Therefore, since everything is a possible object of thought, mind in order . . . to know, must be pure from all admixture; for the co-presence of what is alien to its nature is a hindrance and a block . . . Mind is what it is by virtue of becoming all things . . . Mind in this sense of it is separable, impassible, unmixed, since it is in its essential nature activity . . . When mind is free from its present conditions it appears as just what it is and nothing more: this alone is immortal and eternal." Taken in their context, however, these positive statements leave unresolved many issues about the immortality of the individual human soul.

to the recognition of the nothingness of limit apart from the unlimited source of being.[3] Creatures, in contradistinction to merely limited substances, possess a positive principle of existence, received from another, without which they would not only fail to be of this or that kind of substance but would fail to be at all.[4] This metaphysical web of interlocking principles and causes is the real basis from which Thomas formulates his argument in support of the immortality of the human soul. But, although the web cannot be ignored in the full consideration of his argument, neither can it be treated within the scope of the present article. At best its importance for the proof can only be adverted to at crucial junctures of the argument. In this respect, however, his proof does not differ from any other subtle, complex, and difficult argument. Such arguments never stand on their own, for they cannot contain expressly all of their suppositions and evidences. Such a proof must be taken, rather, as an offering for further reflection upon and examination of principles at once deeper and broader than the stated premises and the conclusion of the proof. The proof stands open to further discourse.

The proof of the immortality of the human soul to which I refer[5] proceeds through three moments: first, it establishes the immaterial nature of the intellectual operations performed by the human soul, their *incorporeity;* then, it establishes the soul's capacity to exist in and through itself, its *subsistence;* and finally, it establishes the actual survival of the soul after death, its *incorruptibility*. An adequate consideration of the three moments would require a larger compass than the present affords, especially in regard to the third moment which involves a great deal of metaphysics. I intend, therefore, to concentrate upon the first moment only, since if it does not bear up, the other two will hold only antiquarian interest.

In establishing the incorporeity of the human soul, St. Thomas sets out from a great "fact"—I am tempted to call it a "transcendental fact," since it is neither a particular datum nor an empirical generalization. It is that human beings are capable of recognizing what it takes to be a physical thing. In his technical language: "It is manifest that by means of his intelligence man can understand what all bodies are": *Manifestum est enim quod homo per intellectum cognoscere potest naturas omnium corporum*.[6] Now, in claiming that we can know "the natures of all bodies," Thomas is not claiming that we have an exhaustive knowledge of each and ev-

---

3. The shift from Greek limit to Christian finitude is traced out by Hegel in ontological terms in *Science of Logic*, Bk. 1, Section 1, c. 2, B: "Finitude."
4. See, for example, St. Thomas, *STh* I, 44, 1 and 2; and *SCG* II, 52–54.
5. See esp. *STh* I, 75, aa. 2 and 6
6. *STh*, I, 75, 2c (i.e., the *corpus* or body of the article).

ery individual body in the universe. He does not even claim knowledge of all the basic kinds of bodies. In a word, he is not making an arrogant claim to omniscience. Undoubtedly, there are bodies in the far reaches of space that may in fact remain forever unknown to us, and basic kinds of materials of which we have no suspicion. After all, in some of its regions the medieval world was even more mysterious and inaccessible than ours. Indeed, no claim is being made to any particular actual knowledge at all. What is being claimed, instead, is that we have the capacity to recognize the basic features which are essential to physical things, and that we can possess general knowledge sufficient to distinguish in principle what is corporeal from what is not. Indeed, this is just what we will be doing in this present essay.

What, then, is the nature of bodies? The ancients stressed the capacity in bodies for other-induced change; but in addition to the capacity for mutation and dislocation and the susceptibility to the modification of qualities and states, we are nowadays more likely to stress features of corporeity such as occupancy in space, dimensionality, externality of relations, and possession of mutable qualities and spatio-temporally definite states. We might well wrap up all of these features into one term: *determinacy*.

But there are at least three kinds of determinacy that come to mind in this context: formal, actual, and material. Formal determinacy is that definiteness of form that Plato has made so famous; actual determinacy is the trans-formal determinativeness of actual existence which Thomas saw as the crowning principle of metaphysics and of reality itself. The determinedness appropriate to physical bodies, however, is material determinacy; but, because its determinateness is rooted in quantified matter, it might better be called physical or formal-material determinacy, since it is the determinacy appropriate to any composite of form and matter. It is that determinacy which asserts its own being by excluding others; it is *other-excluding determinacy*. It is what Hegel called "being-in-itself" *(Ansichsein)*, whose chief characteristics are quality, quantity, and measure.[7] Now, although one form (e.g., red) is *other than* another form (e.g., oblong), nevertheless both co-exist in the same brick; so that from the point of view of real things, formal determinacy is not other-excluding. If actually determinate things are physical, they exclude one another, but not precisely by virtue of their bring actual, since there are other kinds of actual beings that are open to the interior presence of others, as we shall pres-

---

7. The term is introduced in the section on quality (*Science of Logic*, Bk. 1, section 1, c, 2, B, a, 2), but its other-excluding character is developed throughout the whole of the first book, finally precipitating a transition to the consideration of knowledge in the second book.

ently argue. For physically determinate things "to be real," on the other hand, is equivalent to their "excluding others." That is why space and spatial relations play a dominant role in physical nature, since space is the context in which parts and wholes exist outside and alongside one another.

By the "exclusion of others" I do not mean that physical things exist in a vacuum totally untouched by others. Quite to the contrary, the continual mutation of physical things by one another is central to what it means to be physical. Nevertheless, the exclusion of others takes the dynamic form of resistance to encroachment by others: thus, if a thing preserves its own being by appropriating the influence of another as a new property, condition, or state of its own being, we speak of an alteration of a relatively permanent thing; and, if the influence overwhelms the thing's own being, so that it passes away into another, we speak of its corruption. Precisely just because their way of being is to be by excluding others, communication between physical things must take the form of transformation or mutation, i.e., of the acquisition of something by one thing through the loss of it by another. Moreover, just because it is of the essence of physical things to exclude one another, so too their interrelation must take place through external connections, i.e., through means by which they remain outside one another. And in touching one another by these means, they also recoil back upon themselves; so that reciprocity or mutual reaction and interaction is the most complete category of relation among physical things.[8]

Now, Thomas' claim that we can know what it is to be bodily amounts to the claim that we can know that bodies are determinate in the terms just set forth. To be sure, such a modest claim is trivial and uninteresting to physics and other sciences of nature, since it makes no particular contribution to their enterprise; nor is it of interest in the ordinary affairs of human life, and it can be parodied easily. But metaphysics lingers over what is obvious and useless, and draws less than obvious inferences from it. Let us see what St. Thomas draws from this "great fact."

In addition to knowing what *bodies* are, we must also advert to what *knowing* is according to St. Thomas, since it is these two terms that are principal in the "transcendental fact." Now, to his mind, human knowledge results from a union of a distinctive sort between the knower and what is known. Moreover, that union is a sort of identification, so that to know something is to be identified with it in some way.[9] To be sure, not

---

8. See, for example, Kant, *Critique of Pure Reason*, the Third Analogy, and Hegel, *Science of Logic*, Bk. 1, section 2, 3, B, c: "Action and Reaction," and C: "Reciprocity."

9. Cf. Aristotle, *De anima*, III, 5 (430a20): "Actual knowledge is identical with its object."

all theorists of knowledge agree that knowing is a union of any kind, let alone an identification. What is more, many versions of identity theory have emerged in the history of philosophy; and so, if Thomas' argument is to be understood—even if only to be criticized—it is important to grasp the precise version of identity theory that plays its role in his proof.

Here again, Thomas is working with a basic insight. It is: that nothing *happens* to a thing inasmuch as it is known; instead, knowing belongs to and is an actuation of the human knower and not of the thing known. Of course, something may happen to the thing known *because* it is known; captured thieves corroborate that. Moreover, something may have to happen to a thing *before* it can become known; treasure washed ashore from deep dark seas corroborates that, as does knowledge gained by experiment. Or again, something may happen to a thing *while* it is being known; a sequence of events viewed from a passing train corroborates that. But these consequences, interventions, and concomitants are subsequent or preparatory to or concurrent with the thing's being known. Then, too, between conscious beings, especially among the higher animals and man, there is mutual knowing, i.e., knowing that one is being known. Wild creatures who discover themselves spied upon may take fright, tame creatures may return affection, and human beings may respond in mutual recognition: this knowing that one is being known reaches its apex in the intimacy of love and friendship, and of the sinner before God. But these responses in the one being known do not arise, strictly speaking, out of their being known—except in the instance of the sinner, who must first be acknowledged by God; they arise rather out of their knowing that they are being known. If they do not know that they are being known, such responses do not occur. In sum, in the passive state of being known, the thing, insofar as it is an object of knowledge, is not altered. When a thing comes to be known, then, it does not suffer a mutation because it is known. The schoolmen spoke of the relation between knower and known as an *intransitive* relation, since strictly speaking it lacks an external product; and they spoke of the activity of knowing as an *immanent* activity, since it maintains itself "within" the knower. Paradoxically, knowing is an activity that, in itself, is nonproductive, and that, although it may be said to dwell "in" the knower, is literally and spatially nowhere.

In order to make the obvious but easily passed over point more patent—that nothing happens to the thing known precisely insofar as it is known, but that the knower is affected in some way—permit me to have recourse to an absurdity. Suppose that a chair (which has neither brain, nerves, nor sense receptors) were suddenly endowed with the capacity to know, and that it became aware of the various things in the room. The recourse to such an absurdity is for the purpose of shock, so that we might free ourselves from the routine suppositions about receptors, communications systems, and the computer-like brain, suppositions that are contained in the current jargon of popular versions of information theory. Stripped of these familiar consolations, how best could we say what would have happened? It would heap foolishness upon my calculated absurdity if, following some popular presentations of the knowing process, we were to say that suddenly the room itself would now be contained in the chair. For, how would it be contained? on a smaller scale? Such old-fashioned isomorphism won't do; it never did, anyway. What about a more sophisticated analog model that does away with identity theory? This may help us to predict future results and fruitful lines of investigation, but it leaves unsaid the basis of the analog relationship, for it does not help us to understand in intrinsic terms what it is to understand. If we speak of brain waves and electro-chemical stimuli in various regions of the brain, we certainly do not speak foolishly, since many of these interactions have been well attested experimentally, even though much remains vague or unknown about these processes. We only speak foolishly *if* we think that such talk tells us what it means to *know* something. For to know something is not ultimately explained by a detailed account of how we process inputs of energy. Moreover, when popularizing theorists call the stimuli "information," they simply cover over the problem of what it means to know, since they leap magically from relations between definite states and values of energy to relations of meaning, from the order of physically determinate states of input and output to the order of representative meanings. We do indeed receive such input, and the painstaking research that is only now beginning to uncover these processes must be counted among the most precious knowledge we have, since it both throws light upon the material conditions of knowing and provides clues to tragic malfunctions in conscious life. Nevertheless, the precise nature of that awakening which we experience as knowing—even though it requires such input—is not itself experienced anything like these processes.

How, then, would we speak about the chair—this suppositious absurdity which knows? To begin with, is it not that—rather than the room being in the chair—the chair would now be "in" the room in a new and distinctive way? For in addition to the physical and chemical relations it already has with the room and its objects—relations of other-induced mutation and other-excluding determinacy—the chair would now also be related to the objects of the room as in some sort of union with them. And, since the objects would not thereby be altered through the new relation, the shift would have come about "in" the knower, i.e., in respect to this marvelous chair. What are the senses of these two *ins*? That is, the chair in the room (containment), and the chair "in" the room (in a relation with it over and above the physio-chemical relations it already has as a physical occupant of some part of the room)? Now, even though stimuli or input from the room and its furniture might be said to be contained in the chair in the ordinary physical sense of having been received by it within a determinate spatio-temporal context, still the room insofar as it is *meant* could not be "in" the chair in any ordinary sense of containment. We are forced to conclude that, in addition to the determinate state and context of the input received by the chair, we would still have a relation that is of *another order of relations* than the chair has with the room and its objects as a simple occupant of it. In addition to being involved with other things in physically determinate relations (of pressure, heat, light, etc.), the chair would be related to the things in a relationship that, while being determinate, would not be physically determinate. It would be related to them as knower to known. Let us begin by calling this new relationship that is without material determinacy a relation of *presence*, for it is just this that comes about when knowing occurs: the knower comes to be present in an immaterially determinate way to the things he or she knows, even if materially determinate things are the objects of that knowing and even if materially determinate conditions (environs, medium, organs, and processes) are means to that knowing.

To be sure, such an order of relations calls for methods of analysis quite different from those of empirio-mathematical experimental research. It is not unfashionable at this point to throw up one's hands and cry: This is mystical nonsense. For long after the cruder presuppositions of positivism have been abandoned because they proved indefensible, the positivistic temper remains. Now, a critical mitigated skepticism can be a boon to philosophy, but an unreflective dogmatism that will not hear of metaphysical modes of discourse simply yields to the temptation to draw all rational discourse back into the safety of current modes of scientific discourse. It seems to me, rather, that the question we are examining is difficult in the extreme and that we must not approach it with routine predetermined conditions for acceptable discourse. Such a dogmatism is more a bias of psychological taste than a requirement of methodological objectivity. We need instead to be prepared to recover an expanded sense of legitimate rational discourse, and to explore the relationship of presence with as few pre-conditions as possible.

The intuition that nothing happens to the thing known *qua* being known (intransitivity), and that knowing is an affair of the knower (immanence), directs our attention to the knower. And indeed, St. Thomas states a quite general principle about knowers. It is as follows: to be able to know something, the knower must be devoid of the actual physical reality of the thing known. Knowing, after all, is not the substitution of one thing by another, a sort of displacement. It is neither a displacement by means of the original thing known, nor by means of a physical copy of it, nor by any physical substitute. St. Thomas expresses the nature of the identity achieved in and through knowing by a maxim that is quite general to his account of knowing. He takes the principle from Aristotle, but applies it in his own way. It can be called the principle of purity or transparency, though the purity is not here a moral one but a constitutional or metaphysical purity that the ancients called *immateriality*.[10] In his own words: "But whatever is able to know certain things cannot have any of them in its own nature": *Quod autem potest cognoscere aliqua, oportet ut nihil eorum habeat in sua natura*.[11] He then gives the reason why the knower must have nothing of the actual being of what is known in its own constitution as knower: "because that which would be present in it in a physical way would impede the knowledge of other things": *quia illud quod inesset ei naturalite impediret cognitionem aliorum*. Because it is not obvious why the physical being of something would impede the knowledge of that thing, Thomas provides an illustration taken from the sense of taste, and later one from sight, saying that if the tongue is infected with a bitter humor it cannot rightly perceive the sweetness of anything, just as the eye being clouded by a discolored pupil or by a color in the medium cannot rightly perceive the ordinary color of an object. By "rightly" I do not mean to canonize the received categories of taste; nor by "ordinary" do I mean to absolutize the conventional names our culture has given to a certain spectrum of colors and shades. We are well aware today that perception cannot be disengaged from the relativity of both individual subjectivity and cultural selectivity. Nonetheless, it is sufficient for our present purpose that there are objectively discernible differences of taste (such as between spoiled ["sour"] and unspoiled ["sweet"] milk); and that qualitatively different states of light are perceptible under various conditions of daylight. These perceptions need not hold for all times and places, for all cultures and situations, for animals as well as humans. We ought not to look for absolutes where there are none intended, nor ought we to reduce everything to "arbitrary convention" when we fail to find them. Sense perception is through and through conditioned, relative to its conditions, and restricted by the limitations

---

10. Cf. "Immateriality Past and Present," *Proceedings of the American Catholic Philosophical Association*, 52 (1978): 1–15. See chapter 10 above.

11. *STh*, I, 75, 2c.

of its organs. Nevertheless—and this is the efficacious point of the illustrations—within that range, by means of the organ and the medium, and under those conditions, the intervention of a physical being in the organ or medium skewers the "rightness" of any judgments based upon the perception as though it had occurred under "ordinary" conditions. Sugar will, indeed, taste bitter, and blue objects will, indeed, seem green under these unusual conditions; but the judgments based upon those tastes and sights *as though* they were based upon "ordinary" conditions of perception are "rightly" judged to be in error.

The principle of purity or transparency plays its role, then, in a merely relative way in sensory perception. Each sense power has a limited range within which it is receptive: the human ear cannot register sounds heard by the canine ear, ultraviolet rays remain undetected by the unaided human eye. Moreover, men, birds, frogs, and insects see differently the common world in which they live and die. For the basic relativity of sensory perception is species-specific; each sentient organism has its own range and its own selective attention, based upon the needs of its species. But, even within the human species, St. Augustine marveled that each individual saw the sun differently, yet saw the same sun. What is grasped in sensory perception, then, is not the object without qualification, but precisely the object *qua* audible, visible, tactile, etc.[12] And it grasps these qualified objects under the particular physical and perceptual conditions of the perceiver's situation, organs, and media. To speak strictly, the perceiver does not see the apple purely and simply, but the apple insofar as it is illuminated by a particular source of light acting upon a particular organ (with its particular condition and situation) through a particular medium. In perception, then, the principle of purity holds only in a relative and restricted measure. Insofar as perception forms the basis of a judgment, the principle of purity expresses the relative necessity for the perceiving powers, organs, and media to be free from the physical or natural being of what is perceived.

I have called the references to taste and sight "illustrations," since I do not think that they contribute directly to the validity of the principle of purity in its intellectual mode; for there it must stand on its own grounds, grounds taken from the nature of understanding itself. Content that these indications of sensory perception provide a weak analogy with understanding, Thomas now states the principle of purity as it functions in the understanding of things: if the understanding can know all

---

12. In the later language common to the schoolmen, these different perspectives, rooted in the organic constitution of the knower (and so, in our terms, "subjective") are capacities which correspond to what are called "formal objects" *(id quo)*, i.e., aspects or actual determinations, rooted in the thing, through which the thing itself *(id quod)* is known.

bodies in the sense of knowing what it is to be bodily, it must in its own constitution be free of all corporeity. The difference between perception and understanding is that the latter can take account of the very relativity within which the senses are bound, and by going beyond these conditions can strike an absolute note by recognizing the relativity of the perceptual conditions. It attempts to do this each time it utters: *it is*, rather than *it seems*. Or rather, even when it utters: *it only seems*, it holds before itself the possibility of an absolute utterance (which some philosophers express in the familiar periphrastic jargon: *it is the case that . . .*). St. Thomas puts it this way: "The senses indeed do not know being, except under the conditions of *here and now*, whereas the intellect apprehends being absolutely, and for all time": *Sensus autem non cognoscit esse nisi sub hic et nunc, sed intellectus apprehendit esse absolute, et secundum omne tempus.*[13]

We might put the matter thus: When the human intelligence grasps its meanings it transcends the particular conditions from which and within which it discerns them. The meanings of its universal concepts may differ in some respects from culture to culture and age to age. Moreover, a new kind of variety arises within a concept from the various "perspectives" under which it can be considered; as, for example, justice or table salt may be considered "with regard to . . ." or "insofar as. . . ." Nevertheless, the form in which the meanings arise in the understanding is free from the particular conditions in which its instances exist in reality. It is Plato's point once again, but with a difference. The world may fall upon evil days, so that there may not remain a single just man in it, or for that matter any salt; but justice would be justice, if there were any, and salt just what it is. Many such things may come into being and pass away, and their concepts with them. And so, the claim to the self-identical character of the determinacies expressed through our concepts does not entail a doctrine of eternal ideas or eternal species, since eternity belongs, if anywhere, to the order of actual existence and actual duration. Nor need any claim be made that the human understanding has in its innate possession the full range, definition, and scope of the meanings by which it knows. The human mind is an inquiring, learning, discovering intelligence. It can know that much remains unknown to it. But it can also know that its grasp of determinations transcends their particular instantiations, so that its meanings acquire a character absolved from the confinement of real time and real place, even when the thing to which the concept refers is itself bound by particular times, places, and changes. Thus, the earth's atmosphere may alter so that there will never again

---

13. *STh*, I, 77, 6c.

be the pink glow of a sunset; but what that determinateness which we now call "pink" would be—if it were ever once again to be—is just *that* determinateness. The cult of an ancient Egyptian god may die out, but what it *was* can—in principle—be stated by the inquiring intelligence.

Within this transcendental context, the human understanding pursues its meanings, ever amending and refining its comprehension, yet always proceeding in a manner that is not intrinsically bound by particularities of time and place. And, if time and place are part of a complex conception, such as the cult of Osiris in the twenty-fourth dynasty, that time-and-space-bound conception arises within the indefinite horizon of meanings that transcends all particular times and places. In concept-formation the knower stands forth before all past, present, and future instances of the determination, and even those that will never be. Moreover, this absolute quality also appears in judgment, as when we declare that such and such *is* or *is not* the case. There is no guarantee of infallibility in this absoluteness. The knower may make wrong judgments, just as he may malform complex concepts; though he does not make only wrong judgments, nor frame only bad concepts. But, this transcendence is the capacity to stand forth from the particular contexts into an absolutely indefinite horizon of meaning in which the mind forms its judgments. So that the "abstraction" of which the schoolmen were wont to speak is not the extraction of something out of a set of instances; that indeed would bring about a change in the thing known—or rather, the thing could never be known by that process. Abstraction consists, rather, in the knower being able to rise above the particular conditions to discern in a situation determinations that are not exhausted by any of their particular instantiations, and to render judgment in terms of the absolute distinction between *is* and *is not*.

The features that belong to our concepts and judgments—transcendence of particularity, self-identity of determinacies, and absoluteness of context—belong not to the things known, but to our manner of knowing them. And so, even as the mind in its pursuit of meaning and truth raises the significance of a situation into a context that transcends the particularities of place and time, so too does it thereby raise itself into that absolute way of being that is its own by its very nature as an incorporeal being. For this reason, understanding is the root of human freedom: this freedom from particular conditions is sealed within the very dynamism of human thought; by it the knower projects himself beyond those particular conditions towards the comprehension of whatever is. That freedom from (i.e., abstraction) is thereby freedom to *be present in and to* the world in an intransitive, immanent, immaterial identification with it.

Now, because man is free to take up a relation to his own life as a whole, he has concern for his own death and interest in his origins; because man can take up a relation to the whole of his people, even to the whole of his race, he tells myths about the origin, fall, and destiny of man; and because, looking at the seas and the stars and the fossil record, he embraces the whole existence of the universe in the wonder of his thought, he searches heaven and earth for ultimate meaning. This comprehension is not an exhaustive knowledge of detail, nor a complete system of categories, nor a guarantee of certitude; it is rather a promise that is continually being redeemed *in part*. In one sense of the word, this "absolute" must remain an asymptote, since the human knower is already in possession of a horizon absolved from the restrictions of time and place. This tension—between an absolute already in its possession (its mode of understanding) and an absolute forever inaccessible (omniscience)—lies behind St. Thomas' insistence upon *both* the immortality and the embodiment of the human soul. In reaching for what lies forever beyond his grasp man affirms his transcendence of particular situations even as he finds himself rooted in them. It is to this freedom that Thomas points when he says that the intellect can apprehend being "in an absolute manner and for all time": *esse absolute, et secundum omne tempus*.[14]

This freedom has been described as a kind of non-being. Indeed, the negativity of consciousness—its not-being in the sense of not being any physical thing, its being no-thing—is the central point uniting modern dialectical philosophies. Among neo-Marxists, Theodor Adorno has stated the negativity of critical consciousness in the starkest terms. Among Existentialists, Jean-Paul Sartre—for whom reality *(l'en soi)* resembled nothing so much as a prison—made famous the neologism: *néantisir*, to nullify, and heaped up metaphors to indicate the nothingness of consciousness: a wind, a rupture in the fabric of things, the viscous and the formless. Despite the flirtation with materialist shadows, both neo-Marxist and Existentialist thought has grasped the "non-thingly" character of consciousness. Hegel, too, recognized that consciousness is quite other than things, for he conceded to consciousness the ability to confront things (recognition), to hand itself over to them (in order to know them as objects: objectivity), and yet to survive in the result (and thereby reclaim a transformed subjectivity). Consciousness can do this, he insisted, just because it does not enter into the traffic of things in the way in which physical things do.

Nor do only dialectical philosophies recognize the distinctive nature

---

14. Ibid.

of consciousness. Descartes is famous for continuing the tradition that saw the mind as an immaterial substance. And even Kant recognized that the transcendental categories and ideas of critical idealism were of a quite distinctive nature, unlike the content of the objects known, with their temporal, spatial, and empirical qualities. Nor are Husserl's acts to be thought of as just more empirical psychological events. All of these announce a distinctive principle, that of consciousness itself. Indeed, the Vienna positivists implicitly conceded the distinction between the orders of things and consciousness by insulating the principles of verifiability, consistency, and similar logical principles from empirical data. Now, this "no-thingness," this transparency, which Thomas calls incorporeity, is the source out of which arises the distinctive order of knowledge—of signs, representations, and intentionalities.

For it does no good here to speak of electrical charges in the brain as though they even begin to give an account of the *meaning* that is the pronounced characteristic of ideas. These physical impulses play their role in the genesis of conscious representations—percepts, images, memories, concepts—but they do not advance us one step towards the nature of what is meant and what it is to mean. Moreover, there is good reason why in principle they will never do so, for knowledge is not the substitution of one physical thing by another, nor even the transmutation of one physical thing (the brain, nervous system, etc.) by another (stimuli). Another primitive intuition underlies this conviction. It is that I do not become fed by knowing that others are, I do not turn green when I marvel at well-kept lawns, and I do not become just because I can define justice. *Qua* physical stimulus or electrical charge, the physical mutation does not *represent* anything. It does not even represent itself, it *is* itself. Indeed, if properly understood, it could be said that consciousness consists in being what the thing is not and not being what the thing is.[15] In knowing a chemical compound the chemist *is not* that compound (i.e., does not become it physically); if he did, he would come to grievous harm upon discovering an explosive or a poison. Equally, in knowing a chemical compound he or she *is* it "in the manner of not being it." The two senses of "is" express the irreducible otherness of physical being and noetic being. The intentional character (to use the term made current by phenomenology) is not accounted for by the physiological line of explanation; nor (to use Kant's term: *Vorstellung*) is the representative function. In the language of the schoolmen, knowledge is an affair of pure (as distinct from physical) signs, means by which *(medium*

---

15. The suggestion for the formula comes from Sartre's discussion of "Bad Faith" (*Being and Nothingness*, part I, ch. 2), but without his sardonic twist, and from Hegel's precise, if obscure, formulation in regard to self-consciousness (*Phenomenology of Spirit*, B, 4, A).

quo) the knower comes to be present to the thing known in an intransitive, immanent, and incorporeal way.

It seems to me, then, that a basic intuition has emerged in philosophy among very different philosophers: it is that knowing is not an ordinary traffic between bodies, no matter how sophisticated or complex or defined that traffic may be. St. Thomas expresses this as the exclusion of the ordinary nature of physical bodies and their qualities from the knowing power. This is the primary condition for releasing the intentional order, without which there can be no shift from being to representing or signifying. Strictly speaking, nothing *represents* itself. It may use something else to signify itself (as the State uses stop signs), or it may even use a part of itself to stand in for the whole (as a cartoonist selects a salient feature of his victim), but the sign or representation must be *recognized* as significant, and the whole must then be interpreted through the assigned part. Even if another body (e.g., a green light) has been assigned to represent a traffic command, the representative quality is of quite another order from its physical composition, and it takes a non-physical power to pick up that intended relationship.

Nevertheless—even if the human understanding does perform an operation that excludes bodies and is by constitution incorporeal—Thomas still asks whether that rules out the use of an organ in performing that operation? Now, Thomas is well known for insisting that we gain all of our knowledge by means of the senses and therefore from the things we perceive about us. He is, in the Aristotelian sense of the term, an empirical philosopher. Since the soul is the form of the body, the question arises whether, after all, the soul in its understanding might not perform the action of understanding in a way similar to the way in which it perceives, i.e., by means of an organ proper to the intellect and intrinsic to the very nature of the operation of understanding. Today we tend to think of the brain as just such an organ of thought. There is no doubt that the brain is involved in the processes that fill out our conscious life. I have already mentioned that we know this in much more impressive detail than did the ancients, even though the need of the brain for conscious life was not unknown to them. There is no question, then, that injury to the brain may well put an end to any manifest action of understanding in this life. What is at issue, however, is not the fact of the intimacy and reliance between soul and body but the character of that intimate alliance.

Now, Thomas had concluded that the human mind could not grasp the nature of body as such unless its own constitution were free of all body, saying: "if the intellectual principle had the nature of a body as its own nature, then it would not be able to know the nature of body as such": *Si igitur principium intellectuale haberet in se naturam alicuius corpo-*

ris, non posset omnia corpora cognoscere.[16] He adds that it would not be able to know all bodies because "every body has a certain determinate nature": *Omne autem corpus habet aliquam naturam determinatam.* This is why the brain or any other physical organ cannot be an intrinsic constitutive part of the operation of understanding. In Thomas' words: "for the same reason, it is impossible that [the intellectual principle] understand by means of a corporeal organ, because if it were to do so, the determinate nature of that corporeal organ would prevent the knowledge of all bodies": *Et similiter impossibile est quod intelligat per organum corporeum, quia si esset, natura determinata illius organi corporei prohiberet cognitionem omnium corporum.* And so, Thomas concludes that "the understanding alone among the operations of the soul is performed without a corporeal organ": *solum intelligere inter opera animae sine organo corporeo exercetur.*[17]

The absolute purity of the intellectual principle is often attributed to the universality of concepts in distinction from the particularity of sense impressions. But this difference is an *epistemological* consequence of a more basic *ontological* difference. "Every body has some determinate nature": *Omne autem corpus habet aliquam naturam determinatam.* It is the difference between the other-excluding determinacy of physical beings (confined to their particularity) and the openness of knowers present to other beings (in a universal and even absolute context). Knowing is not an affair of substituting one physical thing for another—for example, an input of energy in place of the thing itself, or the alteration of brain states. It is not even a strategy for finding the appropriate set of symbols—mathematical or otherwise—as substitutes for what is known, or models as instruments of prediction. Bodies can and do fulfill extrinsic conditions for understanding, but they cannot be an essential and intrinsic part of the understanding itself and its operations. They cannot, because the material determinacy of one body excludes that of another. Knowing is neither simply resistance to another body nor displacement by it. It is a non-physical identification of the knower with the known, by which the knower is present to the known in and through meaning, representation, significance.

To sum up this long exposition of the first moment of the proof: Taking knowing to be a kind of identification of the knower with the known, Thomas has argued that knowing is an intransitive relation between the two, in which nothing happens to the known; that the activity of knowing remains "within" the knower and "qualifies" him or her; that consciousness is not a physical thing, nor can the knowledge-relation be accounted for by the ordinary coming and going of physical things, nor

---

16. *STh*, I, 75, 2c.
17. *STh*, I, 75, 3c.

by emissions from things; that knowing comes about through a distinctive order of meaning (signs, representations, intentionalities), whereby the knower comes to be present in and to the world in an incorporeal way; and that, while physical organs and objects contribute extrinsic conditions to understanding, understanding cannot be bodily either in its constitution or in its manner of operation.

The requirement of incorporeity, which is absolute in understanding, is the principle of purity. Taken negatively, this purity is the absence of physical being; but it is also the sign of a new order of presence. For, whereas things are present in a primary sense in the world, they are re-present in and through being known, this second "being-present" is a re-existing of real being in the order of intentional being. The full significance of the principle of purity is not grasped, therefore, if it is seen only as an order of "mental" representations. Thomas claims genuine metaphysical vitality for knowing: to be sure, knowing is *immaterial*, but it is immaterial *being*, and all being (for Thomas) has some connection with actuality. Although knowledge is not physically existent and cannot of itself directly enforce the traffic between physical things, its incorporeal mode of being is nonetheless a mode of actual existence, a way of living; it is the life of the human spirit.

This life of knowledge and freedom is manifest through the activity of the human intelligence. In order to appreciate the grounds for his positive claim, we need to look briefly at the second moment of the proof, without being able to consider it adequately in its own right. For he claims that an action performed without the body indicates a kind of being that is itself incorporeal. Now, this indication points to much more than a definition, for action is not merely an affair of natures, kinds, ways, or modes. Action displays an actually existing being; since "there is no performance except that of an actual being": *Non enim est operari nisi entis in actu.*[18] Thomas intends a double sense of *"in actu"* here: in the secondary sense of action or performance *(operatio)*, and in the primary sense of actuality or existence *(esse in actu)*. And so, "a thing exists in the manner in which it acts": *unde eo modo aliquid operatur, quo est.* That is to say, if we discover an action that is performed in which the body does not share, then we *thereby* discover an actual being which exists in and through itself and not in dependence upon the body. "To act through itself belongs to what exists through itself": *per se agere convenit per se existenti.*[19] The human soul, then, by virtue of its capacity for understanding, is not only non-material in its nature or constitution (incorporeity), but is capable of existing without the body (subsistence).

18. *STh*, I, 75, 2c.
19. *STh*, I, 75, 2, ad 2m.

The metaphysical notions of actuality, causality, and agency have been subjected to criticism, of course, but it is from them that Thomas draws his claim to the human soul's subsistence. Having concluded that the human soul is capable of "an operation of its own which it does not share with the body": *Ipsum igitur intellectuale principium, quod dicitur mens vel intellectus, habet operationem per se, cui non communicat corpus*—he then invokes the principle that an agent must act according to its nature; more precisely, "nothing is able to operate on its own, except it subsist (on its own)": *Nihil autem potest per se operari, nisi quod per se subsistit.*[20]

The term *per se* is difficult to render into English. Perhaps: "What operates through itself exists through itself," i.e., out of its own resources, by its own right and in its own name. It is so constituted that it has the capacity (all conditions being favorable) to exist in and through itself, as a tree or animal or element can exist *per se*, in contrast to a color or sound which requires a surface or carrier in which to reside as in a subject (*in alio*). This is a primitive intuitive recognition of the difference between existing in another as in a world, environment, or context *and* existing in another as in a subject, i.e., as an aspect of that other. Thus, parasitic and symbiotic relationships are nonetheless between subsistent things, whereas qualitative modifications, such as colors or lengths, are determinate characteristics possessed by subsistent things. Today, after several centuries of nominalism and Cartesian insistence upon unrelatedness, such a rendering as "on its own" must not be permitted to carry any suggestion of absolute autonomy, as though a thing cannot be called "subsistent" unless it be and be conceived in complete isolation from all other things (after the manner of Kant's famous *Ding an sich* or Spinoza's Substance). Neither Aristotle nor St. Thomas had in mind as a condition for subsistence a complete and total self-sufficiency absolved of all relations. Such exaggerated self-sufficiency is not needed in order that a thing both act and exist *per se* and yet in some context.

Nevertheless, even though the understanding may both be and function without dependence upon the body, still it needs the body in order to have an object to which to relate. Thomas puts the objection thus: "if the soul were something subsistent, it would have some operation apart from the body. But it has no operation apart from the body, not even that of understanding; for the act of understanding does not take place without a phantasm [without an image susceptible to interpretation by the mind]; and such an image cannot exist apart from the body [i.e., apart from the sense powers and their organs]. Therefore, the human soul is not something subsistent."[21]

20. *STh*, I, 75, 2c.
21. *STh*, I, 75, 2, obj. 3.

In meeting the objection, Thomas concedes that "the body is necessary for the action of the understanding," but he hastens to qualify this perhaps surprising concession. The understanding needs the body, "not as the organ by which it performs such as action, but by reason of [its need for] an object": *Corpus requiritur ad actionem intellectus, non sicut organum quo talis actio exerceatur, sed ratione objecti.*[22] Lest this seem a belated concession, if not a fatal one, he continues: the understanding needs objects for its consideration, and it finds them in the images (phantasms) which it has received through the sensory powers from its own body and the bodies about it; nevertheless, the need for objects does not compromise the incorporeal and organ-free character of the understanding and its mode of operation, nor its claim to subsistence. Thomas compares the understanding's relation to its objects to the relation between an animal's sensory perception and its objects. Because an animal needs to perceive objects we do not deny its subsistence; not every kind of dependence undermines subsistence. No more does the understanding's need for objects negate its subsistence, which is established on the grounds of the immanent (self-contained) nature of the operation performed, and not on a dependence upon objects that remain physically as they were outside the circle of that intransitive, immanent activity.

To a modern mind that demands the intrinsic relatedness of everything within a system, the answer may prove puzzling. But it recommends itself to a philosopher who understands subsistence as Thomas does, because the context (principle of totality, i.e., the world) does not so encroach upon individuals that their *relatively* subsistent status is threatened, nor is their independence so exaggerated that it threatens the unity of the world. I say: "relative subsistence," since *creatures* do not possess absolute subsistence, receiving—as they do—their very existence from the source of existence. The pervasiveness of membership in the system (world, ecosystem, society) does not override the constitution of the individuals; for, even though they have been created as members of a world, and even though it may enter to an important degree into the way in which they exercise their subsistence, they are not mere aspects of the totality of which they are members. What is at issue is the relation of the world to the individuals in it. Today we tend to view the unity of the world as systemic, and the claim to subsistent individuals seems to threaten the unity of the world. Of course, if there are no subsistent individuals, then there is no need even to ask about the immortality of individual souls.[23] St. Thomas has argued that, if the intellectual

---

22. *STh,* I, 75, 2, ad 3m.
23. But, if the proof were to do nothing else, it poses the perennial question of the nature of ontological order: Is the unity of the cosmos systematic? Or are systems merely partial (and hence abstract) versions of that unity?

soul performs an action in which the body cannot share *as agent,* then its reliance upon the body for the *object* of its operation does not destroy its subsistence (though, after death, it would require another mode for the presentation of objects).[24] The central claim to subsistence has been made on the basis of agency: where there are agents, there are subsistents; where there are incorporeal agents, there are incorporeal beings.

But although the human soul may be said to be subsistent and to act and live the life of spirit, still it is a very special—one is tempted to say "odd"—sort of substance. Thomas has made famous the formula that the human soul is both the form of the body and an individual subsistent thing: *forma corporis et hoc aliquid.*[25] Nevertheless, although it is subsistent, and hence may be said to be a substance, it is an imperfect one.[26] Something may subsist perfectly as a particular thing of a specific nature (Aristotle's famous primary substance: *tode ti*); on the other hand, something may subsist imperfectly and incompletely. That is, it does not exist as a mere accident or a material form inheres in a subject, but does exist in and through itself, and yet also exists as a part of something else. It is this imperfect mode of subsistence that the human soul possesses, since it is a "part" (i.e., a constituent principle) of the human composite.

What remains to be indicated regarding the third moment of the proof is the ways in which something subsistent can be corrupted. Very briefly: Thomas concludes that death—which is the separation of the life-principle (the soul) from the body—cannot bring about the corruption of the human soul, either by accident (externally through the action of another thing) or by essence (intrinsically by its own self-destruction).[27] The argument invokes the metaphysics of existential act. That is, having established the incorporeal subsistence of the human soul as an actually existing though incomplete substance, Thomas argues that existence comes to the human composite by virtue of its form (the soul): *Esse autem per se convenit formae, quae est actus;* and that the principle of actuality *(esse)* belongs inseparably not to the composite but to the soul by virtue of its own subsistence: *id quod secundum se convenit alicui, est inseparabile ab ipso.* Much more, of course, would need to be said—not only in defense of Thomas' argument—but even in order to state it clearly. If such a task does not lie beyond the present author, it certainly lies beyond the present article.

Moreover, when all is said, a shadow falls upon the human soul, from

---

24. See the extended discussion of the separated soul and the knowledge available to it in *Quaestiones disputatae de anima,* qq. 15–20.
25. *Quaestiones disputatae de anima,* q. 1. See James Robb's excellent introduction to his English translation, based upon his Latin edition: *Thomas Aquinas: Questions on the Soul* (Milwaukee, WI: Marquette University Press, 1984).
26. *STh,* I, 75, 2, ad 1m.
27. *STh,* I, 75, 6c.

within the contours of what has been argued by the proof itself. For St. Thomas recognizes that the survival sustained by the separated soul is not an entirely satisfactory one. As the formal principle of the human composite, it is, after all, intimately bound up with the body. There is no question here, then, of a free-wheeling soul that is gladly rid of its body; quite to the contrary, the human soul is meant to be with its body. Indeed, the soul separated from its body poses an embarrassment that only the religious promise of resurrection can adequately undo. Now, that is a religious hope and a religious reality, which St. Thomas considers as a theologian rather than as a philosopher. It needs to be remembered, of course, that as a Christian St. Thomas does not consider this hope to be a mere hypothesis, tacked on to the divine order as an afterthought. It is, rather, for him the vision of the way things really are, the glory towards which reason gropes, into which faith peers darkly, and in which the blessed take joy. The farthest he can go *as a philosopher* in parting the mysterious veil that lies at the boundary of our present life, however, is expressed in his formula: the human soul, by virtue of its intellectual nature, is both a substance in its own right and yet the spiritual life of the body *(forma et hoc aliquid)*. Without the body, it subsists only as a radically incomplete being, since it is by nature meant to inform, structure, and vivify its human body. In the end, then, St. Thomas' proof delivers to us something not unlike a Greek shade. This is not surprising, however, when we bear in mind the nature of the discourse *(logos* become *ratio)* with which St. Thomas articulates his proof.[28]

28. See "Are there things more important for the human race than survival? The Greek Heritage: Rationality," in *Das europäische Erbe und seine christliche Zukunft*, vol. 16, ed. N. Lobkowicz (Cologne: Hans Martin Schleyer-Stiftung, 1985), 348–56 (German translation: 95–104). For a penetrating, and sometimes surprising, development of St. Thomas' position on the separated soul, see Mary F. Rousseau, "The Natural Meaning of Death in the *Summa Theologiae*," *Proceedings of the American Catholic Philosophical Association* 52 (1978): 87–95, and "Elements of a Thomistic Philosophy of Death," *The Thomist* 43, no. 4 (Oct. 1979): 581–602.

Chapter 13

IS LIBERALISM GOOD ENOUGH?

And so begins a chat (sermo), not about other men's homes and estates, nor whether Lepos dances well or ill; but we discuss matters which concern us more, and of which it is harmful to be in ignorance—whether wealth or virtue makes men happy, whether self-interest or uprightness (usus rectumne) leads us to friendship, what is the nature of the good and what is its highest form.

Horace, Satires II, vi, 70–76

A free market will undoubtedly offer several varieties of goods for sale, including a variety of theories of the good. As we enter the bazaar we can expect to be offered the very best theory of the very best good; nor should we be surprised to find the trademark "Liberal" stamped upon it, and perhaps the logo: "Produced by the Forces of Liberalism." And yet, it seems prudent to look over a few other wares, some older perhaps, some even newer, even some that seem bizarre. The wary customer may be excused if he or she does not by impulse (subliminal or otherwise) take up the most popular brand, but looks about a little. For the advertisements, however insistent, may not be finally persuasive. Indeed, one of them may even claim that the liberal theory is so good that it can't be classified as a mere theory of the good, much in the same way that for a time General Electric claimed to produce "Progress" instead of light bulbs. It may claim that liberalism rises above the fray, stands indifferent to the competing theories of the good and does not abandon its neutrality even when it referees the inevitable competition that arises. So that the good life is best lived without the encumbrance of a theory of the good. Well and good; but the prospective buyer must still test both claims: (1) that liberalism has the best theory of the good, and (2) that it doesn't need one.

It is still wise to ask whether liberalism is the best we can do. It is no secret that liberalism promotes the individual; that headline won't sell

---

Reprinted from *Liberalism and the Good,* ed. Bruce Douglass et al. (London: Routledge, 1990), 86–104. Copyright © 1990 by Routledge.

newspapers. It is said, too, by older voices, that it neglects the common good. My discontent is lodged, however, in its central affirmation, and how liberalism understands the very individual whose interest it strives to promote. What is unsatisfactory about liberalism is neither the central importance it attaches to the individual, nor its pursuit of the individual's good. What is at issue is the nature of the individual's good. What is good for the individual, however, is relative to what he or she is and how he or she is understood. And it is just here, it seems to me, that liberalism fails its clients, because—or so it seems to me again—liberalism does not give full value to the individual. My thesis, then, is that liberal liberty is reductionist.

For there is a richer, fuller understanding of the individual available in the long tradition of so-called Western thought. I go back to Aristotle for the beginning of its career; but I do not mean that we should rest there. For not only has the notion of the individual changed since the citizen of the Greek *polis* has passed into history, but the reality itself has changed. What it is to be an individual has greatly changed, and liberalism has striven to take account of that. By using the words "good enough" in the title, I mean to indicate that I do not reject liberalism outright—whole and entire. Rather, my subordinate thesis is that its account of the massive change we call "modernization" is only partial; and that liberal liberty is reductionist because classical modern liberalism has expressed only the moment of *difference* in that change, even though it has often expressed that aspect with clarity and verve. But the same Aristotle also tells us that change combines novelty with permanence, unites alteration with identity, and bridges discontinuity with continuity. Now, in expressing only what had changed, liberalism caught what was different between old and new, but (so far as it was possible) discarded the old in favor of the exclusive value of the new. Heir to the Renaissance and companion of the Enlightenment, it proclaimed a radical new beginning. Its ahistorical stance is not incidental to it, nor is its antitraditional voice accidental.[1]

It is hardly possible to retain a focus upon such a broad front as "Liberalism," since there are many different versions, even among classical modern proponents. And so, it is fair to ask: Whose ox is being gored

---

1. The call for new beginnings was, of course, quite general during this time, even among those who are not usually associated with liberalism. Thus, Descartes wrote in his *Discourse* (Part II): "Nevertheless, as far as the opinions which I had been receiving since my birth were concerned, I could not do better than *to reject them completely for once* in my lifetime, and to resume them afterwards or perhaps accept better ones in their place, when I had determined how they fitted into a rational scheme" *Discourse on Method and Meditations*, Library of Liberal Arts (Indianapolis, IN: Bobbs-Merrill, 1960), 12; emphasis added. Descartes protests that his revolution should remain within the sphere of ideas alone, but history has shown us that modes of thought may become institutionalized. The myths of the state of nature, made famous by early modern thought, may differ from one another, but they all agree in possessing a prehistorical character that is ahistorical and antitradi-

and which fields are being left unplowed? Moreover, the approach taken will determine in part what is to be considered an essential feature of liberalism and what is not. My own philosophical—indeed, I admit it, metaphysical[2]—analysis casts its net rather broadly, so that important features of liberalism tend to merge with the more general movement of thought associated with the Enlightenment and its antecedents. Yet, despite the variety, there is need to address the question in broad terms. Of course, it does not make the discussion easier that the apostle of change itself has changed: liberalism has not stood still. Indeed, somehow even against its spirit, we can speak now of a liberal "tradition," for it has continued to develop an understanding of the individual on the basis of its early modern beginnings and within that particular horizon. Recent versions of liberalism have displayed imagination and ingenuity in meeting new and stressful circumstances. This is no small achievement. For in the sphere of politics, our century has shown an alarming proclivity towards illiberal regimes, and in economics it has exhibited an insensitivity to minimal government, low taxation, and minuscule national indebtedness. In response to current conditions, some contemporary theorists supply the liberal individual with a social conscience rather different from the one supplied by Adam Smith. He rested conscience upon the implacable cycle that was to bring about general prosperity as evenhandedly against an unwary or unlucky merchant as against the laboring poor, whereas they place it within the context of democratic social policy.[3]

In a variety of versions, liberalism continues to thrive in moral theo-

---

tional. Moreover, this feature has been a propellant for social change, and it still remains in current versions of liberalism. Thus, John Rawls posits a hypothetical "original position" behind a "veil of ignorance." *A Theory of Justice* (Cambridge, MA: Harvard University Press, 1971), 17ff. and 136ff. And although Bruce Ackerman rejects all versions of the state of nature and of contractarianism, and although he permits us to bring the baggage of our opinions and our social conditioning on board his metaphorical "spaceship," and even later permits us to adjust the "perfect technology of justice" to meet real conditions, he stipulates that "no prior conversation has previously established the legitimacy of any claims to the manna [i.e., the primary goods] in dispute." Moreover, we are required to imagine ourselves "on a spaceship that comes upon a new world where the available manna has not, up to now, been claimed by anybody." *Social Justice in the Liberal State* (New Haven, CT: Yale University Press, 1980), 25.

2. It may be objected that I needlessly inject a "metaphysical" reading of the individual into a social context that can be better handled by games theory or social pragmatics. That can, of course, be a matter of discussion, but I reject the positivist tactic of using "metaphysics" as a scare word, or as a form of intellectual contempt. The question at issue is whether the individual is something like what I will set forth or not, and whether such an analysis is relevant to the problem at hand. It will not do, therefore, to arbitrarily put such an analysis out of play in social thought on the grounds that it is "metaphysics" or because Rawls or others did not intend a metaphysical reading, any more than a physician can dispense with diagnoses or an engineer with the physics of forces.

3. Cf. the oft-quoted passage from *The Wealth of Nations*, III, 4: "two different orders

ry, political discourse, and the law; while in economic policy it offers a range of advice from sophisticated free-market capitalism to redistributive social democracy.[4] The accents of public debate also show how deeply liberal values are embedded in our democratic mores.[5] This is not surprising if, as I have indicated and will argue further, liberalism offers a plausible interpretation of the complex of forces that has shaped the modern individual, even though its interpretation is but a partial and deficient expression of that complex. One need not endorse a metaphysics of the Zeitgeist in order to recognize that a prevailing wind does billow forth today, so that shouting into it may seem as pointless as a mere puff of contrary air. Or, to change the image, to look for something better than liberalism pits one against a main current in modern Western life in whose flow the social, political, and economic values of conventional wisdom find their buoyancy. And yet, if the liberal understanding of the individual arises out of profound and interconnected changes in science, technology, and economics; in society, culture, and polities; in philosophy, religion, and art, the general features of liberalism may be brought into higher relief and sharper profile by a consideration of those interconnected changes. I neither can nor wish to doc-

---

of people who had not the least intention to serve the public.... Neither of them had either knowledge or foresight of that great revolution which the folly of the one [the landed proprietors], and the industry of the other [the merchants and artificers], was gradually bringing about." What was further urged by Adam Smith in the eighteenth century as *benevolence* towards the poor becomes in the twentieth a primary feature of *justice* as fairness toward the "least fortunate" or "least advantaged class." Rawls, *Theory of Justice,* 98f.

4. John A. Hall, *Liberalism: Politics, Ideology and the Market* (Chapel Hill: University of North Carolina Press, 1987), 35–62 passim, raises the issue of the connection between liberalism and capitalism. He is not alone in arguing that despite their long-standing historical alliance, the connection is nonetheless contingent. The divergence of their central interests, he argues, puts them in potential conflict; for central to liberalism is the moral worth of the individual, whereas central to capitalism is the maximization of profit. He also notes the change in some versions of liberalism that has been brought about by social democracy, which requires a strong social infrastructure and comprehensive safety net, in order to promote the moral worth of the individual. Thus, John Rawls insists upon the distribution of primary goods, including our inherited talents, in keeping with the needs of the least advantaged and in accordance with the principles of justice as fairness (*Theory of Justice,* 101f., 179).

5. A. MacIntyre, *Whose Justice? Which Rationality?* (Notre Dame, IN: University of Notre Dame Press, 1988), 392, writes: "Liberalism, as I have understood it in this book, does of course appear in contemporary debates in a number of guises and in so doing is often successful in pre-empting the debate by reformulating quarrels and conflicts with liberalism, so that they appear to have become debates within liberalism, putting in question this or that particular set of attitudes or policies, *but not the fundamental tenets of liberalism with respect to individuals and the expression of their preferences.* So so-called conservatism and so-called radicalism in these contemporary debates within modern political systems are almost exclusively between conservative liberals, liberal liberals, and radical liberals. There is little place in such political systems for the criticism of the system itself, that is, for putting liberalism in question" (emphasis added).

ument all of these changes, any more than I can address all versions of liberalism at once and in detail. But I do need to sketch points that are salient for my story of the individual, and salient, I hope, in reality too.

THE SEARCH FOR "ELEMENTARY PARTICLES"

We know that the science of mechanics, and the industrial technology that eventually drew power from it, did much to shape early modern thought and practice. The mechanistic mode of analysis swept other spheres of thought and life along with it in the aura and with the impetus of its brilliant successes. Of course, science and technology were not exclusive agents of change. It seems, rather, that they were bearers and indicators of a deeper movement, which had its immediate antecedents in a broader trend. That drift included a theoretical shift during the late Middle Ages to nominalism in logic and metaphysics, and to empiricism in natural philosophy. Now, modern science and technology drew upon a conception of unity that was shaped by those antecedents and that put its stamp upon what was to become the liberal understanding of individuality.

Against the background of nominalism,[6] and in the spheres of physics, astronomy, and various technologies, sixteenth-century mechanics launched scientific inquiry and technique upon a search for ultimate and elementary particles—at first called *minima*, corpuscules, and more rarely, atoms.[7] It is a search that continues to this day, though it is presently yielding pride of place among some theorists to more holistic approaches. According to its own terms, the search for absolutely ultimate and simple particles has been in vain; and yet its "vanity" has produced the most remarkable, and mostly beneficial, results. My present interest, however, is not directly in its contributions to scientific knowledge and technical application, but in its indirect influence. For mechanism helped to shape and to confirm the underlying conceptions of social interaction and to curtail the scope of rationality by defining rigor in terms of precision. Two features of this bias stand out: the twin demands for *self-sufficiency* and for *separateness*. The mathematization of scientific

---

6. Commenting upon the relatively modern recognition of individual liberty as a conscious political ideal, Isaiah Berlin, in his essay "Two Concepts of Liberty," commends "the valuable discussion in Michel Villey, *Lecons d'histoire de la philosophie du droit*, who traces the embryo of the notion of subjective rights to Occam." *Four Essays on Liberty* (Oxford: Oxford University Press, 1969, 1986), 129, n. 1.

7. For my own account of the shift to elementary analysis, see "Analysis by Principles and Analysis by Elements," in *Graceful Reason: Essays in Ancient and Mediaeval Philosophy Presented to Joseph Owens, CSSR*, ed. Lloyd P. Gerson (Toronto: Pontifical Institute of Mediaeval Studies, 1983),315–30. See chapter 2 above.

inquiry in its early modern phase led to a triumph of the ancient definition of geometrical points of space as "parts outside of parts." It is a victory that instrumental versions of rationality still cling to and that brings with it tendencies to social fragmentation. The search for elementary particles of matter lent support and gave expression to an analytic habit of mind that jealously guarded the principle of differentiation and the self-sufficiency of each particular idea or sensation. Among the intellectualists, Descartes pressed for clear ideas absolutely distinct from one another, Hobbes defined elementary bodies as concrete points in space, and among empiricists, Hume insisted upon the self-enclosed and discrete completeness of each impression. Among the transcendentalists, Kant posited the discreteness of data in the sensory manifold.

Now, a certain kind of unity requires separateness and the consequent externality of relationships. For the nature of the unity of anything determines the character of the relations into which the real or ideal unit (that is, the particle or idea) can enter. The status of an ultimate and elementary particle in mechanism is that it possesses a self-sufficiency which it retains even after it has entered into relations with other elementary particles. For that reason, its relations must remain external to it. In sum, then, the ultimate nature of the differential unity proposed by nominalism and pursued by mechanism consists in its *incomplexity*. For the ultimate nature of such differential units resides in their lack of parts. The ultimate units were ultimate precisely because they were simple in the sense of being the last possible point of analysis. To be one was to be simple, and to be ultimate was to be absolutely one—indivisible and irreducible. All relationships had to fall "outside" of them, therefore, taking the form of attachments to and detachments from a distinct and separate elemental unit.

Translated into the order of freedom, ultimate unity took the form of the discrete movement of the individual will. Moreover, voluntarism, often associated with nominalism, promoted the primacy of the will in the human individual. None celebrated the new sense of freedom more felicitously, however, than the eclectic Platonist, Pico della Mirandola. His *On the Dignity of Man* places that dignity in the lack of a given nature in the human being, who possesses instead the open power of free choice. In more lapidary terms, Descartes espoused a minimal conception of human liberty as the absolute indifference to any and every alternative, an indifference extensive with the infinitude of the individual human will.[8] More generally, the notion of *conatus*, as the spontaneous striving of the

---

8. For Pico, see *On the Dignity of Man,* trans. Charles G. Wallis, Library of Liberal Arts (Indianapolis: Bobbs-Merrill, 1965); for Descartes, see the fourth meditation where he writes: "(God) has given me a volition more ample than my understanding. For as the volition consists of just one body, (its subject being) apparently indivisible, it seems that its na-

individual human appetite (whether passional or rational), runs through the thought of philosophers from Hobbes to Leibniz to Hume and beyond. The conception of natural right is often cast along these lines at this time. Hobbes' dramatic formulas are well known, such as: that in the natural condition of mankind, "every man has a right to everything; even to another's body."[9] And Spinoza understood by natural right: "that every natural thing has by nature as much right as it has power to exist and operate."[10] Even Leibniz, who repudiated the extended separateness of the fundamental units, still understood each self-enclosed monad to be driven by its own wholly internal appetition.[11] Locke takes volition to be a simple rather than a complex idea.[12] And for Hume, a passion is "an original existence," moving the individual prior to rational deliberation, and therefore able to be countered only by another original impulse.[13] Insofar as conatus takes the form of will proper, we may speak of it as the power to choose, but in the broad sense it is appetite, passion, desire, sentiment, or choice. What holds for all variant positions is that the individual human will or conatus is the impetus moving us prior to all else and the ground of all value. Even Kant, who speaks of obligation, means by it self-obligation, the principle of moral autonomy: the relation of the pure self-legislating reason to itself. All other relations must remain external to such a self-will. It follows, then, that everything other than the self is converted into the status of alternatives for choice and potential

---

ture is such that nothing could be taken from it without destroying it." Both Descartes and Pico find the amplitude of the individual human will, its infinitude in scope, to comprise the very image of God in the individual human being (See Pico, 116).

9. *Leviathan* I, 14; also "the right of nature . . . is the liberty each man hath, to use his *own power, as he will himself,* for the preservation of his own nature" (emphasis added). Hobbes' use of the term "will" properly speaking is to designate the last act or decision, whereas my emphasis is meant to draw attention to the primitive conatus that underlies the process of deliberation and will in Hobbes and others.

10. *A Political Treatise*, c. 2, secs. 3–5. Of course, each philosopher embedded the conatus in his own fuller thought, as Spinoza here identifies natural right with the power of God or Nature. See also *A Theologico-Political Treatise*, c. xvi: "The power of nature is the power of God, which has sovereign right over all things; and, inasmuch as the power of nature is simply the aggregate of the powers of all her individual components, it follows that *every individual has sovereign right to do all that he can*, in other words, the rights of an individual extend to the *utmost limits of his power* as it has been conditioned. Now it is the sovereign law and right of nature that each individual should endeavour to preserve itself as it is, *without regard to anything but itself;* therefore this sovereign law and right belongs to every individual, namely, to exist and act according to its natural conditions. . . . As the wise man has sovereign right to do all that reason dictates, . . . so also the ignorant and foolish man has *sovereign right to do all that desire dictates*" (emphasis added). *The Works of Spinoza*, 2 vols., trans. R. H. M. Elwes (New York: Dover, 1951), vol. 1, 292 and 200 respectively. See also *Ethics* I, Definitions I and VII.

11. *Monadology*, paras. 11–15. Cf. also his revival of the notion of *vis activa*.

12. *Essay Concerning Human Understanding*, II, 6.

13. *Treatise on Human Understanding*, II, iii, 3. See the discussion of passional motivation according to Hume in MacIntyre, *Whose Justice?* 300ff.

objects of possession. All else, in the broadest sense, then, becomes potential property. In sum, will, passion, appetite, desire, sentiment, and choice are but various ways of naming and understanding the striving for self-assertion and appropriation of others that, according to liberalism, is the conative element—passional and/or rational—at the moving core of each individual human being.

There is, however, a more basic feature of the archetypal mechanistic science of early modern times that takes us more deeply still into the liberal character of freedom. Modern science was, and still remains, a science of motion. Motion is understood as displacement, and rest is merely the temporary absence of motion; or, in entropy, it is the permanent unavailability for further movement. With the abandonment of final causes in seventeenth-century science, rest was emptied of one of the meanings it had once possessed, namely, that of the fulfillment of the individual through the attainment of its purpose. To the extent that social and political thought were in part influenced by mechanics, and in part themselves expressive of a deeper thrust that was concomitant with mechanics—to that extent the liberty possessed by the individual will becomes not simply the power to choose, the ancient *liberum arbitrium.* The nature of choice itself had changed. Or rather, the character of liberal liberty is not simply the power to choose: it is equally, even primarily, the power to *unchoose.* For what has primacy in this general view of the self is not that it is free to complete itself by choosing a good already somehow prescribed for it or inscribed in it, but rather that it achieves its own highest good by retaining the power not only to choose but also to relinquish that choice and to take up another. For, in retaining *that* power, it retains in the currency of freedom the very mobility that is of supreme import and interest in the science of nature. The foundation and force of liberalism lies in the simplicity of the individual's power to move—the impulse to change one's mind and one's place and, where possible, the world. In this motility lies its exaltation of the freedom of the individual.[14]

THE PRIMACY OF THE SUBJECT

So far, then, I have argued that liberalism is the socioeconomic, moral, and political interpretation of those features by which the modern individual differs from the past. Moreover, in the process that formed the

---

14. Ackerman (*Social Justice,* 198ff.) asks whether the forty-year-old "Shifty" should be bound by contracts he made at twenty, and asserts that the advantage his own liberalism of neutral discourse about power relations has over contractarianism lies in its "courage to question the doubtful notion that a promise, once fairly made, must *always* be kept."

modern individual, liberalism has given pre-eminence to a conception of unity as simplicity and of freedom as mobility. There is no doubt that liberal ideas have won for themselves an impressive authority, in part at least through their promotion of tolerance and defense of civil peace. In guarding the difference, however, liberalism has created the mythology of a discredited pre-liberal past as part of its antitraditional weaponry; and, in catching at the moment of difference, discreteness, and fragmentation that is an operative force in the formation of the modern individual, liberalism has assumed the shape of the distinctions and dichotomies that emerged four centuries ago in Europe. They arose in many fields, but let me remind you of them by telling of their emergence in modern philosophy. Philosophers sometimes trouble their neighbors by raising doubts over what seems indubitable. In so doing, they may articulate a sense of unease wider than their own. But philosophers also live in society, and they sometimes reinforce its certainties. It is likely, too, that those who are or become influential are those who formulate what the society intuits to be the fundamental nature of things.

Consider modern *epistemology*, which is receiving rather rough treatment from deconstructionists these days. According to it, the human subject proclaims itself to be the first and overriding principle. It certifies itself in virtue of its rationality or its experience, and variously according to the criteria of rationalism, empiricism, or transcendentalism. The powerful certainty of self-consciousness purchases for the subject a self-conviction that construes everything else as set over against it: in a word, as *ob-ject*. The canons of objectivity are the protocols by which the subject dominates its objects. On the basis of this certainty (which not even the skeptical Hume denied), various philosophers devised various mental shapes and methods to account for the way in which the object could be represented to the subject—could be brought to the bar of Reason (Spinoza), or into the vivid associations of the senses and passions (some empiricists), or led before the tribunal of the understanding (Kant). What prevails in these positions is the operative primacy of the subject.[15]

It is not surprising, then, that in the *ontology* of the modern period the human subjectivity, so dominant in epistemology, should put its imprint upon the very shape of things perceived, rendering them into ob-

---

15. Obviously, I am critical of any elevation of the distinction between subject and object to a primary and privileged role such as it enjoys in liberalism. At the same time, however, I am reluctant to add my voice to the growing chorus of those hermeneutists, deconstructionists, and neo-Marxists who vent their disaffection with modern epistemology. It seems to me that many critics do not sufficiently relinquish the *effective and operative primacy* of the individual subject, but retain it instead in the form of aggressive critical rationality.

jects admitted to "real" status only insofar as they are able to meet the conditions of subjectivity understood as the primary principle. To the scientists of the time, busy as they were discovering the secrets of nature, it may well have seemed (as Hegel is reported to have said) that the very world was being created before their wondering eyes. But it is also true that the world that was being discovered agreed wonderfully with the emerging dichotomies.

The principal aim of modern *technology* was enthusiastically proclaimed by seventeenth-century philosophers: it was to gain control over nature for human ends. With industrial technology, control easily took the form of active domination of nature which was approached as a passive field for human exploitation. The dichotomy of active manipulator and passive material fitted easily into the reigning parent dichotomy of subject and object. Obviously, it makes a considerable difference in the approach to nature whether a technologue sees himself as a dominant self who sets the agenda according to subjective human wants or as a human being who is situated in a less dominant position and is associated with nature in a more companionable way.

Finally, the very scope and nature of *rationality* came to be determined by the subjective pre-eminence that is inveterate in the parent dichotomy. The unequal status of subject and object can be seen in the double role enjoyed by the subject. On the surface it seems to be an equal and correlative partner in the relation between subject and object; but a deeper look discloses that it colors the whole relationship. That is, the subject functions in both a partial and an integral way: it is a party to the relation but it also lends to things its *own* shape and takes their utility for itself to be *their* significance. In admitting them as objects it validates them according to its demands for mathematical precision, systematic order, and verifiable evidence. In this way, the very limits of acceptable rational discourse come to be drawn closely about what is deemed to fall within the horizon of the individual human subject. Under such limitations it was all but inevitable that everything deemed to be in any way transcendent or mysterious (the matters of religion) should fall outside the pale of "rational" discourse. And this exile was prelude to such matters losing their place in the public discourse. The political disestablishment of any particular church or religion (justifiable on grounds of the freedom of conscience implicit in biblical religions) became the separation of church and state. But that *political* separation was preceded by the *epistemological* eviction of religion from "intellectually respectable" conversation. Reduced to mere opinion or belief, it was to be left wherever other private things are kept.

As we turn to *social thought*, I am aware that the logic of implication does not rule over events, which lend their own weight to the way ideas come to rest in the domain of social actuality. Nevertheless, ideas do offer a pathway along which events may take shape, especially if the ideas represent, express, interpret, or facilitate possibilities already immanent in the situation. At the beginning of the modern period the parent dichotomy of subject and object was rooted in (and gave further credence to) a growing sense of the inadequacy of the established institutions and the received traditions of the late medieval and early modern period—their perceived inability to cope with the unprecedented and burgeoning energies of individual agents. For the latter became increasingly independent of, and in many instances alienated from or hostile to, established authority.[16] Now, the parent distinction between subject and object gave canonical expression to that distance, and gave added weight to what I have called the differential. That differential at once gives distance to the social, cultural, and political "space" between the subject and its objects; but it also opens up a distance between the subject and other subjects. The negative fallout of that distance expresses itself in isolation, fragmentation, and alienation. On the positive side, however, it permits the subject to preserve its own individual freedom, to assert its primacy over objects, and to maintain its inviolability in the face of other subjects. The modern insistence upon individual rights is on its way.

In the classical versions of this view, self-interest (enlightened or not) has prior claim to legitimacy, even though it may require negotiation and qualification to settle rival claims and arrive at a guarded civility.[17]

---

16. In France it came to a head in the attack upon altar and throne. See Hegel, *Phenomenology*, c. vi. Cf. K. L. Schmitz, "Enlightenment Criticism and Embodiment of Values: The Hegelian Background to a Contemporary Problem," in *Indian Philosophical Annual* 18, (1986): 33–53.

17. Ackerman (*Social Justice*, 343–46) presents a current version of liberalism that seems neo-Hobbesian in tone. Rejecting both contractarianism and utilitarianism, he nevertheless finds the former superior to the latter on the score that "individuals have the *right* to put themselves first" (emphasis added). Still, the "true liberal," he writes, rejects the false individualism of Contract (with its hidden privileges and neglect of social influence) and also the false community of Utility ("brothers sharing in some mystical communion with the public good"). Instead the true liberal prefers (the word is mine) to base his position upon (1) the undefined and practically unlimited scope of individuals' subjective wants. In the beginning is the word. but the first words of the Ackerman dialogue are: "I want X!" "So do I!" The second assumption is (2) the scarcity of goods. I cannot help but observe that this is a scarcity by definition; that is, given the practically unlimited desires of individuals, an infinity of goods would not be enough. (3) The resultant conflict and struggle for power (Ackerman speaks of my rights against you, p. 347) needs containment. (4) A neutral dialogue is recommended which would consist of talk about power on the basis of "acceptable" reasons. The "neutrality" of the dialogue, however, remains suspect to me, and my suspicions are heightened by the demand for dialogic competence (p. 70), the obvious advantage of adult status (p. 110), the speculations about a world without

This strategy recognizes the indifferent equality of a plurality of dominant selves, and—out of a prudent fear—negotiates rival claims by contract, by appeal to the maximization of happiness, or more recently by procedural rules. The liberal strategy has as its primary aim to safeguard and promote—not happiness or virtue so much—as the liberty of the differential individual.[18]

Nevertheless, in the classical versions, self-love need not be invariably ungenerous or selfish. On the contrary, the self can extend itself to encompass concern for others. British (notably Scottish) philosophers and moralists placed emphasis upon the softer, gentler passions, while novelists (in eighteenth-century England, France, and Germany) paid tribute to the more tender sentiments.[19] Certainly, the promotion of tolerance in politics and of moderation in social mores marks one of classical liberalism's proudest moments, though it is offset by neglect of the poor, rapacity of unregulated competition, and excess of civil litigation. No doubt, the general spirit of tolerance was shaped at least in part by the pervasive distinction of subject and object mentioned earlier. For within that distinction the built-in primacy of the subject gained for the self a certain privilege in the way in which benevolence was understood. The continuum of loves divided into subjective interest and objective concern and, according to the parent dichotomy, this meant that love divided into egoism and altruism. The very language betrays the double role of self mentioned earlier. Moreover, the primacy of self gives rise to a "hermeneutics of suspicion" that purports to uncover self-love even in the seemingly purest altruistic motive.

---

moral significance, *sans* Creator, and in which we create "the only meanings we will ever know" (pp. 368–69), and the disposition made on several issues, including intergenerational conflict and the role of the family. Being invited to join such a "neutral" and "open" dialogue may turn out to be not unlike an invitation to a nudist camp, in which you are advised to divest yourself of clothes only to arrive at the beach wearing considerably less than your hosts, who have retained what they regard as indispensable beach wear.

18. Brian Barry takes a stern view of these matters. He writes: "Liberalism rests on a vision of life: a Faustian vision. It exalts self-expression, self-mastery and control over the environment, natural and social; the active pursuit of knowledge and the clash of ideas; the acceptance of personal responsibility for the decisions that shape one's life. For those who cannot take the freedom it provides alcohol, tranquilizers, wrestling on the television, astrology, psychoanalysis, and so on, endlessly, but it cannot by its nature provide certain kinds of psychological security. Like any creed it can be neither justified nor condemned in terms of anything beyond it." *The Liberal Theory of Justice: A Critical Examination of the Principal Doctrines in "A Theory of Justice" by John Rawls* (Oxford: Clarendon, 1973), 127. The variety of contemporary interpretations of liberalism can be seen by reading the literature that has arisen around Rawls' book; compare, for example, Barry's study with those of M. Sandel, *Liberalism and the Limits of Justice* (Cambridge: Cambridge University Press, 1982), and R. P. Wolff, *Understanding Rawls: A Reconstruction and Critique of A Theory of Justice* (Princeton: Princeton University Press, 1977).

19. See the discussion of the Scottish thinkers in MacIntyre, *Whose Justice?* esp. 268ff. The novels I have in mind include Richardson's *Pamela*, Rousseau's *Emile*, and Schlegel's *Lucinde*.

In any event, altruistic or not, the high value placed by liberalism upon the individual self is, in my view, continuous with and a distortion of a more general hallmark of so-called Western culture. Christianity and biblical religion generally, so important in the formation of that culture, proclaim the spiritual equality and worth of each person. As well, however, the worth of the individual also has remote origins among the ancient Greeks. For it finds among them an early echo in the honor paid to self-subsistence and in the striving for self-sufficiency and even autonomy *(kath' auto,* cf. *ens per se).* In attempting to recover what, it seems to me, is a more adequate and timely sense of the worth of the individual and the inherent equality of individuals, it is with the Greeks that I begin—and particularly with Aristotle.

THE COMPLEX, CONSTITUTIVE INDIVIDUAL

Now, Aristotle's individual is a complex affair.[20] He calls it "this somewhat" *(tode ti,* cf. *hoc aliquid),* "this something of a certain kind." The two factors, "this" and "what," are distinct in thought and speech, but they are not separate in reality. For the primary realities of Aristotle's world—and of ours as well, I must add—are composite but not composed. They are really complex, but they are not put together out of independent and separate entities. One never meets a this that is not also a that, nor a what that is not in reality a this. The "this" captures the *singularity* of each real and individual thing, while the "somewhat" indicates what it shares with other things, and which I call its *commonality.* By the latter term I do not mean merely the abstract character which comprises its species and genus, but all of the constituent principles that it shares with other things. To Aristotle, the "somewhat" *(ti)* stood in the first instance for the essence or substance of the thing *(ousia,* cf. *substantia, natura).* By calling the "what" *(ti)* "commonality," however, I mean to extend it so as to include the cultural and social constituents that make up our changing individuality. Without attributing the extension to Aristotle himself or minimizing the difference between his problematic and mine, we can nonetheless recognize that for him no individual could be complete without the relationships brought about by life in the *polis.*

To be sure, Aristotle acknowledges the necessity of tradition for building up the skills of artisans and by implication for social life as a whole. Undoubtedly, however, we give more weight today than he did

---

20. For more detailed development of my use of Aristotle, see "Community: The Elusive Unity," *Review of Metaphysics* 37, no. 2 (Dec. 1983): 245–64; "Metaphysics: Radical, Comprehensive, Determinate Discourse," *Review of Metaphysics* 39, no. 4 (June 1986): 675–94; and "Neither with nor without Foundations," *Review of Metaphysics* 42, no. 1 (Sept. 1988): 3–25. See chapters 1 and 4 above.

to the role played by time and history in the constitution of the individual. With the disruption between past and present introduced by historical consciousness and with the emphasis upon the differential that is thought to separate us from the past, we have become aware of the situatedness of the individual in time in general and within a particular cultural and social space-time context. This need not mean, however, that an individual is so radically immersed in the situation that all individuality is lost. The singularity secures its uniqueness. For the singularity and commonality that constitute the *integrity* of the individual do not relate as part to part but as whole to whole. That is, the individual is through and through singular, but also in regard to many of the commonalities he or she is fully and entirely them. The individual is not of French culture or German-speaking or an American citizen with only a part of himself or herself, but is such commonalities whole and entire. So, too, is he or she entirely singular.

Aristotle's complex individual, and the constitutive individual here developed on the basis of it, differ from the primary sense of individuality entertained by the ancient atomists and the late medieval nominalists. As I have already mentioned, the original, primary, and paradigmatic sense of unity was for them the absolutely simple. The unit was a single particular point, irreducible and solitary, radically incomplex.[21] Aristotle's individual, on the other hand, far from being isolated in ultimate self-closure, receives its very constitution—for good and for ill—from and through its causes and in its ongoing relatedness to others. The real and shared presence of others is constitutive of the individual through its commonalities.[22]

I have avoided calling the commonalities "conditions," because an inflationary use of the latter term would treat the commonalities as though

---

21. The contemporary phenomenon of collectivism exhibits, it seems to me, the transference of the nominalist sense of unity (as incomplexity) from the individual members of society to society itself (writ with capital S). Leon Brunschvicg is reported to have commented upon the Nurnberg rallies: "There is Durkheim's religion; the people worshipping themselves. The loss of effective identity on the part of the individuals is not surprising in such a conceptual scheme. If I am correct, then, collectivism is simply (i.e., conceptually, for things are never so simple in actual life) the contrary to liberal individualism, being founded upon the same notion of unity and identity. This may provide the conceptual basis for the recent drift of some liberal theorists towards a collectivist form of socialism under the pressure of the demands for equality and social justice. In opposition, the conservative liberal would hold on to the original identification of basic unity with the individual."

22. Isaiah Berlin ("Two Concepts of Liberty," 158) stresses the need of the individual for status (i.e., for acknowledgment by others). Hegel, too, has disclosed the necessary role of mutual recognition in the constitution of the self (*Phenomenology*, c. iv). No doubt, these commonalities are essential for human individuality, and I should want to include them in my own account; but I would also want to ensure that properly physical and metaphysical factors are operative in their own right and according to their modes.

they were external to an alleged "core."[23] It is not easy to find a suitable name for the primacy of the individual self that can be applied commonly to the varieties of liberalism, and yet such a core is part of liberal understanding. The core is, or would be, a free self: an *elector* self in the root sense of the Latin term. For, as far as possible, and in some sense prior to other individuals and society, it would select the terms under which it relates to them; let us say, then, in shorthand: a *selective* self. It is in some sense a law unto itself: hence we might call it an *autonomous* self, since even Kant's law-obligated moral ego is self-governed. Again it is in some sense a *pre-institutional* self, since the institutions to which it subscribes are in principle its own product and derive their legitimacy in some way from its consent.[24] It is in some sense an *independent* self, since it holds itself in reserve and apart.[25] In contrast, the constitutive individual, whose integrity consists of its singularity and its commonality, has no separate core. It is singular with a singularity that is not something independent, related to its conditions by external relations. The singularity, even as the common-

---

23. In a recent version, even our inherited talents are assets external to the individual self. Discussing Rawls' proposals for the distribution of natural talents as common assets (see note 1 above), Michael Sandel comments: "No longer am I to be regarded as the *sole proprietor of my assets,* or privileged recipient of the advantages they bring . . . I am not really the *owner* but merely the *guardian* or *repository* of the talents and capacities that *happen to reside* in me, and as such have no special moral claim on the fruits of their exercise. . . . By regarding the distribution of talents and *attributes* as a common asset rather than as *individual possessions,* Rawls obviates the need to 'even out' endowments in order to remedy the arbitrariness of social and natural contingencies . . . Although I am *entitled* to the benefits answering my legitimate expectations, I do not *deserve* them, for two reasons: first, given the assumption of common assets, I do not really *possess* the attributes that give rise to the benefits, or if I do possess them, it is only in the weak, accidental sense rather than the strong, constitutive sense, and this sense of possession is inadequate to establish desert in the strong pre-institutional sense" (emphasis added, except for the last three instances). *Liberalism and the Limits of Justice,* 70–72.

24. Locke's solution to legitimacy (viz., that later generations have given their *tacit* consent merely by growing up in the society and accepting its benefits) is no longer persuasive to many liberals, so that the problem of legitimacy receives various and sometimes torturous solutions.

25. *Apart:* Here again I stress the *disengaged* character of the liberal self and the externality of its relations as part to parts (as self to all others, all non-self). Ackerman is perhaps the most radical contextualist, for he insists upon the concrete individual's "interaction with society" (*Social Justice,* 330). He further describes the individual as clothed with "the marks of our encounter with organized society." Still, he spurns any deeper grounding of the individual, because it would require "theological" (i.e., transcendent, and so unacceptable) arguments (p. 331). He rebukes the standing liberal traditions (Contract and Utility) for their appeal to "a hypothetical being who transcends the social situation in fundamental ways" (p. 332). It seems to me that Ackerman has here reached the conceptual limits of liberal individualism, and that in positivist fashion he shuts down the inquiry rather than move it towards an *a priori* self or to an overly situated and immersed self (cf. his critique of Utility, n. 17 above, and my remarks on collectivism, n. 21). Ackerman speaks freely of "our independent identities," despite his "contextualism." Here, it seems to me, lies the obscurity and ambivalence of liberalism, resident in the partial character of its account of modernity.

ality, is an inseparable though distinguishable factor in the constitution of the individual. Once again, these complex constitutive individuals are primary realities; in their own order—the primary order of reality, if Aristotle is right—they are not products, not mere juxtapositions of ultimate, independent, separate components. Rather, such components—taken in themselves and in isolation from their context—are abstractions from concrete, complex, composite (but not composed) individuals.

Nor would I call the commonalities "properties." John Locke gave to the term "property" a wide meaning, to include life, liberty, and estates, and within that, we may suppose convictions, ideas, and free speech.[26] Now, these are among the constituents that enter into the formation of the modern individual, along with other traits, physical, psychological, and spiritual, such as genetic endowment, familial custom, educational formation, social circumstances, and moral ideals. But the way we name things usually indicates the focus of our interest, the ordering of our values, and where our heart or our desires are. Here the two different names demonstrate the contrast between the selective self and the constitutive individual. For to use the term "commonalities" rather than "properties" is to reverse the flow of individual and social life.[27] Now, the term "commonality" looks to the community as an integral part of what it means to be an individual. It names those constituents within the individual by which he or she is released from and enabled to transcend the singularity which is equally constitutive. The term "property," on the other hand, looks back towards privacy and ownership *(proprium)*, and to the exclusivity of the radically selective self. It follows in that view that all of its relationships must fall outside of the individual as special forms of possession.[28] Indeed, in at least one version, the given talents and inherited advantages are alienable by the society, as though they are so much property. My quarrel with liberalism, then, is that, try as it may, and however much complexity it admits, it holds that complexity at arm's length.[29] If it did not, it would have to revise its understanding of the individual and with that it would have to revise what it means by freedom and by choice.

---

26. In respect to *conatus,* Locke places considerable qualification upon the acquisition of property. It is to come about through labor and for use. Nevertheless, the individual's possession of property is central to his thought (see *Second Treatise on Government,* 5, 31–32).

27. For example, Sandel (*Liberalism and the Limits of Justice,* 64) puts Rawls' position thus: "as a person's values and ends are always *attributes and never constituents of the self,* so a sense of community is only an attribute and never a constituent of a well-ordered society. As the self is prior to the aims it affirms, so a well-ordered society, defined by justice, is prior to the aims—communitarian or otherwise—its members may profess" (emphasis added). The parallelism mentioned in n. 21 is explicit in this passage.

28. Cf. n. 4.

29. Sandel (*Liberalism and the Limits of Justice,* 64) writes: "The assumptions of the original position (of Rawls) thus stand opposed in advance to any ('thick') conception of the

The constitutive individual, on the other hand, is not a selective self, fortifying itself by preference or by guarded civility; nor does it hide behind an adroit management of masks *(personae)*. It is a composite unity of singularity and commonality that from its inception is already underway, continually undertaking and undergoing its own constitution—not by election merely, but by participation. I cannot separate out my genetic endowment or my enculturation from me: I do not have them as property. I *am* them; they do not belong to me, they are not mine, they are *me*. This identification does not entail the loss of my identity through submergence in the community, because I am not simply my participation in commonalities; I am also and equally my singularity.

Equality is not only an affair *among* individuals; it is also an ontological parity *within* each individual. This intrinsic, constitutive equality is, in its origins, not only a moral demand. Rather, the moral sanction is grounded in and rises out of an ontological necessity: there can be no *what* without a *this*, no commonality without singularity, and conversely. The equality of integrity constitutive of each individual grounds the moral sanction, on the one hand, against irresponsible singular behavior and, on the other, against repressive collective conformity. From equality within the individual there arises equality among individuals, and that equality sanctions the just freedom of the individual. That is why it is *not* good or just that one be forced against his or her will to die for the people. On the contrary, in the scales of justice, each individual person is equal in right to the whole people and to the entire apparatus of the state. The "hard" choice is not one which forcibly sacrifices the one for the many, but that which refuses to consider such an option.[30]

COMMONALITIES THAT BIND

Of course, nowadays few are likely to deny the influence of the social milieu upon the individual.[31] It is agreed upon on all sides: no man

---

good requiring a more or less expansive self-understanding, and in particular to the possibility of community in the conservative sense. On Rawls' view, a sense of community describes a possible aim of antecedentally individuated selves, not an ingredient or constituent of their identity as such. This guarantees its subordinate status." There is much discussion of whether or in what sense Rawls is Kantian, and there are deontological as well as positivistic readings of his original position. But there can be no doubt of the essentially *pre-institutional* character of the Rawlsian self. I find some such priority of the self to be a constant feature of liberalism, whether "natural" or "postulantional." See also n. 27 above.

30. Jacques Maritain brought the resources of personalism to this issue. See, among other writings, *The Person and the Common Good*. The situation between the individual and society is, of course, a quite different issue from "hard" choices between (inherently equal) individuals, as in health treatment and food aid: but such issues lie beyond the scope of the present essay.

31. Cf. n. 27.

is an island, Robinson Crusoe notwithstanding. The issue is not the social fact, but how we are to understand it, what implications it might hold, and why we understand it variously. For liberals, it seems to me, the social milieu must remain a set of conditions, the complex property of the selective self. If, on the other hand, we accept "commonality" as an initial interpretation of the social milieu, we arrive at a different understanding. Many commonalities are accidental, of course, and even dispensable; nor do all have moral implications, though some do. Nor are all commonalities benign. But in any event, an important number of them are not simply detachable; at least some are not simply preferences to be dealt with in whatever way I choose or on the basis of agreed upon conventions. Some commonalities set up a claim upon me prior to any election on my part; I have not elected them. To be sure, I can, and perhaps may, choose to ignore the claim. But some commonalities give a certain disposition to my life and person and constitute a certain directive for me. I am not entirely free, nor ever am. I am provided with norms prior to my choice, norms that are not simply given and neutral facts, but that come to me already bearing the weight and inclination (*pondus*) of some value and some good.

Commonalities do not so much reside in me as I in them, since I live with them and in them. That I am a male is not simply a fact, nor did it arise by my preference. Nevertheless, it orients me in the social world in definite ways. It would be silly to give moral value to such a status, even though we must admit that in the past, social authority was often denied to women on that basis, and that our own society is not without bias in this and other ways. Such a commonality, without having moral value in itself, nonetheless plays a part in determining the way in which the individual enters into social and moral relationships. Sometimes such a commonality will give rise to moral responsibilities, including those of fatherhood. Consider another commonality, one that binds me to two individuals as their son, and which binds me to them in certain ways by a bond that lies prior to my choice. It would be silly again to give moral value to the mere fact of the bond itself, but from it there arises a certain norm that is directive of my conduct towards them: honor thy parents. Or yet again, I am called to acknowledge teachers from whom I have received a cultural and intellectual formation, and friends who cooperated in the formation of my character. Such commonalities present themselves as dispositive, even directive, even sometimes as normative. They are often prior to any choice on my part, nor is my acknowledgment of them and response to them what for the first time endows them with value. They are not simply benevolences. Liberalism neutralizes such givens, puts them out of play, and then may reappropriate them selectively and by election.

Once again, I do not mean that the influences which we receive through our participation in society and which I have called "commonalities" are uniformly benign; neither we nor our societies are that perfect. Nothing I have said should lead to complacency. To the contrary, our involvement in such processes and relations from the beginning of our formation as individuals should urge us to increased constructive efforts to improve our social as well as our natural environment. I am not pleading for sentimentality and warm feelings, nor for benevolence or altruism, however desirable that may be. I am not directing my argument primarily towards the will or the feelings, but above all towards the understanding. I am arguing that the ground of certain directives is built into and inseparable from our own formation and character. Liberalism can certainly countenance and even recommend benevolent feelings, for not all liberals envisage a rival power struggle that results at best in guarded civility and more likely in disciplined greed. Nor am I urging that the commonalities be treated as common assets to be handed over to the collectivity. The generosity at work in the constitution of the individual lies in the very nature of things, and much of it at a depth prior to the choices of individuals. It is the very dynamic of the natural and social world. The constitutive participation of the individual does not depend in the first instance upon good-feeling, but rather upon the processes by, in, and through which the individual is constituted. The civic friendship that Aristotle thought inseparable from a healthy society is based not simply upon good intentions—though it can hardly flourish without them—but upon the fact of our individual as well as of our social and political constitutions. For, in the end and from the beginning, our individuality is situated in what is neither wholly mine nor wholly yours, but ours. We are none of us self-made, and we owe "debts" that by the nature of time we often cannot directly pay, but are called upon to repay to society and to others than those to whom we are directly indebted.

In liberalism the question of the good seems to be an affair of barter between selective selves on the basis of a negotiated justice; but in fact the human good does not involve humans alone. Among the commonalities that make up the individual are those in which each of us is involved in and with the world of nature. Now, not only is liberalism deficient in acknowledging the contribution of others to the constitution of the individual; it has in the past reinforced the exploitative bent that has been so pronounced an animus in industrial technology from its beginning. While the liberal may negotiate a compromise with other selective selves, nevertheless, in putting the selective self first, it is disposed to approach nature as something to be mastered and put to uses dictated by our preferences. Today's liberal can no longer put his trust in a "hidden hand" that is supposed to rectify imbalance, the happy coincidence of individual wills each pursuing its own interest, apparent or real, and unwittingly to the overall benefit. For just as we, so too has he discovered that the hidden hand is ours. It is no judicious and impartial judge: it is us.

No doubt the power we have accumulated is awesome. For the most part it has been to our real benefit, but lately nature has been showing signs of exhaustion and worse. Now, the putative "law of market forces" puts no brake upon the limitless exploitation of nature to the satisfaction of our wants, real or artificially simulated. To the contrary, advocates still seek solutions through ever-increasing productivity. Eventually, even our politicians will have to stop crying: jobs, jobs, and more jobs! and salesmen stop beckoning: buy, buy, consume still more! It may be demurred that the liberal can always take matters in hand and negotiate the best ways in which to resolve ecological issues such as we face today and are likely to face for years to come. However, his clear-headed but prudent fear may prove too late to be timely, and may be too indecisive in the face of the plethora of individual wants. In retaining the primacy of the selective individual self, he will be tempted to set the limits of choice too wide.

There is need, instead, of a renewed solidarity with nature that liberalism is unlikely to provide. If, on the other hand, we are indeed constitutive individuals, then that solidarity is already there, often unrecognized, but nonetheless working in us and in our dealings with nature. Is not nature telling us something about the good when we treat it well and also when, in our thoughtless pursuit of goods, we treat it ill? That frantic pursuit throws a dark light upon the profile of the good. It is as though we have been treating nature like the dummy hand at bridge, only to realize lately (if not too late) that it has begun to play its own hand and is beginning to deal us some rather unwelcome cards—in the disvalues of pollution, exhaustion of resources, and similar evils. For they in actual fact are commonalities, too. Along with the stimulus of a salutary fear, constitutive individuals, conscious of themselves, may help to return Western attitudes towards the recognition of a deeper solidarity with the very constitution of the earth. On such a ground it would be possible to build our politics towards a renewed integrity.

Such a task does not call upon us to abandon civility; nor does it tolerate a totalitarian imposition of an arbitrary notion of the good. Our various commonalities are too diverse for that! And our freedom is too deeply rooted in the equality of integrity within each individual. Negotiation, discussion, and accountable judgment will still be needed. There will still be greedy, fraudulent, self-serving, and violent individuals, cynics and cheats as well. But the public discussion will not proceed on the basis of what is simply mine over and against what is simply yours, for many things are neither simply mine nor simply yours, but both mine and yours, or rather, ours. The public language will be less directed towards *my* rights than towards *our* possibilities. Instead of the primary language of litigation and private rights, the public language will have to include the recognition of our solidarity with others as well as with nature: with others on the basis of the equality of integrity, and with nature, because in our search for a reasonable individual and social good, we must build the good of nature into our concern as *it has already been built into us.* I do not think that liberalism has the resources with which to do this, since it does not have an adequate notion of the individual or its good. And yet, it needs one that it cannot have. Anyway, we, as individuals and in community, need it.

My strategy in this chapter has not been to ask what moral and social order I might prefer, and then to set out its conditions and presuppositions: that is a liberal strategy. I have tried, rather, to arrive at a more realistic understanding of the individual and to build up my moral and social expectations from there.

PART III
GOD

Chapter 14

THEOLOGICAL CLEARANCES
Foreground to a Rational Recovery of God

Near the beginning of the *Summa theologiae* St. Thomas Aquinas presents the well-known "five ways."[1] The *quinque viae* make up a single proof of the existence of God by way of five approaches: from *motion* concluding to the First Mover; from causative *action* concluding to the First Cause or Source; from *contingent* beings to Something that is absolutely necessary; from *degrees* of actual perfections in things to the Original Source of their existence and goodness; and, finally, from the *regularity* of processes in the world to a Creative Intelligence that implants tendencies towards order in things. At the end of each of these ways he remarks laconically, "And everyone understands this to be God"; or, again, everybody "names" or "calls" such Being "God" and, more intimately, "And we call this, God: *et hoc dicimus Deum.*"

The author of a profound modern treatment of this traditional argument has written of the need to "get God out of the categories."[2] By this he meant that further argument is required: to show that the Prime Mover does not move in any usual sense, to conclude that the action of the First Agent lies beyond ordinary agency, to clarify the absolute nature of Divine Necessity, to arrive at Unmixed Perfection beyond the more and less limited excellences found in the world, and to break beyond the bounds of human intelligence to Creative Intelligence. Of course, St. Thomas sets out to provide such further argument throughout the first part of the *Summa*. But, while we must surely attend to the rigor of this prolonged argument, in order to determine *whether* it proves, we

---

Reprinted from *Prospects for Natural Theology*, ed. E. T. Long, Studies in Philosophy and the History of Philosophy, vol. 25 (Washington, DC: The Catholic University of America Press, 1992), 28–48. Copyright © by The Catholic University of America Press.

1. Pt. I, q. 2, art. 3.
2. Gerard Smith, S.J., *Natural Theology* (New York: Macmillan, 1951), 108–13.

need also to ask about *what* the argument intends to prove. In pursuit of this latter inquiry we need to clear away obstacles to understanding what seems to me the most ambitious intellectual enterprise ever undertaken, namely, the attempt to prove the existence of such a God.

IN CONCLUSION: MYSTERY

For those to whom the reality of the biblical God has been preached, the only God worthy of the highest name is a mysterious living God, a God who reveals and does things unlike anything that has entered into a human head. This is the God who is denied by the biblical "fool," and denied even if he does exist, for the fool is not foolish in any ordinary sense. He is no mere doubter. Rather, he is an atheist who appreciates the importance of God, and who says that such a God cannot, could not, must not be, even if he were. So that, even to the "fool," such a God is the only one worthy of the labor of argument in disproof, if not in proof, of his existence.

For we do not set out to prove or disprove the existence of just any divine being; we do not seek to prove or disprove the existence of Diana or Neptune or Apollo. At best, such gods are mythical interpretations of a people's experience of the numinous. Among the Greeks and Romans, the numinous received celebrated poetic expression. Indeed, its echoes are heard centuries later in the nostalgic effort by various Romantic poets to "revive" the ancient deities.[3] Such numinous presence remains close to human experience, comprising its first exotic fruits. The attractive charm of such *numina* arises from the degree to which they share the human condition, while sharing it in a somewhat strange and larger-than-human way. It is not required to deny the presence of such a *numen*, in order to take seriously the biblical disclosure; nor is it even necessary to claim that these "gods" are purely human fabrications. It is enough to acknowledge that they are no substitute for *the* God, whether or not such a God exists. For they do not even fill out the idea of God. Their ghostly presences remain infinitely far from the high God of whom St. Thomas speaks and to whom the proof is addressed and meant to lead. For many of us, no other God will quite do. It would be better that the throne remain empty than that pretenders receive the title falsely. Better atheism denying the high God than polytheism laying claim to a divinity that is not its own. It is as though, having once tasted a great wine, others may serve lesser purposes without, however, deserving the honor paid to greatness. So, too, once the idea of the high God

---

3. For example, Schiller's *Die Götter Griechenlands*.

is noised abroad, other conceptions of divinity pale. The very wording of the question forces the singular nature of the issue: "Whether God exists: *Utrum Deus Sit.*"

Nevertheless, the living God is not sought for only in faith. Believers may seek him by the paths of reason and argument as well, while—paradoxically—he is also at issue for non-believers. Indeed, atheism has adopted its most vociferous tone in the denial of the biblical God. It was Nietzsche who cried, "If there were gods, how could I endure not being one? Hence there are none."[4] Now, it is clear that he had in mind the high God and not a lesser pantheon. Nor is his protest merely facetious or petulant. It is a cry that rises in the throat and from the heart of a rebellious creature, for it is rooted in the crux of a being that is but need not, even might not, be; it wells up from a being that exists only on the sufferance of Another. Make no mistake: this God, if such there be, is a creator, and there exists nothing without his constant support. Nietzsche's cry, then, is the cry of contingent being, inasmuch as it struggles against a contingency so radical that it leaves nothing to the creature that is entirely its own, or, conversely, leaves it everything that it is as a gift received.

Radical contingency is—according to the biblical disclosure—the condition of every creature, but it takes human form in the cry for liberty. Haunted by the specter of such a God, Jean-Paul Sartre may be understood to have defiantly argued, "If there exists an omnipotent God, how can I be free? But I am free, indeed I must be free; hence God cannot be." This will-to-freedom also has its biblical origins, for it was believers who first saw in human freedom the reflection of perfect divine freedom. Indeed, the biblical freedom of the sons and daughters of God is made in the image and likeness of divine freedom, so that, *qua* image, human freedom is contingent upon its relation to God's creative freedom. On the other hand, the freedom that drew Sartre into defiance is a freedom without God but that yet embodies a kind of infinity within itself, in the sense that there is nothing in its own order that can limit it. In Spinoza's words, though not his sense, "infinite after its own kind." At least in his early writings, Sartre postulates, if I may so put it, a finite freedom without limit and without measure.

The roots of such a conception may also be traced back to the late medieval "liberty of indifference," which was given its first mature and influential modern expression by Descartes when he insisted that the human will, unlike the human mind, is infinite. This insistence upon infinitude is not of itself the Promethean dream of power, but it can eas-

---

4. *Thus Spoke Zarathustra*, pt. II: "Upon the Blessed Isles."

ily turn into it. In its extreme form it can disclose a drive for total power than has haunted modern political thought in the form of totalitarianism and its opponent, anarchy. The dream of total liberty, of a liberty answerable only to itself, has arisen in modern times as a distorted illusion of a discredited divine omnipotence. Thus the issue of God, his nature and existence, stands at the center of the issue of human freedom. The issue is whether human freedom is created in the image of a greater liberty or is rather the self-vindicating warrant of human autonomy.

But if the issue of God is the narrow gate through which one passes to one or the other of these conceptions of human freedom, how does one go about proving or disproving the existence of such a Being? One thing is sure: we must not play at the fiction that we simply start thinking and accidentally stumble upon the argument that, step by step, proves the existence of such a God. God is not an accident, nor is the structure of our thought simply arbitrary. Either God is absolutely necessary for us, or he does not exist at all. That is the crisis posed by the conception of such a God. On the other hand, if he is unconditionally necessary, why do we not everywhere and always naturally and inevitably follow out our reasoning to its logical and onto-logical end? Why does not everyone who thinks arrive at the conclusion that God exists? Why are we able to think of so many things and for so long a time in so many ways other than the thought of God? It was Spinoza, in modern times, who converted "It is necessary that God exist" into "Hence God exists necessarily," turning God into the necessary law of being and of thought, *Deus sive Natura*. In the experience of the believer, however, the biblical God remains more manifest yet more wonderfully hidden and more necessary than the laws of nature. God is at once the ancient glory and the ever new mystery.

Still, if the idea of such a God is neither necessary nor accidental, how does the proof or its denial get started in the first place? For if we do not have any idea of God at all before we begin the proof, how can we know what evidence may be relevant and what may not be? It is in this sense that, unless my memory forsakes me,[5] St. Thomas somewhere remarks that we would not proceed to the demonstration of God's existence unless we first *somehow* knew that he existed. Of course, St. Thomas was a believer, and this seems to be overstating the starting point and begging the outcome—unless, of course, the proof shows us what we already *somehow and necessarily* have been aware of all along. For if such a God exists and exists necessarily, and if we cannot exist without Him—

---

5. I must confess that I have not been able to locate the remark in his biblical commentaries.

and that is the only adequate and acceptable conclusion other than denial of his existence—then he must *somehow* be present in our sense of things all along, and be hidden in the very identity of our own being. The issue resolves into: *somehow already or never at all.*

But there is more trouble yet. For even if the proof succeeds, this "somehow" will never become fully clear. The intelligibility of the reality reached through the conclusion exceeds the concepts employed in reaching it. For the only God worthy of that high name is a mysterious God, a God of will as well as of nature, a God of freedom as well as of necessity, a God who is more than will and nature, more than freedom and necessity. "My ways are not your ways," says the Lord. For our ways are the categories in which we couch the idea of such a divinity, whereas that very idea bends back upon those categories to find them deficient. It is the purgative force of this idea that propelled St. Thomas to distinguish in this matter between the thing signified *(res significata)* and the manner of signifying it *(modus significandi)*.[6] He tells us that the manner of signifying God is inherently human, whereas the reality towards which the idea points lies beyond human signs in the mysterious region of the divine. And so the proof is, for him, a process in which the idea leads the mind beyond its own categories, without thereby ceasing to be intelligible. It can do this insofar as the mind breaks through its concepts into a judgment that lies open to the fullness of existence.

When the schoolmen spoke of faith seeking understanding, they meant, among other things, that they were led by way of such a concept towards its reality. But if the idea and its reality will never become fully clear or even as clear as other ideas can become, nevertheless the proof is meant to purchase a conclusion that is to become ever more necessary and convincing. Here is a non-Cartesian divide between clarity and certainty. The proof, then, is a process that is meant to prove a mystery without destroying it. In the words of the poet, its reach is meant to exceed its grasp.

Now, the term *mystery* may mean many things. It can be used offhandedly to indicate a question that puzzles a mind ignorant of its solution: "It's a mystery to me." In midnight horror films, it may name the uncanny that is contrived to lie beyond our ken. Or it may be simply another word for obscurity. On the objective side, it may stand for what is dark and stubbornly unenlightening, and, on the subjective side, for a mind that is left in the shadows of doubt and ignorance. This is the negative meaning of mystery. Among the great Christian doctors, however, one finds a positive meaning to the term. For they celebrate the mystery of a

---

6. See, e.g., *STh* I, 13, 3c.

great Light. Here the mind is also in a state of confusion, but it is a kind of delirium brought about by a light too bright for clear sight. The mind is confused, not because there is too little to know, but because there is too much to be known. The mind cannot take it all in. An increase in understanding does not decrease the mystery, for the mystery stems from the inexhaustible abundance of meaning that shines from the mysterious reality. Aristotle tells us that philosophy begins in wonder, but his wonder seems to diminish with an understanding of the causes. At any rate, among Christian philosophers and theologians, the greater the understanding, the greater the wonder. Understanding fuels the wonder.

In reality, what is this great light supposed to be? It is not the light of objectivity. The proof does not conclude to an object set over against the human subject. Ordinary categories of objectivity cannot capture the outcome of this proof, not even in the way in which Plato's *Sophist* may be said to have caught the primary Forms, and certainly not in the way in which Hegel's categories in the *Science of Logic* may be said to have articulated the absolute system. These formal categorial names, if they name anything at all, name too mundane a reality. Eugen Fink used to say, half-facetiously, that at least the ontological argument did prove, but he quickly added that what it proved was the existence of the world. Of course, neither St. Augustine's nor St. Anselm's nor St. Thomas' proofs intended such a cosmology; for they did not seek to prove what they thought needed no proof, but rather the existence of the utterly transcendent biblical God.

It is no thing that is reached by such arguments, if anything is reached at all, not even a vast "Thing" such as the entire universe. The proof proves no thing, not even the "greatest or highest Thing," whatever that might be. A similar recognition had already nurtured the long tradition of negative theology *(via negativa)* that finds in the name "Nothing" *(Nihil, Nada,* etc.) the most appropriate name for the utterly transcendent God.[7] Nevertheless, while St. Thomas also understands the proof to prove no thing, it is not because the proof falls short of rational standards, but, on the contrary, because its subject is filled with a surcharge of intelligibility that in its conclusion challenges our entire understanding of reality.

---

7. While the via negative is rightly associated with neo-Platonism, on the one hand, and with mysticism, on the other, the works of Josef Pieper have brought out the negative element resident in St Thomas' thought as well. In *Scholasticism* (New York: McGraw-Hill, 1964), 53–54, he emphasizes the influence of Dionysius the (Pseudo-) Areopagite by citing several comments of St Thomas, such as: "God is honored by silence not because we cannot say anything or understand anything about Him, but because we know that we are incapable of comprehending Him" *(Commentary on Boethius' De Trinitate,* 2, 1 ad 6). Cf. also Pieper's *The Silence of Saint Thomas,* trans. John Murray and Daniel O'Connor (New York: Pantheon Books, 1957).

AT THE START: LIMIT NOT YET FINITUDE

If the end is mysterious, the beginning is problematic. For at the initial point of the argument we cannot begin with a finitude of such a character that we could never reach the infinite. Thus, for example, by stipulating the self-enclosed and distinct impressions that purportedly make up human experience, David Hume made it impossible in principle to ever reach the actual infinite, permitting us to postulate at most an isomorphic and otiose parallel with the world of impressions. Instead, the proof must begin as far as possible without arbitrary presuppositions and more simply with whatever is, without declaring beforehand that what is is so thoroughly finite that it is inescapably enclosed within itself. In other words, we must not pre-empt the possibility of proof by defining the starting point in such a way that a transcendent order of reality is excluded from it a priori.

In fact we must not begin with finitude at all. It is enough to acknowledge the principle of limit in the things we directly encounter: as moved, caused, contingent, more or less adequate, and more or less regular in behavior. For there are two stages in defining the starting point. First (A), it is required to establish in what sense, and on what evidence, we may conclude that what is limited is indeed finite. Secondly (B), once that is done, to establish the nature of the relation between the finite and the infinite in order to determine in what sense the finite is finite. Neither of these tasks is easy or obvious.

(A) First, if the limit is taken to be atomistic, that is, if we start with an impregnable and irreducible finitude, with a plurality of impervious self-enclosed units—whether they be separate Humean psychic impressions or supposedly real indivisible ultimate particles—then no such argument as St. Thomas has in mind is possible. What is in question here, then, is the nature of unity. If in accordance with the tendencies of nominalism, unity is identified with simplicity, so that the basic units of reality are defined as ultimate incomplex particles, then there can only be displacement of units within the totality or at most intrusion of an alien and external force after the manner of classical Deism, the so-called "god of the philosophers," that is, a functionary in the service of certain metaphysical systems. Such a God would exist at the borders of time and space, and would sustain the only kind of relation admissible in such a totality, namely, an external relation to it as part to part within a greater totality (pantheism) or as whole to whole (Deism). But such a mechanistic definition of the starting point risks being gratuitous and at best dubious, given the transformative energy of the perceptible universe, in which real transmutation does take place. Even the methodological advantages of such a mechanism seem nowadays to have all but exhausted themselves. Certainly, physics seems to have moved away from this unreal restriction of thought, away from the search for ultimate particles towards larger wholes, towards waves, fields, and holographic structures.

But if the more systemic approach of the physical and chemical sciences, the more organic and ecological approaches of the biological sciences, and the more holistic approach of the social and human disciplines are more adequate to our experience, they do not of themselves translate the limited nature of the data into finitude. And although cosmological thought requires a reversal of perspective from the part to the whole, its theories about the beginning of the present condition of the universe presuppose an antecedent totality of potential forces, so that its explanations (whether the so-called Big Bang or the Bubble) move among the limited categories of thought. They attempt to describe the relative beginning of the present order of things, rather than to give an account of the absolute origin of reality. And so the concern for totality does not lend itself easily to translating our experience of the limited nature of things into recognition of their finitude. For scientific explanations show how the elements of things pass on into new forms, rather than how the things themselves may cease to be. Nothing short of the explicit concern for being seems able to articulate this radical nothingness.

(B) But even if it can be shown that what is limited is a finite that finishes, where does it finish?[8] Does it finish by passing over into the infinite? And into what infinitude? With Hegel it is the infinitude of the absolute system, so that the finite does not so much transcend itself as it, rather, integrates itself into membership in the totality of being, essence, and spirit. Or does the finite end by passing over into nothing? So that all is mere sound and fury, signifying nothing? Hegel thought that such a fate was senseless, since it led to nothing constructive, but he located the failure of such a negation in a non-dialectical conception of finitude. He called such a negation merely positive, a sterile, simple, negative self-identity that leads nowhere.

(C) Before banishing this nothing, however, we ought to look more closely at it. It may tell us that the finite, considered in itself, does indeed lead nowhere, passes over into nothing, has no issue or result. Still, such a consideration can help us to discern the tension in the finite: it both is and is not. Its *is* teeters on the brink of an *is not* that—far from being Hegel's all-inclusive infinite—is radically ambiguous. On the one hand, it is sheer non-being. Hegel had his own reasons for branding this non-dialectical negation a dead end, since the "where" to which such

---

8. The references to Hegel are from *Science of Logic,* pt. I, bk. I, chaps. 1 and 2.

a dead end does *not* lead is his dialectical absolute system. For it does not lead in Hegelian fashion to the mere indeterminacy of Hegel's primal negative category, *das Nichts*. Instead, the metaphysical conception of negation leads to non-being in its emptiest sense, to sheer nihilation, not merely to a relative moral nihilism, but to the most radical metaphysical nihilism. But suppose that, following upon this recognition of metaphysical negation, the proof succeeds, then it will turn out that this radical nothing is the dark harbinger that leads us, on the other hand, to the Nothing who is the high God. This "Nothing and/or nothing" draws out the radical ambiguity of contingency.

Now, if in this root-like darkness we can still raise up the question "Where is this nowhere to which such sheer contingency leads?" then there must be more in that contingency than sheer non-being. For questions can arise only from the base of a questioner who, in all his or her fragility, is present there in that darkness. For the darkness is the darkness of contingency, of an *is* that is yet an *is not*. And the questioner asks: What is the value of such an *is*? Does it provide a starting point? What is this *is* that simultaneously simply *is not*? For we must not divide the questioner into half *is* and half *is not*, as though he or she were made of two parts, an *is* that is not negative and a negation that is in no way affirmative. The existence of the questioner is one singular existence, an existence that (taken in itself) is simultaneously a non-existence. That is the precise character of contingent being: it is an is that simultaneously is not.

Moreover, the simultaneous identification of is and is not is not a convenience of our making; it belongs to the character of contingent being itself. We rightly recognize the distinction between is and is not, for that is the lifeblood of reality and thought. But we are not entitled to make over the distinction between the negative and affirmative character of such a being into a separation. On the contrary, in the contingent being itself, its very being is shot through with the fragility of nihilation. The bearers of that possibility within the being include its merely formal and potential factors. But its existential being is of one texture: a being that in its very being exists in such a way that its non-existence is always a real and constitutive possibility.

And yet, if the question can be raised by such a being, there is a point of light in its darkness after all. Suppose that the point of light is reflected from an order of being that does not teeter on the brink of annihilation? Suppose that contingent being is an *is* that is in continuous communication with a quite different order of *is*? Of course, this supposition is just what needs to be proven, or disproven. It is not yet proven in the saying of it, though if or when we are entitled to say it, we can also say: Q.E.D. These prolegomena are meant to clear the ground of current and conventional obstacles, so that the true issue of the proof may be laid bare. The genuine difficulty, as distinct from barriers or obstacles due to misunderstanding, is first of all to bring ourselves to see in what lies before us whether there is evidence of such a simultaneous *is/is not*, of the real possibility of annihilation, and only then of a parlous affirmation.

We ought not to assume that we can easily take to heart the annihilation of a being, let alone our own demise. Consider the simplest change. If I eat an apple, I can imagine its elements continuing to exist under new forms; and this continuity is true. But is it not also true that the apple ceases to exist in reality? It may continue to exist in memory and in its effects; but *it* is no longer. And that possibility is a real possibility during its entire existence, and during ours as well. It is a negative possibility that is constitutive of its existence; so that we can characterize its existence, even as it exists, as being really able to cease to exist throughout the duration of its whole existence. Without the recognition of such radical contingency there can be neither proof nor disproof of the high God.

These reflections are meant to chart the course required if the proof is to reach safe harbor or encounter shipwreck. In sum, to say "limit" is not yet to say "finite," for, far from starting obviously with the finite, it must start simply with what is limited. The proof then requires that we establish that what is limited is in truth finite. More clearly than any other philosopher, Hegel has charted the transition from the category of the "limit" *(die Grenze)* to that of the "finite" *(das Endliche)*. There is no change in the content of the two categories, but there is a change in emphasis, internal structure, perspective, and ontological status. The difference of meaning arises through a change in the conception of the infinite *(das Unendliche)*. Now, although the Hegelian conception of the infinite as absolute system is not the same as the traditional Christian conception of the Infinite Being, nevertheless Hegel does take account of the changed meaning introduced into the term by the Christian conception of God.

FROM FINITE TO INFINITE

For the Greeks, the infinite was the indeterminate, essentially a negative term. The Greek mind gave positive weight to formal *limit*, so that the limit was the innermost boundary that separated one thing or form from another, each constituting part of the whole economy of being and of thought. Limit butted upon limit, even the gods being "parts" of the cosmos. With the interposition of the concept of the high God, however, the term "infinitude" came to acquire a positive and determinate meaning. The biblical and especially the Christian mind placed the positive weight upon the infinite glory of the high God, so that what had been seen positively as limited now came to be seen negatively as finite. For in the wake of this conception, to call something that is limited "finite" is to name it from the vantage point of the unlimited divine fullness. The term "finite," then, properly signified the radical and unqualified dependency of the creature upon the Creator.

Nowadays, however, as seen in the previous reference to Sartre, the term "finite" has been claimed also with deliberate resolution in order to name the autonomy of the human sphere taken in itself and with exclusion of that theological vision; hence, "finite without limit." And so nowadays, to say "finite" is not thereby to imply "infinite" in any but a merely conceptual and verbal sense, leaving it open whether the latter is grounded in the former or vice versa. But equally, to say "the limited is finite and the finite is not infinite" does not rule out the possibility that the finite may be grounded in the infinite. There may yet be an infinite without which there would be no finite. That is the current nub of the proof. For proof always exists in context, and the challenge today is not, as it once was, to establish finitude against limit (though that too must be done); but also, even when what is limited is shown to be finite, it is still required to show that the finite is such that it must acknowledge the reality of the infinite precisely as the high God. The proof, then, is an inquiry into the finite—that there is the finite and what its character is—as much as, or even more than, it is a proof of the infinite. For whether the proof succeeds or not, it will tell us even more about ourselves than it will about God. And if it does succeed it will have shown that the *alpha* (qua limited starting point) must harbor within itself (qua finite) the *omega,* that is, the Infinite Being reached through the conclusion.

ST. ANSELM'S CLARIFICATION

It is just this putative pre-presence that makes the ontological proof so attractive—attractive yet problematic. It is a curious feature of the ontological proof that, since its first formulation, it cannot be quite banished from the human mind. It returns again and again in various forms: in St. Anselm, if not earlier in St. Augustine; in St. Bonaventure and Blessed John Duns Scotus; in Descartes, Spinoza, Leibniz, and Hegel; and in the recent lively philosophical discussion of proof. The idea that motivates it is so powerful that it cannot quite be relinquished, yet so unique that it does not submit easily to demonstration.

The ontological proof is *sui generis,* both as an argument and in its conclusion.[9] First of all, as an argument: In his *On Behalf of the Fool*, that is, the atheist, the monk Gaunilo of Marmoutiers objected to the proof in the form presented by Anselm of Bec in the *Proslogion*. Using the analogy of a perfect island, Gaunilo hoped thereby to refute Anselm's argument on the grounds that the mere possession of the idea of a perfect island in no way warrants the assertion that such an island actually exists. Anselm readily granted the point but replied that the idea he had in mind—of a Being than which none greater can be conceived—is not at all like the idea of a perfect island (which in truth is not a coherent idea at all); and that it is as unlike every other idea as the Being it presents is unlike every other being. The trouble with Anselm's reply, however, is that our language moves by analogies, by likenesses and their correlative unlikenesses. Indeed, Anselm himself appeals to the distinction between a painting in the mind and a painting in reality in order to set up the distinction between the unique idea existing in the mind and that same idea also existing in reality. He thereby recognizes that our terms are embedded in a web of other terms, so that one does not break out of them any more than one breaks out of the whole interconnectedness of language, except into silence. To say "light" is to suggest "dark," and to say "is" is to imply "is not."

It seems, then, that to the extent to which the argument is unique, it forsakes the common logic needed for the demonstration even while it draws the force of its conclusion from that same logic. It would be too much to charge Anselm with a straightforward inconsistency, and yet it is at least curious that he rejects the argument from analogy in the reply to Gaunilo, even while he relies upon a general analogy in order to determine the names of God in the remaining chapters of the *Proslogion*. And yet such a criticism somehow misses the force of the argument. In its own way the argument accommodates the correlative nature of linguistic terms by reducing thought to the contrast of absolute being and absolute non-being. The force of the argument is meant to carry thought through the irreducible linguistic correlation of *is* and *is not*, in which both have equal status as terms, to the absolute non-reciprocity in reality of *is* over *is not*.[10]

This non-reciprocity is disclosed in the conclusion, too. As to what is concluded: if the Being than which none greater can be conceived is so unique that it stands in relation to none other, does not that status violate the very dynamism of proof that seeks to establish relationship? And yet, the power of the idea carries us beyond the idea itself, provided we can in some sense extend ourselves towards what is more intelligible than any possible conception. It is in this sense—which I do not

9. St. Anselm, *Proslogion* and *Reply to Gaunilo*, as well as Gaunilo, *On Behalf of the Fool*.
10. In the later chapter of the *Proslogion*, Anselm employs the principle: God is whatever it is (absolutely, i.e., in every respect) better to be than not to be.

claim was acknowledged by Anselm, except perhaps in the prayer with which he entered upon his proof—that Anselm's form of the ontological argument approaches the *via negativa*, carrying us beyond the web of language and thought. For both positions have in mind the same divine being. It is here, too, that—once again surprisingly—Anselm must meet Nicholas of Cusa. For Anselm's God, no more or less than Nicholas', stands in no comparative relation with others, not even in a negative or differential relation with them.[11] *The* God is beyond otherness, beyond Plato's form of the Other, and beyond the Other articulated by recent students of religion. As has already been pointed out, the God indicated by Anselm's idea is no part of the totality of being. That does not mean that he is "outside" that totality, for that would simply constitute a new and greater totality of which he would be an integral part. He simply is not to be identified with either of such purported totalities or with any part of them. It is this denial that leads to the *via negativa*.

It is by a similar denial that Jacobi found "nihilism" to be truer than Fichte's transcendental system of philosophy.[12] It is this, too, that led John Scotus Eriugena[13] to the strange conclusion that, in the words of the master to his disciple, not only do we not know this high God, but God does not know himself. That is, God does not know *what* he is, not because he lacks knowledge, but because he is not a what, that is, because he transcends utterly all categories of being and knowledge. Such a conclusion is at once more negative and more positive than the pale Nothing *(Nichts)* waiting to be filled with the categories of Hegel's dialectic. It is sheer transcendence. And yet when we read St. Anselm we are reminded that this transcendence is, after all, Being. Now, the distinctiveness that Anselm finds in the Idea, St. Thomas finds in existential supereminence: Being at once most determinate yet utterly unlimited *(Esse infinitum primum et perfectum)*. It is of this Being that we must say that creation does not add a whit more being than there is in God alone; indeed, an infinity less. And to this existence St. Thomas gives the name of Pure Act of being, *Ego sum qui sum*.

TRANSCENDENCE AND IMMANENCE ARE REALLY IDENTICAL

It is clear that such a God is no mere part of what is, nor even a whole within a larger whole. But when we speak of the transcendence of God

---

11. See Anselm's *Monologion*, chaps. 15 and 16.
12. *Friedrich Heinrich Jacobis Werke* bd. 3, Leipzig: 1816: *Jacobi an Fichte* (1799). This "Open Letter" is available in English: *Fichte, Jacobi, Schelling: Philosophy of German Idealism*, ed. E. Behler, The German Library (New York: Continuum, 1941), 119–41.
13. *On the Division of Nature*, bk. II, chap. 28f.; cf. III, 19–23.

today, the Enlightenment intervenes to cloud the issue. For it has translated the term "transcendence" into "that which is supposed to lie beyond this world"; so that "transcendence" is commonly understood as "otherworldly." In truth, however, nothing can falsify the conception of divine transcendence more than a separation between the terms "transcendence" and "immanence." If we take the etymological sense of the term "immanence" to mean "indwelling," "dwelling within oneself," we may, of course, extend it to mean "being contained within the universe, this-worldly." Now, the strategy of Enlightenment thinkers has been generally to narrow the horizon of interest by driving a wedge between "this world" and "the next," abandoning the term "transcendence" to the "otherworld," which is in turn taken to be inaccessible, except perhaps to private belief. Considerations of transcendence can then be set aside in public discussion as mere personal opinion. And "transcendence" is then reduced in rational discourse to a non-serious term.

The reduction of the term "transcendence" to the periphery is further completed by the rejection of both terms; so that "this world" comes to mean not "that which stands in opposition to the next world" (the initial sense given to the terms by Enlightenment thinkers), but "the only world." And this sole world can be taken to be "the only world we can be sure of" (the sense given to the term by agnosticism), or "the only world we need consider" (the sense given by secular humanism), or "the only world open to rational discourse" (the sense given by positivism). Once this reduction of the term "transcendence" has been completed, it can once again be put to domestic use in what has been called "horizontal" transcendence (intentionality) in place of "vertical" transcendence (participation).

All of this stands in contrast to the meaning given these twin terms in the long Christian discourse that preceded the Enlightenment and that formulated the idea of the high God. Among the schoolmen of the Middle Ages the term *"transcendens"* was used in a number of different contexts. Said of the relation of God to his creatures, however, it did not designate a different relation in reality from his intimacy with and immanent presence to his creatures. We may say, then, that, when said of the divine, the two terms "transcendence" and "immanence" designate one and the same relation in reality. They do not differ *in re*, but only *in mente*, only in definition. The distinction of terms is a concession to the human mind as it deals with the real relation of creature to Creator.

In the schoolmen's tradition, the term "immanence" generally signifies the specific activity proper to organisms by which they can act so as to transform themselves. Such activities as wanting, feeding, and perceiving originate within the organism and have as their term a change within that organism. Immanent activity of this sort is a primitive auto-determination. With human persons, immanent activity becomes the ability to communicate with another without loss of self, as when I teach someone geometry without losing the knowledge of it myself. With this too, however, there can be change, development, and devolution, for I can gain new understanding through that teaching, but I can also forget what I have once known. This "newness," however, is of quite another order than my new coat or my new suntan or my new figure. To be sure, we undergo change and are only imperfectly immanent. Thus, the activity of perception is shot through with physical interaction. Nevertheless, precisely *qua* perceiving (as distinct from the transmission of light, the activation of nerve cells, etc.) it is immanent in the sense that an agent initiates a process that alters itself. And so a complex activity that is partly transitive and partly immanent can be said to be "immanent" in that respect in which no diminution of being results from it. In the jargon of the day, it is a "win-win" situation. Thus, immanent activity means exchange without loss, as when in friendship I may come to know myself better through knowing another well. "Indwelling" here means "dwelling with" and is the basis of both friendship and citizenship. Indeed, the goods proper to civilization, as distinct from its physical products, are built up through the interplay of immanent and transitive activities, that is, of self-determination and those other-determining activities that terminate in products independent of their producers.

In the high God envisaged by St. Thomas' proof, however, immanence and transcendence do not merely interplay with one another, they coincide. Complete beyond measure, his perfection does not guard Him against change, but rather pre-empts the grounds for it. In this fullness consists his transcendence. In such a divine abundance, immanent activity is in the form of rich and intimate self-presence. We must, however, obviate possible misunderstanding. In his self-presence, the Creator is acutely concerned with his creatures, for this is no longer the self-contemplating God imputed to Aristotle, indifferent to a universe he has not created. Such unawareness is clearly seen to be unworthy of the absolute perfection of the Creator God. St. Anselm tells us that this is the God of infinite compassion who entertains the highest interest in the good of his creatures. His presence to self is so fully and actually conscious that he is present to others by their being present to him within his own self-presence. The divine concern does not wait upon contact with his creatures, but arises rather in that creative self-presence in which creatures are present to the transcendent Source of their being. The real identity of divine transcendence and immanence calls us to recognize that the creature consists wholly and entirely in its relation to this transcendent-immanent "No-thing," as though to say, *"esse creaturae est adesse Deum,"* the being of creatures consists in presenting themselves to God.

Ordinarily, of course, relations presuppose terms. Thomas called such relations "categorial" or "predicamental." He also spoke of "transcendental" relations, such as those of the one, the true, and the good, relations that transcend all categorial relations and are confined to no type of being but are found throughout the whole range of being. But the relation of creation is unique. It is a non-reciprocal relation, a one-way dependence of the creature upon the Creator. For the creature participates in the creative gift of existence communicated by the Creator. The closest analogy is the relation of offspring to parent. But it is only an analogy, in which the difference outweighs the similarity. What is more, the believer attains religious maturity when he or she passes over from conceiving God in terms of parents to understanding parents in terms of God. Properly understood, the reversal discloses the unique character of the Creator God, on the one hand, and of the relation of creaturehood, on the other.

As to the relation, in it the creature has no existence independent of the relation, being constituted wholly and radically in, by, and through that relation. And yet, just because the unique relation of creation is the free and generous communication of *being—that* whereby each thing is and is everything it is—the creature receives its own integrity in and through that relation. The being of the creature, then, is that of a one-term, subsistent relation, or again, being in which the second term is the very relation itself.

The unique character of the relation called creation derives from the transcendent-immanent nature of the Creator. For God is not *a* being, like and unlike others. Nor is he the "highest being," the apex of the much discussed onto-theo-logical pyramid. God is, in the words of Nicholas of Cusa, so transcendent that he is not even "other" from his creation. He is not that Other so popular among recent philosophers and phenomenologists of religion. He is, says Nicholas, *nonaliud;* by which is meant, not that he is the same as us, but that he is so transcendent that he cannot be fitted into the correlation of same and other. God escapes the categories, even the fundamental ontological ones. For that very reason, however, God is closer to his creatures than they are to themselves. God, said St. Thomas, and St. Augustine before him, is most intimate to his creatures. Robert Sokolowski[14] says of the conception elaborated by

---

14. Robert Sokolowski, *The God of Faith and Reason* (Notre Dame, IN: University of Notre Dame Press, 1982), especially chaps. 1–5.

St. Anselm of a Being than which none greater can be conceived that such a God is no part of the universe at all, takes up no room in it, displaces no creaturely being, and hence can be more intimately with and in his creatures than they can be with and in themselves. Creative presence is, to be sure, a unique order of presence.

To sum up, then, the unique character of this relation redounds upon the meaning of the terms "immanence" and "transcendence." Different in meaning, they are identical in reference and reality. The divine immanence is such that it transcends its creation utterly and absolutely, so that it is not even other to it. Here the spatial imagery at the root of the terms fails and the dissimilarity between God and creatures becomes explicit. By virtue of being no part of the universe, neither within it nor outside of it, by virtue of taking up no room or displacing any creature, such a perfectly determinate and actual Infinite Godhead can be said to be closer to each creature than it is to itself.

TWO PATHS WITHIN

In physical imagery, what is near is not far; closeness and distance oppose one another. Not so in human relationships. Physical proximity may go hand in hand with coolness and disdain, while physical separation need not diminish the intimacy of friends. Nor is the divine closeness spatial either. The search for such a God does not require a search beyond into some other world. It frequently takes religious form as a search within, but this religious interiority needs to be distinguished from a modern form of human interiority with which it is sometimes confused.

At the beginning of modern times the anthropological turn received decisive shape in the writings of Descartes, who undoubtedly gave expression to a widespread shift of interest. If early modern astronomy displaced man from the physical center of the universe, even more, for reasons too complex to enter into here, the upshot of the uncompromising mechanism of early modern physics—only recently coming under criticism from a minority of physicists—exiled from the physical world all that had been associated with the specifically human, so that "nature" was no longer conceived as a familiar world of colors and sounds, of finality and form. The Cartesian retreat within to an individual human interiority ended in the indubitable certainty of the *ego cogito*. This mental fortress was to be given other names by later philosophers: "self," "association of impressions," "mind," "transcendental consciousness," "ego," and "will to power." Among its names is "subjectivity," a concept that seeks to preserve what is distinctively human by a retreat from an alien world given over to "objectivity." The modern sense of "intentionality" is a newer concept that seeks to move out once again into the world from which consciousness had fled, but it rests upon that earlier flight.

Religious interiority is also a movement within, but it differs radically from such modern inwardness, for it does not fall back upon itself in retreat from the external world. Rather, it takes the whole world, spiritual as well as physical, along with it back to its creative source. Instead of anchoring the retreat in some defensive form of the inner self, religious interiority brings one out onto the "broad field" that lies open before God. This breadth infinitely transcends the distinction of inner and outer, of physical and psychic, as the infinite Source transcends its finite consequents. The relation is non-reciprocal just because the finite stands in absolute dependence upon the infinite. Once again, we anticipate such a relationship in our experience of parentage. We often look back to the adults familiar to our childhood and wish that we might have been able to relate to them in more equal fashion, as we would now were they still alive. This is the sometimes bitter and always sad recognition of a certain non-reciprocity between human generations. But these sources of our own personal formation are only relative sources, and so the relation is not pure non-reciprocity. Or again, we also anticipate such non-reciprocity in the experience of receiving a gift. Reception is no simple physical transaction, for the only adequate "return" is that of gracious acceptance. But the "reciprocity" of reception is itself non-reciprocal, that is, it does not conform to the law of equal action and reaction. It is a free acknowledgment that adds nothing physical to the original communication.[15]

THE PRESENT CONTEXT OF THE PROOF

I have dwelt upon the issue of the relation of creation to the Creator God in order to point out that the proof cannot be effectively presented or understood or even refuted as though it were a straightforward argument from nature as currently understood. The argument implicates a whole context and subtext including the human dimension of reality as well. Thus, the first way *(prima via)* cannot proceed from motion and nature in the sense presently given to them. The "nature" of which St. Thomas speaks contains within itself efficient, formal, and final causalities, and its "motion" is to be understood within an ontological context that recognizes immanent activity as well as transitive activity and dis-

---

15. K. L. Schmitz, *The Gift: Creation,* The Aquinas Lecture (Milwaukee, WI: Marquette University Press, 1982).

placement. Moreover, the term *natura* is broader and richer than our present term *nature*. The former is used of human and divine as well as of physical being. It simply means "the various modes of being appropriate to things, humans, or God." And we still preserve that meaning in such sayings as "It is in the nature of things," though we have largely emptied the terms of its metaphysical meaning.

Nowadays "nature" tends to refer to what is neither God nor man but is simply physical. Indeed, it is usual to think of nature as over against, or at least distinct from, the human, the social, the cultural, and the religious. A proof that would begin with a conception of nature devoid of causality and principles is unlikely to convince. Nor should it. The traditional proof, on the other hand, moves within a context of agency, and of agency that is not reduced to mere mechanical force.

And so those who have some misgiving about the effectiveness of the five ways today are not entirely without grounds. To the extent that the rich polyvalence of the term *natura* (said of physical things, human beings, and God) remains intact, so that the intelligible nexus and the real context within which the proof moves is taken to be polyvalent, to that extent the proof may reach its goal. However, once modern dichotomies—such as the Cartesian dualism between the affairs of the mind and those of the body, or the Kantian between understanding and will—were able to force a separation of distinct (though related) meanings formerly associated within the term nature, the proof needed restatement, in order to overcome the new situation. Instead, it has frequently received a reduced statement, as though one could rise to the high God from the new sense of "nature," that is, from "mere nature," from nature alone devoid of ontological constitution, from a nature from which the human has been methodically excised, from a mechanical nature separated from intelligible principles.

Once the distinctions inherent in the polyvalence of the term nature had been broken down into separations, dichotomies, and oppositions, there could be no resolution into the transcendent-immanent unity provided by the Source. Instead, the unity was sought for in other ways: through dialectical argument that broke down oppositions by synthesizing them into an architectonic unity (Kant), by sublating them into absolute system (Hegel), by returning them to their mythical ground (Schelling), or by suppressing the question (positivism). None of these reached towards the high God to whom St. Thomas' proof is directed.

The finite, whether taken as a hard shell exclusive of radical otherness or as system conceived as self-contained totality, remains impervious to such an argument. If rational argument is able to move only within such an enclosure (as many Enlightenment and post-Enlightenment thinkers insist), the rational recovery of God is unlikely. For then the issue of God must be handed over to a faith out of touch with the highest capacities of human thought. It is likely, then, that the question of God will be surrendered to feeling, perhaps to a "transcendental" feeling, such as that expounded by Schleiermacher or the earlier misreading of Rudolf Otto. Or perhaps it will be reduced to a merely private matter, of no great general import for human affairs. Or, again, reason may be robbed of its integrity, without an end of its own, and in the form of instrumental reason it may be pressed to serve interests ultimately inimical to it (ideology): the interests of power, arbitrary will, emotion, greed, preference, or one or another form of irrational faith. The challenge of the proof—namely, of the rational recovery of the high God or its failure—puts everything to the test. For it tests not only the concept of God, but reason itself and the scope of rationality. Indeed, in the end it confronts our very selves, since the nature, character, and destiny of our humanity is at stake in the outcome. The greatness of Nietzsche was to recognize this even as he sought to overcome it.

It may not be true that, as the Grand Inquisitor put it, if there is no God, everything is permitted. But it is true that if there is no God, very different things are permitted. To which the secular humanist replies, If there is a God, is anything permitted? Can anything at all be done by human agency? Here again we meet the question of human liberty and divine will, and the issue of human dignity. To which a human reason, unburdened by unfounded obstacles, has every right to ask, If the proof proves that there exists the high God as an unconditional necessity upon which the very existence of the finite depends, can there be indignity in acknowledging such an absolute Giver and such an absolute endowment? That is the issue upon which the proof ventures, and its outcome is nothing less than the answer to the question, Who are we anyhow?

Chapter 15

GOD, BEING, AND LOVE
New Ontological Perspectives
Coming from Philosophy

In keeping with the theme of *Fides et ratio*, I am impelled to complete the subtitle: "New Ontological Perspectives Coming from Philosophy," with the following: "Coming from Philosophy in its Encounter with the Proposals of Faith." For the strict substance of the argument in the encyclical insists that nothing truly and profoundly new—it speaks of the "radicality and newness of being"—will come to philosophy except through its encounter with faith. On the contrary, it insists that reason acting as though independent from, indifferent to, or hostile to faith is not stimulated to seek *ad novitatem et radicalitatem ipsius "esse."*[1] The argument insists, too, that the long quest for meaning holds, not only philosophers, theologians, and other intellectuals, but each and every person in its grip, inasmuch as the search for ultimate meaning is inscribed in the very constitution of the human person. Indeed, the encyclical defines the human being as the one who seeks the truth: *ille qui veritatem quaeritat.*[2]

John Paul's intense interest in the person as the central reality is already discernible in the dramas of his youth. They deserve a moment of attention in regard to the present theme. They are dramas of the living word, so that their atmosphere and medium is the Word spoken by and incarnate in Jesus Christ. For the divine Word is present within the words spoken by the characters in the plays. The dramatic weight, the playwright later tells us,[3] is carried, not as in traditional theater by

---

Reprinted from *La Razon Creyente, Actas del Congreso Internacional sobre la Enciclica Fides et Ratio*, ed. J. Pradez and J. Ma. Magaz. (Madrid: Studia Theologica Matritensia, 2002), 240–87. Copyright © 2002 by Studia Theologica Matritensia. This also appeared in *Revista Espanola de teologia* 60, nos. 2–4 (2000): Spanish, 169–95; English, 303–29.

1. *Fides et ratio* 48 (hereafter FR).
2. FR 28.
3. See Karol Wojtyla's 1952 essay "On the Theatre of the Word," in *The Collected Plays*

the scenery and plot, nor even by the development of character.[4] The weight is borne by the words alone, spoken in their proper, intelligible medium: that is, at the level of meaning and insight proper to the person. For the person is the concrete human subject *(suppositum)*, the instigator of discourse and drama, in keeping with the rational and spiritual manner of human existence. Much later, as a philosopher, Karol Wojtyla will speak of the distinctive character of the human act *(actus humanus)* and of the irreducibility of the human person.[5] It is what Gabriel Marcel has called the truly "existential" dimension of human life. In this dimension, the truth and truthfulness of the person play the decisive role; and they continue to play that role throughout the later writings, including *Fides et ratio* (hereafter FR) For the splendor of truth (cf. *Veritatis splendor,* hereafter VS) is the distinctively personal value from which all others flow. Without truth, the good is debased, beauty is disfigured, and unity itself disintegrates. Moreover, living in the experience of the truth, the presence of the person is at the vital center of the culture of life (cf. *Evangelium vitae*), even as its absence leads inescapably to the culture of death.

As already said, and speaking theologically, the words in the dramas are centered in the person of Jesus Christ. Indeed, He makes a decisive appearance in all but one of the five extant plays.[6] To a philosophy aware of the Word of faith and sensitive to its proposals, an intimacy between language and truth is disclosed that can bring a new depth to the fascination with philosophies of language and hermeneutics. And even to a philosophy not open to those proposals, the fact of the cultural influence of the Word in history presents a crisis in which word and truth may fall apart. That separation constitutes the present "crisis of *meaning*" (*discrimen significationis;* FR 81) and the "crisis of truth" (*crisis circa veritatem;* FR 98) of which the encyclical and its predecessor, *Veritatis splendor* (VS 32), speak. Either way, faith points up the issue; it is the reef on which the relation between faith and reason may shatter,[7] or through which it may pass to new explorations (FR 23).

---

and Writings on Theatre, translated and edited by B. Taborski (Berkeley: University of California Press, 1987), 371–78 (hereafter CP).

4. Ibid.

5. "Subjectivity and the Irreducible in Man," in *Analecta Husserliana,* series 7 (1978): 107–14; also in *Person and Community: Selected Essays,* ed. T. Sandok (New York: Peter Lang, 1993), 209–17. Originally published as "Podmiotowosci i 'to, co nieredukowaine' w czlowieku," *Ethos* 1, 2–3 (1988): 21–28.

6. I say "all but one," since there is no actual appearance of Christ in *Jeremiah,* though His presence is felt throughout, as when the Jesuit priest, Father Piotr Skarga Paweski, after the long lament "Were I in Jeremiah . . ." concludes with the words: "Let the Lord fortify you—Let the Lord guide you, through Jesus Christ, our Lord. Amen" (act 2; CP,115).

7. The Latin puts it more starkly still: "ad quem 'naufragium' facere potest" (FR 23). The encyclical describes the believer as an "explorer" *(exploratorem)* in search of truth (FR 21).

The dramas are themselves explorations. In the first of them, bearing the title: *Job*, the Prologue and Epilogue speak of "the Word—the Word inspired by the Lord." It is the Word that comes from eternity, that penetrates time, embraces it, makes it fruitful, and gives it direction.[8] Directed to the oppressed people of Krakow in 1939 it pleads: "Behold, my people—and listen to the Word of the Lord, you who are downtrodden, you who are flogged, sent to the camps, you—Jobs—Jobs."[9]

And the play ends with the counsel: "Take these words against the storm; hold them when darkness descends. They will be for you like the silent lightning cutting the sky above Job . . . Nourish your heart today, brother. This is a tragedy of suffering—the sacrificial circle is closed. Depart—with a song in your heart."[10]

For in the dark days of 1939, the people of Krakow had only the Word of faith with which to nourish their hope.

In the second play, entitled: *Jeremiah*, the words of the prophet ring out above the loud clamor of the propaganda that filled the airwaves in the Krakow of 1940: "One must throw truth across the path of lies. One must throw truth into the eye of a lie."[11]

Yet despite the importance of words, and in the same play, the Jesuit priest warns that "Words are not enough, not enough . . . One must catch hearts to kindle them, furrow hearts as with a plough, and root out the weeds, root them out."[12]

And the Crown Hetman adds: "At the feet of truth one must erect love; at the foundations, low in the ground, it will take root even in a wilderness, will build, uplift and transform all things."[13]

For while words express the human dimension of the dramatic action, something more must lend weight to them: that "something more" is love.

The drama entitled: *Before the Jeweler's Shop* probes the difference between words proclaimed, on the one hand, and on the other, love lived in the covenant of marriage. Therein we hear of the tension that takes

---

8. The foreword to the drama reads: "The Action Took Place in the Old Testament Before Christ's Coming. The Action Takes Place in Our Days in Job's Time for Poland and the World. The Action Takes Place in the Time of Expectation, Of Imploring Judgment, In the Time of Longing for Christ's Testament, Worked Out in Poland's and the World's Suffering" (CP, 25).
9. CP, 29, 72.
10. *Epilogue;* CP, 73.
11. *Jeremiah,* act 1 (CP, 109; cf. 101–103).
12. *Jeremiah,* act 1 (CP, 98); act 2 (CP, 121). In *Reflections on Fatherhood*, Adam, having heard the word of the catechism many times before, cries out: "All this I know. But is it enough? Knowing, I can continue to substitute for everything the same common denominator of my loneliness—my inner loneliness, chosen so that I can remain myself alone and nobody else" (CP, 368). Such knowledge changes nothing radically.
13. *Jeremiah,* act 2 (CP, 121).

form between the noetic and ontological dimensions of love, the "distance" that separates intention from fulfillment. We are told that the first ingress of love may be all passion, the parties being swept away by surface feeling; but the fruit of that passion is a fulfilling love that leads the lovers into surprising depths, beyond themselves, beyond each other, and into a new mode of being.[14] For within every "horizontal" and passing feeling of love there is a "vertical axis" that cuts across and through every love.[15] It challenges the lovers to pass beyond the borders of passion to the uplands of that compassionate friendship that constitutes every faithful marriage bond; to a love lived in the aura of a distinctive intimacy, even to participation in the compassion which St. Anselm—and Karol Wojtyla as well—associates with God.[16]

It is similar with the religious love that is explored in *Our God's Brother*. There, Brother Albert, towards the end of a long life in the compassionate service of the poor, knows not where he is being led, but knows that it is Love itself that draws him towards Itself, and towards a greater, truer, better freedom.[17]

Now, I have drawn attention to these early plays because they contain the figure of an existential connection between knowledge and freedom, between truth and love. They are dramatic seeds that bear doctrinal fruit later in Karol Wojtyla's philosophical, theological, and papal writings and that ripen into maturity in *Fides et ratio*.

In his first lectures as a young professor of ethics at the Catholic University of Lublin in the 1950s,[18] he undertook a sort of grand tour through the history of ancient, medieval, and modern philosophy, with particular attention to the factors that go into the constitution of human action. His interest was caught by a significant transformation of the classical, pre-Christian understanding of the Good. Plato had raised the Good above the other forms; indeed, even above Truth itself.[19] As

---

14. Cf. the threefold analysis of love (metaphysical, psychological, and ethical) in ch. 2, "The Person and Love," of *Love and Responsibility*, trans. H. T. Willetts (San Francisco: Ignatius, 1993), 73–140. Originally *Milosc i Odpowiedzialnosc* (Krakow, 1960).

15. *Before the Jeweler's Shop*, act 3, scene 3 (CP, 316).

16. In the *Proslogion*, using the principle that it is permissible to attribute to God whatever it is "absolutely" better to be than not, St. Anselm attributed compassion without [sensible] passion to Him. *The Jeweler's Shop* speaks of Love Itself in absolute terms reserved to God.

17. *Our God's Brother*, act 3 (CP, 266). As the younger brothers tell of the violence that has broken out in the city among the poor, the play closes with Brother Albert's words: "Ah well. You know that anger has to erupt, especially if it is great.... And it will last, because it is just.... I know for certain, though, that I have chosen a greater freedom."

18. *Lubliner Vorlesungen*, ed. J. Stroynowski (Stuttgart Degerloch, 1981), 196–97, 244, 177 (hereafter LV).

19. *Republic* VI, 508d–09b: "So that what gives truth to the things known and the power to know to the knower is the form of the good. And though it is the cause of knowl-

Wojtyla reviewed the history of philosophical thought, he came upon St. Augustine's transformation of the Platonic Good. For, in embracing Plato's Good, the saint went on to identify the supreme form of the Good with the very being and personal presence of the Christian God. Wojtyla remarks that this identification alters the relation of man to the highest Good. For with the transformation, a cosmic admiration and inspiration gives way to a deeply personal love. And that love gives rise in turn to the praise that comes to Augustine's lips: "Only he who loves sings!"[20]

In a similar vein, others have remarked that Christian poets of the fourth and fifth centuries—although not so eminent poetically as their earlier pre-Christian counterparts; after all, Prudentius did not rival Virgil, nor Paulinus Pindar—nonetheless these Christian poets had suffused the very structure of their poetic lines with a new intensity of feeling.[21] The older, stately rhythms gave way to a deeper, more personal passion, while magnanimity was converted to *agape*.

In the same *Lublin Lectures* (hereafter LV) Karol Wojtyla is concerned to formulate a philosophical anthropology of the human person as it plays itself out in the field of human action, and as it integrates knowledge and love, truth and freedom, in a fully human search. As he passes from St. Augustine's linkage of love with the highest Good, Wojtyla arrives at St. Thomas Aquinas. Already in *Before the Jeweler's Shop*, the somewhat mysterious character Adam, speaking perhaps as Everyman, had observed that "every person has at his disposal an existence and a love. The problem is to build a sensible structure from it. But this structure must never be inward looking. It must be open in such a way that . . . it always reflects the absolute Existence and Love; it must always, *in some way*, reflect them. That is the ultimate sense of our lives."[22]

And it is in St. Thomas, within a deepened Aristotelian dynamic of human action, that Wojtyla finds a recognition of the depth that secures

---

edge and truth, it is also an object of knowledge. Both knowledge and truth are beautiful things, but the good is other and more beautiful than they. In the visible realm, light and sight are rightly considered sunlike, but it is wrong to think that they are the sun, so here it is right to think of knowledge and truth as godlike but wrong to think that either of them is the good—for the good is yet more prized. . . . Therefore, you should say also that not only do the objects of knowledge owe their being known to the good, but their being is also due to it, although the good is not being, but superior to it in rank and power."

20. Cited by J. Pieper in the preface to *Only the Lover Sings: Art and Contemplation* (San Francisco, 1988).

21. H. O. Taylor, *The Classical Inheritance of the Middle Ages* (1901; New York, 1958), ch. 4, esp. 262–84, documents the shift from classical quantity to Christian accent and rhyme in late Latin and medieval poets. Cf. A. Cameron, *Christianity and the Rhetoric of Empire: The Development of Christian Discourse* (Berkeley: University of California Press, 1991), esp. ch. 2, for other changes of language brought on by Christian experience.

22. *Jeweler's Shop*, act 3, scene 5 (CP, 321).

love to existence as part of the realism that suffuses both the plays and the philosophical writings.

It is in the existential Thomism of the Lublin school that he finds the metaphysical anchor for his analysis of human action, the anchor embedded in the understanding of being as existential act. He notes that the principles of act and potency are of universal importance for a metaphysics of the human act, and of import for an adequate anthropology, once act is understood metaphysically as the act of being in the sense of existential actuality. This same conviction is prominent in the encyclical *Fides et ratio*. And so, it is important to observe that John Paul's frequent calls in the document for a recovery and renewal of the metaphysics of being is not merely a general call for the recognition of being as entity, for a *philosophia entis;* it is precisely the call for a metaphysics of *esse*.[23]

I have attempted to sum up this recognition elsewhere as follows:

> Thomas Aquinas deepens the standpoint of Augustine ... by wedding Augustinian participation to Aristotelian realism (LV 197, 245). But he goes beyond Aristotle, too, with his insight into the existential nature of the good (LV 197). Existence is the definitive feature that is constitutive of the good (LV 244). For Thomas, the good is good only insofar as it in some way actually exists: *esse actu*. Indeed, the more complete the existence of something, the more complete is its being, and thereby the greater is its goodness (LV 196). The absolute perfection of the good is rooted in *esse* as act (LV 177).[24]

So far, then, with reference to the pre-papal writings, including the plays and the *Lublin Lectures*, we see an insistence upon the personal na-

---

23. Given that the use of a term such as *philosophia entis* is readily available, the use throughout *Fides et ratio* of the Latin verbal form *esse* confirms the judgment that the verbal use is deliberate. So that, without closing off existential metaphysics in the tradition of St. Thomas from further development and dialogue with modern philosophies, the term points to a definite notion of metaphysics (already endorsed in the *Lubliner Vorlesungen*). See, for example, the following references in *Fides et ratio* to the usage: the warning against abandoning the investigation of *esse* (5); furthermore St. Thomas arrived at a *philosophia essendi* and not merely at a knowledge of appearances (44); reason unobservant of faith is not inclined to look *ad novitatem et radicalitatem ipsius "esse"* (48); God as Creator is a truth "which has been so crucial for the development of philosophical thinking, especially as *philosophicam respicientem esse"* (76); "the person constitutes a privileged *locus* for the encounter *cum actu essendi"* (83); "the metaphysical interpretations of things opens up before [enquirers]: in truth, in beauty, in moral goods, in other persons, in *esse*, and in God" (83); scientism has erroneously revived the positivist rejection of the *essendi notio* (88); nihilism rejects the sense of *essendi* (90); its neglect *(neglectum ipsius "esse")* leads to the loss of truth, dignity, and man as the image of God (90); the *intellectus fidei* lays claim upon a *philosophia essendi* (97); *philosophia essendi est philosophia actuosa seu dynamica;* such a philosophy is strong and enduring because it is sustained by the very act of being itself *(actu ipso "essendi")* (97).

24. K. L. Schmitz, *At the Centre of the Human Drama: The Philosophical Anthropology of Karol Wojtyla/Pope John Paul II* (Washington, DC: John Paul II Institute, 1993), 51.

ture of the supreme Good, which calls forth the response of love; but we see also the identification of the good with existential actuality, resident in the created being which the Creator Himself looked upon as "good" (Gen 1:10–31). In sum, then, there is an indispensable link between the person, love, the good, and existence: the medium within which they dwell and in which they complete themselves is the Truth.

Fides et ratio fills out the portrait of that Truth as it manifests itself in the transcendental conditions of philosophical inquiry. And so, in reproducing that portrait it is well to begin with the conditions under which the search for truth is undertaken. We are in realist territory immediately, for we are told at the very onset that being itself is not indifferent to the quest for meaning *(inquisitione de sensu ipso;* FR 1).[25] Drawn by the "desire to know the truth" *(veritatis cognoscendae studium)*, the human spirit rises on the paired wings of faith and reason to contemplate the truth about itself, others, and God.

Now, philosophy itself arises out of this desire for truth *(veritatis cupiditatem)*. This desire actualizes itself in the quest for the deepest meaning of reality, of history, and of human life itself (FR 1). It is desire touched by passion. What is sought here is meaning as the *logos* of the heart *(hominis animus;* FR 1); so that we are, from the beginning, implicated in the "logic of love." That is why, immediately following its inception, the letter speaks in the language of "gift" *(donum)* and of "service" (FR 2); and it is worth noticing that it is precisely in the service of Truth *(Veritatis diaconiam)*. In its own name, philosophy takes that search to itself, bringing the light of reason to bear upon the work of love. Aristotle spoke correctly of wonder *(thaumatzein)* at the gate of philosophy, but Plato spoke more tellingly of eros,[26] and Augustine still more fully when he spoke of *amor*.

By its very character such truth enters intimately into the movement of history.[27] In words of faith, reminiscent of the dramas, we are told that

---

25. "Interrogatio de significatione rerum suaeque ipsius exsistentiae" (FR 1).

26. Cf. J. Pieper, "Divine Madness," in *Plato's Case Against Secular Humanism*, trans. Lothar Krauth (San Francisco: Ignatius, 1995); originally "Göttlicher Wahnsinn," in *Eine Platon-Interpretation*.

27. Speaking of Revelation, the letter insists upon the historical character of faith. "God's revelation is therefore immersed in time and history... The truth about himself and his life, which God has entrusted to humanity, is immersed therefore in time and history... For the people of God, therefore, history becomes a path to be followed to the end..." (FR 11). "History therefore becomes the arena where we see what God does for humanity. God comes to us in the things we know best and can verify most easily, the things of our everyday life, apart from which we cannot understand ourselves" (12). For its part, reason finds itself poised between its own embodiment in history and the lure of a mystery which lies beyond its own powers (14). And so we are free to choose a path "which begins with reason's capacity to rise beyond what is contingent and set out towards the infinite" (24).

"the Eternal enters time, the Whole lies hidden in the part, God takes on a human face."[28]

And so, at the same time that truth is encountered in history, in that very encounter human reason gains access to that which transcends the conditioned flow of time. Now, such a transcendence, by which truth lays a claim upon us and binds us beyond the changing conditions of time and place, is proclaimed by faith and experienced by philosophy in its search for a lasting sense of life and existence.

With seemingly boundless confidence, the encyclical endorses the endless advance into the meaning of life and existence, witnessed by the affirmative progress of philosophical insight throughout its history up to the present day. For, even in the midst of errors, the growth of philosophical insight points to an inexhaustible richness of intelligibility in the truth of the being that is sought. Beginning in wonder (FR 4), reason opens out onto a legitimate plurality of ways in which the search for meaning and truth is carried out in various philosophies and in various cultures.[29] Modern thought has not been simply an unmitigated series of errors. On the contrary, it is clear to anyone who looks at the historical development of philosophical inquiry that, despite its dangers and wrong turns, there have been new acquisitions of insight. That is why, even though the document accords a certain privilege to St. Thomas' metaphysics, it looks positively, though not uncritically, upon other philosophies as well. Indeed, there can be no one exclusive and exhaustive system of philosophy (FR 4); the truth is too large, too rich, and too full for that.

This may remind us of Gabriel Marcel's "definition" of being: as that mystery which necessarily resists—or should resist—any attempt at exhaustive analysis.[30] The encyclical finds in any such claim a "philosophical pride" *(superbiam philosophicam)* which seeks to present its own partial and imperfect view as the complete reading of all reality.[31] What outstrips every system is "the primacy of philosophical enquiry."[32] Nevertheless, the rejection of a single system does not commit us to relativism

---

28. "Aeternum ingreditur tempus, quod est Omne absconditur in parte, Deus hominis suscipit vultum" (FR 12).

29. The letter endorses a "legitimate plurality of positions" *(Licita sententiarum varietas;* FR 5) but warns against the danger of an indiscriminate pluralism *(indistincto pluralismo).* At FR 38, we read that the ways to the one and same truth are many.

30. "The Ontological Mystery," in the English collection: *The Philosophy of Existentialism* (New York: Citadel, 1966), 14: "being is—or should be—necessary. It is impossible that everything should be reduced to a play of successive appearances which are inconsistent with each other ('inconsistent' is essential), or in the words of Shakespeare, to 'a tale told by an idiot.'"

31. FR 4.

32. Ibid.

and historicism, but to a recognition of the plural condition of rationality.[33] That plurality is not rooted in the transient flow of time, however, but in the plenitude and *richesse* of truth, which escapes the human search on all sides.

We ought to stop here for a moment and appreciate the subtle way in which Christian Revelation has in this way expanded the horizon of the philosophical quest. It is Hegel who has brought this insight to clarity. In the *Wissenschaft der Logik* he renders explicit the distinction between the concepts of the limit *(die Grenze)* and the finite *(das Endliche)*.[34] The former is associated with Aristotle and generally with Greek thought and culture whose refined sense of the limits of things still holds us in the spell of their beauty.[35] To consider the limited as finite, however, requires a shift of horizon, for it is only from the point of view of an affirmative infinite that the limit appears as finite.

Now this "point of view" was alien to the Greek mind, for which infinitude meant indeterminacy and indefiniteness. Recent attempts to articulate a "philosophy of finitude" presuppose this shift. If we look for the underlying mover of that shift, we are led to the effective presence of biblical Revelation and precisely in its Christian form. Moreover, this factual presence is operative even in the thought of those philosophers who do not believe in the Revelation. This is an instance of faith expanding the horizon of philosophical inquiry, perhaps after the manner of an *objectum motivum* in St. Bonaventure's sense of the term.

Because human reason in its quest touches that fullness, however imperfectly, the human mind can arrive at universal truths that pervade all cultures: such truths as those of "non-contradiction, finality and causality, as well as the concept of the person as a free and intelligent subject, with the capacity to know God, truth and goodness."[36]

This knowledge, along with certain moral norms—some enshrined in "national and international legal systems" which regulate the life of society (FR 3, 4)—points to an implicit philosophy that belongs to all humanity (FR 4). It is reflected in the several cultures as well as in the various systems of philosophy within different cultures. Without the capacity to satisfy this passion for the truth, however imperfectly, life would become a sterile routine lacking personal vitality (FR 4).

---

33. *Rationality Today: La Rationalité Aujourd'hui*, ed. Th. Geraets (Ottawa, 1979), sets forth many of the current conceptions of rationality, by representatives of philosophical thought, including Gadamer, Habermas, Appel, and others.

34. *Wissenschaft der Logik* (2nd ed.), vol. 1, bk. 1, ch. 2, the transition from determinate being to finitude to affirmative infinity.

35. "Place *(topos)* is the first unmoved limit *(peras akineton proton)* surrounding a thing" (Aristotle, *Physics* 212a 20).

36. FR 4.

We pass on from the desire for truth to the power it has to draw us and to obligate us. For while the transcendent character of truth is explicitly proclaimed by faith, it is also presupposed by philosophy's own submission to the truth, since truth binds human reason to its service. What is more, truth is celebrated in art, literature, and poetry as well as pursued in science and ordinary reflection. Now, in their common regard for the universality and transcendence of truth, both faith and reason share a value and a common meeting ground. For the authentic desire for truth is nothing less than the desire for access to its fullness.[37] It is this aspiration that led Marcel to wish that philosophers had spent less time on the problem of how the many issue from the one, and more on the appreciation of the mystery whereby the full permeates the empty. And in this community of concern for the fullness of truth, shared by faith and reason, faith entices reason to press its search with more vigor and with indefeasible hope.

In that search for the meaning of life we are called beyond ourselves to the truth of being (*veritatem existentiae;* FR 5). In *The Acting Person,* Karol Wojtyla had already called each person to the double task of integration and transcendence.[38] In this search for ultimate meaning, it is the truth that offers us the way out of ourselves; and this is philosophy's "original vocation" (*pristinam suam vocationem;* FR 6). Its role is to call persons and whole cultures to the quest for truth (FR 6). In responding to the call, the philosopher, wittingly or unwittingly, cooperates with and contributes to the call of faith, which is the call to fidelity and to holiness.

The call to truth, of course, is not simply an invitation to collect ideas or patterns of information; it is the call to an existential encounter *(con-*

---

37. The unconditioned search for truth is the search for a full and final answer. And this is also the intent of philosophy itself: fundamental inquiry into the fullness of truth (FR 27).

38. "Part of our fulfillment consists in a horizontal transcendence, that is, in our going out to the things around us, in coming to know them, in interacting with them and being affected by them. But such horizontal transcendence is only a condition of our fulfillment: it is not its key. The threshold that we must cross is upwards; it lies beyond us. We are called therefore to vertical transcendence, that very transcendence. . . . At the very source of every love" (*At the Centre of the Human Drama,* 86). See the full discussion in chapters 2 and 3 of *The Acting Person,* esp. regarding obligation and conscience. In particular p. 181: "Man as the person both lives and fulfills himself within the perspective of his transcendence. Is it not freedom, obligation and responsibility which allows us to see that not only truthfulness but also the person's surrender to truth in judging as well as in acting constitute the real and concrete fabric of the personal life of man?" At the same time, the task of integration brings the principle of immanence into play in the *actus humanus* (see esp. ch. 5). In *Fides et ratio* (23) we read: Of itself, philosophy is able to recognize the human being's ceaselessly self-transcendent orientation towards the truth: "philosophia, quae iam ex se agnoscere potest perpetuum hominis ascensum adversus veritatem."

gressio) with the life-giving source. For the truth which the "sapiential" character of philosophy seeks is not mere correctness but a dramatic presence.[39] It is, to be sure, truth as the guide to good order, for wisdom orders things rightly; but far more, it is the source of love (*fons amoris;* FR 7). The search, then, is not driven by idle curiosity, but is the movement of love itself within the inquiring person. And here we gain a glimpse of that personal Good that (out of an abundance of love: *ex abundantia caritatis*) desires "friendship" with all who inquire.

Paradoxically, the authentic philosophical experience is one in which, after all of his efforts, a truth-bearing insight comes to the inquirer as a gift.[40] For truth is a kind of grace received to which the philosopher is called to respond.[41] And just because truth is a gift (*donum*) received, and not merely the recognition of a given perceived (*datum*), there stands behind that gift the fullness of the Giver.

It is proper to philosophy, not simply to seek the truth as one might seek food or some other desirable object, but to pursue the truth wholeheartedly, in a deliberate and self-conscious way. Within visible creation, man is the only creature who not only is capable of knowing but who knows that he knows, and is therefore interested not only in what he possesses but in the real truth of what he perceives. No one can remain genuinely indifferent to the question of whether what one knows is true or not. As St. Augustine reminds us, there are many who may wish to deceive but none who wish to be deceived.[42]

What is it that we seek when we seek the truth without conditions? It does not consist simply in "getting things right," though getting them wrong may block the way to the truth sought. In reflecting upon this question, the metaphysics of *esse* recognizes that the truth does not add any real factor to what is sought after; it is characterized, not by some-

---

39. FR 7.
40. ". . . a question as dramatic as the question of meaning cannot be evaded" (n. 26). In ch. 4 of *The Acting Person* (p. 168) we read: "[Obligation] introduces the person through his actions into that characteristic drama enacted in the context of reality of which it makes him the subject (*dramatis persona*)."
41. A number of Catholic philosophers have stressed the paradoxical nature of existence, knowledge, and love. This is inherent in the incommensurable analogy between the philosopher as seeker and the truth as immanent-transcendent and unconditional. Peter Wust puts the issue starkly when he relates the search for truth to a prayerful attitude: "Wer die Wahrheit sucht, muss bereit sein vor der Wahrheit niederzuknien. Er muss lernen, den philosophischen Reflektionsakt mit dem religiösen Devotionsakt in eine ganz enge Verbindung zu bringen. . . . Oro ut intelligam." *Im Sinnkreis des Ewigen* (Graz, 1954); *Existenz vor Gott* (Berlin, 1971); cited by H. Westhoff in *Christliche Philosophie im katholischen Denken des 19. und 20. Jahrhunderts*, ed. E. Coreth et al., vol. 3 (Graz, 1990), 117. Cf. also F. Ebner's "paradoxical logic of the Word," and also the work of Erich Pryzwara, Hans Urs von Balthasar, and others.
42. N. 25; citing *Confessions* X, 23.

thing additional to and other than being, but by the relation which the knower has to that which is known. For, while it is not incorrect to account for knowledge as the acquisition of ideas, it is closer to the nature of truth to understand knowing as the spiritual openness to the way things really are. My knowledge of this room does not effectively put the room in my head after the manner of a miniature picture gallery. Rather, knowing calls me forth into the room in a distinctive way. Now, this transcendental relation belongs to the order of spirit, and brings its perfection to the knower precisely as to a spiritual being. Indeed, the entire medium of the search for meaning is in the modality of spiritual existence.

In reflecting upon that medium, we are in the position of one who is both too distant and yet too near the reality of spirit. It seems distant because intangible; yet near because we are caught up in its very activity and receptivity. Perhaps the most succinct characterization of our spiritual mode of questing is to notice that its reciprocity obeys laws quite other from those of physics. For, in our search for meaning, the proper nature of our interpersonal communication does not consist in the exchange of physical energy, though that attends the psycho-physical unity of our composite being. Rather, in our communication we establish relations with others without loss of physical matter. In short, the emblem of the spirit might be: communication without loss.[43] The truth that is "in" the knower is not in him in the same way as the physical energy that he discharges in physical actions. This is evident from the fact that our communication of meaning in a conversation does not diminish our knowledge; indeed, the communication may even increase it. It was this observation that led the schoolmen to characterize knowing as immanent activity.

Now, this "in" is not strictly speaking any location within the knower as in a physical space. Yet the truth is not simply absent from the inquirer. Philosophy as fundamental inquiry would not have arisen were truth entirely absent from the human constitution: "Human beings would not even begin to search for something of which they knew nothing or for something which they thought was wholly beyond them."[44]

Indeed, as already mentioned, the human person is one who seeks the truth: *ille qui veritatem quaeritat . . .*[45] We might say that even when, fearing its consequences, we try to avoid the truth, it is present in our evasive action, after the manner in which a warplane seeks to avoid the ground defenses.

Or we may put the matter in other terms. Milan Kundera has writ-

---

43. I have developed the analysis at more length in "The First Principle of Personal Becoming," *Review of Metaphysics* 47 (1994): 757–74. See chapter 11 above.
44. FR 29.
45. FR 28.

ten the postmodern novel *The Unbearable Lightness of Being*, in which being is emptied of all serious meaning. Now, even if we were to accept the "lightness" of being as a description of much of the pettiness of everyday life,[46] we need to ask: Why should this "lightness" be experienced as "unbearable"? Why, indeed, if not for the hidden presence of an unacknowledged sensibility to meaning in the depths of the human person? So that even the loss of hope and the consequent despair give negative witness to the inevitable desire for the meaning of life.

In this regard, it is worth noting that the encyclical rejects the supposition, commonly held today, that we entertain profound and unavoidable desires which are in principle inevitably frustrated. Here we encounter a difference of atmosphere between the encyclical and the very loss of confidence in reason that is the occasion for its promulgation. We might put it this way: In Plato's *Symposium*, the desire for beauty, goodness, and truth is difficult of access and requires the help of another (Diotima), since it is a loving gift to be received; but, for all the self-discipline and self-sacrifice required on the part of the lover, the good is in principle and somehow accessible or receivable.[47]

Too often in the modern and postmodern intellectual atmosphere, the contradiction is endorsed that we can be possessed of, driven by, tormented through a desire that cannot possibly be fulfilled. On the contrary, the letter speaks against this mind-set: "It is unthinkable that a search so deeply rooted in human nature would be completely vain and useless."[48] Indeed, the very putting of the question implies "the rudiments of a response."

The *situs* of that search and that response, however, is not to be found in the isolated individual, which has served as a model for much of modern philosophical thought. More recently there has been a greater acknowledgment of the "relational" character of knowing. Pressing more deeply still, however, the context for knowing the truth is to be found rather in the community of persons *(communio personarum)*.[49] And here we come upon one of the advances in the portrait of truth, in the emphasis given to its communal nature. For, if the search for the truth is undertaken by one who cares for the truth, by one who loves the truth, the search is already embodied in relationship with others. It is principally a relationship of trust *(fiducia)*: "The perfection of human life does not consist in simply acquiring an abstract knowledge of the truth but

---

46. See also his *Art of the Novel* (New York, 1993), a translation of *L'Art du roman* (Paris, 1986). See in particular his opening reflection on "The Depreciated Legacy of Cervantes."
47. Cf. J. Pieper, "Divine Madness."
48. FR 29.
49. Ibid.

also in a living relationship of dedication and fidelity to others."⁵⁰ So that the human person—the one earlier characterized as one who seeks the truth—may now be described as one who lives by trusting others: *ille qui vivit alteri fidens.*⁵¹

This is the *communio personarum*, worked out in other writings, but now in the context of the search for truth. First of all, in regard to ordinary knowledge, the still prevalent model for the acquisition of knowledge is too individual, as though we know only that which we have acquired and verified through our own efforts. Anything less tends to be looked upon as imperfect knowledge (*imperfecta cognitionis forma;* n. 32). But this is surely not the case. We claim to know (and not simply to believe) all sorts of things that we have not ourselves checked out. Thus, for example, we know there is the continent of Antarctica, even without having visited it. We don't simply believe that there is such a continent, we are sure we know it. We know it by report. Much of our richer knowledge is arrived at in just this way: through relations with others in a medium of trust. Such trust need not be credulous, since we have many ways of testing such knowledge other than by personal inspection: for example, through the credibility of what is said in relation to other knowledge, as well as the credibility and authority of the one who communicates it to us. This interpersonal character of knowledge, then, leads us to acknowledge the communal nature of truth and the truthfulness of its witness. To reiterate this important point: "the human being—the one who seeks the truth—is also the one who lives by trust."⁵²

The truth, so deeply sought in the quest for the ultimate meaning of existence and life, draws out of philosophy its inherently sapiential character. The kind of truth that the search for ultimate meaning entails differs from truths that are acquired by the ordinary knowledge of things and events (*veritates. . . . adeptas ad rerum gestarum*) or in the ordinary course of philosophical investigation (*vel philosophiae ordinem*).⁵³ The interpersonal context discloses that "what is sought is the truth of the per-

---

50. Ibid.
51. Ibid.
52. FR 31. "In believing (*in credendo*), we entrust ourselves to the knowledge acquired (*adeptae*) by other people. This suggests an important tension (*intentio*). On the one hand, the knowledge by way of trust (*cognito ex fiducia*) can seem an imperfect form of knowledge, to be perfected gradually through personal accumulation of evidence (*quae paulatim per evidentiam singillatim comparatam perfici debet*); on the other hand, trust (*fiducia*) is often richer than simple evidence (*simplex evidentia*), because it involves a close interpersonal relationship (*necessitudinem*) and brings into play (*statuendo*) not only a person's capacity to know but also the deeper (*penitiorem*) capacity to entrust oneself to others (*sese aliis personis confidendi*), to enter a close relationship (*necessitudinem*) with them which is intimate and enduring (*validiorem et intimiorem*)" (FR 32).
53. FR 32.

son *(ipsa personae veritas)*." For what is at issue is human perfection, and that is served, not by merely abstract knowledge, but "in a dynamic relationship of faithful self-giving with others." Knowledge through trust *(cognitio per fiduciam)* is grounded on the assessment of character between persons *(existimatione interpersonali)*, and is not present except in relation to truth; so that, in believing, we are brought into union with *(committitur)* the truth to which the other gives witness.[54]

This portrait of the truth shows philosophy in its own integrity, even as it shows the fullness of that same truth lying beyond the reach of philosophy. The portrait, the search, and the letter are premised upon the seamless infinitude of truth. For it is the same truth that faith testifies to and that philosophy searches for and imperfectly adumbrates. As the letter moves towards its completion, it calls with increasing urgency for a metaphysics capable of acknowledging philosophy's open integrity; it is a metaphysics of *esse*. With such a philosophy in mind, the latter sections of the letter reap a harvest planted from the beginning by the sturdy confidence that faith and reason, theology and philosophy are partners in the same search for the selfsame ultimate meaning and truth.

In keeping with the integrity of philosophy, two images come into play. The one, long familiar in Thomistic circles, is that of the border *(limes)* that distinguishes the two disciplines, philosophy and theology, grounded in reason and faith. We are told that the border ensures their distinctive natures, but that it also establishes a "space" in which the two may meet.[55] There is operative, however, a second and not quite as explicit image, which bears an affinity with the thought of Maurice Blondel.[56] Moreover, this second image is needed in order to complete the argument for the interrelation between philosophy and theology. For the "place" *(locus)* in which they may meet (*ubi ambae ipsae con gredi possunt*, FR 23) is a place of encounter *(congressus)* and that is a more dynamic image.

Indeed, the architectonic image that presides over the letter and that wends its way from beginning to end is the dynamic image of the "search," the search for meaning. So, the more static image of a border,

---

54. FR 32. "Eodem tamen tempore, cognitio per fiduciam, quae existimatione interpersonali nititur, non datur quin ad veritatem referatur: homo, credendo, veritati quam alter ostendit committitur" (n. 32). The letter cites martyrs as "the most authentic witnesses to the truth about existence" ("Martyr, enim, integerrimus testis est veritatis de exsistentia"; 32).
55. FR 23.
56. See P. Henrici, "The One Who Went Unnamed: Maurice Blondel in the Encyclical *Fides et ratio*," *Communio* 26 (1999): 609–21. This absence is perhaps the more unusual in view of the eulogy given by John Paul II in memory of Blondel, who was praised as a model contemporary philosopher/theologian (L'Osservatore Romano).

which initially serves to preserve the distinction between philosophy and theology, is completed by the more intimate and existential image of the encounter, with its emphasis upon the search. This is in keeping, too, with the "interpersonal" character of the truth sought for in that search. There can be no doubt that the present John Paul's turn to phenomenology and its exploration of intimacy and interiority has helped to articulate this dynamic encounter.

It is, however, with some surprise that I have come to the conclusion that the deeper, newer, and more radical "ontological perspective" in *Fides et ratio* has come about primarily by way of the metaphysics which John Paul invites us to consider. It must be recalled that in a metaphysics of existential act, being rooted in *esse* is what is most comprehensive and most intensive, for it embraces everything in its comprehensive universality, while at the same time it penetrates most deeply and intensively into the environs of each and every being,[57] and most excellently into personal being.

The importance of history, highlighted by the encyclical,[58] has been accentuated in modern times. It follows that the history that has unfolded in the past seven centuries since St. Thomas must be understood as the history of being, "for nothing has actuality except insofar as it is."[59] I suggest that this understanding of being accounts in large measure for the boundless confidence with which John Paul advocates a not uncritical but primarily positive engagement with the philosophical currents of the present time. Just as believers are called to bring everything that is "beautiful, good and true"[60] to the feet of Christ,[61] so too philosophers

---

57. St. Thomas, *STh* I, 8, 1c: "Esse autem est illud quod est magis intimum cuilibet, et quod profundius omnibus inest, cum sit formale respectu omnium quae in re sunt..." and *STh* 1, 4, 1 ad3: "ipsum esse est perfectissimum omnium..."

58. See, for example, FR 11: "God's Revelation is therefore immersed in time and history... The truth about himself and his life which God has entrusted to humanity is immersed therefore in time and history... For the people of God, therefore, history becomes a path to be followed to the end..." And FR 12: "History therefore becomes the arena where we see what God does for humanity. God comes to us in the things we know best and can verify most easily, the things of our everyday life, apart from which we cannot understand ourselves." And for the impact of Revelation in history upon philosophy (14): "Revelation therefore introduces into our history a universal and ultimate truth which stirs the human mind to ceaseless effort; indeed it impels reason continually to extend the range of its knowledge until it senses that it has done all in its power, leaving no stone unturned." "A point of reference both for philosophy and theology" is given by St. Anselm's notion: "O Lord, you are not only that than which nothing greater can be conceived... but you are greater than all that can be conceived."

59. *STh* 1, 4, 1 ad3m: "Dicendum quod ipsum esse est perfectissimum omnium; comparator enim ad omnia ut actus. Nihil enim habet actualitatem, nisi inquantum est..."

60. FR 21.

61. "Leaning on God, they [the explorers] continue to reach out, always and everywhere, for all that is beautiful, good and true" ("semper et ubique ille adversus ea omnia quae pulchra sunt, bona et vera"; FR 21).

who are metaphysicians of *esse* are urged to enter into respectful dialogue with philosophies that differ from or even contradict the metaphysics of *esse*.

Indeed, the turn to phenomenology, so characteristic of Wojtyla's earlier philosophical work, has undoubtedly drawn his attention to an ontological interiority in the concrete and historical order of being itself. For there is operative in being as existential act an interiority that is neither religious in form nor introspective in the modern sense, but that is the very "radicality" of being itself. This, above all, it seems to me, is the most significant "newness" that *Fides et ratio* brings to our attention. It is nothing short of the "dearest freshness deep down things."

For, in the metaphysics of *esse*, it is the insight into the nature of being that sustains the search for truth. The bond between knowledge and love, between the true and the good, is certified by the actual richness of being itself. Moreover, it is in the transcendentals that we see the intrinsically differential unity of being in all its richness. Being is really one with the good, the true, and the beautiful; it is only the finitude of our approach that is the source of their distinction *(ratione)*. And it is this intimate "convergence," which is already an identification, that gives attractive power to truth.

For the search for ultimate truth is a sapiential search for the completion of the human journey, ordered to the good as to that which attracts, and to being as the actuality of the good. Beauty adds to the good that innocent attraction that points towards the glory of truth itself. Philosophically, it is in the communion of the transcendentals that we find the adumbration of that absolute plenitude and person who is at once both giver and goal of the search.

The primary new ontological insight, then, is into the ontological interiority disclosed by the metaphysics of *esse*. It seems to me that, in his earlier philosophical work, especially in *The Acting Person*, metaphysics had been construed as indispensable but somewhat "objective," betraying an unintended infection from the modern primacy given to the distinction of subject and object. The difference between metaphysics and phenomenology remains. Metaphysics gives its account within the horizon of the community of beings, whereas phenomenology has as its horizon human experience as such.

In turning to phenomenology to interpret human interiority, Karol Wojtyla brought subjectivity to prominence, a prominence that has continued to characterize his writings on work, society, and interpersonal relations. But, it seems to me that in *Fides et ratio* there is evidence that the "soft" exteriority of metaphysics has given way to a more permeable and intimate metaphysical discourse under the influence of a phenomenology that, without altering the character and vocabulary of a metaphysics of existential act, has nonetheless had an impact upon it. It is as though the turn to phenomenology has acted as a catalyst to release the metaphysics of *esse* from any residual exteriority attendant upon the modern sense of objectivity. And, indeed, this is to restore that metaphysics to its pristine character prior to the modern primacy given to the distinction of subject and object. Is this a simple return? By no means, since the impact of a phenomenology of experience has released from within the traditional metaphysics of *esse* a new and more radical appreciation of the ontological interiority of being itself: *adnovitatem et radicalitatem ipsius "esse."*

Chapter 16

THE DEATH OF GOD AND THE REBIRTH OF MAN

Metaphors of language sometimes express a reality that stricter and more modest conceptions do not express so well. Moreover, some striking metaphors, such as the "death of God," can give expression to real conditions in our culture. The intention of this essay is to sketch a current problematic—the widespread acceptance of the absence of God in the cultures of technologically advanced societies of the so-called Western type[1]—and to suggest a strategy for a metaphysical intervention in that problematic. The temporal field within which the paper moves is the *process* of modernization over the past four hundred years, principally in European and Anglo-American societies. Within this very complex process, which engages us all in manifold ways, there is discernible a certain passage of thought—a strain or skein—which has attempted to define the nature of this process and to provide a *profile* of it.[2]

In this profile the metaphorical expression "the death of God" articulates not one death—the death associated with Nietzsche's famous phrase—but three deaths. They are familiar to students of modern thought: first, the death of a *superfluous* God: this is the charge of Enlightenment atheism; second, the death of a *dangerous* God who threatens human freedom and dignity: this is the accusation of an ideology widespread in the nineteenth century; and third, in the past century, the death of a *negligible* God, that is, one who can be ignored in the de-

---

This article was first read at the international conference *Metafisica verso il terzo millennio*, held in Rome, Sept. 5–8, 2000. It has been slightly revised by the author.

1. On the importance of the issue of modern atheism, see the remarks of Karol Wojtyla during the Vatican Council (Acta Synodalis Sacrosancti Concilii Vaticani Secundi, VI-2 (Typis Polyglottis Vaticanum, 1972), 14, 661–63).

2. I distinguish between the *process* which is the actual current of modern life, and which admits of a variety of interpretations in accordance with the various disciplines—history, sociology, natural science and technology, political science, literature, art, religion, and philosophy—and the *profiles* which attempt to interpret and define it. The "death of God" is such a profile.

termination of fundamental issues of human life and destiny: this is the speculative rethinking of some postmodernist intellectuals and increasingly the disregard that presides over the practical ideology of much of contemporary culture.[3]

The widespread dismissal of the importance of God is not without consequences regarding the meaning of man. Indeed, it has led, not to man's florescence but to—and here is another metaphor—the very "death of man," a death that is somehow no mere metaphor, but that can be seen in the crises of our culture. The threefold series of divine deaths has been accompanied by a threefold series of human deaths. In short: philosophical anthropology has recapitulated philosophical theology.

The reflection will proceed along three lines: (1) It traces the threefold development of the rejection of God among a number of influential modern philosophers. In this development Nietzsche's slogan is not only dramatic, but plays a pivotal role. (2) In parallel fashion a threefold demise of man—literally, the idea of man—accompanies the threefold demise of God. In our own day, some postmodern thinkers have enlarged Nietzsche's fierce criticism of Christianity to become a critique of all humanisms, that is, has led to the third death of man.[4] For what

---

3. Among philosophers the issue is much more complex than in popular culture, but Nietzsche, Freud, and Heidegger provide a background. Derrida rejects any theology based upon metaphysical "self-presence"; Foucault accepts Nietzsche's proclamation of the death of God; and Jacques Lacan remarks that "if for us God is dead, it is because he has always been dead." For Lacan, the idea of God (in the wake of Freud's *Moses and Monotheism* revisited) belongs to the field of psychological trauma. Moreover, Lacan continues to speak of the "Great Man," but it is by no means in the usual sense of a humanism. Nevertheless, as with other philosophers, the question of God haunts much of postmodern thought. Graham Ward observes that postmodern thought is free of the secularity of modernity and offers possibilities for "thinking about other, alternative worlds" (ed., *The Postmodern God: A Theological Reader* [Oxford: Blackwell, 1997], xxii). There is no doubt, however, that something "other" is intended than the mystery of God as it is adumbrated by traditional metaphysics and its intrinsically related humanism. Among some, the idea of God is so formless, so beyond being, that it is difficult to affirm *philosophically* how and in what way God might play a determinate role in human affairs, except perhaps—and this is not unimportant—by holding in reserve the boundless depth in things.

4. This is especially pronounced in Jacques Derrida, for whom the *sign* incorporates a fundamental alteriety and difference that is irreducible to what is for him the self-affection of the logic of presence (logocentrism). For him, the relation to the other is constituted, not by the promise of enrichment of the terms in union or communion, but in an unbridgeable *différance*. Since any attempt to conceive man as a complex unity is impossible, so are all humanisms; hence the symbolic "death" of man, a "death" whose symbolism both expresses and reinforces the absence of any substantial unified structure underlying human life. See, for example, his lecture "The Ends of Man." In *Speech and Phenomena*, he writes: "The possibility of the sign is this relationship to death. The determination and effacement of the sign in metaphysics is the dissimulation of this relationship to death, which nevertheless [through its incorporation of otherness] produced signification." And in *Of Grammatol-*

is intended by the phrase, the "death of man," is not the denial that two-legged, tool-using animals have ceased to exist, but that all prior attempts to recognize a stable human structure and purpose in human life have failed. Its proponents insist upon the bankruptcy of man's own self-understanding as a rational human being. In these latter-day hands, Nietzsche's polemic and his spirited advocacy of the Overman have not led to a *superhumanism* as he intended, but to the demise of *all* humanisms. (3) After tracing this link, I will suggest a metaphysical proposal for entry into the problem.

In brief, then: the three stages of modern atheism, paralleled by the death of man, and finally the possibility of a rebirth of man in dialogue with this widespread strain of atheistic thought.

Philosophical atheism received its modern public endorsement among Enlightenment authors of the seventeenth and eighteenth centuries. In the full-blown flush of the brilliant successes of the sciences of nature this is perhaps not entirely surprising.

It was for the most part a theoretically grounded atheism,[5] which assumed the form of a denial of the reality of God as one might deny the existence of an object. Of course, such a denial was not unknown to classical and medieval thought. St. Thomas had already formulated the position in a counterargument to his five ways.[6]

In the eighteenth century the position is stated, sometimes with the calm confidence of a supposedly scientific materialism, as by Diderot, or with passion, as by d'Holbach.[7] The position applies the principle of economy. Only two principles are needed to account for everything in our experience. The sciences of nature have made motion the first and

---

ogy: "The subordination of the trace to the full presence summed up in the logos [through a logic of presence, of identity characteristic of speech] . . . [is] another name for death, historical metonymy where God's name holds death in check." The metonymy accords with Nietzsche's charge that the Christian belief in God is the product of fear of death.

5. But by no means always theoretically motivated!

6. "Quod potest compleri per pauciora principia, non fit per plura. Sed videtur quod omnia quae apparent in mundo, possunt compleri per alia principia, supposito quod Deus non sit, quia ea quae sunt naturalia, reducuntur in principium quod est natura; ea vero quae sunt a proposito, reducuntur in principium quod est ratio humana vel voluntas. Nulla igitur necessitas est ponere Deum esse" ["For what can be accomplished by a few principles is not brought about by many. But it seems that everything in the world can be accomplished by other principles, on the supposition that God does not exist. For the things of nature can be reduced to one principle which is nature and voluntary things can be reduced to one principle which is human reason or will. Therefore there is no need to posit the existence of God."] (*STh* I, q. 2, art. 3).

7. Denis Diderot, "Entretien entre D'Alembert et Diderot," written 1769, published 1830; and Paul Heinrich Dietrich Holbach (Baron d'Holbach), *Systeme de la nature* (1770) and *Systeme sociale* (London 1773).

sufficient principle that accounts for all natural phenomena and that requires no further explanation. And in human affairs—in history, psychology, and sociology—the human will is the first and sufficient principle that accounts for whatever is not accounted for by nature, that is, for culture and its attendant attitudes and values.

Here, by the "death of man" is meant the dying of that classical humanism that had its origins in pre-Christian Greece and Rome and its transformation under Christian auspices in the Middle Ages. This first "death" is the "death" of *metaphysical* man. I do not exaggerate in using the term "death," since it here signifies the destruction of what for two millennia had been considered to be definitive of what it meant to be human: and this was, in the main current of thought, the rational, intellectual, and spiritual principle that made man what he is and is meant to be.[8]

Nevertheless, this ontological structure, prevalent in much of classical and medieval thought and life, was disassembled with surprising rapidity during the first half of the seventeenth century. The chief philosophical architects of this deconstruction were Descartes, Bacon, and Hobbes. Of course, they did not spring up from nowhere. Indeed the demolition was already underway in the immediately preceding centuries, highlighted by the quarrel between the upholders of the old way of thinking, the *via antiqua*, and the new, more nominalistic way, the *via moderna*.

This took the form of the dismissal of the four causes. What is important, however, is not so much the dismissal of the causes—effective, formal, final, and material—as the residue of that dismissal. For matter congealed into seemingly solid, self-identical units, *minima* or *corpuscula*, which sponsored the centuries-long search for ultimate particles in physics and chemistry; form surfaced as design or structure; agency was restricted to initiatory impulses of motion; and the range of final causality was foreshortened to human purpose.

Now the motivator in this shift was an alteration in what it meant to understand: it was a displacement of reason as it had previously been understood. The advocates of the new way of thinking, more or less in line with the up-to-date nominalism of the *via moderna*, had challenged the metaphysical conception of man, as understood by the proponents of the old way, the *via antiqua*. The success of this challenge was secured by the multiplication of particular questions in the science of nature—

---

8. That is, the four causes ceased to be considered principles *(archai)*, in the sense of sources of a composite order, and were replaced by analysis into elements or components.

during the fourteenth and fifteenth centuries[9]—detailed questions to which the old metaphysics and its physics had far less to contribute than the precise, hypothetical language of mathematics. In a more concrete fashion, during the fifteenth and sixteenth centuries, the successes of the rapidly developing practical-theoretical science of mechanics reinforced this shift in the nature of explanation.

What is of capital significance in this displacement is the determination that justified knowledge was to be found in a study of motion in and for itself, as in the newly emerging sciences of physics and astronomy, optics and chemistry.[10] This displacement made of motion a first principle which explained everything else, but which itself neither needed nor could receive explanation in terms of other causes.[11] During the seven-

---

9. See Olaf Pedersen, *Early Physics and Astronomy* (Cambridge: Cambridge University Press, 1993), esp. ch. 15–17, for a discussion of late medieval statics; and also for the distinction between *dynamics* (as the study of causal forces of motion: *quo ad causam*) and *kinematics* ("the description of how a motion proceeds in space and time": *quo ad effectum*, p. 193). The former gradually gave way to the latter. The discussions also bore upon the distinction between physical and mathematical theories of astronomy. That difference had already been remarked upon by Thomas Aquinas who had "a clear insight into the hypothetical nature of [mathematical] astronomical theories. [In his view] they are designed to 'save' phenomena, but are insufficient as descriptions of the physical nature of the universe" (p. 237). To Thomas' mind, only physical or metaphysical causes [*ad causam*] could do that.

10. What counted as valid knowledge was not knowledge as such, but *justified* knowledge certified by the appropriate method; thus, epistemology replaced metaphysics as first philosophy. No doubt, it is true (as R. Ariew demonstrates in *Descartes and the Last Scholastics* [Ithaca, NY: Cornell University Press, 1999], 188–205) that the reception of Descartes' new ideas during the seventeenth century were taken up with metaphysical issues, and that attention to the principle *cogito ergo sum* was less than it has been in the more recent course of modern philosophy. Nevertheless, time is, as it were, the great "logician" in the sense that it strips bare a central idea from the complex context in which it first announces itself and lets it engage subsequent thought with its own power.

11. Pedersen, *Early Physics*: "The one person to whom [causal] force was not an obvious essential to motion was William of Ockham. He and some of his Nominalist followers considered the concept of motion to presuppose nothing but a material body which, at different times, is found at different places. To them, particular forces are unnecessary as causes of motion; a body moves, they argued, simply because it is moving, and there is nothing more to be explained" (p. 203). Ockham is in many ways a transitional figure. In his magisterial *The Philosophy of William of Ockham in the Light of Its Principles* (Toronto: Pontifical Institute of Mediaeval Studies, 1999), and with reference to the principle "What is moved is moved by another," Armand Maurer attributes the first move away from the unexceptional status of the principle to John Duns Scotus. For Ockham, in the matter of projectile movement: "The motion of a projectile, then, is different from gravitational motion. As we have seen, a body naturally moves downward through its heaviness (*gravitas*), which is an accidental quality of the body really distinct from its substance. In the unique case of projectile motion, the body does not move itself through an added quality but through its own substance. This is a remarkable solution of the problem of projectile motion. Ockham seems to have been the first to propose it, but Duns Scotus cleared the way for it by denying the universal principle that everything that is moved (or moves) is moved by another... If this is the case with projectile motion, it would seem that there can be local

teenth and eighteenth centuries, many of the best minds sought to formulate the various laws of the behavior of the basic particles or elements of nature. Newton's famous laws of motion were exemplary, but more important still was the conviction that the very nature of explanation itself consisted in proving and formulating precise laws of motion.[12]

This understanding of the task of reason has become almost second nature to us, so that we need to make clear what a profound shift this was in the conception of reason and its tasks. For in the previous philosophical understanding, including the philosophy of nature, motion was not a first principle; on the contrary, it was a derived mode of being, which could be made intelligible only by tracing its derivation back to a cause or causes that in themselves transcend motion, and ultimately to the Unmoved Mover or First Uncaused Cause of all motion.[13] This metaphysical resolution of motion into its causes understood them ultimately in terms of the categories of being, which in and of itself was the ground of all that was moveable and immoveable.

In sum: the focus of rationality had shifted from ontological causes to relations closer at hand. In regard to the physics of motion, Descartes knowingly sought to restrict the explanation of things to factors that possess the same level of being as the things they were to explain.[14] The

---

motion without a cause. But does not local motion always require a cause? . . . To Ockham, however, the question is wrongheaded, for it assumes that local motion is *something*, whereas it is only an abstract term signifying that a movable body is verifiably in different places at different times without resting in between." The entire nuanced discussion deserves careful attention (pp. 435, 425–39).

12. Thus redirecting the aim of knowledge to *formulation* rather than to *origin* in the sense of source. The metaphysical understanding of principle as source *(archē)* gave way to law as expression of a formal order.

13. The metaphysical distinction between primary and secondary causality, once it took the form of a discussion of forces in the explanation of motion *ad causam*—while properly metaphysical and physical—provided the ground for a further movement towards immanent explanation *ad effectum*.

14. In *Descartes: An Intellectual Biography* (Oxford: Clarendon, 1995), 70–71, discussing Descartes' "apprenticeship with Beeckman 1618–19," S. Gaukroger remarks that Beeckman insisted "that macroscopic mechanical phenomena be explained in terms of microscopic mechanical processes which are essentially similar to them, in that they invoke entities and processes familiar to us from the macroscopic level, as opposed to the Aristotelian procedure, which requires that the explanation invoke states or processes different in kind from those being explained." John Schuster (*Descartes and the Scientific Revolution 1618–1634* [Ann Arbor: University of Michigan Press, 1977], 60) remarks that "Beeckman's corpuscularianism reflected and reinforced these beliefs, because it permitted him to see on an ontological level that only motion need be asserted as the cause of motion, and that only displacement of parts need be asserted as the essence of change." Ariew, *Descartes and the Last Scholastics*, 136ff., remarks that "Unlike Basso, Descartes is not an atomist. His matter is indefinitely divisible: 'every body can be divided into extremely small parts . . . It is certain that it [the number of these small parts] is indefinite.' But like Basso, Descartes uses atomist modes of explanation; he explains the visible by the invisible—macro-phenomena by reference to micro-phenomena; as Descartes says in *Le Monde,* not only the four qualities

implicit loss of a more robust sense of transcendent causality was not lost immediately, of course: but Descartes' argument for the existence of God (as cause of ideas and initiating cause of motion) aimed principally at securing support for the unfolding of the set of relations that made up his philosophy and physics. As a result, God was on the way to a reduced role as initiator who would be invoked less and less as the transitional God of Deism, and to eventually wither away. Spinoza equates God with nature: *Deus sive natura.* And, as Hegel has shown in his brilliant analysis of the conflict between reason and faith in the Enlightenment, transcendence was banished to an elusive and dubious "otherworld."[15]

Two observations will complete this brief sketch. First, part of the attraction of the new way was pragmatic, for unlike the allegedly unproductive quarrels of the scholastic metaphysicians and their opponents, the renewal of the sciences promised a new "commodity" of life.[16]

The second observation is less obvious; indeed, is paradoxical. For if what is central in this development is the displacement of reason as it had been previously understood, then, having been stripped of its former power to delve deeply into the transcendental nature of things, this same curtailed cognitive reason was now raised to an unprecedented height. Spinoza sums up the spirit: Everything, he insists, must be brought before the bar of reason. But this very reason whose status is now inflated to the exclusion of any other power, and of which much is expected, is the very reason that simultaneously has been disempowered.

The result of this simultaneous and paradoxical downgrading and upgrading did not appear until towards the end of the eighteenth century.[17] Kant was to tell us that such a reason in its cognitive mode could

---

called heat, cold, moistness, and dryness 'but also all the others (and even all the forms of inanimate bodies) can be explained without the need of supposing for that purpose anything in their matter other than the motion, size, shape, and arrangement of its parts.'" Of course, Descartes still clung to a residual metaphysical sense of causality, since he held matter to be inert, thus requiring an external impulse contrary, for example, to d'Holbach, who took issue with him on this point.

15. *The Phenomenology of Spirit,* ch. 6: "Faith and Pure Insight."

16. Not only Francis Bacon, who counseled the productive power of knowledge, and Hobbes, who scorned "idle speculation," but Descartes, too, looked towards practical results. In his Letter (to Abbé Picot) that forms the Preface to the *Principles,* he points to the fruits of knowledge in the products of medicine, morals, and mechanics. This new practicality tends to obscure the *praxis* that was intended to be the result of speculative knowledge in the *via antiqua,* namely, the inculcation of the virtues that sustained a fully rational and human life. The practical results of the older way were interior and were manifested in and through human action, whereas the desired results that were to contribute to a more modern commodiousness of life were viewed much more objectively as products.

17. I make no pretense here to accommodate the varied voices of that rich century of

reach only so far as the appearance of things, and even before him David Hume had demonstrated the narrow limits of its competence. Indeed, whether we think in terms of the conventional types of rationalism and empiricism or Kantian critical idealism, none permitted entry for reason into the transcendent field into which an earlier reason had thought it could enter.[18] Now this restriction had profound effects among many very different thinkers and was to spill over into the next phase.

Nietzsche—who made the death of God his signature—represents the second phase. No doubt, the first phase paved the way for the second. Indeed, Nietzsche was keenly interested in natural science, read widely in it, and was no doubt influenced by it.[19] But he was not so much a plain, ordinary, "garden-variety" atheist as he was an *anti-theist*. For him, the question of God was never a straightforward factual question. His denial moved more within the orbit of the biblical fool who said in his heart: there *shall* be no God, nor will I serve him.[20] In the section on the "Blessed Isles" in *Thus Spoke Zarathustra*, Nietzsche's Zarathustra complains that, *if* there were gods, how could *he* not be one; adding that, having drawn this conclusion, it now draws him. God is, for him, a mere "conjecture," born of weakness, pity, love of the small, equality born of resentment, and hostility to the power of life.

More generally, in the nineteenth century, what I have just called anti-theism is found among several prominent thinkers, above all, Marx and Nietzsche. During the second phase of modern atheism, a growing

---

lights. The present reflection is not a history of philosophy, which would be obligated to give a detailed and balanced account of the intellectual scene, but a philosophical reflection upon a skein of influential thought and its logic, which nevertheless is drawn from that fuller scene.

18. The lingering presence of a captive transcendence in the idealist tradition is found in Descartes and Leibniz among others; muted because it is tied metaphysically to its role in respect to the cosmos and morally to its function as judge.

19. In order to appreciate how the second stage drew upon its predecessor, one ought not to neglect the extensive reading that Nietzsche himself did in the natural sciences of the day, including the work of Boscovich, *Philosophiae naturalis Theoria . . .* (1759), as well as a critical review of his system (1772), much consulted by Nietzsche; also H. Kopp, *Geschichte der Chemie* (1844); A. Ladenburg, *Vorträge über die Entwicklung der Chemie in den letzten hundert Jahren* (1869); Fr. Mohr, *Allgemeine Theorie der Bewegung und Kraft als Grundlage der Physik und Chemie; ein Nachtrag zur mechanischen Theorie der chemischen Affinität* (1859); and J. H. v. Mädler, *Der Wunderbau des Weltalls* (1867). Indeed, Nietzsche read copiously in the theory of knowledge and natural philosophy during the years 1872–74. (K. Schlechta, *Nietzsche-Kronik* [Munich, 1984], for the year 1873.) Michel Foucault's reflections on power throw light back upon Nietzsche. It seems to me that the unanalyzed understanding of power characteristic of modernity carries over in an important way to Nietzsche's thought.

20. Nietzsche's deliberate allusions to the Bible are palpable throughout *Thus Spoke Zarathustra*, most obviously in the sections "Upon the Mount of Olives" (III), "On Old and New Tablets" (III), and "The Last Supper" (IV).

consensus emerged which subjected modern reason (the downgraded/ upgraded reason of modernity) to non-rational powers. In their antitheism, Marx and Nietzsche are not as far apart as first appears. Marx demanded of every revolutionary that he look upon the relevant past as the exclusive product of human agency. Only in that way would the revolutionary regard the present and the future as a project subject to human will alone, and thereby act as though the present and future were open to total and radical alteration by a revolutionary will.

In this second phase of atheism, what these two thinkers share is an opposition to belief in God because it is deemed incompatible with human agency, human freedom, and human dignity.[21] Nor is this attitude entirely surprising, given the almost geometric accumulation of human power that can be experienced increasingly in almost every aspect of contemporary life. But this subordination of reason brought about what, without too much exaggeration, we might call the second "death" of man, the death of *rational* man, of the confident and sovereign reason of the Enlightenment.[22]

Marx had reduced reason to the revolutionary principle of action;[23] but Nietzsche was more radical still, for he made reason subservient to a rightly attuned will to power. It should be noticed, however, that it is the reduced reason of the Enlightenment that Nietzsche (and his later followers) have in mind when they consign cognitive reason to a subservient role.

Now, Nietzsche might be asked: Why did God have to die? Why did the ugliest man murder him? And why must you and I bear the consequences of this murder? Among his many answers, he has replied that God had to die in order to free man from the moral order. But, as we have remarked of the first phase, this destruction of the moral order meant that something else died along with God. That something was not simply the moral order, but the broader sovereignty of a rational order that was more extensive than the moral order with its distinction of good and evil.[24] What died was the guiding power of reason in its cog-

21. Later, Sartre will continue this view, concluding that if an omnipotent God were to exist, Sartre could not himself be free; but since he will be free, there can be no God, although hatred of the idea of God could be the basis of a kind of negative unity of mankind.

22. Around the turn of the century (1800), the challenge to the sovereignty of reason was mounted by Romanticism, but largely in terms of the imagination, expressing itself sometimes in nostalgic memory of a past that never was, sometimes passing over into fantasy.

23. This is already adumbrated in the sketchy *Theses on Feurbach* (1845), in particular III and XI.

24. Zarathustra has learned that "man needs what is most evil in him for what is best in him—that whatever is most evil is his best power and the hardest stone for the highest

nitive mode.²⁵ Reason was subjected to the will and its passionate desire to appropriate all that was and is and shall be—subsumed into its own project, that is, into the going under of man and the passing over to the Overman.²⁶

Once that fatal inversion of will over reason was proclaimed most tellingly by Nietzsche, the creative will was called to surmount the restraining limits of good and evil, not as with Marx through a programmatic ideology,²⁷ but in fulfillment of the destiny of the will of one or another creative genius.²⁸

In sum, then, we can distinguish between an intellectual and theoretical atheism characteristic of the rationalism of the eighteenth century and a practical anti-theism of defiance, affirmed by Nietzsche and Marx in the nineteenth century.

But, if Nietzsche is not so much an intellectual atheist in the rationalist fashion, neither is he simply a repetition of the biblical fool, the practical atheist, who rejects God as an encumbrance upon human free-

---

creator; and that man must become better and more evil: "dass alles Böseste seine beste Kraft ist und der härteste Stein dem höchsten Schaffenden; und dass der Mensch besser und böser werden muss." (*Zarathustra* III, "The Convalescent," no. 2; K. Schlechta, *Friedrich Nietzsche. Werke in Drei Banden* [Munich: Carl Hanser, n.d.], vol. 2, 464; Eng. trans. W. Kaufmann, *The Portable Nietzsche* [New York: Viking, 1958], 330.) (Hereafter, the Schlechta pagination is given first, followed by the Kaufmann: 464/330.) "Thus the highest evil belongs to the highest goodness: but this is creative" ("On Self Overcoming," *Zarathustra* II, 372/228). "The greatest evil is necessary for the Overman's best" ("On the Higher Man," *Zarathustra* IV, 524/400).

25. When Zarathustra is asked for his reasons *(meine Gründe)*, he replies: "What are reasons to me?" ("On Poets," *Zarathustra* II, 382/238). This is not surprising, given that his grounds are rooted in and rise out of his will to power over what is thinkable. "God is a conjecture; but I desire that your conjectures should be limited by what is thinkable. Could you *think* a god? But this is what the will to truth should mean to you: that everything be changed into what is thinkable for man, visible for man, feelable by man. You should think through your own senses to their consequences" ("On the Blessed Isles," *Zarathustra* II, 344/198).

26. This is most patent in Zarathustra's teaching of the eternal recurrence of the same. Overcoming his nausea at the prospect of the return of the small, he determines "to recreate all 'it was' into a 'thus I willed it'—and that alone shall I call redemption: *alles 'Es war' umzuschaffen in eine 'So wollte ich es'*" ("The Welcome," *Zarathustra* IV, 394/251). "To redeem what is past in man and to recreate all 'it was' until the will says, 'Thus I willed it! Thus I shall will it'—this I call redemption" ("On Old and New Tablets" *Zarathustra* III, 445/310).

27. By way of a broad parallel, as Nietzsche looked to the going-down of the old order in light of the "great Noonday" (*Zarathustra* I, 340/191; IV, 556/435, and throughout), so did Marx look to the advent of socialism followed by true communism, and in milder form August Comte looked to the triumph of positivism supplemented by the social sympathy of human love.

28. This reduction of modern reason to non-rational forces found variations, such as the primacy of instinctual drives (including the thanatos drive) in Freudian psychoanalysis and the sovereignty of choice in Sartrean existentialism.

dom. An elemental force, he straddles the second and third phase; that is why Nietzsche is pivotal in the present problematic. For, while he is an anti-theist, he is also by intention a meta-theist, for he looked towards the day when the term "atheism" would have lost its meaning, the sense of *theos* having been forgotten. If in the anti-theist phase, God had to be killed, in the meta-theist phase, he could be ignored, simply buried and forgotten. Not even a tomb was to mark his place; not even the famous slogan.

This view was shared by others. August Comte in the previous century had already hoped to pass beyond what he took to be the sterile quarrel between theists and atheists.[29] That quarrel belonged to an outmoded metaphysics which persisted in asking the primordial question 'Why?' when it should turn from such profitless inquiry and ask the procedural question 'How?' He planned to replace the Christian God with the only reality worthy of worship, the Absolute Divine Being, Humanity Itself.

All of these—Nietzsche, Marx, Comte—are proponents of the third phase in the development of the rejection of God: it is not simple atheism, or even anti-theism, nor is it merely post-theism; it is meta- or trans-theism. And here man, along with God, suffers a third "death." For, with Comte in the spirit of positivism, reason gives up its right to inquire into the deeper issues of human destiny, and, already having become an instrumental reason, it increasingly becomes a technical reason.

Whereas Nietzsche looked forward to a kind of *superhumanism* in which reason served the will to power of those strong enough and hard enough to exercise it, in the era of this negligible God the third meta-theistic, postmodern "death" of man occurs. It may take one or another form. Robbe-Grillet has written what has been called the first postmodern novel, *Jealousy* (1957). In it all human characters are absent, except in and through and by their absence. We read of place settings at table, empty chairs—all meticulously described in excruciating detail, but we never meet a single human being. The absent humanity parallels absent divinity. This, it seems to me, is the literary description of the third death of man. Or again, in Jean-François Lyotard we are led through the deflation of reason into technique—a deflation in which reason serves willed ends projected as the immediate satisfaction of perceived needs, but a reason that does not touch the deeper issues of what it is to be human.[30] Everything that lay within the power of reason in the first two phases dies; only

29. The point is expressed in several writings; for example, in *A General View of Positivism* (1848), ch. 1 and 6, which prefaced his larger work.

30. Jean-François Lyotard has described this demotion of reason in *The Postmodern Condition*, and Gabriel Marcel has criticized it in such works as *Les hommes contre l'humain* (*Man against Mass Society*). But already as early as John Stuart Mill, the possibility of rational dis-

the instrumentality of reason remains, along with what Marcel has called the "metaphysical unease" of the present age.[31]

When pondering how one might enter into this philosophical development, Plato comes to one's aid; for did he not describe philosophy as essentially a *meditatio mortis?* Then too, in shaping this culture, Christian Revelation has illumined the existential passage through the valley of death. For Christians have faith in a non-metaphorical death of God on the Cross, which has brought about a quite different result: not a retrieval or a recurrence, such as Lessing had in mind, or even a rebirth, but a totally transformative resurrection. It is a dark and continuing mystery, and a testament to the deep formative influence of Christianity upon this culture, that the skein of atheism over the last four centuries has played out the drama of the death of God, although in a distorted and self-destructive fashion.[32]

What, then, has a traditional metaphysics to say to this issue? And precisely a metaphysics that has dwelt with this *meditatio mortis?* For in what follows I do not mean to suggest that the metaphysics of being remained unaltered throughout this trial of thought; in fact, it too suffered distortion in its central insights.[33] In making its modest contribution, however, a revitalized metaphysics encourages reflection upon the very texture of being itself. Since it professes that this texture is present in any and every development, the texture ought to be discernible in this latest modern development. For, if being is the very ground and character of all that is,

---

course about human ends was denied and rational discussion was reduced to the determination of instrumental means in pursuit of ends chosen on other grounds (such as utility, pleasure, or power). This downplaying of reason was already heralded by David Hume, who insisted that a passion could not be controlled by reason but only by another passion. It is common in eighteenth- and early nineteenth-century literature (such as Stendahl's *The Charterhouse of Parma,* or Sarah Fielding's *The Adventures of David Simple*) to find the passions characterized with slight or no reference to the rational factor.

31. See "The Ontological Mystery" (in the English collection *The Philosophy of Existentialism* [New York: Citadel, 1966], 12); commenting upon the loss of the sense of being and the prevalence of the category of function, he writes: "Besides the sadness felt by the onlooker, there is the dull, intolerable unease of the actor himself, who is reduced to living as though he were in fact submerged by his functions."

32. This, of course, is the theme of Henri de Lubac's *Drama of Atheistic Humanism.*

33. One must acknowledge this, without simply discounting the often helpful labor of the great commentators among the schoolmen. It is a complex story; but Hans Urs von Balthasar has tellingly exposed the emptying out of the fullness of being as actuality into the neutral, univocal concept of being in the baroque neo-scholasticism of Suarez and others. (*The Glory of the Lord:* V: *The Realm of Metaphysics in the Modern Age,* trans. O. Davies et al. [San Francisco: Ignatius, 1991], 21–29; *Herrlichkeit* III, 1, *Teil* II, *Neuzeit,* Einsiedeln: Johannes, 1965). Etienne Gilson had also traced the passage of being into what he termed "essentialism" in *Being and Some Philosophers,* 2nd ed. (Toronto: Pontifical Institute of Mediaeval Studies, 1952).

its comprehension and intension, its inward depth and all-embracing horizon, then it must include the history of the past four hundred years—however complex and varied—*precisely as the unfolding history of being.*

For that reason we cannot simply surrender that history to a negative judgment, as though being itself has not been present in and throughout its phases. We must not concede the death of *being*.[34] It is all too easy to point to the failures in modern culture: the erosion of classical values, the breakdown of traditional institutions such as the family, the gap between rich and poor in the face of unparalleled plenty, the ready resort to exceptionally destructive violence, the past century of unprecedented death, the anxiety that lies below the surface for many, and the evanescence of meaning as it touches the deepest levels of human existence and desire.[35]

But something new and positive has also emerged in the past four centuries. It is as though the ontological understanding of man and being at the end of the Middle Ages still left aspects to be developed. This surely is the fate of the finite condition of human understanding. In any given complex, as one aspect is brought forward, another may be pushed into the background. A legitimate kind of infinity—not simply Hegel's "bad infinite"—accompanies every philosophy as a sign of its incompleteness. There is yet something to be discovered in and through the unfolding of being. Aspects that had not been lived out or thought out before the modern experience include: On the side of ontology and cosmology: a greatly increased knowledge of the detailed workings of the forces of nature; a greatly expanded appreciation of the enormous magnitude and protracted age of the universe; the general historicity of existence, including that of the earth; and the fragile nature of the environment. On the side of ontology and anthropology: a sharpened sense of individuality, not simply as an idea but as a way of living; an expansion of options open to the individual; a new relation to the earth in the experience of unprecedented mobility; a cultivation of the imagination in the novel, of experiment with form in the plastic arts, and of the nonverbal modes of communication in music. At the same time, human life itself has become problematic and its value ambiguous: the human person is in some respects appreciated in new ways, while at the same time is threatened and cheapened by an indiscriminate use of human power drawn from newly exploited physical forces.

---

34. Any more than it can be conceded that the evil of non-being annihilates the good of being.
35. The call to a recovered confidence in an intellectual metaphysics as wisdom has been a principal theme in Pope John Paul II's *Fides et ratio*.

296   GOD

The question is whether a traditional metaphysics of being and its anthropology can accommodate and integrate these aspects, and whether they can be shown to be present even in their denial. It seems to me that, although the threefold development I have outlined may have weakened the metaphysical sense, it has not destroyed the texture of being.

This is by no means obvious; and in such a brief presentation I can only suggest a series of probes or *topoi* for further thought. In traditional metaphysics it is the transcendentals that make up the texture of being. You are familiar with them: being itself, unity, otherness, the true, the good, and the beautiful. Not all of them have fared equally well in the course of modern thought.[36]

Consider the *good:* Plato had placed the good at the height of reality, arguing that, while we might accept a plausible story as true (witness his *Timaeus*), no one is happy to accept a merely apparent good; we want the real thing (even if the higher good may be difficult of attainment).[37] Aristotle (and Aquinas after him) held that in principle no natural desire could be in vain.[38] But, since Freud, the suspicion has grown that such desires are in fact not what they seem to be and that as such they are not able to be realized.[39] Milan Kundera has given expression to this contradiction in his novel *The Unbearable Lightness of Being*. This "lightness" consists in the absence of meaning in our experience of reality. Yet the desire persists, for why should the "lightness" be "unbearable" if an implicit and ineradicable expectation were not present? In a word, the

---

36. Otherness *(aliquid)* has received considerable attention under the general rubric of *relationality* as in Heidegger's *In-der-Welt-Sein* and *ontologische Differenz*. Derrida tells us that unity and contradiction are the same, and presses the neologism *différance* into service in order to name an unbounded equivocity. Foucault tells us that to think is to think differently. In words read by Deleuze at Foucault's funeral: "What is philosophy today—philosophical activity, I mean—if it is not the critical work that thought brings to bear on itself? In what does it consist, if not in the endeavor to know how and to what extent it might be possible to think differently... The 'essay'—which should be understood as the assay or test by which, in the game of truth, one undergoes changes...—is the living substance of philosophy, at least if we assume that philosophy is still what it was in times past, i.e., an 'ascesis', *askesis,* an exercise of oneself in the activity of thought... The object was to learn to what extent the effort to think one's own history can free thought from what it silently thinks, and so enable it to think differently" (*The History of Sexuality*, vol. 2: *The Use of Pleasure,* trans. R. Hurley [New York: Vintage, 1990], 9; *L'Usage des Plaisirs* [Paris: Gallimard, 1984], 14–15). Regarding difference, the metaphysical sense of analogy as "unlike likeness" could be brought to bear upon this contemporary primacy of difference. See Erich Przywara, *Analogia entis*.

37. *Republic* VII.

38. St. Thomas, *STh* I, 75, 6: "Naturale autem desiderium non potest esse inane."

39. Derrida, too, tells us in *Glas* that "desire is theoretical, but as such is tortured by a contradiction that makes it practical. In effect, theoretical consciousness (death) has only to do with the dead." This contradiction is rooted in the very structure of the sign, which leaves knower and knowable, self and other, in irreconcilable *"différance."*

good is still operative, in however a secret way; in its power to awaken human desire.[40]

Or consider *truth*: Is the desire for truth an unrealistic dream? Or is there not, with every serious philosopher, a striving after truth, not just this or that particular truth, but truth itself? For philosophy differs from the special and positive sciences just in this: that it seeks *the truth of truth*. To be sure, in the spirit of critical reason, the very notion of "truth itself" can be and has been challenged. But, surely too, it has been challenged in the name of a better truth, in the name of truth itself; and if the inquiry into the nature of truth is abandoned, philosophy itself ceases to have a *raison d'etre*.[41] The essential link between philosophy and truth has been recognized, at least implicitly, by those who, despairing of truth, have sounded the death knell of philosophy itself.[42] And indeed, it has been shown that positivism requires certain presuppositions whose validity it cannot itself judge and which for it must remain unexamined.[43]

---

40. Plato, *Republic (Respublica/Politaieas)* 505d: "Is it not apparent that while in the case of the just and the honorable many would prefer the semblance without the reality, yet when it comes to the good nobody is content with the possession of the appearance but all men seek the reality, and the semblance satisfies nobody?" (Paul Shorey translation, 1931).

41. In a recent Oxford volume, entitled *Truth: Oxford Readings in Philosophy* (ed. S. Blackburn and K. Simmons [Oxford: Oxford University Press, 1999], 3–4), its editors discuss the problem of the general nature of truth. They recognize that the very notion itself, and the question "What is truth?" has been dismissed by most of the contributors to the volume. Referring to the position of "deflationism" (which holds that one ought not to raise the general question of the nature of truth but confine one's inquiry to the search for particular truths), the editors remark: "All such views agree that a general inquiry into the nature of truth as an abstract [i.e. general] property [sic!] is wrong headed . . . The issue is amongst the most baffling and the most important in contemporary philosophy. For deflationism is both disconcerting and surprising. It is disconcerting, because if truth disappears as a general topic, then too much else may seem to disappear with it. Our awareness of the world is at least largely an awareness *that* various things are true; that we are in a room of some shape and size, surrounded by people like ourselves and so on. An awareness of our situation is just an awareness that various things are so, and that others are not . . . So if there is nothing to say about truth in general, this may seem to imply that there is nothing to say about the relationship between mind and world in general. And if that topic is denied to us, then much of philosophy seems to disappear with it . . . Conversely, if these topics [about the relation of our mind to the world] are indeed vivid and real, why should they not be described as inquiries that, by throwing light on the nature of our representation of reality, thereby throw light on the nature of truth?"

42. See, for example, the discussions in K. Baynes et al., *After Philosophy: End or Transformation?* (Cambridge, MA: MIT Press, 1987), an anthology of contributions from Appel, Derrida, Foucault, Gadamer, Habermas, Lyotard, Ricoeur, Rorty, and others. See also *Rationality Today: Le Rationalité Aujourd'hui*, ed. T. Geraets (Ottawa, 1979).

43. I refer to the critique by F. Copleston and others in the debates over Alfred J. Ayer's *Language, Truth and Logic*, which forced Ayer and other positivists to emend their position, on the grounds that, by their own stipulation, their canonical postulates were themselves "nonsensical." There is a curious acceptance of existence as *facticity* in Nietzsche for whom: "Indeed, the truth was not hit by him who shot at it with the word of the 'will to ex-

No doubt, positivism itself is part of philosophy's own history. That is testament to the radical character of philosophy as fundamental inquiry that must press its inquiry into first things. And these include the nature and existential character of truth, whose illuminative gift is *not only normative for the mind but perfective of man as well*. This is so, especially when we summon up the courage to face unpleasant truths.[44]

But suppose that truth is not rooted in a positively conceived existence, a mere being-there *(Dasein)*, a plastic field or *tabula rasa* open to some other power than reason: to agency by Marx, sympathy by Comte, will to power by Nietzsche? Suppose that being is a *gifted* texture that houses the transcendentals open to development but not indifferent to finite conditions? And suppose that reason is *receptive* of that structure; so that reason is neither sovereign nor subordinate, neither simply instrumental nor in the unquestioning service of technology, but rather that the presence of truth in the texture of being—the intelligibility of being—is the window through which, however refracted by human finitude, there passes to the mind the light of the way things are? Is not this why truth is still pursued by dedicated philosophers, who try to "get it right" and grow in being through the process? Nothing short of philosophy itself is at stake in the question.[45]

The most stunning instance among the transcendentals, however, is that of *beauty*, where the true and the good gather in a moment of celebratory unity and joy. It is noteworthy that, whereas the good in the form of morality is ostensibly overcome by Nietzsche and truth is subordinated to will, beauty escapes his transvaluation of values. Again and again he rallies us to the standard of beauty.[46] More generally still, while many may debate about what concrete object or setting or work is beautiful, even those confused about the good and skeptical about the true, for the most part still instinctually retain an aesthetic interest. This may be rooted, unless all but completely dulled by exhaustion or distorted by envy, in the capacity for admiration.

Nevertheless, insofar as being itself has undergone a recent history in the process of modernization, so too must metaphysics. The good sur-

---

istence' *(Dasein)*: that will does not exist. For, what does not exist cannot will; but what is in existence, how could that still want existence? Only where there is life is there also will: not will to live but—thus I teach you—will to power *(Wille zur Macht)*." "On Self-overcoming" *(Selbst-Überwindung)* in *Thus Spoke Zarathustra* II (372/227).

44. Cf. Marcel's reflection on this point in *The Mystery of Being*, vol. 1: *Reflection and Mystery* (Chicago: Henry Regnery, 1960).

45. Of course, such dedication is not reserved to philosophers but is shared by scientists and all who seek to know.

46. "Where power becomes gracious *(gnädig)* and descends into the visible—such descent I call beauty" *(Zarathustra* II, 374/230). "It is not in satiety that his desire shall grow silent and be submerged, but in beauty" (ibid.).

vives but is transformed by its passage through the modern reduction of the good to rational technicity. Truth survives but with a keener recognition of the contingency of a world that requires an experimental verification of much of our knowledge of it. Beauty also survives, but not without incorporating into itself the ugly and the dissonant. In the past two centuries, the ugly has received an aesthetic presentation that integrates it in beauty even as beauty strives to overcome its incongruent. For beauty is that which gives joy in the experience of an *unearned rightness* that points to truth and that draws us towards and into its presence, where truth exercises power over us that is not only normative but also perfective. In its perfective power, truth is the bearer of the good of being. In the presence of beauty we have the gathering fellowship of truth, goodness, and being, the texture of being itself.

The transcendental texture of being, then, offers purchase points for engagement with the passage through the valley of death. For in recovering the texture of being we are on the way to a recovery of God as its fullness and source and of man as a person who is a member of the larger and deeper community of beings. It may be objected that the transcendentals do not settle specific questions about truth, goodness, and beauty. Quite rightly so. The discussion as to the specific character of these will continue among philosophers as long as philosophy lives out its destiny. What the transcendentals provide is the texture and the context for that discussion, which in contrast to the destruction of all humanisms, holds promise for the rebirth of man.

Chapter 17

THE WITNESS OF BEAUTY
The Profile of God

THE PERCEPTION OF BEAUTY,
THEN AND NOW

In 1939, during the early horrible days of the Nazi occupation of the Polish city of Krakow, the young Karol Wojtyla wrote to an older friend, replying to his request for information regarding mutual friends, those who had disappeared during the initial terror. Wojtyla provided him with what meager information he could, for no one knew whether the victims had emigrated, gone into hiding, been murdered, or been transported to the camps. After addressing the list of the missing, Wojtyla then invited his friend to come to Krakow to create, in the midst of the suffering that engulfed the people, what he called a Christian Athens that would dramatize the faithful presence of Christ among his people, and illuminate God's unconditional love in such a dark and desperate milieu. What is striking is that, in the midst of such unprecedented ugliness and pain, the young Wojtyla closes his letter with the words: "I send you greetings in the name of Beauty, which is the profile of God, the cause of Christ, and the cause of Poland."[1]

But what is this profile? We might begin by recognizing that it is the final Christian hope to see the beautiful Face of God. Many centuries ago, St. Anselm of Canterbury had cried out from his monastic cell: "Your face, O Lord! I long to see your Face; I was made to see your Face, and I

A talk given to Cardinal Maida's Center for Youth and Family, Detroit, June 2003.

1. A letter of Nov. 2, 1939, written to Mieczyslaw Kotlarczyk, in *The Making of the Pope of the Millennium,* ed. A. Boniecki, MIC (Stockbridge, MA: Marian Press, 2000), 63. A priest recalls the young student Wojtyla arriving to serve the priest's mass at the outbreak of the war, Sept. 1, 1939: "The morning air raids of Krakow caused a panic among the workers of the Cathedral, so I had no one to serve mass for me. Karol came along just then. I will never forget the first wartime mass, at the altar of Christ Crucified, amid the howl of sirens and the blasts of explosions" (p. 62).

have not yet done that for which I was made." For us today, this call for vision is the call to courage, to "be not afraid," words spoken by Pope John Paul II at his inauguration.² It remains the call to make out of the present ugliness of much that we hear and see on the nightly news—to make out the features of that Beauty, ever old yet ever new, aged in years yet shining with youth. We saw it in Toronto during the World Youth Days, shining in the lined face of the aged and fragile Pope. If the Pope finds enthusiasm in his encounter with the young, does he not see in their face and in their energy, the selfsame manifestation of that Beauty?

The schoolmen of the Middle Ages saw it too, and none more keenly than St. Thomas Aquinas. He reflected upon the very fabric of reality itself, and saw in the texture of being the enduring presence of the true, the good, and the beautiful, for they served as companions on his journey, as they serve today on ours. With his contemporaries he saw images of that selfsame beauty in the round of daily activities: in song and prayer and in the drama of the mass, but also in the cycle of feast days. How reassuring, too, the beauty of what men's hands had built: the village church, the cathedral in the city, and more dramatically the drama of the liturgy and the festive color of saint's days, as God's Face shone forth, both within, in prayer and contemplation, and without, in stained glass and stone. The costumes of the guilds and sodalities contrasted with the drab quality of many ordinary days, giving a visual reassurance of future joys. St. Thomas' contemporaries heard the austere plainsong, recapping in its simplicity the sounds of nature; and they heard, too, the cultivated chant of choirs whenever they were able to come in from their labors.

Removed from the Middle Ages in time but not in spirit, Gerard Manley Hopkins has given voice to the beauty of the world and its Source:

> The world is charged with the grandeur of God.
> It will flame out, like shining from shook foil;
> It gathers to a greatness . . .
> And for all this, nature is never spent;
> There lives the dearest freshness deep down things;
> And though the last lights off the black West went
> Oh, morning, at the brown brink eastward, springs—
> Because the Holy Ghost over the bent
> World broods with warm breast and with ah bright wings.³

---

2. This is the express theme and principal motivation for the promulgation of John Paul II's encyclical letter *Fides et ratio*, which calls for a renewed courage of mind and will, heart and spirit, echoing the words of the angel Gabriel to Mary at the Annunciation: Luke 1:30–31: *Me phobou!;* Vulgate: *ne timeas Maria.* ["Do not be afraid, Mary."]

3. "God's Grandeur," in Gerard Manley Hopkins, *Poems and Prose* (New York: Penguin, 1985), p. 27.

But the people of the Middle Ages saw, too, the beauty of a nature that could be harsh and cruel in its frequent famines, fires, and floods; but that could yet blaze forth with the terrible glory of God. How welcome, after the dreary cold months, was the early spring sun whose warmth awakened the flowers in the field, and whose summer heat promised to satisfy the gaunt and hungry flesh that had weathered the dead cold of winter days. They were familiar, too—all too familiar—with the constant presence of death in their midst, that dark and looming shadow that snatched away the young and the old, purloined the weak and not seldom even the strong. No doubt, the contrast of light and shadow, joy and grief, made for a release into the order and radiance of beauty that was more surprising still. A society such as ours, that has elevated comfort to a first principle, is not likely to savor the beautiful as keenly. In such a setting as St. Thomas experienced, on the other hand, it is not strange that he defined beauty as that which being seen pleases: *id quod visum placet*.[4] Still, this only scratches the surface of beauty, since, properly speaking, such a description is called a merely nominal definition which does not penetrate to the thing itself; it refers back to us and to the effect that beauty has upon us, rather than disclosing the essence of beauty itself.

But, if this is the world that God has made, we might rightly expect that it would bear some distant resemblance to *His* beauty and not only present itself for our satisfaction. We would expect the world to be that mirror of which St. Paul speaks.[5] And is this mirror of faith not the pro-

---

4. St. Thomas, *STh* I, 5, 4, ad 1m: "pulchra enim dicuntur quae visa placent." To the objection that the good cannot be a final cause, because it is praised as beautiful, whereas beauty implies the notion of a formal cause, Thomas replies: "Dicendum quod pulchrum et bonum in subiecto quidem sunt idem, quia super eandem rem fundantur, scilicet super formam; et propter hoc, bonum laudatur ut pulchrum. Sed ratione different. Nam bonum proprie respicit appetitum; est enim bonum quod omnis appetunt. Et ideo habet rationem finis, nam appetitus est quasi quidam motus ad rem. Pulchrum autem respicit vim cognoscitivam; pulchra enim dicuntur quae visa placent. Unde pulchrum in debita proportione consistit, quia sensus delectatur in rebus debite proportionatis, sicut in sibi similibus, nam et sensus ratio quaedam est, et omnis virtus cognoscitiva. Et quia cognitia fit per assimilationem, similitudo autem respicit formam, pulchrum proprie pertinent ad rationem causae formalis." ["Beauty and good in a subject are the same, for they are based upon the same thing, namely, the form; and so good is praised as beauty. But they differ in meaning, for good relates to the appetite; good being what all things desire. Thus it has the aspect of an end, for appetite is a kind of movement towards a thing. Beauty, however, relates to the knowing power, for beautiful things please when seen. Hence beauty consists in due proportion, for the senses delight in things duly proportioned, as things similar to themselves, for even sense is a sort of reason, as is every knowing power. Because knowledge by assimilation and likeness relates to form, beauty properly pertains to formal cause."]

5. First Letter to the Corinthians 13:12: *Blepomen gar arti di esoptrou en ainigmati*. ["For now we see in a mirror, dimly."]

file to which the young Wojtyla had pointed? Indeed, this very word, *mirror*, occurs later in Wojtyla's major philosophical work.[6] The word describes the way in which the objects of our mind and heart, having been "constituted in the field of consciousness" by the dynamics of the mind, acquire a properly human and spiritual way of being. For in the attentive reception of the objects of consciousness we become aware of their beauty and receive beauty into our own personal hearth and home at the center of our conscious life. To be sure, in this life, we do not see Beauty "face to face," but rather "as in a mirror darkly"; yet for all that we see it luminously and are caught up in its gladsome and wondrous light. Jerome LeJeune, the Catholic biogeneticist who isolated the Down syndrome gene, spoke of man as the animal who could be filled with admiration, the *animal admirante* who could be swept up by the radiance of the beautiful.

Still, neither the natural nor the religious setting of the Middle Ages is quite ours today, and so we must dust off that mirror and look again. After several centuries of industrial and post-industrial economy and its increasing urbanization, and during the recent flood of information and misinformation, and the virtual presences of television, the Internet, and the communications revolution, most of us live in an environment almost exclusively of planned and unplanned human design. Precise straight lines are nowhere to be seen in nature, yet they are everywhere before our eyes as we walk along our streets; nowhere in nature yet everywhere in the city. They intend to remove us from nature to a more abstract world, more comfortable and more controlled, and they succeed in doing so. They surround us with manmade comfort in place of a more robust and less predictable confrontation with nature. Please don't misunderstand me! Almost no one wants to go back!! But, the question arises: whether the profile (of which the young Wojtyla spoke) is actually so clearly to be seen in the contemporary mirror that through a secular prism reflects our own image back upon us from the glass towers, the neat suburban lawns, the shopping malls, and the superhighways that dominate the cityscape.

The media guru Marshall McLuhan wryly commented that, whereas the Gothic cathedral pointing skyward to God was the exemplary architectural form of the thirteenth century, the model form of the twentieth is the multi-lane freeway. And indeed, the latter does express our love of the freedom of movement, just as the modern sciences are scienc-

---

6. *Persona e atto*, ed. Giovanni Reale and Tadeusz Styczen (Ruscon Libri, 1999; a bilingual redaction of the 3rd edition of *Osoba i Czyn*), 101ff. Cf. the 1st edition in English, *The Acting Person*, 31ff.

es of the study of movement, whether in the classical modern form of Newton's laws of motion, or Einstein's postmodern relativity of motion. But, if beauty is everywhere according to St. Thomas, then it should be found in movement as well and in our present environment. For the "good news" remains what it always has been, even though the condition of those who hear it alters; as does the shape and the manner in which beauty manifests itself. And so we come to our question: What has beauty to tell us about our present condition and the profile of God?

BEAUTY AS ALWAYS

Beauty delivers itself to us at three levels. There is most obviously the surface charm that first strikes the eye, ear, and mind and stirs the emotions. But then there is a second level at which the very nature and essence of beauty offers itself to be understood and celebrated through a devoted and sustained philosophical meditation. And finally, there is the unmerited and mysterious presence of beauty in the life of grace, the spiritual beauty that is revealed to us in faith. Everyone is familiar with the surface level of beauty, and so I pass on to the philosophical reflection on its nature. What, then, is beauty?

Although we cannot restore to its fullness the actual architectural and liturgical scene of St. Thomas' day, nor should we even attempt to do so, we can still learn something from the way he understood his environment which, like ours, manifested all three levels. Indeed, this can prove valuable for us in our situation; and so, it is helpful to gain a little clarity about the very nature of beauty. For the schoolmen speak of beauty as one of the transcendentals. By this word they mean that it overflows every special and restricted kind or type of being. They mean that beauty is omnipresent in the very texture of reality itself. This is a bold claim, if not an outright absurdity! And we instinctively draw back from it. Surely they couldn't mean that everything is beautiful? And yet that is just what they did mean, though not necessarily in our terms. We can hardly expect you to find beauty in a savage beast about to eat you. Yet scientists in their laboratory will speak admiringly of the beauty of a deadly virus. The schoolmen meant that, properly understood, being itself, *esse* or existence, in its depths is beautiful, and things *(res)* are more or less beautiful in varying degrees.

Given the plentiful evidence of the many ugly things we encounter, such a claim is difficult to understand. Nevertheless, it provides a sort of compass to guide our thoughts back towards the Source of reality and along the path that links our present world to that divine Source. If we accept that God made the world and saw it as good and well-formed

(Genesis 1–2),[7] we may begin to see in what sense beauty is the profile of God Who made everything in the heavens and on the earth. St. Thomas, commenting on the treatise on *The Divine Names* by Dionysius, found beauty to be the motive and reason for God's creating the world in the first place. He wrote:

> Because God possesses His own beauty, he wished to multiply it as far as possible through the communication of his own likeness [which every being bears]: Quia (Deus) propriam pulchritudinem habet, vult eam multiplicare, sicut possibile est, scilicet per communicationem suae similitudinis.

And he adds:

> For all things are made so that they may portray the divine beauty in some way: *Omnia enim facta sunt, ut divinam pulchritudinem qualitercumque imitentur.*[8]

It is time to undertake a fresh attempt at grasping beauty in its deeper vein and more hidden manifestation, the second level of its manifestation. And here we look to what St. Thomas denotes as the transcendental features of the nature or essence of the beautiful. In more than one text, he tells us that its properties are three: clarity or radiance, proportion or harmony, and integrity or wholeness.

Clarity or radiance[9] is what first draws us to a beautiful object, whether it be a painting, a scene from nature, or a person. By clarity, however, we do not simply mean ordinary brightness, for even the darkest of nights may call forth an experience of the beautiful lit by a pale and fleeting moon, and the sunless depths of the sea under certain conditions may disclose its marvelous treasures. But those necessary conditions tell us something about beauty. For some light, of greater or lesser brilliance, and from some source must play upon the distinct figures and forms or we have nothing to see, nothing to marvel at. I recall a dusty, shabby carved foot of a bureau in my room in Qom, Iran, where I had been invited to give a talk. It was uninterestingly drab throughout

---

7. The Hebrew text reads: *tov*, which can mean well-made, fair, or good-looking (Armand Maurer, CSB, *About Beauty: A Thomistic Interpretation* [Houston, TX: Center for Thomistic Studies, 1983], 46); the Septuagint reads: *kalon*, with the double meaning of good and beautiful; while the Vulgate reads: *bonum*. In a related usage, Ps. 103:1 uses *decor* as does 92:1; but 95:6 reads *confessio et pulchritudo in conspectus eius* (and the version for liturgical use from Pius XII reads: *majestas et decor*).

8. *In Div. Nom.*, ch. 4, lect. 5, n. 352; and n. 353; cited by A. Maurer in *About Beauty*,65. Maurer's whole work, with references to contemporary art, is rewarding, and was of great use in the preparation of this paper. Incidentally, *imitor* is part of the classical vocabulary of *pulchritudo*.

9. The terms are drawn from vision and light, but can be applied analogously as when we might remark upon the clarity of a horn solo or the crispness of a dancer's movements.

the day until the rays of the late afternoon sun played upon its unremarkable contours to make its rough shape shine with the radiance of pure gold. The appreciation of beauty arises in and through the relation of some thing to our senses or our mind, and it emerges in the thing itself from a source of inner or outer light that releases its beauty.

This intimate association of light with beauty marks, for St. Thomas, the ingredient of knowledge that is present in beauty, so that the beautiful always has a cognitive element in it, though not necessarily in a form that can be expressed adequately in ideas, concepts, and words. It is this insight that has led artists, particularly in the twentieth century, to create works of art that are deliberately non-representational, so-called abstract art. This development challenges many who are puzzled by the intent of such works. There is no need to accept everything that claims to be abstract art. Dada is almost always bad art, as is every attempt to gain an immediate shock value; but at its best abstract art strives to meet the cognitive demands of a vision of beauty that moves in a more intellectual atmosphere. The break with representational art that disturbs many is also a confirmation of its cognitive character as long as it remains subject to the three criteria of beauty. For each thing that is really beautiful possesses some degree of truth, even though it may challenge us to see its truth and to appreciate it. This is what the poet Keats observed, when he wrote, "Truth is beauty, beauty truth." In many intellectual circles today, far removed from the robust sense of the Renaissance or even from the softer melancholic enthusiasm of the Romantics, even the driest of academics will at some point declare that such and such a thing or topic is "interesting," that is, in some sense attractive and even perhaps fascinating *(fascinans)*. This is the pale mark of beauty in a muted and overly rationalized world.

The second feature of beauty, Thomas tells us, is the intrinsic order of parts, i.e., proportion or harmony.[10] And indeed, as we look out at the waters of a lovely lake into the light of a setting sun or an evening moon, we are struck with an inner order that composes the scene, a harmony that lends its gracious luminosity to the scene. We experience a certain "rightness" or unity that we also find in a well-played symphony, a well-performed dance, a well-composed painting, or a well-directed life. The parts and stages somehow fit together. Nevertheless, that "fit" may accommodate a very different set of elements and aspects. For we appreciate the beauty of some things precisely because of the intrinsic contrast

---

10. These terms are drawn above all from the domain of sound, though they can also be applied analogously to the composition of a painting, the arrangement of wild or domestic plants, and the congruence of colors in a painting or structures in a building.

of their parts. Every tragedy expresses the conflict of pain and pleasure, of freedom and necessity, of happy fortune and ill outcome, of good and evil, and gains through the contrast.

And the third feature of beauty, Thomas tells us, is the integrity of the object, a certain wholeness that spells completion and that gives us at least a fleeting sense of rest.[11] Nothing in our experience, of course, is perfectly complete, and few artists are entirely satisfied that they have communicated the full beauty of their vision to the canvas or the score, to the building or the performance. Yet what is beautiful stands out in an imperfect world because it reaches towards a distinctive fullness even as it may promise something more. That is why painters continue to paint, gallery-goers continue to watch, and concert-goers continue to listen. Yet we experience a kind of coming to rest in the relative totality of a plenitude that suggests yet more.

I think that with these three characteristics, St. Thomas has drawn a very sound profile of the general character of beauty. It draws us towards itself insofar as it presents itself as something true and authentic, and as something good and attractive. And in this lies the unitive power of genuine beauty.[12] It is the integrative power to embody the companionate transcendentals of unity *(unum)* and relation *(aliquid)*, and above all, to draw together the honesty of truth *(verum)* and the value of the good *(bonum)* and thereby to give them a face. And this drawing power is always ready to be placed at the service of the truth, the goodness, and the beauty of the Gospel. In sum, then, the radiance of beauty attracts us, its goodness empowers us, and its integrity perfects us. Integrity is the capstone of the fullness of beauty; for if we let the radiance alone cast a spell over us, we fall into a superficial pursuit of pleasure; and if we separate the good from its attractiveness we reduce the good to a joyless moralism of imposed duty. In its threefold fullness, on the other hand, we are lured by the beauty of nature, art, and liturgy.

BEAUTY AND ITS COMPANIONS

Now the schoolmen saw that, inasmuch as genuine beauty brought together both truth and goodness, it does not stand alone. It is the companion of the other transcendental features of reality, and is above all a friend of the good and the true. And so, to understand what beauty is in

---

11. This feature seems to be associated above all with being and unity, since it seals the ontological identity of the natural thing as well as the work of art. It too must be acknowledged in analogous ways, since what is integrity for a person and a life is not the same as that for a work of art or a display of nature.

12. See David Schindler, "Is Truth Ugly?" *Communio* 27, no. 4 (2000): 701–28.

its very nature, we need to give some thought to the company it keeps.[13] Now Aristotle tells us that the good is that which all desire because it is that which can fulfill our emptiness in one way or another. But this description tells us more about ourselves than it tells us about the nature of the good; for we can go on to ask: But why and how is it that the good is that which satisfies our desire?

Plato was enamored of the good, for he thought it towered above all other considerations. And he tells us that, while we might put up with a plausible story if we can get nothing better, no one wants a merely plausible or apparent good; we want the real thing.[14] Herein lies the mystery of the evil and the ugly. Even the serial killer commits his foul crime for what he takes to be a good: a perverted pleasure in inflicting pain upon others; a misguided sense of power inducing fear and a savage control over the daily lives of thousands; or yet again, futile revenge against imagined ills. We don't have to live long to come to see that we may be mistaken about the true good that is able to improve our humanity; but Plato's point is that though we may be mistaken because we are fallible, we will pursue even our illusions, not because we take them to be illusory, but because we mistake them for what is genuinely good. The need for a real good still holds us under its spell. And here we glimpse the first stage in understanding the good; for, like all transcendental properties of being, we find that its call is unavoidable, even if we distort it. We may pursue false goods, but we pursue them because, through carelessness or perversion, deliberately or inadvertently, we take them to be real. And this unavoidability indicates that the good is intrinsic to the texture of reality itself and of relevance within our own structure as persons.

This inescapable pre-eminence of the good, in the very texture of reality and of our lives as God intended them, may not be so easily seen today as we may like to think it might have been in St. Thomas' time. The reason is that there has been a shift in expectation that is widely operative in our culture and that directly affects our emotional life. Let me explain. For almost two thousand years in Western culture, from Aristotle to the Renaissance, it was held to be undeniable that every essential desire rooted in the very structure of human nature could not be entirely empty of the realization it promised.[15] And so, for example, it was held

---

13. In St. Thomas' technical language (*STh* I, 5, 2c), the transcendental properties of being differ *secundum rationem but not ad rem;* they are one in being, though they differ in conception. The same is said of all the transcendentals: *ens, res, unum, aliquid, verum,* and *bonum.* (See *Quaestiones disputatae de Veritate* I,1).
14. *Republic* 505d.
15. See, for example, the argument that man is possessed of an incorruptible, spiritual principle because he is an intellectual creature who is capable of grasping the significance

that because we desire existence as such from the very depths of our being, this desire was a sign *(signum)* pointing towards its realization in immortal life.

What has happened, however, is that with the development of critical reason and what has been called the hermeneutics of suspicion, the dark conviction has arisen that such desires cannot be fulfilled, that they are empty. This differs greatly from ancient authors such as Plato, for whom, however difficult the climb towards the virtuous life, the expectation of fulfillment was in principle realizable. With the modern hermeneutics of suspicion, on the other hand, the conviction, or at least the suspicion, has grown that our deepest desires are themselves illusions, including our basic desire for knowledge and for happiness.[16]

We need simply to recall Freud's *The Future of an Illusion,* in which he interprets our fundamental desires as deceptive masks for the sexual drive (libido) and the death instinct (thanatos drive). Milan Kundera's novel *The Unbearable Lightness of Being* graphically expresses the sense of emptiness. It details a series of sexual affairs that lead to nothing, to utter meaninglessness. But here again, the transcendental and omnipresent character of the good that ought to perfect us becomes manifest in the novel; for why should the failure of desire be felt to be empty except by the suppressed expectation of something better, the irrepressible hope that is buried in our very bones: the expectation, namely, of a good that can perfect our very humanity?

I have spent some time depicting the nature of the good, because the attractive power of beauty presents itself as a kind of good. It is as though, in their association, beauty and the good are twinned, though in the same being and so in Siamese style. But the friendship of the good and the beautiful embraces also that of truth, so that we ought perhaps to speak of transcendental triplets.

For St. Augustine said something similar about the unavoidability of truth. He remarks that he has known many who would like to deceive others but none who wish themselves to be deceived.[17] We need only recall the recent indignant uproar over the market shenanigans at Enron. Though we ought to recall also that it is easier to complain when others have betrayed the truth, while we sometimes struggle to accept an un

---

of a continued and trans-temporal existence *(esse absolute et secundum omne tempus).* If not a fully demonstrated argument, it was at least a strong sign and a firm principle. (St. Thomas, *STh* I, q. 75, a. 5c: *Naturale autem desiderium non potest esse anane.*)

16. This prevalent disillusion is a major theme of the encyclical *Fides et ratio* See note 2 above.

17. *Confessions* X, 23, 33 (Loeb Classical Library [Cambridge, MA: Harvard University Press, 1912]): "Multos expertus sum, qui vellent fallere, qui autem falli, neminem." (Cited in *Fides et ratio* 25.)

welcome truth in our own lives.[18] Or to change examples, when Marxists criticized so-called "bourgeois" truth, they did it in the name of what they took to be a greater, better truth. Or again, when Einstein criticized and improved upon Newton, he did it in the name of a truer vision of the cosmos. Nietzsche, too, tried to reduce the good operative in nineteenth-century European culture to an allegedly outdated Christianity in the interest of what he took to be a greater good; and he dismissed the truth which he identified with Kant's philosophy of mere appearance in order to secure what he thought was a greater truth. And so, he preached the Overman and the will to power in the name of a better good and a truer truth.

It is significant, however, that when he came to beauty he could not overcome it. For he defines it truthfully, telling us that when power descends graciously, there is beauty.[19] Perhaps this insight anticipates the present condition of the broader secular culture within which we live and think, and indicates the present frontier for a common public discourse between believers and non-believers regarding serious issues required for a fruitful life together. For in our present culture we can talk neither metaphysics nor morality, neither about creation nor about right and wrong, and expect to share even enough agreement to carry on a mutually serious conversation regarding such issues as abortion, divorce, or celibacy.

BEAUTY AS PERSONAL CALLING AND PUBLIC DISCOURSE

Can the face of beauty help us to enter into a more serious public discourse with a variety of our fellows? It would be a mistake to think of the three characteristics (clarity or radiance, inner order or harmony, and integrity or wholeness) as merely formal and empty criteria that lose their relevance when we seek to apply them. On the contrary, there are more or less definite conditions for what is beautiful that distinguishes it from the simply ugly or tasteless. For even though we may disagree over particular concrete embodiments of the beautiful, we respect

18. Marcel provides telling examples in the struggles of the would-be monk to discern whether he has a true vocation, the young couple with the gravely handicapped child who come to the realization that he needs institutional care, and the scientist who refuses to "betray" the conclusion of his research despite its contravention of the ideology of a repressive regime. (*The Mystery of Being*, vol. 1, ch. 4: "The Intelligible Background.")

19. *Thus Spoke Zarathustra* II (*Friedrich Nietzsche. Werke in drei Bänden*, ed. K. Schlechta [Munich: Carl Hanser, n.d.], vol. 2, 374; Eng. trans. by W. Kaufmann, *The Portable Nietzsche*, [New York: Viking, 1958], 230): "Where power becomes gracious *(gnädig)* and descends into the visible—such descent I call beauty." And: "It is not in satiety that his desire shall grow silent and be submerged, but in beauty." For an extended treatment of beauty as the principle theme of Nietzsche's philosophy, see Rüdiger Görner, *Nietzsches Kunst* (Frankfurt am Main/Leipzig: Insel Verlag, 2000).

beauty enough to argue about it under its governance in a way in which we are not likely to find many in the prevailing culture who will discuss metaphysics or even find agreement on basic moral values. In this sense, metaphysical language (about being and non-being) or moral discourse (about right and wrong) is more easily dismissed in the prevailing relativism of our culture.

Perhaps Nietzsche's insight into beauty anticipates the present condition of the broader secular culture within which we live and think. For in our present situation we can talk seriously only about procedural issues rather than substantive ones and hope to meet with any agreed upon consensus. But beauty still calls us, still attracts us, still interests us, still has an existential pull upon us. For the three beauty marks of clarity, order, and wholeness still invite us to participate in making our own lives beautiful. The presupposition, not an easy one, is that beauty can introduce a certain order and purposiveness in our lives, what was wont by the ancients to be called a virtuous life.

For the disagreements about what is beautiful or not beautiful do not arise from a mere relativism of taste. Rather, there are both subjective and objective conditions that account for our disagreements. There are perimeters and parameters to the effective presence of these criteria in any given object or situation.

The subjective conditions may lead us to find little or no interest in a work of art that others would almost die for. This is because of factors that differentiate us, one from another. We may give the easy examples first. If one is tone-deaf he will not likely be drawn to a love of music, although even here there are remarkable instances of music appreciation through touch. Or if one is colorblind she is not likely to appreciate the beauty of a painted sky or a sunset.

But there are more subtle differences as well, such as a lack of knowledge of more intricate musical patterns and sounds; or more or less interest in and previous knowledge of the historical setting of a novel; or again, more aesthetic interest in natural representation than in formal design. But such differences tell us more about the degree of our openness and ability to enter into an appreciation of a particular manifestation of beauty than it tells us about the actual presence of beauty in the object itself, be it a novel or a painting or a building.

On the objective side of the beautiful artwork itself, there are concrete requirements, since not every material is suitable in successfully producing a particular work. We can argue about the content of an artwork and whether the materials used have served it well. Thus, for example, the artist's vision of what he intends to create may be much looser if he is working in oils than if he is engraving on a copper plate, since an unsatisfactory brush stroke in oils can be altered whereas the stylus that draws a line in the copper is fixed once and for all. Or again, in music, the composer directs which instruments best express the desired sound; and in architecture the very function and site of the building must be taken into account.

What is more, at the personal level affecting each of us intimately, as distinct from the public and social level, this understanding of beauty is no merely academic profile. It touches us at our core. For it is the task of each of us to unite these transcendentals within our own lives. That task is laid upon us by the very texture of reality and the given structure of our own being.[20] It is part of the task of personal integration and transcendence of which John Paul speaks in *The Acting Person,* and which the young Wojtyla intimated in his vision of a new Athens. If, instead, we separate out the truth from its companions, it becomes merely correctness, coherence, and validity; if we separate out the good from its associates, it becomes merely what we desire, subjective opinion, or pleasure; but if we are drawn into their unity in and through our "disinterested interest" in beauty, not simply to possess it but to praise it as we admire it,[21] then we are free to realize a more fully human perfection and perhaps even work towards a more fully human community. Our lives will undergo an upward thrust rather than continuing along a merely horizontal line. The foregoing portrait of beauty is meant to help us both understand it and understand the grounds for our admiration of it, and thereby help us to participate in it. But it is up to us to cultivate an interest in beauty, to pursue it, to care for the natural environment, and to support artists and liturgists in their work, so that we might create what the young Wojtyla had in mind when he spoke of a new Athens.

SACRED BEAUTY

Now, Nietzsche would agree that beauty is not simply "that which, being seen, pleases." And we too are called upon to enlarge our understanding of what St. Thomas' characterization of beauty expresses. And here, the very Christianity that Nietzsche so rebelled against has had its say, even in our secular culture. For it has expanded and deepened the range of what might be considered beautiful. This is evident in the work of artists (such as Goya) who take up what is ordinarily ugly and give it

---

20. See Karol Wojtyla, *Persona e Atto* part III, ch. 5 and 6, 445ff. (*The Acting Person,* 189ff.) It is through free action that we are called to integrate the various levels of our bodily and mental dynamisms (physical happenings and processes, the emotional, subconscious, intellectual, and voluntary drives) in and through our freedom (autodetermination). As we do this, we transcend to a new inner threshold of our being.

21. The paradoxical term "disinterested interest" derives from Kant, who sought to distinguish the desire of possession from the attitude of non-possessive admiration, but it is already acknowledged in the classical profile of beauty.

an aesthetic context and value. A composer may incorporate high levels of dissonance in a work without destroying its radiance and integrity.

Nevertheless, a truly unprecedented mode of beauty is revealed to the believer as he or she gazes upon the stricken face of the Lord on the cross. The anonymous seventeenth-century German hymn *Fairest Jesus* expresses this beauty with touching simplicity:

> Fair are the meadows! Fairer still the woodlands...
> Jesus shines clearer than all the heavenly host on high.

For the believer has learned that, while there is little that is immediately pleasing in the wizened face of the poor, the sick, the leprous, or those dying of AIDS, there can be a greater beauty hidden within the pain and the suffering. It is this sense of beauty that led the young Wojtyla to commend it as the very profile of the Face of God in the face of inhuman ugliness and evil. We have many examples of such beauty in the two-thousand-year history of the faith. When St. Francis descended from his richly adorned horse to kiss the leprous beggar, was this not in some unusual sense a beautiful gesture and an even more beautiful act? To be sure, something deeply human in our nature revolts when confronted by what is ugly and diseased, and disfigured by suffering, and this is no doubt initially a healthy response, since we are not called to value the ugly as such. Yet, for all that, there is something beautiful in the wedding of poverty with the riches of mercy; something gracious in the kindness that does not overlook the needs of the most unfortunate; something beautiful about the figure of Mother Teresa cradling a wasted and unwashed child in her arms, or Jean Vanier tending to the needs of the mentally handicapped. It is here that we are invited to a new level of contemplation of the beautiful, and not simply to a reversal of values, but to a transvaluation of ordinary values, to an extraordinary transcendence of the ordinary. Indeed, a specifically Christian art is called to redeem the ugly by situating it in an aesthetic context, not simply in order to heighten the lovely by contrast, but to place it in the service of agapic Love. It is here, as a character says towards the end of the film *Babette's Feast*, that beauty and mercy kiss. But this requires a continuing and fresh attempt at grasping beauty in its deeper vein and more hidden manifestation. It is this beauty that calls us to holiness and to evangelization, for it is the beauty of sanctity.

In this way, each of us, and in a special way the artist, is called to serve beauty as a witness to the "good news."[22] Now just as the Gospel calls

---

22. See, on the occasion of the completion of the restoration of the Sistine Chapel, John Paul's remarks on the artist as participating as *imago Dei* in and through his creative activity, and also his appreciative comments in the *Letter to Artists* (April 1999, Libreria Editrice Vaticana).

everyone to a new life in grace, so too beauty reveals a new and gracious face unlike that of any other. Indeed, with the entry of Christianity through the Incarnation, everything has changed and keeps changing according to the providential guidance of God. John Paul tells us that history and the history of culture are very important for Christianity and for mankind.[23] Having entered time, Christ calls us not merely to a reversal but also to a transvaluation of values. And we see that transformation in the depths and configurations of beauty as affected by the values of the Gospel. Beauty thereby is revealed as present to and in much that by ordinary standards is held to be ugly. Is it too much to say that, just as the Gospel calls us as sinners to a new life, it calls even the ugly to a new face? By ordinary standards, Mother Teresa was scarcely a fashion model, yet must we not acknowledge that her life was in the deepest sense a beautiful life, and that it was not so much her life as her Lord's life, so that through her there shone the profile of divine beauty, as it does in the lives of the saints?[24] By ordinary standards Jean Vanier's work with the mentally handicapped of L'Arche was not the work of a successful entrepreneur; yet we admire his lifestyle in much the same way we admire other striking persons, places, and things. Here beauty acquires a pronounced quality of nobility and magnanimity.

Christianity has worked its disclosive influence far beyond the borders of the Church, in what *Dominus Jesus* calls "the kingdom of God." For its presence, even in our secular culture, has had both obvious and hidden effects, reaching out to touch even those who are not Christian. A former student told me of a cultivated Zen Buddhist master who confronted a livid Crucifix of the Suffering Christ, and who turned with anger to my friend, saying: What kind of a God could do that to his Son? In this sensitive non-Christian, the representation was enough to challenge the ordinary values associated with the sacred. And I recall a startling Crucifix in a restored church in Warsaw that had no arms, legs, or head! It had been found among the rubble of the bombed-out church, and was about to be cast away, when the pastor was struck with the appropriateness of this statue that had been robbed of its initial beauty by the savagery of war, and he saw in that the unseen and unseeable image of the suffering Christ who had given his very substance for us. Of a sudden, the broken crucifix was seen to have a transformed sense of clarity, order, and integrity, the integrity of the divine gift of redemption reaching out to all mankind.

Indeed, the liturgy calls us to move from its radiance to the inner order, proportion, and harmony of its parts and stages so that we might

---

23. *Fides et ratio* 11–12.
24. St. Paul, "Life to me is Christ..." (Phil. 1:21), and "not I but Christ lives in me."

come to rest in the realization of the perfect, complete, and integral sacrifice and sacrament of the Eucharist, and to carry this in and through the witness of our lives.[25] This personal journey is given to us through personal prayer and the prayer of the Church, as well as through the solidarity of communal action with others and the witness of the saints. If our witness is clarion, then that passage may attract others by its radiance to penetrate to the transcendent order of God's ways, ways that are often disturbing by ordinary standards, and yet further towards the fullness of His grace. This is the call to a strange and wondrous beauty that discloses in the most intimate possible way the very profile of God, of a beauty which "eye hath not seen, nor ear heard," but which is glimpsed in a mirror darkly as the very profile of an Unconditioned Love.

In sum, then, having reflected upon the three levels of beauty: that of charm, essence, and grace, we have sought to enter into an appreciation of its three characteristics, those of radiance, harmony, and integrity; and through a consideration of its most intimate companions, the true and the good, we have seen the power of beauty to follow a path which leaves nothing behind, carrying its radiance with it to its interior harmony, so as to come to rest in the appreciation of the wholeness and integrity of the sacredness of reality itself. In this way, through its own prism we glimpse that beauty which is greatest of all: the beauty of unconditioned, gratuitous, and fairest Love.

25. We have here the universal call to holiness expressed also in Karol Wojtyla's call to personal integration in and through the transcendence of our present state towards a growing maturity and love of God.

Bibliography

Ackerman, Bruce. *Social Justice in the Liberal State.* New Haven, CT: Yale University Press, 1980.
Adorno, Theodor W. *Gesammelte Schriften.* Frankfurt am Main: Suhrkamp, 1981.
Adorno, Theodor W., and Max Horkheimer. *Dialectic of Enlightenment.* Trans. J. Cumming. New York: Herder and Herder, 1972.
Anselm. *Monologium.* Trans. and ed. J. Hopkins and H. W. Richardson. Toronto: Edwin Mellen, 1975.
———. *S. Anselmi Opera Omnia.* Ed. F. S. Schmitt. Stuttgart: Frommann, 1968.
Ariew, R. *Descartes and the Last Scholastics.* Ithaca, NY: Cornell University Press, 1999.
Aristotle. *The Basic Works of Aristotle.* Ed. Richard McKeon. New York: Random House, 1941.
———. *De anima.*
———. *Metaphysics.*
———. *Physics.*
Athanasius. *Contra Arianos.* Oxford: Clarendon, 1844.
———. *De Decretis.* In *The Nicene and Post-Nicene Fathers.* Reprint, Grand Rapids, MI: Eerdmans, 1987.
Augustine. *The Confessions of St. Augustine.* Trans. John K. Ryan. Garden City, NY: Doubleday, 1960. Also trans. William Watts, 1631; reprinted Loeb Classical Library. Cambridge, MA: Harvard University Press, 1912.
Ayer, Alfred J. *Language, Truth and Logic.* London: Gollancz, 1936.
Bacon, Francis. *Novum Organum.* Ed. T. Fowler. Oxford: Clarendon, 1889.
Balthasar, Hans Urs von. *The Glory of the Lord.* Trans. O. Davies et al. San Francisco: Ignatius, 1991.
Barnes, Jonathan. *Early Greek Philosophy.* New York: Penguin, 1987.
Barry, Brian. *The Liberal Theory of Justice: A Critical Examination of the Principal Doctrines in "A Theory of Justice" by John Rawls.* Oxford: Clarendon, 1973.
Baynes, K., J. Bohman, and T. McCarthy. *After Philosophy: End or Transformation?* Cambridge, MA: MIT Press, 1987.
Berlin, Isaiah. "Two Concepts of Liberty." In *Four Essays on Liberty.* Oxford: Oxford University Press, 1986.
Blackburn, S., and K. Simmons, eds. *Truth: Oxford Readings in Philosophy.* Oxford: Oxford University Press, 1999.
Boethius. *Contra Eutychen.* Trans. H. F. Stewart and E. K. Rand. Loeb Classical Library. Cambridge, MA: Harvard University Press, 1962.
Boniecki, A., ed. *The Making of the Pope of the Millennium.* Stockbridge, MA: Marian Press, 2000.
Bosanquet, B. *The Essentials of Logic.* London: Macmillan, 1895.

Bourke, V. J. *The Pocket Aquinas*. New York: Washington Square, 1960.
Burnet, John. *Early Greek Philosophy*. London: Adam and Charles Black, 1930.
Burtt, E. A., ed. *The English Philosophers from Bacon to Mill*. New York: Modern Library, 1939.
Cameron, A. *Christianity and the Rhetoric of Empire*. Berkeley: University of California Press, 1991.
Chenu, M. D. "Création et Histoire." In *St. Thomas Aquinas: 1274–1974 Commemorative Studies*. Toronto: Pontifical Institute of Mediaeval Studies, 1974.
Clarke, Norris. *Person and Being*. Milwaukee, WI: Marquette University Press, 1993.
Comte, August. *A General View of Positivism*. Trans. J. H. Bridges. New York: R. Speller, 1957.
Della Mirandola, Pico. *On the Dignity of Man*. Trans. Charles G. Wallis. Indianapolis: Bobbs-Merrill, 1965.
De Lubac, Henri. *Drama of Atheistic Humanism*. Trans. Edith M. Riley. New York: Sheed and Ward, 1950.
Denzinger, H. *Enchiridion Symbolorum*. Freiburg: Herder, 1963.
Derrida, Jacques. *Margins of Philosophy*. Chicago: University of Chicago Press, 1982.
———. *Of Grammatology*. Baltimore: Johns Hopkins University Press, 1976.
———. *L'Usage des Plaisirs*. Paris: Gallimard, 1984.
De Saussure, Ferdinand. *Course in General Linguistics*. La Salle, IL: Open Court, 1986.
Descartes, Rene. *Oeuvres de Descartes*. Ed. C. Adam and P. Tannery. Paris: Cerf, 1904.
DeVogel, Cornelia J. *The Concept of Personality in Greek and Christian Thought*. Studies in Philosophy and the History of Philosophy, vol. 2. Washington, DC: The Catholic University of America Press, 1963.
Diderot, Denis. "Entretien entre D'Alembert et Diderot," written 1769, published 1830.
Diels, H. *Die Fragmente der Vorsokratiker*. Ed. W. Kranz. Berlin: Weidmann, 1934–54.
Fabro, Cornelio. *La nozione metafisica de participazione*. Turin: Marietti, 1963.
Feiblemann, James K. *The Pious Scientist: Nature, God and Man in Religion*. New York: Bookman Associates, 1958.
Ferré, F., J. Kockelmans, and J. E. Smith. *The Challenge of Religion*. New York: Seabury, 1982.
Finance, Joseph de. *Etre et agir dans la philosophie de saint Thomas*. Paris: Beauchesne, 1945.
Forest, Aimé. *La structure métaphysique du concret selon S. Thomas d'Aquin*. Paris: Vrin, 1931.
Freud, Sigmund. *The Basic Writings of Sigmund Freud*. Trans. and ed. A. A. Brill. New York: The Modern Library, 1938.
Garceau, Benoit. *Judicium: Vocabulaire, sources, doctrine de saint Thomas d'Aquin*. Paris: Vrin, 2002.
Gaukroger, S. *Descartes: An Intellectual Biography*. Oxford: Clarendon, 1995.
Geiger, L. B. *La participation dans la philosophie de St. Thomas*. Paris: Vrin, 1953.
Gerson, Lloyd, ed. *Graceful Reason: Essays in Ancient and Mediaeval Philosophy Presented to Joseph Owens, CSSR*. Toronto: Pontifical Institute of Mediaeval Studies, 1983.
Gilby, Thomas. *The Phoenix and the Turtle*. London: Longmans Green, 1950.

Gilson, Etienne. *Being and Some Philosophers.* Toronto: Pontifical Institute of Mediaeval Studies, 1952.
———. *The Christian Philosophy of St. Thomas.* Trans. L. K. Shook. New York: Random House, 1956.
Görner, Rüdiger. *Nietzsches Kunst.* Frankfurt am Main/Leipzig: Insel Verlag, 2000.
Grillmeier, Alois. *Jesus der Christus im Glauben der Kirche.* Freiburg: Herder, 1981.
Hall, John A. *Liberalism: Politics, Ideology and the Market.* Chapel Hill: University of North Carolina Press, 1987.
Hegel, G. W. F. *Glauben und Wissen.* Hamburg: F. Meiner, 1962.
———. *Hegel's Phenomenology of Spirit.* Trans. A. V. Miller. Oxford: Clarendon, 1977.
———. *Wissenschaft der Logik*, 2 vols. Hamburg: F. Meiner, 1967. (*Hegel's Science of Logic*. Trans. A. V. Miller. New York: Humanities Press, 1969.)
Heidegger, Martin. *Wegmarken.* Frankfurt: Klostermann, 1967.
Henrici, P. "The One Who Went Unnamed: Maurice Blondel in the Encyclical 'Fides et Ratio.'" *Communio* 26 (1999): 609–21.
Hobbes, Thomas. *Body, Man and Citizen.* Trans. R. S. Peters. London: Collier-Macmillan, 1962.
———. *Leviathan.* Ed. C. B. Macpherson. New York: Penguin, 1985.
Holbach, Paul (Baron d'Holbach). *Systeme de la nature* and *Systeme sociale*. London, 1770, 1773.
Hopkins, Gerard Manley. *Poems and Prose.* New York: Penguin, 1985.
Hume, David. *Treatise.* Ed. L. A. Selby Bigge. Oxford: Clarendon, 1988.
Hyppolytus. *Against Noetus.* Patrologiae graeca (PG) 10:818.
Jacobi, Friedrich Heinrich. *Fichte, Jacobi, Schelling: Philosophy of German Idealism.* Ed. E. Behler. The German Library. New York: Continuum, 1941.
John Damascene. *On the Orthodox Faith.* PG 94:964.
John Paul II (see also under Karol Wojtyla). Encyclical *Fides et ratio.*
John Scotus Eriugena. *On the Division of Nature.* Trans. and ed. Myra L. Uhlfelder. Indianapolis: Bobbs-Merrill, 1976.
Kant, Immanuel. *Critique of Pure Reason.* Trans. N. Kemp Smith. London: Macmillan, 1950.
Kelly, J. N. D. *Early Christian Doctrines.* San Francisco: Harper and Row, 1960.
Kundera, Milan. *Art of the Novel.* New York: Harper and Row, 1993.
———. *The Unbearable Lightness of Being.* New York: Harper Perennial, 1991.
Leibniz, Gottfried. *The Monadology and Other Philosophical Writings.* Ed. R. Latta. Oxford: 1898.
Levinas, Emmanuel. *Totality and Infinity: An Essay on Exteriority.* Pittsburgh, PA: Duquesne University Press, 1969.
Locke, John. *Essay Concerning Human Understanding.* Ed. J. W. Yolton. London: Dent, 1964.
———. *Second Treatise on Government.* Ed. Thomas Peardon. Indianapolis: Bobbs-Merrill, 1952.
Long, Steven A. "Personal Receptivity and Act: A Thomistic Critique." *The Thomist* 61 (1997): 1–31.
Lyotard, Jean-Francois. *The Postmodern Condition: A Report on Knowledge.* Minneapolis: University of Minnesota Press, 1984.
MacIntyre, Alasdair. *Whose Justice? Which Rationality?* Notre Dame, IN: University of Notre Dame Press, 1988.

Marcel, Gabriel. *Being and Having: An Existential Diary.* Trans. Katherine Farrer. New York: Harper and Row, 1965.
———. *Du Refus à l'Invocation.* Paris: Editions Gallimard, 1940. (*Creative Fidelity.* Trans. Robert Rosthal. New York: Farrar Straus, 1964.)
———. *Homo Viator: Introduction to a Metaphysics of Hope.* Chicago: Henry Regnery, 1951.
———. *Man against Mass Society.* Trans. G. S. Fraser. Chicago: Henry Regnery, 1951.
———. *Metaphysical Journal.* Paris: Gallimard, 1927.
———. *The Mystery of Being.* Vol. 1, *Reflection and Mystery*, trans. G. S. Fraser. Vol. 2, *Faith and Reality*, trans. R. Hague. Chicago: Henry Regnery, 1960.
———. *The Philosophy of Existentialism.* Trans. Manya Harari. 6th ed. New York: Citadel, 1966.
Maritain, Jacques. *Antimoderne.* Paris: Editions de la Revue des jeunes, 1922.
———. "Compagnons de route." In *Étienne Gilson: Philosophe de la Chrétienté*, 275–95. Paris: Cerf, 1949.
———. *Creative Intuition in Art and Poetry.* New York: Meridian, 1957.
———. *Existence and the Existent.* New York: Doubleday, 1957.
———. *The Person and the Common Good.* Trans. John J. Fitzgerald. Notre Dame, IN: University of Notre Dame Press, 1966.
———. *Religion and Culture.* London: Sheed and Ward, 1931.
———. *Three Reformers: Luther-Descartes-Rousseau.* New York: Scribner's, 1929.
———. *True Humanism.* Trans. Margot Adamson. London: Geoffrey Bles, 1946.
Maurer, Armand. *About Beauty: A Thomistic Interpretation.* Houston, TX: Center for Thomistic Studies, 1983.
———. *The Division and Methods of the Sciences* (translation of Questions V and VI of Thomas Aquinas' Commentary on Boethius' De Trinitate). Toronto: Pontifical Institute of Mediaeval Studies, 1963.
———. *The Philosophy of William of Ockham in the Light of Its Principles.* Toronto: Pontifical Institute of Mediaeval Studies, 1999.
McMullin, E. *The Concept of Matter.* Notre Dame, IN: University of Notre Dame Press, 1977.
Mounier, Emmanuel. *Personalism.* Trans. Philip Mairet. Notre Dame, IN: University of Notre Dame Press, 1952.
Nédoncelle, M. "Prosopon et person dans l'antiquité classique." *Revue des Sciences Religieuse* 22 (1948): 277–99.
Newton, Isaac. *Principia.* Trans. Andrew Motte. Ed. Florian Cajori. Berkeley: University of California Press, 1966.
Nicholson, G. "Camus and Heidegger: Anarchists." *University of Toronto Quarterly* 41 (1971): 14–23.
———. "The Commune in *Being and Time.*" *Dialogue* 10 (1971): 708–26.
Nietzsche, Friedrich. *Friedrich Nietzsche. Werke in drei Banden.* Ed. K. Schlechta. Munich: Carl Hanser, 1956.
———. *The Portable Nietzsche.* Trans. Walter Kaufmann. New York: Viking, 1958.
Owens, Joseph. "Aquinas as Aristotelian Commentator." In *St. Thomas Aquinas: 1274–1974 Commemorative Studies.* Toronto: Pontifical Institute of Mediaeval Studies, 1974.
———. *St. Thomas and the Future of Metaphysics.* The Aquinas Lecture. Milwaukee, WI: Marquette University Press, 1957.
Pedersen, Olaf. *Early Physics and Astronomy.* Cambridge: Cambridge University Press, 1993.

Pelikan, J. *The Christian Tradition*. Vols. 1–3. Chicago: University of Chicago Press, 1971–78.
Peters, F. E. *Greek Philosophical Terms: A Historical Lexicon*. New York: New York University Press, 1967.
Pieper, Josef. "Göttlicher Wahnsinn," in *Eine Platon-Interpretation*. ("Divine Madness," in *Plato's Case against Secular Humanism*. Trans. Lothar Krauth. San Francisco: Ignatius, 1995.)
———. *Guide to Thomas Aquinas*. Notre Dame, IN: University of Notre Dame Press, 1957.
———. *Scholasticism (Scholastik)*. Trans. Richard and Clara Winston. New York: McGraw-Hill, 1964.
———. *The Silence of Saint Thomas*. Trans. John Murray and Daniel O'Connor. New York: Pantheon Books, 1957.
Plato. *Republic*. Trans. Paul Shorey. Loeb Classical Library. Cambridge, MA: Harvard University Press, 1931.
Przywara, Eric. *Analogia entis*. Freiburg: Einsiedeln, 1966.
Ramsey, Ian. *Religious Language*. London: SCM, 1957.
Rawls, John. *A Theory of Justice*. Cambridge, MA: Harvard University Press, 1971.
Richardson, Samuel. *Pamela*. Ed. Peter Sabor. New York: Penguin, 1980.
Robb, J. *Man as Infinite Spirit*. Milwaukee, WI: Marquette University Press, 1974.
Rossi, Osvaldo. "Der christliche Personalismus." In *Christliche Philosophie*, ed. E. Coreth et al., 550–63. Graz/Vienna: Styria, 1990.
Rousseau, J. J. *Oeuvres complètes*. Ed. B. Gagnebin and M. Raymond. Paris: Gallimard, 1959.
Rousseau, Mary F. "Elements of a Thomistic Philosophy of Death." *The Thomist* 43 (Oct. 1979): 581–602.
———. "The Natural Meaning of Death in the *Summa Theologiae*." *Proceedings of the American Catholic Philosophical Association* 52 (1978): 87–95.
Sandel, M. *Liberalism and the Limits of Justice*. Cambridge: Cambridge University Press, 1982.
Schindler, David. "Is Truth Ugly?" *Communio* 27, no. 4 (2000): 701–28.
———. "Norris Clarke on Person, Being and St. Thomas." *Communio* 20, no. 3 (1993): 580ff.
Schilpp, A., and L. E. Hahn, eds. *The Philosophy of Gabriel Marcel*. La Salle, IL: Open Court, 1984.
Schmidinger, Heinrich M. "Max Scheler und sein Einfluss auf das katholische Denken." In *Christliche Philosophie*, ed. E. Coreth et al., 89–111. Graz/Vienna: Styria, 1990.
Schmitz, Kenneth L. *At the Centre of the Human Drama: The Philosophical Anthropology of Karol Wojtyla/John Paul II*. Washington, DC: John Paul II Institute, 1993.
———. "The Authority of Institutions: Meddling or Middling?" *Communio* 12, no. 1 (1985): 5–24.
———. "Community: The Elusive Unity." *Review of Metaphysics* 37 (1983): 243–64.
———. "Enlightenment Criticism and the Embodiment of Values: The Hegelian Background to a Contemporary Problem." *Indian Philosophical Annual* (1986): 33–53.
———. "Faith and Practice: The Nature and Importance of Religious Activities." In *The Life of Religion: A Marquette University Symposium on the Nature of Religious Belief*, ed. Stanley H. Harrison and Richard C. Taylor, 39–60. Lanham, MD: University Press of America, 1986.

———. "Gibt es für Menschen Wichtigeres, als zu überleben? Das Erbe Griechenlands: Rationalität." In *Das europäische Erbe und seine christliche Zukunft*, ed. N. Lobkowicz, 99–104 (German), 348–56 (English). Cologne: Hans Martin Schleyer-Stiftung/Pontificum Consilium pro Cultura, 1985.
———. *The Gift: Creation*. The Aquinas Lecture. Milwaukee, WI: Marquette University Press, 1982.
———. "Intimacy and the Knowledge of Persons." *Filosofia e Comunicação* 7 (1981): 87–90.
———. "Natural Imagery as a Discriminatory Element in Religious Language." In *Experience, Reason and God*, ed. E. T. Long, 156–76. Studies in the Philosophy and History of Philosophy, vol. 8. Washington, DC: The Catholic University of America Press, 1980.
———. "Natural Wisdom in the Manuals." *Proceedings of the American Catholic Philosophical Association* (1956): 160–81.
———. "On a Resistant Strain within the Hegelian Dialectic." *The Owl of Minerva* 25 (Spring 1994): 147–54.
———. "Philosophical Pluralism and Philosophical Truth." *Philosophy Today* 10 (1966): 3–18.
———. "The Philosophy of Religion and the Redefinition of Philosophy." *Man and World* 3 (1970): 52–82.
———. "Restitution of Meaning in Religious Speech." *International Journal for Philosophy of Religion* 5 (1974): 131–51.
———. "The Roots of Catholic Intellectuality." *CCICA* (Catholic Commission on Intellectual and Cultural Affairs) *Annual* (1984).
———. "Selves and Persons." *Communio* 18, no. 2 (1991): 184–206.
———. "La transcendence coincident: fondement de l'interrogation religieuse." In *Urgence de la philosophie*, ed. T. De Koninck and L. Morin. Quebec: University of Laval Press, 1986.
———. "What Has Clio to Do with Athena?" In *Etienne Gilson: Historian and Philosopher*. Toronto: Pontifical Institute of Mediaeval Studies, 1988.
Schürmann, Reiner. *Heidegger on Being and Acting: From Principles to Anarchy*. Trans. Christine-Marie Gros and Reiner Schürmann. Bloomington: Indiana University Press, 1987.
———. *Le principe d'anarchie: Heidegger et la question de l'agir*. Paris: Editions de Seuil, 1987.
Schuster, John. *Descartes and the Scientific Revolution 1618–1634*. Ann Arbor: University of Michigan Press, 1977.
Sextus Empiricus. *Outlines of Pyrrhonism*. Ed. R. C. Bury. Loeb Classical Library. Cambridge, MA: Harvard University Press, 1976.
Smith, Adam. *The Wealth of Nations*. Ed. Edwin Canaan. London: Methuen, 1950.
Smith, Gerard, and Lottie H. Kendzierski. *The Philosophy of Being*. New York: Macmillan, 1961.
Smith, N. Kemp. *New Studies in the Philosophy of Descartes*. New York: Russell and Russell, 1953.
Sokolowski, Robert. *The God of Faith and Reason*. Notre Dame, IN: University of Notre Dame Press, 1982.
Spiegelberg, Herbert. *The Phenomenological Movement: A Historical Introduction*, 2 vols. 2nd ed. The Hague: Nijhoff, 1969.
Spinoza, Baruch. *The Works of Spinoza*. Trans. R. H. M. Elwes. New York: Dover, 1951.

Stevens, Wallace. *Poems.* Ed. S. F. Morse. New York: Vintage, 1959.
Taylor, H. O. *The Classical Inheritance of the Middle Ages.* New York: Harper, 1958.
Taylor, Mark C., ed. *Deconstruction in Context: Literature and Philosophy.* Chicago: University of Chicago Press, 1986.
Thomas Aquinas. *De principiis naturae.*
———. *De potentia Dei.*
———. *De veritate.*
———. *Expositio in Libros Sententiarium.*
———. *Expositio super librum Boethii de Trinitate.*
———. *In Boethium De hebdomadibus.*
———. *Quaestiones disputatae de anima.*
———. *Sententia super Metaphysicam.*
———. *Summa contra gentiles.*
———. *Summa theologiae.*
———. *Thomas Aquinas: Questions on the Soul.* Trans. James Robb. Milwaukee, WI: Marquette University Press, 1984.
Wallace, William. "Immateriality and Its Surrogates in Modern Science." *Proceedings of the American Catholic Philosophical Association* 52 (1978): 28–83.
Ward, Graham, ed. *The Postmodern God: A Theological Reader.* Oxford: Blackwell, 1997.
Wojtyla, Karol. *The Acting Person.* Trans. Andrzej Potocki. Dordrecht: Reidel, 1979.
———. *Letter to Artists.* April 1999. Libreria Editrice Vaticana.
———. *Milosc I Odpowiedzialnosc.* Krakow: 1960. *Love and Responsibility.* Trans. H. T. Willets. San Francisco: Ignatius, 1993.
———. "On the Theatre of the Word." In *The Collected Plays and Writings on Theatre,* trans. and ed. B. Taborski. Berkeley: University of California Press, 1987.
———. *Person and Community.* Ed. T. Sandok. New York: Peter Lang, 1993.
———. "Subjectivity and the Irreducible in Man." *Analecta Husserliana* (1978).
Wolff, R. P. *Understanding Rawls: A Reconstruction and Critique of "A Theory of Justice."* Princeton, NJ: Princeton University Press, 1977.
Wust, Peter. *Sinnkreis der Ewigen.* Graz: Styria, 1954.
———. *Ungewissheit und Wagnis.* Munich: Josef Kösel, 1937.

Index

Abelard, Peter, 173
Ackerman, Bruce, 223n1, 228n14, 231n17
Adorno, Theodor, 46–51
Alain of Lille, 154n4
Albert the Great, 200
Anaximander, 43n7
Anselm, St., 121n56, 255–57, 268, 300
Apel, Karl-Otto, 60
Aquinas, Thomas, 8, 16, 18, 23–31, 34, 35, 43n9, 44n10, 51n20, 63–65, 73, 74n1, 77, 88, 106–11, 115n39, 116n43, 121n54, 123–27, 140, 154n4, 165, 166, 184n1, 192n14, 200–220, 245–51, 270n23, 280n57, 285n6, 302n5, 305
Arata, Carlo 133n4
Ariew, R., 287n10
Aristotle, 6, 8, 10, 15, 17, 18, 22, 23, 29, 35, 40n5, 42–45, 55–57, 64, 65, 71, 73, 121n53, 132, 152, 170, 184, 194n19, 222, 233, 273n35
Athanasius, 122n57, 123n59
Augustine, 132, 140, 157, 209, 260, 269, 309n17
Ayer, Alfred J., 297n43

Bacon, Francis, 16, 22, 24, 30, 33, 75, 186
Balthasar, Hans Urs von, 294n33
Barry, Brian, 232n18
Battaglia, Felice, 133
Baynes, K., 39n2, 55n1
Berdyaev, N., 133n4
Bergson, Henri, 133n4
Berkeley, George, 103
Berlin, Isaiah, 225n6, 234n22
Bernard of Clairvaux, 157, 191
Blackburn, S., 297n41
Blondel, Maurice, 133n4, 191n12, 279n56

Boethius, 24, 132, 154n3
Bohman, J., 39n2, 55n1
Bonaventure, 74, 144n26, 273
Boniecki, A., 300n1
Bosanquet, B., 101n5
Bourke, V. J., 23n7
Bozzetti, Guiseppe, 133n4
Buber, Martin, 124
Burnet, John, 43n7
Burtt, E. A., 33n34
Busch, T., 174n7

Cameron, A., 269n21
Cassirer, Ernst, 124
Cicero, 43n9, 151
Clarke, Norris, 107n3, 108n7, 124–26
Comte, Auguste, 54, 188
Copleston, F., 297n43
Cusa, Nicholas of, 257, 260

Damascene, John, 122n57
Darwin, Charles, 33
de la Mettrie, 133
Deleuze, G., 296n36
de Lubac, Henri, 294n32
Denziger, H., 109n11
Derrida, Jacques, 39n1, 56, 112n24, 133
de Saussure, Ferdinand, 37, 62, 124n61
Descartes, René, 16, 23, 32, 40, 75, 89, 140, 157, 186, 188–91, 213, 222n1, 226n8, 288n14
de Vogel, Cornelia J., 150n1
Diderot, Denis, 285n7
Diels, H., 43n7
Dionysius, 305
Douglass, Bruce, 221

Ebner, Ferdinand, 133n4, 275n41
Eckhart, Meister, 172

325

Einstein, Albert, 304
Eriugena, John Scotus, 257n13

Fabro, Cornelio, 114n30
Feiblemann, James K., 110n16
Ferré, F., 3n1
Fichte, J., 188n8
Finance, Joseph de, 114n31, 120n51
Forest, Aimé, 114n29
Foucault, M., 133
Freud, S., 309

Galileo, 33, 75, 117n44
Garceau, Benoit, 115n39
Gaukroger, S., 288n14
Geiger, L. B., 114n32
Gilby, Thomas, 114n34
Gilson, Etienne, 43n9
Goya, Francisco, 312
Grillmeier, Alois, 150n1
Guardini, Romano, 113n25, 133n4, 144n27
Guzzo, Augusto, 133n4

Hall, John A., 224n4
Hegel, G. W. F., 6, 8, 10, 11, 29, 57, 62, 77, 90n2, 92n3, 110, 125n68, 133, 142, 166, 170n2, 176n11, 183, 185, 190n11, 202–5, 213, 230, 234n22, 252–55, 263, 273n34, 289n15
Heidegger, Martin, 10, 14, 37, 39–50, 55, 60, 61, 70, 73, 77, 89, 112, 124, 133, 142
Heraclitus, 9
Herodotus, 42
Hildebrand, Dietrich von, 133n4
Hobbes, Thomas, 16, 22, 24, 32, 35, 75, 227n9
Homer, 42, 46
Hopkins, Gerard Manley, 301n3
Horkheimer, Max, 46–51
Horace, 221
Hosea, 155
Hume, David, 40, 112, 133, 227n13, 290
Husserl, Edmund, 14, 62, 77, 78, 112n23, 133, 166, 188n8, 213
Hyppolytus, 122n57, 153n2

Jacobi, F. H., 257n12
Jaeger, W., 55

Jaspers, Karl, 133n4, 175
John Paul II, 265n1,2, 271–81, 301n2, 313n22. *See also* Wojtyla, Karol
Julius Caesar, 152

Kant, Immanuel, 10, 14, 34n37, 40, 57, 62, 77, 78, 84, 90, 112, 131, 133, 140, 142, 170, 175n9, 185n3, 189n9, 194n19, 213, 217, 263, 289
Keats, John, 306
Kelly, J. N. D., 153n2
Kierkegaard, Soren, 132, 141n21
Kockelmans, J., 3n1
Kowalczyk, S., 134
Kuhn, Thomas, 168
Kundera, Milan, 112n23, 277n46, 309

Lacan, Jacques, 284n3
Lazzarini, Renato, 133n4
Leibniz, Gottfried, 6, 10, 32n32, 77, 84, 227n11
Le Jeune, Jerome, 303
Levinas, Emmanuel, 112n24
Lobkowicz, N., 4
Locke, John, 32, 89, 157, 227n12, 235n24, 236
Long, E. T., 3n1
Long, Steve, 107n6, 108n8
Luther, Martin, 137
Lyotard, Jean-Francois, 110n18, 113n25

MacIntyre, A., 224n5, 268n19
Malebranche, N., 158, 191n19
Marcel, Gabriel, 72, 106n1, 107n5, 111n20, 114, 116n41, 120n52, 122n58, 125n64, 126n69, 131n78, 133–45, 161n14, 174n7, 195, 272n30, 274, 294n31, 310n18
Maritain, Jacques, 43n9, 109n14, 111n22, 115n35, 136n11, 141n17, 237n30
Marx, Karl, 39, 188n8, 290–93
Matthew of Aquasparta, 158
Maurer, Armand, 118n45, 119n49, 192n14, 305n7
McCarthy, T., 39n2, 55n1
McLuhan, Marshall, 303
McMullin, E., 172n5
Mill, John Stuart, 101n5, 293n30
Moliére, 33
Mounier, Emmanuel, 109n13, 132n1

Nédoncelle, Maurice, 109n13, 150n1
Newton, Isaac, 124n60
Nicholson, G., 40n3
Nietzsche, Friedrich, 39, 54, 113n25, 137, 142, 247, 283, 290–93, 298, 310n19

Ockham, William, 31, 137, 287n11
Otto, Rudolf, 264
Owens, Joseph, 21n1, 24n10, 36n40

Pareyson, Luigi, 133n4
Parmenides, 158
Pascal, Blaise, 132
Paul, 302n5, 314n24
Paulinus, 269
Paulson, J. J., 24n9
Pederson, Olaf, 117n44, 187n6, 287n9
Peguy, Charles, 133n4
Pelikan, J., 153n2
Peters, F. E., 43n7
Philo of Alexandria, 153
Pico della Mirandola, 137, 226n8
Picot, Abbé, 23
Pieper, Joseph, 115n36, 269n20, 271n26
Pindar, 42, 216
Plato, 5, 17, 22, 23, 35, 44, 121, 158, 170, 172, 268n19, 294, 297n40, 308
Plotinus, 172
Prudentius, 269
Przywara, Eric, 113n25, 144n27

Ramsey, Ian, 123n59, 162n16
Rawls, John, 223
Renouvier, Charles-Bernard, 132
Rheinfelder, H., 150n1
Richardson, Samuel, 156n6
Ricoeur, Paul, 133n4
Rigobello, Armando, 133n4
Rilke, Rainer Maria, 139
Robb, J., 175n10, 219n25
Robbe-Grillet, A., 293
Rorty, Richard, 38, 60, 133n3
Rossi, Osvaldo, 133n4
Rousseau, J. J., 158, 232n19
Rousseau, Mary F., 220n28
Royce, Josiah, 109, 133n4

Sartre, J. P., 137–38, 141n18, 213, 247, 291
Sandel, M., 232n18, 235n23, 236n27
Scheit, H., 4n2

Scheler, Max, 13n2
Schelling F., 133, 142, 263
Schiller, F., 246n3
Schindler, David, 107n3, 124–26, 307n12
Schlegel, F., 232n19
Schleiermacher, F., 264
Schmidinger, Heinrich, M., 132n2
Schmitz, Kenneth L., xi n1, 4n2, 18n4, 21n1, 35, 52n22, 66n12, 68n14, 74n1, 110n17, 114n33, 121n56, 155n5, 156n7, 158n8, 159n12, 161n13, 162n15, 164n19, 178n13, 220n28, 270n24
Schürmann, Reiner, 39–50, 60n7, 61, 70
Schuster, John, 288n14
Sciacca, Michele Federico, 133n4
Scotus, John Duns, 172, 287n11
Sextus Empircus, 42n4
Shakespeare, William, 152
Simmons, K., 297n41
Siewerth, Gusta, 113n25
Smith, Adam, 223n3
Smith, Gerard, 28n25, 125n67, 245n2
Smith, J. E., 3n1
Socrates, 60, 61
Sokolowski, Robert, 52n22, 260n14
Solomon, 155
Spinoza, Baruch, 16, 75, 186, 217, 227n10, 247
Stevens, Wallace, 83, 94n4

Taylor, Mark, 39n1, 269n21
Teresa of Calcutta, 313
Tertullian, 132, 153
Thales, 67
Tyler, Ralph Flewelling, 109

Vanier, Jean, 313, 314
Villey, Michel, 225n6
Virgil, 269
Voltaire, 33, 158

Wallace, William, 169n1
Ward, Graham, 284n3
Whitehead, Alfred North, 63
Wittgenstein, Ludwig, 37
Wojtyla, Karol, 110n14, 136n11, 193, 266–70, 283n1, 300n1, 303n6, 312n20. See also John Paul II
Wust, Peter, 275n41

www.ingramcontent.com/pod-product-compliance
Lightning Source LLC
Chambersburg PA
CBHW032302300426
44110CB00033B/270